DIACHRONIC ~~SYNTAX~~

Models and Mechanisms

Edited by

Susan Pintzuk, George Tsoulas,
and Anthony Warner

OXFORD

UNIVERSITY PRESS

OXFORD
UNIVERSITY PRESS

Great Clarendon Street, Oxford OX2 6DP

Oxford University Press is a department of the University of Oxford.
It furthers the University's objective of excellence in research, scholarship,
and education by publishing worldwide in

Oxford New York

Athens Auckland Bangkok Bogotá Buenos Aires Calcutta Cape Town
Chennai Dar es Salaam Delhi Florence Hong Kong Istanbul Karachi
Kuala Lumpur Madrid Melbourne Mexico City Mumbai Nairobi
Paris São Paulo Shanghai Singapore Taipei Tokyo Toronto Warsaw

with associated companies in Berlin Ibadan

Oxford is a registered trade mark of Oxford University Press
in the UK and in certain other countries

Published in the United States
by Oxford University Press Inc., New York

British Library Cataloguing in Publication Data

Data available

Library of Congress Cataloging in Publication Data

Data applied for

ISBN 0–19–825026–6
ISBN 0–19–825027–4 pbk.

1 3 5 7 9 10 8 6 4 2

Typeset in Times
by Peter Kahrel, Lancaster
Printed in Great Britain
on acid-free paper by
Biddles Ltd., Guildford and King's Lynn

Preface

The chapters in this volume are based on a selection of papers originally presented at the Fifth Diachronic Generative Syntax Conference (DIGS 5), held at the University of York, 30 May–1 June 1998. We would like to thank all who attended for their enthusiastic participation. We gratefully acknowledge the financial support of the Department of Language and Linguistic Science, the Linguistics Association of Great Britain, and the British Academy (for a British Conference Grant), and the generous donations of Oxford University Press and Cambridge University Press. Many thanks to the graduate students who helped at the conference: Cecile de Cat, Melody Clark, Elizabeth McCoy, Mel Silverstone, Jen Smith, and Daisy Zhu. We would like to thank the anonymous reviewers selected by OUP for their helpful comments and suggestions, and we thank the following colleagues for their assistance with refereeing: David Adger, Kersti Börjars, Anna Cardinaletti, Lisa Cheng, Thierry Etchegoyhen, Jacqueline Guéron, Eric Haeberli, Steve Harlow, Caroline Heycock, Geoff Horrocks, Þorbjörg Hróarsdóttir, Ans van Kemenade, Anthony Kroch, Murat Kural, David Lightfoot, Ana Maria Martins, Ian Roberts, Alain Rouveret, Beatrice Santorini, Ann Taylor, Nigel Vincent, Fred Weerman, Wim van der Wurff and Jan-Wouter Zwart. Finally, we thank John Davey of OUP for his expert advice, enthusiasm, and general good-naturedness, and the contributors for their patience, commitment, and understanding, during the long process of bringing this volume to press.

Susan Pintzuk, George Tsoulas, and Anthony Warner

Contents

Contents

Notes on Contributors

MONTSE BATLLORI is Professor of Spanish Grammar (Diachrony) at the Universitat de Girona. She received her Ph.D. in Spanish Philology at the Universitat Autònoma de Barcelona in 1996. She has published articles on the properties of Old Spanish verbal auxiliaries, noun phrases and verb phrases (impersonal constructions). Her current work focuses on the syntactic properties of determiners within noun phrases and on verb phrases in Old Spanish.

TED BRISCOE has been University Lecturer at Cambridge University Computer Laboratory since 1989. From 1990 until 1996 he was an EPSRC Advanced Research Fellow undertaking research at Macquarie University, University of Pennsylvania, Xerox European Research Centre, and the Computer Laboratory. His research interests are computational and theoretical linguistics and automated speech and language processing, including (nearly-) deterministic, statistical, and robust parsing techniques, defaults and constraint-based approaches to linguistic description, models of human language learning and parsing, and evolutionary simulations of language variation and change.

LARS-OLOF DELSING is a Research Fellow in the Department of Scandinavian Languages, Lund University. His 1993 doctoral dissertation was *The Internal Structure of Noun Phrases in the Scandinavian Languages: A Comparative Study*. His research interests include the structure of noun phrases, and language change in Old and Early Modern Swedish (1225–1732), in particular the loss of the genitive case and OV word order, the rise of preposition stranding, and changes in adjectival morphology. He is currently investigating the breakdown of the Swedish case system.

ERIC HAEBERLI has recently moved from the University of Geneva to become Lecturer in Linguistics in the Department of Linguistic Science at the University of Reading. His main research interests are syntactic theory, diachronic syntax (in particular English historical syntax), and comparative Germanic syntax, domains which are explored in his recent Ph.D. dissertation from the University of Geneva entitled *Features, Categories and the Syntax of A-Positions: Synchronic and Diachronic Variation in the Germanic Languages.*

CHUNG-HYE HAN received her Ph.D. in linguistics from the University of Pennsylvania. Her main areas of research are syntax, semantics and their interface, and the syntax of Korean. Her Ph.D. dissertation (Han 2000) is a cross-linguistic investigation of imperatives and related constructions. She has also worked on negative polarity items, the semantics of questions, and counter-factuals. She is currently a postdoctoral fellow at the University of Pennsylvania working on issues in the diachronic syntax of English, and the development and implementation of a grammar of Korean within the framework of Tree Adjoining Grammars.

ÞORBJÖRG HRÓARSDÓTTIR is a postdoctoral scholar in the Department of Linguistics, University of Tromsø. Her 1999 doctoral dissertation was entitled *Verb Phrase Syntax in the History of Icelandic*. She has published articles on the change from OV to VO in the history of Icelandic. Her research interests include the implicational relationship of language acquisition and language change, OV/VO word order in conjunction with non-canonical complementation, ellipsis and gapping in OV-languages, and object agreement in Icelandic.

ANS VAN KEMENADE is Professor of English Language and Linguistics at the University of Nijmegen. She has published *Syntactic Case and Morphological Case in the History of English* (Foris/Mouton 1987) and numerous articles, mainly on Old and Middle English syntax. She has edited a number of collections of articles, including *Parameters of Morphosyntactic Change* with Nigel Vincent (CUP 1997), and is currently working on a monograph on verbal syntax and negation in the history of English.

ANTHONY KROCH is Professor of Linguistics at the University of Pennsylvania, and specializes in theoretical syntax and in the historical syntax of English. His historical work has focused on the use of statistical methods to trace the time course of language change and to tease apart the contributions of competing grammars in mixed texts. He and Ann Taylor are responsible for the design and construction of the Penn–Helsinki Parsed Corpus of Middle English. He has also worked on the grammatical description and analysis of major syntactic constructions of the West Germanic languages.

ANA MARIA MARTINS is Assistant Professor in General and Romance Linguistics at the University of Lisbon. Her main area of teaching and research is historical linguistics, in particular historical syntax. Other connected research areas she has devoted attention to are theoretical linguistics, philology, and dialectology. She has worked and published on different topics in Romance diachronic syntax: clitic placement, clitic climbing, word order, negation and negative words, and the Portuguese inflected infinitive.

SUSAN PINTZUK is Lecturer in Linguistics at the University of York. She has research interests in syntactic variation and change in the history of English and other Germanic languages. She is currently working on a research project on the syntax of Old English poetry and (with Anthony Warner and Ann Taylor) the York–Helsinki Parsed Corpus of Old English. She has published articles on Old English syntax, and *Phrase Structures in Competition: Variation and Change in Old English Word Order* (Garland 1999).

FRANCESC ROCA is Professor of Spanish Syntax at the University of Girona. He received his Ph.D. in Spanish Philology at the Universitat Autònoma de Barcelona in 1997. He has published articles on the properties of Spanish pronominal clitics, the structure of noun phrases, and the syntactic and morphological processes of quantification in Spanish. His current work focuses on the syntactic properties of determiners and noun phrases in Spanish and in the morphophonological processes of Basque case morphemes.

ANN TAYLOR is a Research Fellow at the University of York. Her research interests include second-position clitics, especially in Ancient Greek, and the syntax of Middle English. She is the co-creator, with Anthony Kroch, of the Penn–Helsinki Parsed Corpus of Middle English and is currently at work producing the York–Helsinki Parsed Corpus of Old English in conjunction with Anthony Warner and Susan Pintzuk.

GEORGE TSOULAS is Lecturer in Linguistics at the University of York. He has published articles on the interpretation of pronouns and the syntax of non-finite sentential complementation. His recent research is concerned with the formal theory of quantification, the syntax and semantics of pronominal anaphora, and the syntax of scrambling and multiple subject constructions in Korean and Japanese. He has edited (with David Adger, Bernadette Plunkett, and Susan Pintzuk) *Specifiers: Minimalist Approaches* (OUP 1999).

NIGEL VINCENT is Mont Follick Professor of Comparative Philology at the University of Manchester. His recent research has been concerned with Lexical-Functional Grammar and the potential of an Optimality Theory inspired version of LFG for modelling morphosyntactic change. His specialist language areas are Latin and Romance, especially Italian. He directs a British Academy funded research project on 'Archaism and Innovation in Syntactic Change', and co-edited with Ans van Kemenade a collection of articles, *Parameters of Morphosyntactic Change* (CUP 1997).

ANTHONY WARNER is Professor of English Linguistics at the University of York. He has a major interest in variation and change in the history of English syntax. He is the author of papers in syntactic change and in phrase structure grammar; and of *Complementation in Middle English and the Methodology of Historical Syntax* (Croom Helm 1982), and *English Auxiliaries: Structure and History* (CUP 1993).

JOHN WHITMAN is Associate Professor in the Department of Linguistics at Cornell University. He teaches historical linguistics, Japanese and Korean linguistics, and syntax. His publications include (with Koichi Takezawa) *Nichieigo hikaku sensyo, vol. 9: Kaku to gojun to tôgo kôzô* (Kenkyûsha 1998).

ALEXANDER WILLIAMS is a student at the University of Pennsylvania. His current research concerns subjecthood and inverse constructions in English and Chinese. He has also written on the compositional structure of demonstrative phrases in Mandarin, and on the semantics of adverbial quantification over embedded interrogatives in English. He is interested in language contact in Eastern Turkestan, where he has done fieldwork on Uyghur.

DAVID WILLIS is Lecturer in Linguistics at the University of Cambridge. His main publications are *Syntactic Change in Welsh: A Study of the Loss of Verb-Second* (Oxford University Press, 1998) and journal articles on the history of Welsh word order. He is currently working on auxiliary systems in Slavonic, and relative clauses and related *wh*-phenomena in Welsh.

1

Syntactic Change: Theory and Method

SUSAN PINTZUK, GEORGE TSOULAS, and ANTHONY WARNER

The starting point for discussions of syntactic change in Chomskyan generative syntax is acquisition, specifically the individual's acquisition of a grammar distinct from the one which underlies the output of the preceding generation. The investigation of changes which can be understood in terms of an abrupt shift at acquisition has proved the most straightforward and fruitful way of relating historical and theoretical syntax, partly because the Principles and Parameters paradigm provides a formal framework in which to interpret differences between successive grammars.

But historical syntacticians are also interested in the linguistic variation which is characteristic of recorded historical data, in the diffusion of change across time and through populations, and in the factors underlying both synchronic and diachronic variation (for example, the influence of language contact and the impact of sociolinguistic pressures on the behaviour of adult speakers). The diffusion of change must be carefully distinguished from the notion of change arising within the individual, although successive acquisition by individuals may indeed be a component of diffusion. What is normally identified as language change in the most general sense is in fact the result of diffusion as well as acquisition, and evidence for both aspects of change is provided by the written records which are the historian's typical data. In the past ten years or so there have been revolutionary developments in the methodology which permits the quantitative analysis of syntactic variation, both synchronic and diachronic. Indeed, an impressive aspect of the present volume is the extent to which statistically based argumentation for grammatical structuring and for the interpretation of variation and change in recorded language (external 'E-language') as evidence for underlying changes in the internalized 'I-language' is deployed. This approach to historical data has clearly come of age.

The conjunction of these two central aspects, acquisition and diffusion, and of the theoretical approaches which interpret them will be explored in this chapter. We will outline issues that are relevant to acquisition and diffusion from the particular perspective of the research represented by the chapters in this book. Our first section introduces some basic concepts. Then we move on, first to recent theoretical developments within the Minimalist Programme and their interface with diachronic syntax, and then to aspects of the methodology of diachronic syntax. We consider the problems posed by the gradualness of recorded syntactic change, and address questions arising from the investigation of variation and the diffusion of change. Finally, we sum up the contributions of the individual chapters in this volume and show how they relate to the issues presented.

1.1. PARAMETERS, ACQUISITION, AND CHANGE

In the Principles and Parameters paradigm, researchers have sought to reduce differences between languages to a small number of more abstract differences or 'parameters' which are part of Universal Grammar (UG). These have typically been associated with functional projections encoding such abstract properties as tense, mood, agreement, definiteness, number, etc., that is, with traditionally grammatical properties which recurrently find morphological expression in individual languages. These parameters are sufficiently abstract for a difference in their value to have multiple surface reflexes in syntactic patterns.

For example, consider the 'Split IP Parameter' of Bobaljik and Thráinsson (1998). The parameter here is whether a language has one or two functional projections above VP to encode the inflectional system of the verb. Bobaljik and Thráinsson claim that if a language has distinct functional projections for Agreement and Tense (AgrP and TP), then several consequences follow: the language will have two subject positions available outside VP (one in the specifier of each functional projection), one of which may be occupied by an expletive in transitive constructions; the verb will be required to move out of VP into at least the lowest of these positions, thus crossing left-periphery adverbs such as *always*; and the language may have multiple inflectional morphemes on the verb stem. These characteristics can be illustrated from earlier English.

(1) (*a*) Peter, knowing . . . that there woulde some Iewes reprove this his doing
  (Udall *et al.*, *Paraphrase of Erasmus upon the Newe Testament* (1548), Acts 43 b, cited from *OED There* 4b)

  (*b*) This most precious bloud that he shed on the Crosse, cryeth always mercye for sinners . . .
  (John Fisher, *English Works* (1535), ed. J. B. Mayor, Early English Text Society ES 27 (1876), 412)

  (*c*) Syr, sowedest not thou good seed . . .?
  SOW+PAST+2SG
  (W. Tyndale, *The Four Gospels* (1525), Matt. 13: 27)

On the other hand, if a language has only one projection for both agreement and tense (IP), as is the case in Bobaljik and Thráinsson's analysis of today's

English, then it will lack all three of these characteristics. There will be only one subject position outside VP, and this will be occupied by the lexical subject in transitives, so that an expletive construction such as (1*a*) is not possible. The verb will remain in VP and will therefore not cross left-periphery adverbials; and there will be no systematic attachment of multiple morphemes to the verb stem. This general contrast is claimed to hold across Germanic: for example German, Dutch, Afrikaans, and Icelandic show Split IP properties, whereas Swedish, Danish, Norwegian, and modern English lack these properties. Clearly the question of how to encode information about agreement and tense in the lexicon is fundamental to a series of differences.

Within this framework, the learner's task in the acquisition of a language includes establishing the relevant parameters and their settings, in accordance with the principles of UG. The input for acquisition, the Primary Linguistic Data (PLD), is interpreted by the learner to provide evidence on the basis of which the parameters of the particular grammar acquired are set.

(2)   UG parameters set to their default values (or unset)
         + trigger evidence of PLD →
         Grammar with parameters set

Thus a child faced with the task of learning earlier English might conclude from evidence like that given in (1) above that the language had a split IP. There is, however, a series of issues here about the nature of this evidence, as well as about the process of acquisition. One view has been that learners seek a match between the PLD and the output of candidate grammars: overall 'input matching'. A second, recent view is that the evidence for parameter setting is found in the presence of quite specific structural properties (triggers or cues) in the learner's partial analyses of input strings (see e.g. Fodor 1998, Dresher 1999, Lightfoot 1999). Thus Lightfoot argues that in acquiring the verb second constraint, learners will look for main clauses with a finite verb in second position, following a phrase in initial position which is not the subject. Here the cue consists of the partial structural analysis of a sentence. But cues will not all be equally weighted, in spite of the fact that the sentences encoding the cues are present in the input data, and a cue may need to reach some threshold to be effective. Consider the acquisition of the movement of V to a higher functional projection in earlier English (let us call this 'V-to-I', focusing on the movement and setting aside the possibility that IP was split). It seems likely that the presence of rich inflectional contrasts provided important evidence for this movement. But Lightfoot (1997) has argued that the presence of such orders as *I heard not your answer*, with finite V + *not* order in negative clauses, did not provide learners with a sufficient cue for this movement after the decline of systematic multiple inflections, even though negative clauses are common. The possibility of a difference between the effectiveness of cues helps us to interpret the motivation for the change and the timing of its actuation: thus questions about acquisition are important for any approach to an understanding of the causes of linguistic change. Whatever view of acquisition is taken, however, it is clear from the model above that the immediate cause of a change involving functional categories must lie in some alteration to the PLD. Change in the PLD may itself be the result of some antecedent change (such as the loss or weakening of overt morphological contrasts), or due to 'external' factors, such as contact or sociolinguistically motivated alterations in frequency, or perhaps arising as a chance fluctuation in frequency. This approach implies that (as Lightfoot has consistently maintained) there is no separate 'theory of change' per se; or in Hale's words: 'Syntactic change should fall out from an adequate theory of syntax along with a learning algorithm' (1999: 1). But this is change in the narrow sense, and we need to add some understanding of processes of diffusion and variation to deal generally with the facts of E-language change.

The central notion of parametric change is simply illustrated by the English cases discussed above. If Bobaljik and Thráinsson are right, then the inflectional projections of the English verb underwent a parametric change in the Modern Period: there was a reduction in the number of functional projections above VP, with a concomitant loss of movement. Another account of a parametric shift at this period interprets the loss of V-to-I as resulting from a change in the feature composition of a functional projection, as in Roberts (1999), who suggests that the V feature of I was formerly 'strong' (hence requiring the movement of V to I) but became 'weak', so that V subsequently remained in VP. Parametric changes typically have a series of surface reflexes. But changes may also occur without showing a major surface reflex, as when some item is recategorized or a structure is reanalysed in a way that does not alter the surface string. A rather dramatic example is a recurrent type of change found in Chinese and elsewhere and discussed by Whitman (in this volume), where a subject resumptive pronoun is reanalysed as a copula. This involves more than a category change of the pronoun (since the pronoun must also change its structural status from specifier of the clausal projection to head of a verbal projection), but it may leave the surface string intact.

Parametric change (and the other types of change just considered) are commonly taken to be abrupt, at least as they are manifested in the individual (although see the discussion in §1.4 below). But the broad types of change known as grammaticalization are characteristically gradual in recorded data. Grammaticalization is traditionally the semantic bleaching and distributional generalization of some item, so that it moves from lexis to grammar: typically a word becomes a particle or an inflection (Meillet 1912), 'formerly autonomous elements evolve into markers of grammatical function' (van Kemenade and Vincent 1997: 22). Such changes include the development of the Old English negative adverb *nawiht/nowiht* 'not at all' into the functional head *not* (discussed by van Kemenade, in this volume, in a case study of grammaticalization), and further into the inflection *-n't*, and the development of determiners out of earlier demonstratives (see Philippi 1997, Vincent 1997, Batllori and Roca, in this volume). There has been much detailed work on histories of grammaticalization with attention to the recurrent changes in profile of the properties of the forms involved across time, including phonological, morphological, semantic, and pragmatic properties as well as grammatical ones (see e.g. Traugott and Heine 1991, Hopper and Traugott 1993). Work in this tradition has not interpreted the associated syntactic changes within a generative model, so that we have lacked a formal account of the processes involved at points of discrete change in such grammaticalization. The recurrence of this type of change poses an interesting challenge to formal theorists, and this will be further discussed below.

1.2. THE MINIMALIST PROGRAMME

1.2.1. *Introduction to the Minimalist Programme*

In this section, we briefly present the basic concepts of Minimalism, and show how syntactic change can be represented within this most recent Principles and Parameters model. The Minimalist Programme (MP), as outlined in Chomsky 1993, 1995 and later and related work, is an attempt to define the basic elements of the syntactic component within a restrictive set of assumptions. Although earlier Principles and Parameters models such as Government and Binding (GB) provided broad empirical coverage, the concepts and technology had become increasingly complex, and in many cases were motivated solely by theory-internal considerations. MP has highlighted the importance of economy in grammar in an attempt to rid linguistic theory of superfluous constructs, including unnecessary levels of representation, relations of government, and specification of phrase structure. Under MP, lexical resources are related to the interface representations Phonological Form (PF) and Logical Form (LF) by the computational system. PF and LF are the only levels of representation; other levels familiar from GB which are internal to the computational system, such as D-Structure and S-Structure, have been eliminated. PF and LF are interfaces in the sense that they are representations that are readable by other systems of the mind/brain: the articulatory-perceptual system and the conceptual-intentional system, respectively. The mapping between lexical resources and PF and LF is 'optimal': it is as efficient as possible given the interpretability constraints imposed by the interfaces.

The basic components of the computational system can be described as follows. There is a universal domain V of features (phonological, semantic, and syntactic). Out of this domain, an operation O constructs lexical items, which are simply bundles of features. The set of all such lexical items for a language constitutes that language's lexicon. We will assume that operation O applies during language acquisition (and in fact is the entire substance of language acquisition, as is discussed below).

For each sentence, a set of lexical items is selected from the lexicon to form a Numeration. The mapping between the Numeration and the output representations PF and LF is a sequence of applications of two core syntactic processes, Merge and Move, which create configurations in which features of the lexical items are checked and eliminated. Merge builds structure by combining pairs of elements, either elements from the Numeration or structure previously built. Move extends structure by displacing an element from within a complex structure to another part of the structure. Spell Out is the point at which the object formed in the Derivation is handed over to the interfaces, PF for morpho-phonological interpretation and LF for semantic interpretation; the derivation converges if all non-interpretable features have been eliminated prior to Spell Out. Thus the components of the computational system can be represented as in (3).

(3)

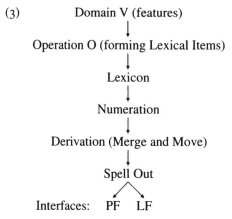

Domain V (features)
↓
Operation O (forming Lexical Items)
↓
Lexicon
↓
Numeration
↓
Derivation (Merge and Move)
↓
Spell Out
╱   ╲
Interfaces: PF   LF

Although GB and MP are both models within the Principles and Parameters paradigm, there are important differences in the way the two systems function. For example, GB allows movement to apply freely, generating one or more representations for a particular sentence, which are then tested for well-formedness. In MP, movement applies only when necessary for feature-checking, and there are no conditions for well-formedness other than the elimination of non-interpretable features.

With respect to cross-linguistic variation, differences between languages have been interpreted within the Principles and Parameters paradigm in terms of a small number of specific parameters. One further, major difference between GB and MP is that the concept of parameter is not at all the same in the two systems. In GB, parameters (like the Split IP Parameter of Bobaljik and Thráinsson discussed above) typically encode clusters of properties and descriptive generalizations: for example, *pro*-drop languages allow long *wh*-movement while non *pro*-drop languages do not;[1] languages with head-final VPs generally allow scrambling while languages with head-initial VPs do not. It is assumed that these clusters of

---

[1] See the discussion of the *pro*-drop parameter and its associated properties in Chomsky 1981: 253-75.

properties are the reflex of a single parameter, together with independent principles of UG. But with the development of the MP model, parameters require the same scrutiny as other grammatical constructs. As a result, parameters within MP are not logically independent entities; instead, parameters are expressed as features on functional entities within the lexicon, and the grammatical coverage of a single parameter is therefore constrained and may be less wide-ranging in nature. This has important consequences for the way that we view the evidence for syntactic change, and the way that we interpret the change within a formal syntactic framework. The fact that a cluster of diverse surface effects is typically involved in parametric change can be represented in MP only if these effects are directly attributable to a feature difference in a single functional category. It is not yet clear to what extent this apparent reduction in the scope of the notion 'parametric difference' will prove compatible with the desire to characterize the unity of clusters of surface differences.

Let us now consider where within the MP model syntactic change may occur. Change is of course manifested at the PF and LF interfaces; but since these are derived levels of representation, they cannot be the locus of change. Similarly, the position of Spell Out cannot be an independent parameter of change: linguistic objects are handed to PF and LF as soon as checking requirements are met, and therefore the position of Spell Out is reducible to the properties of features within the Numeration. Merge and Move, the computational mechanisms responsible for creating and manipulating structure, are unlikely to be subject to change in historical time; they may change in evolutionary time, but this is an entirely different matter. The universal domain V of features might change by addition or loss, although evidence for such change would be difficult to find. We are left with operation O and its output, the lexicon, and this must be the locus of syntactic change in MP: change can be described simply as the reorganization of the featural content of the lexical items of the language. Thus by necessity, cross-linguistic variation within the MP model, and by extension variation through time, is confined to properties of lexical items; and the origin of any given syntactic change can only be located at operation O, which combines features into lexical items.

1.2.2. *Syntactic change and the learner in MP*

In this section we take a closer look at the learning process under MP, since acquisition is the central locus of syntactic change. We will not review here the many different approaches to the formal theory of language learning. Instead, we will build on the generally accepted assumptions about language acquisition remarked in §1.1 above, as well as two additional assumptions: first, that learners are conservative in that they attempt to reduce the computational burden of the grammar; second, that the learning algorithm has a built-in preference for simplicity.[2]

---

[2] Similar assumptions are argued for in Clark and Roberts 1993.

The process of acquisition crucially involves the acquisition of a lexicon. This may include those functional heads which trigger overt movement, which requires more computational effort than either Merge or covert movement. Within a framework which seeks to minimize computational effort, it makes sense to suppose that functional heads triggering overt movement are not the default, but rather are admitted only in response to cues, or to the need to provide derivations for inputs which would otherwise violate economy conditions. Functional heads triggering overt movement will therefore be constructed by operation O only as a response to a lack of simplicity in the grammar required for the target language, in line with the commonly accepted view that the lexicon is the repository of irregularity. Where movement is involved, this clearly echoes the view that parameters correspond to functional elements.

Since differences between languages are located in the lexicon, the learning process can be regarded as the (perhaps repeated) revision of the featural composition of lexical entries. Within this view the loss (or gain) of movement has a straightforward interpretation, as does the central process of grammaticalization. Loss (or gain) of movement arises when functional items in the lexicon are assigned a different featural composition, thus losing or introducing the triggering of overt movement. With respect to grammaticalization, the most important work to date within a Minimalist framework is Roberts and Roussou (1999). They develop an account of grammaticalization in terms of the diachronic development of substantive heads into functional heads driven by the computationally conservative nature of the learner. They argue that this view accounts for all the standard properties of grammaticalization listed by Lehmann (1985). In addition, they account for the striking regularity and frequency of grammaticalization by proposing that it always involves structural simplification, since loss of movement entails reduction in structure under the assumption that all movement is adjunction (Kayne 1994). To understand their approach, consider their example of the development of *thélo* + CP to *tha* + VP in the history of Greek. In ancient Greek *thélo* is a main verb selecting a (purpose) CP complement introduced by the complementizer *ina*. In Modern Greek, the corresponding structure is monoclausal and *tha* is a functional element heading a MoodP or TP projection selecting a VP. The grammaticalization of *thélo* to *tha* therefore involves the structural simplification shown in (4):

(4) $[_{CP} [_{VP}$ thélo CP $]] > [_{CP} \ldots$ tha VP$]$

If their approach is plausible, then this aspect of grammaticalization falls naturally within the framework sketched here, since the core mechanism of change consists in featural recomposition which provides a structural simplification with economy-related advantages. Whitman (in this volume) presents related ideas concerning reanalysis, and shows that the only structural change that may be associated with categorial reanalysis is pruning, that is, structural simplification.

Considerations of economy of derivation seem then to be particularly important in the discussion of syntactic change. But economy and simplicity must be carefully distinguished, even though their effects are interrelated. The learning algorithm has a built-in preference for simplicity, and ensures that the simplest grammar will be selected. The notion of economy which is relevant to particular derivations provides in part the grounds on which that grammar will be selected.

The above scenario provides plausible key elements to explain change within an individual speaker, and tracking I-language change through E-language records is the topic of the next two sections. We begin by considering the data of historical syntax.

1.3. HISTORICAL SYNTAX AND ITS DATA: FROM E-LANGUAGE TO I-LANGUAGE

From one perspective, historical syntax is simply a branch of comparative syntax which happens to involve dialects that are closely related temporally. But one crucial difference between historical syntax and other types of comparative syntax is that the central empirical data of the former is E-language, the data of the historical texts, whereas the essential object of the latter is I-language, the internal grammar (Hale 1998: 1). This presents a methodological problem: how is the E-language of historical texts to be interpreted with respect to the I-language of its speakers? Clearly aspects of E-language data can be interpreted as the output of an underlying grammar (or grammars) in cases where we can reasonably set aside the effects of performance factors. An early insight (Lightfoot 1979) is that a relatively abrupt shift in the historical data, involving a cluster of related changes, may point to a single abstract difference. This may reflect a different parameter setting in the I-language of individuals, which will typically result in a range of surface differences, including the obsolescence of established patterns and the development of new ones. Lightfoot (1991: 166; 1999: 105–6) presents a list of the characteristics of parametric change, some perhaps arguable, which are in effect diagnostics for identifying change in parameter settings, taking as evidence the effects that are visible in the E-language data of historical texts.

But the relevance of E-language changes that occur at the same time, or over the same period of time, is actually much wider than is implied above, in two respects. First of all, a single abstract difference may account for sets of surface differences between temporal dialects without the change necessarily being parametric in nature in the sense of §1.1. As an example of such a change, Williams (in this volume) shows that a sudden drop in the use of verb-initial structures in English takes place in the thirteenth century, and that this correlates with the sudden loss of silent expletive subjects in existential sentences. This is not a parametric difference: verb-initial structure and silent expletives are not two reflexes of a single parameter. Rather, Williams argues that verb-initial structure provides the licensing environment for the silent expletive; and when the environment is lost, silent expletives must necessarily be lost as well. Here then, a deduction about the analysis of two stages of the language (and broader deductions relevant to Germanic) depend partly on evidence of the simultaneity of apparently distinct developments. Williams's approach is an application of the general methodology familiar from synchronic studies which seeks to attribute complexes of differences between dialects to a single underlying distinction.

Secondly, the analysis of variation in E-language, in particular variation over time, can reveal I-language differences. The basic notion here is that as a language changes we can follow the path of the change, and that this path provides information about the nature and organization of the grammar (of the language in particular and of languages in general) that is not available from synchronic comparative research. Much recent work in historical syntax has moved away from a focus on abrupt parametric change toward an emphasis on synchronic syntactic variation and the implications of gradual syntactic change as they can be interpreted within the Principles and Parameters paradigm. Thus the detailed study of patterns of variation is one method of establishing conclusions about I-language on the basis of the facts of E-language.

The use of quantitative data in exploring and understanding gradual change has initiated a large research programme into the time course of change, and into the use of historical data as evidence for the underlying grammars of users. When the syntactic variation found in historical texts is analysed using quantitative methods, we find 'orderly heterogeneity' (Weinreich, Labov, and Herzog 1968): the variation is systematic and the patterns are revealing. When the distributions of forms are analysed in detail, either synchronically during a particular historical stage of a language or else diachronically over a period of time, the results can provide support for the choice of one grammatical analysis over another (see the chapters in this volume by Haeberli, Han, Hróarsdóttir, Kroch and Taylor, Williams; also Pintzuk 1999, Taylor 1994), permit the tracking of syntactic variation and change over time (Delsing in this volume, Kroch 1989*b*, Pintzuk 1996*a*, 1999, Santorini 1993), and uncover dialect differences (Haeberli, and Kroch and Taylor in this volume, Kroch and Taylor 1997). This research programme has been made possible by two developments: first, the construction of syntactically annotated historical corpora, such as the Penn–Helsinki Parsed Corpus of Middle English (Kroch and Taylor 2000, henceforth 'PPCME') and the Brooklyn Parsed Corpus of Old English (Pintzuk *et al.* 2000, henceforth 'the Brooklyn Corpus') which facilitate detailed and precise searches for syntactic structures. The second development is the application of quantitative methods to syntactic data, including those based on sociolinguistic methodology, ranging from the simple examination and comparison of distribution frequencies to more complex multivariate analyses.

Such quantitative studies of syntactic variation over time have provided strong support for the 'Constant Rate Effect' (Kroch 1989*b*): during a period of change, when two linguistic options are in competition, the frequency of use of the two options may differ across contexts, but the rate of change for each context is the same. In other words, while some contexts may favour the innovating option and show a higher overall rate of use, the increase in use over time will be the same in all contexts. It should be emphasized that the word 'constant' in the Constant Rate Effect does not refer to a constant rate of increase in the frequency of the innovating linguistic option. Most syntactic variation and change that has been studied quantitatively has been shown to follow an S-shaped curve, where the rate of change over time is not constant: the replacement of old forms by new ones occurs slowly at the beginning of the period of change, then accelerates in the middle stage, and finally, at the end of the period, when the old form is rare, tails off until the change reaches completion. But where distinct linguistic contexts show different frequencies of new forms over old, the S-shaped curves associated with change in each context have been found to be parallel, so that the contexts maintain a stable relationship with each other. Thus what is 'constant' in the Constant Rate Effect is the relationship between linguistic contexts relevant to the change, so that the frequency of the new form changes in the same way in all contexts. This leads Kroch to an important deduction: 'Contexts change together because they are merely surface manifestations of a single underlying change in grammar. Differences in frequency of use of a new form across contexts reflect functional and stylistic factors, which are constant across time and independent of grammar.' (1989*b*: 199)

Perhaps the best-known case illustrating the validity of the Constant Rate Effect is that of periphrastic *do*, first studied quantitatively by Ellegård (1953). Periphrastic *do* is generally analysed as a semantically null auxiliary that carries tense in contexts where the association of I and the main verb is blocked, i.e. in negatives and questions. The use of *do* was variable in Middle English and Early Modern English, and it has been argued (Kroch 1989*b*, Roberts 1985) that the rise of periphrastic *do* was a reflex of the loss of the raising of finite main verbs to I. Kroch (1989*b*) demonstrates that the frequency of periphrastic *do* proceeded along parallel curves in each of five syntactic contexts (negative declaratives, negative questions, and three types of affirmative questions) between 1410 and 1575, despite the fact that the five contexts exhibited different frequencies of use over the period.

Now remember that the grammatical analysis underlying the change and the contexts in which the forms are manifested may be quite abstract. So if we take Lightfoot's point (noted above) that a difference in I-language is reflected in a variety of surface differences, we can extend it by applying it to syntactic variation over a period. For example, Kroch (1989*b*) builds on and extends the work of M. Adams (1987*a*, *b*) and Priestley (1955) for Middle French to show that three very different surface changes—the loss of subject-verb inversion, the loss of null subjects, and the rise of left dislocation structures—can all be analysed as reflexes of the same underlying grammatical change, the loss of verb seconding. These three surface phenomena can then be regarded as three different contexts in which variation between options is exhibited. The Constant Rate Effect predicts that all three surface alternations will proceed at the same rate during the period from 1400 to 1700, as indeed Kroch demonstrates. Similarly, Taylor (1994) shows that in three periods of Classical Greek, the distribution of clitics and weak pronouns produces the same measure of verb-medial vs. verb-final clause structure as an independent estimate of that ratio derived from the distribution of NP and PP complements and the rates of postposition. And Hróarsdóttir (in this volume), in her analysis of the change from OV to VO in the history of Icelandic, demonstrates that the frequencies of preverbal DPs, PPs, and non-finite main verbs all decline at similar rates, and that all of these can be analysed as the loss of the same syntactic movement (PredP to Spec,PredP). These studies demonstrate that when two or more constructions are reflexes of a single underlying structure or syntactic process, the frequencies of these constructions change at the same rate. We can therefore be confident that the tracking of usage frequencies is a valid methodological tool for research in syntactic variation and change.

1.4. GRADUAL CHANGE: FURTHER METHODOLOGICAL AND THEORETICAL IMPLICATIONS

Many major parametric changes such as those involving shifts of word order like the loss of V2 or the switch from OV to VO order involve a lengthy period of variation; for example, three of the chapters in this volume investigate such long-term variation in verb-complement order in earlier stages of English (Kroch and Taylor), Icelandic (Hróarsdóttir), and Swedish (Delsing). Thus E-language shows variation in the use of word orders and structures, and yet optionality in I-language should ideally be ruled out by economy conditions within the MP. There are in principle two ways of dealing with such variation in E-language at the level of I-language: establishing competing (incompatible) parameter settings, or setting up two or more equally economical derivations.

Kroch interprets the type of structured variation reviewed in the last section as the reflex of 'competition' between grammars with distinct parameter settings which are strictly incompatible within a single grammar, in a situation in which language users are bi- or multi-dialectal. Thus the variation occurs within the individual, and is to be understood in terms of a recurrent linguistic phenomenon, that of code switching or register switching. The way in which the competing options are analysed and described depends upon the syntactic framework being used. In a GB framework, options frequently correspond to contradictory parameter settings: for example, head-initial vs. head-final structure, verb second vs. non-verb second. Within the Minimalist Programme, competing options can be described in terms of the presence of lexical items with contradictory features; note here the parallel with the morphological doublets discussed in Kroch (1994). Thus it is not entire grammars that are in competition, but rather incompatible options within a grammar. The question immediately arises as to the number of different parameters (or features) that can vary simultaneously. In principle there should be no limit (beyond that of learnability), and in fact Pintzuk (1999) shows that both IP and VP vary between head-initial and head-final structure during the Old English period, and Kroch and Taylor (in this volume) demonstrate the same variation for early Middle English.

An alternative characterization of variation within MP would involve the possibility of optionality in derivations which are truly equivalent in terms of economy, as has been suggested recently by van der Wurff (1997) for the loss of OV order in English. Associated with these alternatives of characterization is the question of why a change should progress once variation has arisen. One possibility is that social and stylistic factors, or discourse factors, control the occurrence of variants, and that these factors are subject to successive reweightings over time, for example as an incoming vernacular variant makes headway against established literary evaluations. Another broad view is that change is due to some aspect of communication between mature users (production or reception, especially parsing), in line with traditional suggestions that much language change is in some way 'functional', so that in the choice of variants a more communicatively effective variant is preferred. A further possibility is that the change might progress because of the favouring of one alternative in the process of acquisition, so that with each generation there is a shift towards the incoming variant.

If the choice between structures is truly optional in grammatical terms, as van der Wurff (1997) argues, then, if nothing else were involved, we might expect to find random fluctuation in usage rather than the steady progress of an S-shaped curve. Since this is not what we typically find, there must be factors external to the grammar which are responsible for this progress. So the hypothesis of grammatical optionality is consistent with the relevance of sociolinguistically driven, or processing, or other communicative pressures to the progress of change. And this is in turn consistent with Labov's suggestion that syntactic change is typically 'communal', in that a community moves together in syntactic change, without showing a stratification by age which reflects differences established at acquisition (1994: 84).

In this complex web of possibilities, we want to focus on some aspects of the potential relevance of functional (specifically parsing) pressures to change. A recent attempt to work out the relevance of parsing pressures for change is Sprouse and Vance (1999), who follow the account of change in Kroch (1989*a*). They make the reasonable assumption that users accommodate their production of variants to the frequencies that they perceive in other users, and they point out that given two variants, the first of which is generally parsed successfully while a steady proportion of the second fails to be parsed, the first will eventually replace the second. But we should note that the mechanism of change in this case need not involve language use across a community, as Sprouse and Vance have it. It could be localized in acquisition; both mechanisms permit a steady proportion of the evidence to be reinterpreted, or 'lost' in the sense that it does not contribute to the establishment of relative frequencies of usage. So Kirby (1998, 1999) models the impact of differential success of parsing in acquisition on a population over time, with results which broadly show an S-shaped curve of development (1998: 373–4; 1999: 42 ff.); and in his modelling of acquisition and change, Briscoe presents a rationalization for input matching of perceived frequencies in learners, from which he derives the familiar S-shaped curve of change.

Other results reported in Briscoe's chapter in this volume are also important here. He is initially concerned to model the progress of change through populations. Since this is partly dependent on the properties of learners, Briscoe discusses the possibility that learners show 'inductive bias'. Within a theory of parameters this is equivalent to the idea that a parameter may have an unmarked value which will form the basis of acquisition in the absence of contrary evidence.[3] (For defence and implementation of this type of view see Roberts 1999, Kiparsky 1996, 1997.) In answer to the question 'How likely is it that the language faculty incorporates inductive bias?' Briscoe replies that general learning theory considerations make it likely, but he provides a more speculative modelling of how such biases may have originated: he allows for the differential survival and reproduction of speaker-hearers who vary as to whether specific grammatical information is encoded as an invariant principle or as a parameter which needs to be set. As he notes, such a bias will make functional sense in terms of the linguistic situation which obtained when it became part of the language faculty. But the functional underpinning which established the original bias need no longer obtain today. So change may look at first blush as if it might be functionally driven, when it is actually taking place in accordance with an inductive bias which encodes a differentiation which was functionally relevant during the period of adaptation for language. So even properties which seem to favour communicative function, or ease of parsing, or which correspond to typological universals with some functional interpretation, need not reflect the existence of such pressures on modern usage. Instead they may reflect the continuing genetic relevance of properties of language as used during the period when the linguistic faculty was established. Here it is worth reflecting on recent developments in syntactic theory. As Newmeyer has pointed out, Government and Binding includes conditions which 'have a plausible . . . origin in communication, in so far as they speed up the identification of structure' (1998b: 314), so that GB is a theory consistent with a period of adaptation as the genetic basis for the human language faculty became fixed. The Minimalist Programme, however, is more consistent with the view that UG has disfunctional properties, that it arose by 'emergence' and not through a process of adaptation (Berwick 1998, Chomsky 1998). A question that is relevant for historical linguists here is how to interpret apparently functional effects: are they potentially truly functional in some sense,

---

[3] This is not the same concept as that modelled in Niyogi and Berwick 1997, where a change may result even in the absence of triggering data (see Briscoe's discussion in Chapter 4).

or do they simply reflect the establishment of parameter settings to correspond with function during a period of adaptation?

There is a further important issue for any attempt to account for change directly in functional terms. As noted above, the Constant Rate Effect of Kroch (1989*b*) establishes that a change will typically follow parallel S-shaped curves in different surface contexts. But if the contexts differ in functional potential, as we might suppose would commonly be the case, then there is an *a priori* problem for any suggestion that the change could make progress because of functional considerations. If this were true, it should lead to a divergence of underlying rate of change in the different contexts, as was indeed the initial proposal of Bailey (1973). In such cases we need a more abstract understanding of the unity of grammar and the impact of 'functional' mechanisms, or perhaps an account in which change is itself more abstractly conceived, with apparent functional effects arising as part of its implementation rather than as its engine, as argued by Kroch (1989*b*). Thus there is here a complex area in which a wide range of considerations is relevant, and major issues are quite unresolved, including the question 'What drives change forwards?'

A rather different series of issues is raised by grammaticalization and the long-term tendencies to change apparently associated with this type of development. The recurrence of overtly similar types of change has indeed been clearly established in work by grammaticalization theorists. But questions arise as to how unitary such phenomena may be, how much of this generative syntacticians should attempt to model, and how they should tackle this modelling.

One approach is to focus on the point of discontinuity at which a full lexical form becomes a functional head. This is the position taken by Roberts and Roussou (1999) in the paper discussed above, in which grammaticalization is interpreted as a consequence of the learner's preference for simplicity. A second approach is that taken by van Kemenade (in this volume). By choosing the grammaticalization of markers of sentence negation in English for a case study, she seeks to hold the semantics of the relevant forms steady; then she interprets change within the framework supplied by the contrasts between functional and lexical projections, and between specifier and head positions within functional projections. From this perspective, what is crucial in grammaticalization is that its fundamental component is morphosyntactic weakening. Acquisition remains central, but she offers a framework for interpretation not just of the crucial points of reanalysis, but also of the long-term change more broadly conceived. This aims to give us an overview of Jespersen's negative cycle (1917), not just of a single transition in the status of negative markers which is fundamental to it. Vincent (in this volume) aims for a yet fuller analytic scope. He follows Bresnan (1998*a*, *b*) in setting up constraints (on pronouns) on form, on content, and crucially, on their interrelationship, within an Optimality Theory account couched in Lexical-Functional Grammar. These constraints include implicational scales having a universal default hierarchy which may be overridden in individual

languages. The constraints can be seen to constitute a structuring of the
typological space that contains possible systems, so that semantic/pragmatic and
(morpho)phonological properties are (universally) related to syntactic properties.
Within such a framework, changes in the nonsyntactic properties of items may
have consequences for their syntactic behaviour. This type of approach embeds
the phenomenon of grammaticalization within a wider account, aiming to provide
an articulated framework within which major aspects of recurrent changes noted
by grammaticalization theorists have a place.

In discussing change over a period of time in this section we have stuck to the
spirit of Hale's comment quoted in §1.1, avoiding appeal to historical tendencies
to change, being careful to distinguish what can be formally accounted for. A
sceptical view of some attempts to account for apparent long-term tendencies in
change has been voiced by Lightfoot (1999: chapter 8 and elsewhere), who
rightly calls attention to the major difficulties of establishing appropriate explanatory principles. But this does not mean that gradual change cannot fruitfully be
discussed, and we have looked at several approaches in this section. Lightfoot
goes on to point out that a further important area of work which may give us
some insight into the progress of long-term changes is the computer modelling
of gradual change across populations where the modelling includes the process
of acquisition. Briscoe's discussion of 'inductive bias' (referred to above) is an
example of such work. So is Kirby's (1998) modelling of the development of
dialects in an originally randomly distributed population. This type of work provides us with new, detailed, and sophisticated ways of thinking about change in
language systems and cross-linguistic typological generalizations; see Briscoe's
discussion below about treating languages as 'complex adaptive systems'. So
despite the fact that the diffusion of change raises difficult issues, requiring us
to distinguish what can appropriately be accounted for, there are real advances
in our understanding on a series of fronts.

1.5. AN OVERVIEW OF THIS VOLUME

1.5.1. *Frameworks for the Understanding of Change*

This section contains three chapters which focus on the development of frameworks that contribute to our understanding of syntactic change. The research
presented in these chapters involves two themes: they investigate the appropriate-
ness and usefulness of particular syntactic frameworks for explanations of
linguistic change, and they incorporate results and insights of research outside
the realm of generative syntax—in particular, grammaticalization theory and the
computer modelling of language change in populations.

Vincent (Chapter 2) incorporates both themes in his analysis of the licensing
of null arguments in Latin and Romance. He adopts Optimality Theory (OT) as a
general theory of combinatorial cognitive systems such as human language, using
Lexical-Functional Grammar (LFG) as his specific account of syntax, arguing

that an LFG architecture within the OT notions of constraints and constraint ranking provides the best model for the analysis of syntactic change. He demonstrates that, within this framework, the changes in the potential for null argument licensing from Latin to Romance can be modelled as constraint rerankings, interpreting (for example) the loss of the Latin null object pronouns as a consequence of the development of the clitic systems for object pronouns in Romance. Here he follows Bresnan's account of pronominals (1998*a*, *b*), assuming that correspondences between the form and content of pronouns are subject to a set of universal constraints, themselves ranked on a universal scale from which individual languages may depart. Different rankings may correspond to differences in pronoun inventory, and the interconnection between the morphophonological development of clitic status and the disappearance of null object forms follows. He argues that the LFG/OT (correspondence/competition) model provides a better understanding of change and linguistic dynamics than derivational frameworks, because the notion of competition of forms is built in to the model and does not need to be stipulated.

Van Kemenade (Chapter 3) provides a detailed account of the progress of the negative cycle (Jespersen 1917) in Old and Middle English, embedding her analysis within a substantial discussion of the process of grammaticalization, and demonstrating that the structuring of functional projections permits a precise account of the historical developments. In her interpretation the negative cycle involves the reanalysis of an Old English negative adverb as the functional head *ne* of NegP, with subsequent reduction to a verbal inflection. There was a concomitant development of a second negative form (Middle English *not*, from Old English *nawiht/nowiht*) which, like the first, was initially licensed in a specifier position and later reanalysed as the head of NegP when *ne* was lost; ultimately, we may suppose, *not* became inflectional *-n't*. Van Kemenade interprets these developments as morphosyntactic weakening, and uses this history to argue for a view of grammaticalization as a fundamentally morphosyntactic process rather than one that is semantically or pragmatically motivated. Her analysis of the negative cycle in the history of English is entirely compatible with the Minimalist perspective of our discussion in §1.2.2, in which the relevant differences would be those characterizing the feature structure of negative elements as lexical head and functional head.

Briscoe (Chapter 4) models the diffusion of syntactic change through populations. He presents a sophisticated treatment both of the process of acquisition and of the changing nature of populations, and he demonstrates the consequences of different assumptions for modelling. With respect to acquisition, he shows that a learning procedure which selects between grammars on the basis of single trigger instances (Gibson and Wexler 1994, Niyogi and Berwick 1997) predicts random dynamics in language change. In contrast, if acquisition is modelled so that the learner is sensitive to the relative frequencies of different constructions in the input, then the familiar S-shaped curve of change may result from competition between individuals with the incoming grammar and individuals without it. With respect to populations, Briscoe presents 'microscopic simulations' which model the properties of real populations: in particular, he allows for overlap between generations, adult immigrants (and hence contact situations), and variant proportions of learners to non-learners in a population. Within this more articulated framework, he makes a convincing case that creolization is not a special process distinct from other language change, but rather a normal selective change in a context of radical demographic change. In addition, he models the situation in which change spreads from a random fluctuation in a small pocket of the data, so that the choice of which variant will eventually replace the others is indeed arbitrary, which gives an interesting perspective on the possible role of chance in change. Briscoe presents a picture of language as a 'dynamic adaptive system' which evolves in historical time, creating altered circumstances and contexts which then lead to and condition subsequent change; within the framework he establishes, variation and change seem inevitable and inherent rather than peripheral and accidental.

1.5.2. *The Comparative Basis of Diachronic Syntax*

The three chapters in this section highlight the relationship between comparative syntax and diachronic syntax, and demonstrate that an understanding of syntactic variation has broad implications for analyses of parametric differences between dialects and languages. These chapters provide particularly clear examples of how statistical techniques can be used to investigate historical data and provide quantitative support for a formal analysis. They all focus on syntactic variation in the history of English, and they all use data from syntactically annotated electronic corpora: the PPCME and the Brooklyn Corpus.

Haeberli (Chapter 5) investigates a word-order pattern which has previously received little attention in the literature: V–(adjunct)–subject. He shows that the Germanic languages vary as to whether they permit adjuncts to intervene between fronted finite verbs and their subjects, and he argues that the variation is the result of the syntax of subjects rather than the syntax of adjuncts. He demonstrates that Old English provides crucial evidence, lacking in other languages, for the proper analysis of this word order in the Germanic languages as a group. The analysis that he proposes in turn resolves several long-debated questions about the syntax of Old English, in particular the position of topics, subjects, and finite verbs in verb-second clauses. Haeberli then turns to data from Middle English; and based on V–subject (non-)adjacency, he provides evidence for the same two dialects as those identified by Kroch and Taylor (1997) on the basis of the syntax of verb movement. Like Kroch and Taylor, he links the difference between the two dialects to the absence of overt agreement morphology in the north. His analysis and methodology highlight the relationship between the comparative syntax of modern languages and the diachronic analysis of older ones: comparative syntax poses questions for diachronic syntax, while the analysis of historical data can often be used to resolve issues in the analysis of modern languages and in syntactic theory in general.

Kroch and Taylor (Chapter 6) investigate verb–object order in Early Middle English. Contra standard analyses of a sudden break from Late Old English to Early Middle English, they show that both stages of the language exhibit variation in the headedness of IP and VP, although at different frequencies; this suggests more continuity between Old and Middle English than is generally assumed. Similarly, they demonstrate that two Early Middle English dialects, the South-east Midlands and the West Midlands, show a difference in frequency of use of the available syntactic options, but not a difference in underlying grammar. Their approach, combining standard diagnostics for structure with quantitative evidence, demonstrates that careful and creative quantitative analysis of variation in historic texts can provide evidence for the choice of one analysis over another. For example, they show that the frequency of preverbal non-quantified objects in Early Middle English is too high to permit an analysis of scrambling from postverbal position, but rather supports an analysis of underlying OV structure. Moreover, their results support the interpretation of the E-language data of historical texts as a reflection of I-language. They show that six measures of underlying structure all provide evidence for the hypothesis that the language of the South-east Midlands was more conservative (i.e. closer to Old English) than the language of the West Midlands. These results would be a coincidence if the language of the texts was not systematically related to the internal grammars of their authors, but they are only to be expected if E-language reflects I-language closely in the relevant respects.

Williams (Chapter 7) uses a careful and sophisticated interpretation of the statistical patterns in Middle English to propose the existence of a silent expletive and to justify its restriction to specific sentence types; his chapter provides another clear demonstration of the use of quantitative data to support a particular grammatical analysis. Williams shows that two sudden changes are aligned: the decline of clauses with a silent expletive, and the decline of narrative verb-first sentences. He argues that this alignment points to an interpretation in which the loss of the silent expletive is not a function of the loss of case and agreement, but rather a function of the loss of verb-first word order and structure. His analysis provides evidence for the resolution of several general questions in Germanic syntax: most importantly, that silent expletives in Germanic occur in the c-command domain of a finite verbal feature, and that the finite verb in Old and Middle English c-commands a pronominal subject that follows it but not a pronominal subject that precedes it. This in turn, like the results of Haeberli (in this volume), has direct implications for the debate on the clause structure of the early stages of English (van Kemenade 1997*a*, Kroch and Taylor 1997, Pintzuk 1999).

1.5.3. *Mechanisms of Syntactic Change*

The seven chapters of this section develop ideas and issues that have emerged from within the Principles and Parameters paradigm (and in particular from the Minimalist Programme), applying them to the analysis of specific languages and language groups. The principal theme of Chapters 8 and 9 is the synchronic and diachronic consequences of changes in features and of categorial reanalysis. Chapters 10 to 14 deal with the consequences of the loss of overt movement. As was discussed in §1.2, all of these changes can be interpreted as a reorganization of the properties of items in the lexicon, but they have been grouped here on the basis of their most obvious syntactic characteristic: a change in features vs. the loss of movement. A strong claim emerges from these seven chapters: syntactic change typically and recurrently involves loss: loss of structure, or loss of derivational steps involving movement. We have discussed Roberts and Roussou's (1999) proposal that grammaticalization involves simplification, and, in particular, loss of movement; here we see a broadening of the relevance of loss in a wider collection of instances.

Martins (Chapter 8) analyses the distribution and the degree of variable underspecification of negative and positive indefinites in Romance. Her findings, that negative and positive indefinites become more specific over time with respect to their licensing environments, provide a clear example of the lexical revision process underlying language acquisition discussed in §1.2. In this particular case, negative and positive indefinites are in competition in non-negative modal contexts, which become neutralized and eventually disallow negative polarity items. Martins argues that these contexts are less salient and eventually cease to be identified as licensing contexts for NPIs.

Whitman (Chapter 9) focuses on a class of changes that cannot be described as simply the gain or loss of movement operations. These changes are all categorized as reanalysis, which involves a change in syntactic category without a correlated change in surface form. He challenges the traditional view of reanalysis as a change in the repertory of basic structural patterns made available by the grammar of a particular language, and he argues that the process of reanalysis should instead be interpreted as 'relabelling', a change in the categorial feature of a lexical item. This interpretation captures the fact that we observe a change in category without a change in structure; the only structural change involves pruning, which may accompany reanalysis as a result of thematic changes or a change in status from specifier to head. Within this framework, Whitman analyses as relabelling several examples of changes that involve serial verbs, the *ba*-construction in Chinese, and pronoun to copula reanalysis. In keeping with the Minimalist Programme, he presents a lexical account of change that has been traditionally viewed as syntactic.

Batllori and Roca (Chapter 10) present an analysis of the development of the Modern Spanish definite article from the Latin demonstrative. The structure that they propose for nominals in all stages of the history of Spanish involves (at least) two levels of determination, DP dominating DemP, with heads D and Dem that have distinct syntactic and semantic properties. They show that the development of Modern Spanish *el* from Late Latin *ille* involved the loss of syntactic movement: lexical items once generated in DemP with movement to DP were later generated directly as the head of DP. The change exhibits characteristics of grammaticalization—semantic bleaching, fixing of distribution, loss of movement, and gradualness—and Batllori and Roca suggest that it proceeded via grammatical competition, since in Old Spanish these lexical items exhibit variation in their syntactic and semantic characteristics. Their analysis can be interpreted as a change in the feature structure of lexical items which has consequences for their syntactic behaviour.

Delsing (Chapter 11) presents an analysis of variation in verb–complement order in Old Swedish. He demonstrates that by the end of the fourteenth century, the position of the object, preverbal vs. postverbal, is to a large extent determined by its form: DPs with filled heads are almost invariably postverbal, while DPs with empty heads may occur either preverbally or postverbally. Delsing proposes that objects can be licensed in one of two ways: by filling D by Merge or Move, thus permitting the object to remain in postverbal position and deriving VO word order; or, if D is empty, by leftward movement to Spec,AgrOP for licensing in a Spec-Head relationship with the verbal chain, thus deriving OV word order. Optionality in verb–complement order under Delsing's analysis is therefore accommodated within a single grammar, since head movement to D and DP movement to Spec,AgrOP are equally costly (cf. van der Wurff 1997 for a similar approach to optionality in verb–complement order in Middle English). Delsing links the loss of OV to the loss of V movement to I, which occurred about the same time and which entailed the loss of V movement to AgrO and therefore the loss of object movement to Spec,AgrOP.

Han (Chapter 12) solves a puzzle in the development of periphrastic *do* in the history of English: as the frequency of use of *do* increases in questions and negative declaratives in the sixteenth century, imperatives do not show a parallel development but remain distinct. Then at the end of the sixteenth century, at the point identified as the loss of V-to-I movement (Kroch 1989*b*, Roberts 1985), negative imperatives suddenly start to behave like other negatives. Han first demonstrates that negation may occur in two different positions in Middle English, and then proposes a differentiated structure with intermediate functional projections AspP, M(ood)P, and TP. This structure permits her to divide V-to-I movement into two different movements: V-to-Asp and M-to-T. She shows that the distinct behaviour of *do* in imperatives is modelled if the higher movement (M-to-T) is lost first, and the loss of V-to-Asp does not begin until the end of the sixteenth century. Her analysis highlights the explanatory power of more articulated theories of structure (see also van Kemenade in this volume), and may provide an interesting approach to the apparent dislocation in the development of *do* in negatives and questions which occurs in the sixteenth century, and which is difficult to analyse simply as the loss of a unitary V-to-I movement (Lightfoot 1997, Warner 1997).

Hróarsdóttir (Chapter 13) investigates the change from OV to VO in the history of Icelandic, but the Icelandic data require a different analysis from that of Delsing (in this volume) for Swedish. Hróarsdóttir demonstrates that while a uniform head-initial analysis with optional leftward movement adequately describes synchronic variation in the position of complements in Older Icelandic, such an analysis cannot explain the fact that the frequencies of preverbal DPs, PPs, and non-finite main verbs all decline at similar rates over time. Hróarsdóttir instead builds on the proposal of Kayne (1998) that all syntactic movement is overt: Kayne shows that scopal relations in particular, often derived in the generative literature by covert movement, can be derived instead by overt remnant-VP fronting. Hróarsdóttir extends Kayne's analysis, with remnant-VP fronting applying obligatorily in all clauses in VO languages. She proposes an analysis of Older Icelandic in which VO order results from the obligatory fronting of a remnant VP, while both OV order and main verb–auxiliary verb order are derived by optional PredP fronting. All of the variation is thus a direct result of the optionality of PredP fronting; and as PredP fronting is gradually lost, there is a decline and simultaneous loss of the head-final orders. Hróarsdóttir's analysis is grounded on one of the most important principles in diachronic syntax: when two or more constructions change in the same way over the same period of time, they are almost certainly reflexes of a single underlying change.

Willis (Chapter 14) discusses the conditional in Slavonic, where conditional mood is expressed by using the auxiliary *be*, which is itself inflected for conditional mood and may be attracted to C by an appropriate complementizer. In one group of Slavonic languages, exemplified by Old Russian, a form of conditional *be* is reinterpreted as an uninflected marker of that mood, and is generated directly in C. The reanalysis occurs in those contexts where a particular configuration of three conditions creates potential ambiguity for the learner. First, for the second and third person singular of *be*, movement of the conditional to C has become obligatory. Second, the inflections for mood which characterize the moved forms are identical and the forms are open to reinterpretation as uninflected. Third, in the third person singular, the perfect can be expressed without an overt form of *be*, its normal auxiliary. Hence the possibility arises of analysing the third person singular form of *be* as a clause-initial mood marker, followed by a perfect without overt auxiliary. We might note that under the assumption that learners acquire grammars that minimize movement (Roberts and Roussou 1999, discussed in our §1.2.2), the structural ambiguity in these particular contexts results in reanalysis. Willis's account also has interesting consequences for the status of 'paradigm', since in acquiring Old Russian, learners did not treat the uninflected forms as belonging to the paradigm of the inflected forms.

PART I

Frameworks for the Understanding of Change

2

Competition and Correspondence in Syntactic Change: Null Arguments in Latin and Romance

NIGEL VINCENT

2.1. INTRODUCTION

The vast preponderance of work to date on syntactic change from the perspective of formal linguistics has been couched within the Principles and Parameters framework—see Battye and Roberts (1995) and van Kemenade and Vincent (1997) for representative collections of papers. Inevitably, too, given the time at which the research reported in these volumes was conducted, both principles and parameters were construed in absolute terms. A parameter was either on or off, and once set could not be overridden; principles had to be obeyed absolutely. Put in other terms, the constraints on such a system were of the 'hard' variety. In the present chapter we suggest instead that a number of classic issues in the study of grammar change come into sharper focus once we (a) adopt the assumptions of a different analytical framework, namely Lexical-Functional Grammar (LFG), and (b) interpret the system of grammatical constraints as 'soft' or violable along the lines of Optimality Theory (OT). Two fundamental concepts—Competition (drawn from OT) and Correspondence (drawn from LFG[1])—will receive

This chapter was given as a plenary talk at the Fifth Diachronic Generative Syntax Conference at the University of York, 30 May–1 June 1998. I am grateful to those who discussed it with me there, especially Tony Kroch, Aditi Lahiri, David Lightfoot, and Cecilia Goria, to the organizers of the conference for inviting me, and—in their editorial capacity—for their suggestions for revising the written version. Thanks also to the publisher's referees for their helpful comments and for catching a couple of potentially embarrassing errors. Ana Maria Martins made a number of very perceptive observations, without which the chapter would certainly have been a great deal worse. Steve Parkinson and Þorhallur Eyþórsson helped me with the Portuguese and Icelandic data respectively. I have benefited, as always, from discussion of my ideas with Joan Bresnan, whose assistance was also invaluable in formulating some of the technical parts of the analyses reported here. Parts of this material were also presented at a symposium on Methods in Historical Linguistics convened by the Copenhagen Linguistics Circle on 17 May 1999. The chapter was prepared while I was in receipt of a British Academy Research Readership, and part of it was written while I was a visitor at the Romansk Institut of the University of Copenhagen. Many thanks to all concerned; responsibility for errors and misinterpretations remains, of course, solely mine.

[1] There is an unfortunate terminological ambiguity that has arisen around the term 'correspondence' in the recent literature. Within OT work on phonology and morphology, correspondence (and

particular attention in what follows. Conversely, we will argue that the evidence of change provides further support for such an LFG/OT conception of linguistic systems. The specific case study around which the argument is built concerns some of the changes that take place in the licensing of null and overt arguments as Latin develops into the Romance languages.

The structure of the chapter is as follows. In §2.2 and §2.3 we review some basic concepts of OT and LFG respectively and situate the notions of competition and correspondence in a wider theoretical context. §2.4 reviews the theory of pronominals presented in Bresnan (1998b) and gives a first sketch of the role it can play in accounting for syntactic change. §2.5 refines this model while §2.6 sets out the patterns of change in the pronominal system between Latin and Romance that are the principal empirical focus of this study. In §2.7 we elaborate a formal account of these changes drawing on the ideas introduced in §§2.2, 2.3 and 2.4. Finally, in §2.8 we reflect on the general lessons for the theoretical modelling of syntactic change that can be learnt from the material presented here. §2.9 sums up our conclusions.

2.2. OPTIMALITY THEORY AND SYNTAX: THE NOTION OF COMPETITION

We begin then by briefly rehearsing the general features of the OT approach to characterizing linguistic systems.[2] As is by now well known, the key constructs are Constraints and the Ranking of constraints. The universal set of constraints, under a ranking which is language-particular, apply to a set of Candidate forms generated (by a function GEN) for a given Input. The EVAL(uation) function defined by the constraint ranking then determines the successful Output, which is thereby identified as the grammatical expression of that content (or input) in the language in question. A grammar of a language on this view is then a ranking of constraints consistent with the attested outputs.

Correspondence Theory) has come to refer to the relation of identity between a pair of linked forms, whether input and output or output and output (see Kager 1999: 248–52 and ch. 6 for a convenient summary and references). In a framework such as LFG, by contrast, correspondence holds between the representation of abstract grammatical relations (in LFG, f-structure) and their expression in linguistic form (or c-structure) (Bresnan 1997, 1998a, b). It is this latter sense that is intended here. Correspondence in this sense is very similar to realization (Matthews 1981: ch. 12) or exponence (Matthews 1991: ch. 9). A piece of linguistic form realizes/is the exponent of/corresponds to a piece of linguistic content but there is no reason at all for the representation of the form to be couched in the same metalanguage as that which used to represent the content. In this sense LFG enshrines the syntactic equivalent of what in morphology Aronoff (1994: 8 ff.) calls the 'separationist hypothesis'. For an elaboration of the latter from the perspective of LFG, see Börjars, Vincent, and Chapman (1997) and Vincent and Börjars (1996).

[2] Small capitals indicate technical terms within OT. Their precise sense will become clear as we proceed. For a basic introduction and references see Archangeli (1997) and Kager (1999).

OT may not have had everything its own way in syntax as seems to have happened in phonology (Archangeli 1997: 25–6), but an impressive body of work nonetheless by now exists.[3] In an already classic paper,[4] Grimshaw (1997) demonstrates how a minimal predicate-argument structure input such as {*see (John, who)*} is paired with the output *Who did John see?* via the interaction of constraints which require, amongst other things, that an operator be in a specifier position, that the operator c-command the clause over which it has scope, that X-bar heads be filled, and so on. Here is not the place to repeat all the details of Grimshaw's intricate and elegant analysis. I will focus instead on just one constraint to illustrate the flavour of the argumentation. Grimshaw postulates a constraint STAY which privileges non-movement of syntactic categories. In the example just given, STAY is in conflict with the requirement that an operator be in a suitably c-commanding specifier position (the constraint OP-SPEC). If *who* remains in object position, OP-SPEC will be violated; if not then STAY suffers the violation. The form of English interrogatives shows us that in this conflict it is OP-SPEC which wins out and hence that this constraint must be ranked higher than STAY in the grammar of English. Consider now the different input in which the functions of the arguments are reversed: {*see (who, John)*}. Now *John* fills the object position and *who* already fills Spec,VP, so *who* can satisfy the requirements of OP-SPEC without movement, thus at the same time satisfying STAY. One striking and attractive consequence of this approach is that only as much structure as is necessary is projected: *Who did John see?* is a CP but *Who saw John?* is a VP, and by parity of argumentation *Who will John see?* is an IP. Note too that of these structures, only *Who saw John?* is free of any constraint violations, yet all are perfectly grammatical. In other words, the interaction of constraints works according to a principle of optimality to determine the best candidate in the circumstances, but once chosen, the best candidate, however many constraint violations it has incurred, is absolutely grammatical.[5] Different constraint rankings generate different languages, so that reranking of constraints provides a mechanism for encoding both typological variation (Ackema and Neeleman 1998) and diachronic change, as we will see in what follows.

Despite the unconventional nature of some of Grimshaw's conclusions, the underlying logic of her analysis is not in fact far removed from Minimalist

---

[3] See the papers collected in Beckman, Urbanczyk, and Walsh (1995), Archangeli and Langendoen (1997), Barbosa *et al.* (1998), Dekkers, van der Leeuw, and van de Weijer (2000), plus others mentioned in the course of the present chapter for a representative selection.

[4] It may seem strange to label so recent a paper as 'classic' but in fact it had been circulating for a number of years in earlier versions and had elicited much discussion and reaction prior to its eventual appearance in print towards the end of 1997.

[5] One apparent consequence of this logic is that there should never be absolutely ungrammatical sentences, since there will always be a 'least worst' output for every input. For discussion of this problem, see Ackema and Neeleman (to appear).

ideals. The spirit of Economy is well met by banning movement except where necessary and even then only over the shortest distance (since each step in a movement chain such as V-to-I-to-C incurs a separate violation penalty), and by projecting no more structure than is strictly needed to satisfy independent requirements. This point is made *in extenso* by Speas (1997: 180–5), who notes:

PPT/MP [i.e. Principles and Parameters Theory/Minimalist Program] claims that the principles of UG are inviolable, but . . .
• all of these principles contain hedges which restrict the domain in which the principle is inviolable.
• the Minimalist Program makes violability explicit in its economy principles. (Speas 1997: 185)

Some aspects, then, of the OT philosophy of grammatical analysis and description chime with current views within generative syntax.[6] At the same time, it is important to appreciate that OT is not itself a theory of syntax (or indeed of phonology). It is a theory of how combinatorial cognitive systems such as natural languages may be characterized. This fundamental point is perhaps less obvious, and less crucial, in phonology where constraints refer for the most part to aspects of structure that are directly translatable into more or less theory-neutral concepts such as Voice, Onset, Left/Right, etc. In syntax, the matter is more complex since we do not have an independently observable universal domain parallel to phonetic substance to fall back on. The traditional assumption that semantics can fill such a role for syntax, while not without its attractions or its modern advocates (cf. Langacker 1987, Anderson 1997 to name but two works in this vein), is much more fraught with difficulty. OT syntax, therefore, will inevitably vary according to the theory in which the analysis is conducted. For instance, Grimshaw's already mentioned constraint STAY presupposes an account in which movement is an option within the grammatical metalanguage; a model which has no analogue of Case Theory will not require her CASE constraint; and so on. Different researchers therefore may well agree on the desirability of adopting an OT approach to syntax, while diverging radically from each other on the framework in which the account is cast and therefore on the constraints proposed. It is instructive in this respect to compare Grimshaw's (1997) account of the English *wh*-construction with Bresnan's (1997) reanalysis. Alternatively, scholars may largely share theoretical frameworks but differ on the role, if any, which OT may play in their analyses: compare, from the perspective of the Minimalist Program, Speas's (1997) wholehearted embracing of OT with Pesetsky's (1997) more cautious distinction between areas where the OT remit may run and

---

[6] In other respects large controversies still loom, which I will not go into here. In particular, how much is OT ultimately driven by a connectionist, neural network approach to cognitive phenomena which is radically at odds with the deep-seated innatism which has inspired generative grammar since the beginning?

areas where it may not. Many others no doubt remain unreservedly sceptical of the whole enterprise.[7]

2.3. LEXICAL-FUNCTIONAL GRAMMAR AND THE CONCEPT OF CORRESPONDENCE

If we wish to explore the consequences of OT in the diachronic domain, therefore, we must first choose a particular framework within which to construct the analysis and thus define the constraints. I will adopt L(exical)-F(unctional) G(rammar): for details see the papers collected in Dalrymple *et al.* (1995), notably Kaplan and Bresnan (1982), and for recent OT-inspired developments within the framework see Bresnan (1997, 1998*a, b*) and references therein. This choice is not arbitrary, but is based on a fundamental asymmetry between function-based systems such as LFG and a position-based system such as Principles and Parameters,[8] namely that all positions have a function but not all functions have a (phonetically expressed) position. For a system like Principles and Parameters this means that empty categories/positions have to be postulated to bear the overtly unrealized functions and a separate subtheory, Case Theory, has to be recruited to constrain the links between positions and functions. Consider for example the problem PRO poses for Case Theory under the Visibility interpretation (Chomsky 1986*b*: 93–5) and the artifice that is then required of assigning null Case to the empty category in order to ensure that it is kept in grammatical play (see Chomsky and Lasnik 1993 (= Chomsky 1995: 119) and the excellent critique in Hornstein 1999). None of this is necessary if PRO is seen simply as the unexpressed subject function of an infinitival predicate (Bresnan 1982, Culicover and Wilkins 1986).

A further objection to a configuration-based metalanguage, of particular relevance in what follows, is that it privileges those languages that realize function through position over those that adopt some form of morphological encoding. We will assume instead that abstract grammatical relations—subject and object will be all that will concern us here—can be expressed in one of three possible (and sometimes overlapping) ways, namely:[9]

---

[7] It may of course be that certain types of model are more open to an OT interpretation than others, so that if for independent reasons the OT approach were to prove preferable, then models which were more easily compatible with it would at once be privileged.

[8] In this respect, compare also the model developed in Kiparsky (1997) and recent versions of Relational Grammmar as in Gerdts (1993).

[9] Generative grammar has been a configuration-based system right from the outset, as witness Chomsky's early arguments against the primacy of relations (1965: 68–9). However, in recent instantiations it has oscillated between a reliance in addition on government, essentially a dependent marking strategy (Nichols 1986) and on agreement (essentially head marking, Nichols 1986). Whereas within the Government and Binding approach head marking languages require the postulation of additional governors in INFL, as perceptively noted already by van Valin (1985: 370), under Minimalism arguments have to move to an agreement position to be licensed. A more straightforward

1. configuration/position: e.g. English, Italian, Turkish;
2. dependent marking (cases and adpositions): e.g. Latin, Chechen (Nichols 1986);
3. head marking (agreement and incorporation): e.g. Mohawk (Baker 1995), Abkhaz (Nichols 1986).

Moreover, the particular options employed from within this broad typological range may vary with the passage of time (Kiparsky 1997), as we shall see quite clearly in the present study.

LFG then distinguishes f(unctional)-structures expressed in terms of attribute-value matrices (features) and c(onstituent)-structure expressed in terms of X-bar. Since c-structure serves only to define surface form, it may be freely substituted by morphology or by no marking at all depending on the language. Grammatical relations of the kind which require c-command, *wh*-movement, Case-checking, etc. in a Principles and Parameters type of architecture are expressed in the f-structure without recourse to configuration. The relation which holds between an f-structure and the c-structure and/or morphology which expresses it is one of correspondence or realization.[10]

Adopting a system like LFG where there are no empty positions and no movement will obviously have drastic effects on the standard Principles and Parameters typology of null elements. In anybody's system, the phenomenology of *wh*-constructions constitutes a class apart and we will not be concerned with them here. Intra-clausal NP-traces (passives and middles) are treated lexically and will only impinge marginally on the present analysis; inter-clausal NP-traces (or 'raising') are relevant to our account and following the proposals of Bresnan (1982) will be assimilated to the analysis of control constructions. In sum, therefore, we will be focusing on the changes in the distribution of *pro* and PRO, the [+ pronominal] elements of the standard Chomskyan typology, and integrating these into a broader account of the changes in the distribution of various kinds of overt pronominal. The unified nature of the resulting diachronic analysis can in turn be seen as a further argument in support of the way the grammatical phenomena are divided up under the assumptions of LFG rather than those of Principles and Parameters.

2.4. A THEORY OF PRONOMINALS

It is important to be clear about the relation of non-overt pronominal elements (i.e. those referred to above as PRO/*pro*) to various kinds of phonetically real-

approach would be the traditional one, namely that, in English at least, objects are governed and subjects agree. There is no reason that I know of other than the Procrustean dictates of changing theoretical fashion to require both the internal and the external argument to be licensed by the same formal mechanism. Indeed, we may even wonder, as the discussion below (§2.7) will make clear, if the notion of licensing itself is necessary once the configurational perspective is abandoned. For valuable discussion of the differences between head-marking and dependent-marking non-configurationality, see Nordlinger (1998: ch. 3).   [10] Cf. note 1.

ized pronouns. To this end, we will adopt the correspondence theory of pronominals proposed in Bresnan (1998*b*), which contains the following components:

1. *A universal scale of pronominal form.* Elements which have pronominal function can be ranged along a scale according to the degree of (prosodic and/or morphological) independence they exhibit, namely:[11]

(1) zero < bound < clitic < weak < pronoun

In this conception of things, 'zero' means having no overt realization at all, whether morphological or syntactic. Examples include the marking of subject and object in Chinese and Japanese, and of object in Latin. By contrast, the encoding of subject in Latin via a system of person inflection here falls under the heading 'bound'. 'Clitic' is to be understood in the sense of Zwicky's (1977) 'special clitics', that is to say elements whose syntactic positioning is determined by rules other than those which dictate the position of full nominals. The well-known clitics of the Romance languages are a clear case in point. 'Weak' pronominals are syntactically free in the sense that their distribution for the most part parallels that of full NPs but they are prosodically subordinate to another word (in this respect they behave very like 'light' verbs, articles and some prepositions). A pronoun in the sense intended here is by contrast both distributionally and prosodically indistinguishable from a full NP/DP.

2. *A universal set of features for pronominal content.* In similar vein the possible dimensions of pronominal content may be broken down into three:

(*a*) semantic: pronouns have meaning in virtue of reference internally within a text or externally to entities in the real world. This aspect of their function is treated in terms of values of a feature PRO.[12]

(*b*) information-structural: the status of all (pro)nominals varies from discourse context to discourse context. This is captured as values for a feature TOP.

(*c*) morphosyntactic: pronominal phi-features, which express their grammatical content, are treated as values for the class of features here subsumed under the label AGR (i.e. person, number, etc.).

---

[11] Bresnan does not in fact identify a scale here but simply a range of possible pronominal forms. That, from a diachronic point of view at least, the items in (1) form a cline of grammaticalization is of course well known (Hopper and Traugott 1993: ch. 6). In §2.6 we will see evidence for a scalar interpretation in OT terms, and thus that the stronger position, namely that (1) identifies a scale (or ordered set) rather than simply a range (or unordered set), is justified in the present context.

[12] Note that on this account the distributional differences between so-called 'big PRO' and 'small *pro*' are not handled by recognizing two categorially distinct entities, respectively in the standard Chomskyan view [+ anaphoric] and [– anaphoric], but by differing constraints on the property bundles which describe pronouns of all types. In the notation that follows, therefore, PRO labels a feature that all pronouns have and not a particular type of pronoun. Note in any case that the conclusion that PRO and *pro* are not distinct categories in terms of their featural content has often been canvassed within the Government and Binding framework (cf. Wyngaerd 1994 and Petter 1998 for reviews of the relevant literature—and diametrically opposed conclusions!). See also the OT analysis of Speas (1997).

All such features are privative and a feature may be absent from the representation of the content of a given item: for example, there is no AGR in Japanese verb forms. Thus, the feature constellation [PRO, TOP] defines the class of items that have variable referentiality (PRO) and topic anaphoricity (TOP). It subsumes [PRO, TOP, AGR], the class of items which also have grammatical properties like person and number, and is subsumed by [PRO], the class of items which simply have variable reference. Constellations of these features will provide the input for evaluation by a language's constraint hierarchy, and thus be linked to members of the class of possible pronominal forms identified in (1) above. To this end we further need:

3. *A universal set of constraints on form–content correspondences.* These constraints express recurrent patterns of correlation between the content of an argument type and its expression across languages. There are two important dimensions here. The first limits which elements on the scale in (1) can be encoded overtly and the second those which can be encoded by elements which are in some sense segmentally or prosodically reduced. Thus we have two contrasts as follows:

(2) (*a*) Overt (all except zero) vs. non-overt (zero)
     (*b*) Reduced (all except pronoun) vs. non-reduced (pronoun)

Table 2.1 shows the relations between the constraints in (2) and the items in (1).

TABLE 2.1.

non-overt zero	⎤	
	⎡bound⎤ *reduced*	
overt	⎢clitic⎢	
	⎢weak ⎦	
	⎣full *unreduced*	

We are now in a position to formulate the following (families of) constraints:

(3) HARMONY constraints:
     (*a*) Reduced ⇔ TOP: pronominals are reduced iff they are specialized for topic anaphoricity.
     (*b*) Overt ⇔ AGR: pronominals are inherently specified for person/ number/gender iff they are overt.

(4) STRUCTURAL MARKEDNESS constraints:
     (a) Cross-linguistically the unmarked pronominal is a full pronoun.
     (b) Zero or a bound element associated with PRO violates ICONICITY (since separate pronominal content is not matched by separate form).

(*c*)   A clitic or weak element associated with PRO violates ALLOTAXY[13]
        (since there is more than one way of expressing pronominal content).

(5) FAITHFULNESS constraints: require that all and only the content of the
    input be expressed in the output.

The initial state of the language learner is assumed to be one in which the following dominance relations hold between these (families of) constraints:

(6) HARMONY ≫ STRUCT ≫ FAITH

To determine the correct output for a given language, we start with a featural
characterization of the input—e.g. [PRO, TOP]—and evaluate possible form–
content pairings under the constraint ranking that is postulated to hold for the
language in question. Thus, assume that we are dealing with a language in which
the learner has not acquired evidence to alter the default rankings in (6) which
characterize his/her initial state. This situation is represented in Tableau I.[14]

TABLEAU I

Input [PRO, TOP]	HARMONY	STRUCT	FAITH
Zero: [PRO, TOP]		*!	
Bound: [PRO, TOP]	*!	*	
Pronoun: [PRO, TOP]	*!		
☞ Pronoun: [PRO, AGR]			*

In other words, in such a language, of which English is an example, if we want
to express a pronominal topic, the constraints predict that the free pronoun is
required even though this in fact does not express only topics. A zero pronominal with this function would violate the iconicity member (4*b*) of the structural
markedness constraint family, whereas overt pronominals without phi-features
violate the harmony constraint (3*a*). The remaining candidate is one which does
not exclusively express the desired content. It nevertheless ends up the optimal
form since the violation thus incurred is of the lower ranked faithfulness constraints, and according to the postulated dominance hierarchy in (6) it is more
important to respect structural markedness and harmony than to exactly match
input and output.

---

[13] The term ALLOTAXY is taken from Haiman (1985: 162), and refers to a situation in which there
are multiple realizations for the same syntactic content, i.e. the extension into the syntactic domain
of the notion of allomorphy. Constraint (4*c*) excludes situations in which there is no overt realization
of grammatical content while the complementary (4*c*) blocks more than one such realization. Taken
together, the two constraints privilege the idea of 'one form one meaning' or what is sometimes
called 'Humboldt's Universal'.

[14] Tableau I is a reduced version of Table 1 in Bresnan (1998*b*). Here and in subsequent tableaux
I only include those candidates that are directly relevant to the discussion at hand.

4. *Language particular constraint rankings.* Languages may deviate from the above universally unmarked constraint ranking if the constraint rankings are changed. Thus a *pro*-drop language like Italian is generated if one of the STRUCT constraints, namely that which bans the association of an affix with PRO(nominal) value, is ranked lower than FAITH, as is shown in Tableau II. (For the Chinese type of *pro*-drop, by contrast, in which there is no overt agreement morpheme to do pronominal duty, switch the columns headed *∅ [PRO] and *af [PRO] in Tableau II.) In other words, it is more important to be faithful to the input than to avoid violating the particular member of the structural markedness family of constraints which penalizes the morphologically bound expression of pronominal content.

TABLEAU II

Input [PRO, TOP]	HARM	*∅ [PRO]	FAITH	*af [PRO]
Zero: [PRO, TOP]		*!		
☞ Bound: [PRO, TOP, AGR]				*
Pronoun: [PRO, AGR]			*!	

On this ranking, appropriate for Italian or Latin subjects, the affix emerges as the best candidate for expressing topic anaphoric pronominal reference. However, for non-topic pronominal meaning we still require a full pronoun as Tableau III shows.[15]

TABLEAU III

Input [PRO]	HARM	*∅ [PRO]	FAITH	*af [PRO]
Zero: [PRO, TOP]		*!		
Bound: [PRO, TOP, AGR]				*!
☞ Pronoun: [PRO, AGR]				

Expansion of the pronominal inventory can thus be modelled by constraint reranking. When the purpose of the exercise is to compare the different pronominal systems of languages as geographically and genetically separate as Chinese and Chichewa, the effect of constraint reranking is to permit us to capture typological generalizations. When, on the other hand, the languages being compared form a historical progression, as in the case of Latin and Romance, then the outcome is the first step towards a constraint-based model of syntactic

---

[15] The analysis here essentially encodes the account of Italian pronominals argued for by Samek-Lodovici (1996) but in a non-configurational system which does not require reference to abstract Case or specifier positions.

change. We will seek to develop this insight further in what follows, but first we consider a revision in one aspect of Bresnan's system.

2.5. THE PRONOMINAL MODEL REFINED

Bresnan's model needs to be refined to deal with the double role of Latin and Italian verbal inflection as both the expression of pronominal content when there is no overt subject and as markers of agreement when an overt subject is present. As Cecilia Goria (p.c.) has pointed out to me, the account offered in §2.4 seems to fail in one important respect, namely that the use of an overt pronoun in a non-topical context does not suppress the corresponding affix but simply pre-empts its pronominal function. The affix remains but its function shifts from encoding a pronominal argument to expressing agreement with an independent argument whether pronominal or nominal. To see the implications of this point, consider the following Italian example, an instance of so-called clitic left disloca-tion (Cinque 1990):

(7)   Io   Valerio non lo   voglio   sposare
       I-NOM V.   not OBJCL-3SGM want-PRES-1SG marry-INF
       'I don't want to marry Valerio.'

The precise informational status of such an example, which has two fronted arguments *io* 'I' and *Valerio*, is a complex matter and need not concern us here. Rather, we should note the discrepancy between the status of the clitic *lo* which picks up the fronted object *Valerio* and the inflection *-o* which encodes the fronted subject *io*. Omission of the clitic is possible in other contexts; indeed it is obligatory if the object is overt and in the canonical postverbal position. Thus:

(8)   Voglio sposare Valerio
       'I want to marry Valerio.'

(9)   Lo voglio sposare
       'I want to marry him.'

(10)   *Lo voglio sposare Valerio[16]

Whatever the context, on the other hand, the person/number inflection *-o* is never omissible. The constraint at work here might be thought to be a morphological one which determines the well-formedness of Italian inflected verb forms inde-pendent of the circumstances of their use. While such a solution would in fact work for modern Italian verb inflection, it would not generalize to the data from

---

[16] The string in (10) is acceptable if *Valerio* is treated as a right dislocated element with a pause and intonation break after *sposare*. This however is a different structure with a different informational value.

the inflected infinitive construction we consider in §2.6.2 where the presence of the inflection is in certain contexts optional. At the same time there are languages in which the verbal morphology, albeit 'rich', does not serve to license null arguments or, in our terms, does not have pronominal value. Sigurðsson (1993) shows convincingly that Icelandic is a case in point. And of course many languages with no overt agreement do not allow *pro*-drop, as for instance Danish and Swedish. In fact all logical possibilities exist, as the following table demonstrates:

TABLE 2.2.

	Overt agreement	Zero agreement
Null argument	Italian	Chinese
*Null argument	Icelandic	Danish

Something similar is observable in some clitic systems, namely those characterized by so-called clitic doubling, where a clitic and an overt argument co-occur. Naturally, since zero clitics by definition do not occur, we only find two rather than four possibilities if agreement is of the clitic rather than the morphological type.

Bresnan (1998*b*: 22, note 16) proposes that the agreement property noted here can be handled by letting the PRO value be optionally parsed. In this way, morphological endings and clitics with pronominal content count as arguments and those without do not (cf. Börjars and Chapman 1998). In the Italian type of system exemplified in (8)–(10) clitics do not allow for optional parsing of their pronominal content, and thus they always assume argument status when they occur. In a clitic doubling system, by contrast, the option exists and the clitics are to that extent more grammaticalized and partake already of the properties of an agreement system. The optional parsing solution, however, would not easily generalize to cover optionality of morphological endings.

An alternative account involves postulating an Agreement Hierarchy as in (11) which can be linked to the pronominal hierarchy by the Alignment Constraint in (12):

(11)   AGREEMENT HIERARCHY: zero < affix < clitic

(12)   ALIGN PRO-AGR (zero/affix/cl)

The three terms on the Agreement Hierarchy match the lower end of the pronominality scale, but as we have seen the agreement and pronominality do not have to be aligned. If there is no alignment, agreement has no pronominal effect (the case of Icelandic). When ALIGN PRO-AGR is sufficiently highly ranked, by contrast, it will determine for the language in question at what point, if any, agreement and pronominality coalesce. Thus (12) subsumes the constraint hierarchy in (12′):

(12′)   ALIGN PRO-AGR (zero) ≫ ALIGN PRO-AGR (bound) ≫
          ALIGN PRO-AGR (cl)

Interaction with faithfulness determines which parts of the hierarchy are expressed in overt linguistic form. In the same way, we can envisage that the presence of agreement is expressed by a constraint, which for the sake of argument we will dub 'Realize Agr'. Languages may vary in the way they interleave this with the finiteness hierarchy discussed in §2.7.3. A high rank for such a constraint would ensure that all verb forms, finite and non-finite, bear agreement markers—an example would be Old Neapolitan—while a low rank would mean no overt agreement of any kind, as in Danish.

The advantage of this kind of approach is that it captures the implicational structuring of the typological space that contains the possible systems. If a language aligns the agreement hierarchy and the pronominal hierarchy at the clitic point then the two hierarchies will also be in alignment at all lower points. Thus, a clitic doubling system such as River Plate Spanish will have pronominal Agr as well, whereas Standard Italian, which also has pronominal Agr does not have clitic agreement. The prediction therefore is that a language will not have clitic agreement combined with non-pronominal Agr; in other words clitic doubling would not be an option for a language like Icelandic even if it were to develop a clitic system. In the same way, the interleaving of the expression of agreement within the finiteness hierarchy would allow us to capture the typological implication stated in Vincent (1998: 147) to the effect if a language has subject–verb agreement for non-finite forms, then it also has it with finite forms, but not necessarily vice versa.

The concept of alignment of hierarchies is further explored in Aissen (1998) and Artstein (1998), and forms the basis for the foregoing discussion. The key idea that emerges from their work is that while different hierarchies may align or interleave at different points in different languages, thus leading to typological variation, the terms in the hierarchies may not shift their positions relative to each other. This is important since the fixedness of the relative values of the hierarchically organized items reflects a language external ontological patterning which limits the nature of possible constraints and constraint interactions. In this way we are enabled at one and the same time to respond to a frequent criticism of OT, namely 'What are the constraints on the constraints?', and to embark on the enterprise of grounding a formal model of grammar in conceptual categories (see also below §2.7.2).[17]

---

[17] My use of the idea of 'grounding' here is similar to that of Archangeli and Pulleyblank (1994) in phonology, where grounding refers to the phonetic motivation of phonological categories (cf. also Kager 1999: 11 on the importance of grounding in the definition of OT constraints). The idea that there is a parellellism between the phonetics/phonology relation and the semantics/syntax relation is of course not new. It is in particular associated with Louis Hjelmslev and the so-called Copenhagen School (see for instance Hjelmslev 1954). However where Hjelmslev sees arbitrariness we would see hierarchical structure, following more closely in this respect John Anderson (1997, esp. 5). For a different approach to the problem of constraining constraints based on a more syntactic view of primitives, see Grimshaw (1998). Note too that on this hierarchical view we would not be able to postulate a simple switching of *Ø [PRO] and *af [PRO] as a way of distinguishing the '*pro*-drop'

2.6. PRONOMINALS IN LATIN AND ROMANCE

Bresnan (1995, 1998) develops accounts of competition between different pronominal elements within the synchronic grammars of different types of languages and in the genesis of pidgins and creoles. A third obvious arena in which to test this model is provided by diachronic changes in the form and function of pronominals. Here too it is natural to hypothesize that patterns of grammatical attrition and renewal should work themselves out as shifts in the priority of individual candidates for morphosyntactic expression. The historical developments which took place in the transition from Latin to modern Romance are a clear case in point. We shall look at two case histories. The first concerns the differential status of null arguments of finite verbs—'small *pro*'—in Latin and Romance. The second involves the relation between the non-overt subject of inflected and non-inflected infinitivals. In this section we offer a pre-theoretical sketch of the data before developing a formal analysis in §2.7.

2.6.1. *Subject and object* pro

As is well known, Latin is a classic (and classical!) null subject language, and the well-described null subject properties of Italian, Spanish, etc. are, from a diachronic perspective, simply the continuation of this earlier state of affairs (which can in turn be reconstructed right back to Proto-Indo-European). French and the Northern Italian dialects, by contrast, have in their different ways (M. Adams 1987*a*, Vance 1997, Roberts 1993*a*, Benincà 1994) innovated new systems of pronominal subject marking which are in some sense a compensation for, but at the same time crucially not a direct replacement of, the loss of the Latin agreement morphology. We will seek to show how an OT-inspired approach can model both the continuity and discontinuity evident in such a diachronic profile.

Less often noted than the null subject property of Latin syntax is the fact that it also exhibits null objects (but cf. van der Wurff 1993, Luraghi 1997, Pieroni 1999). There is a striking difference from the null subject cluster of effects in that Latin does not exhibit any system of verbal inflection which might be said to license null objects. By contrast, the Romance languages, all of which exhibit systems of clitic pronouns unknown to Latin, systematically exclude null objects.[18] Thus consider the following ((13) = (2), (14) = (20) in Luraghi (1997); (15) = (18) in Pieroni (1999)):

patterns of subjects in Chinese and Italian as was suggested above. We will leave this problem for resolution on a further occasion.

[18] It is true that Portuguese displays null objects (cf. Farrell 1990 for recent discussion) but this is a later development peculiar to the history of Portuguese alone and does not undermine the generalization that at the time when the Romance languages emerge from Latin they are all characterized by the twin, and as we will argue related, properties of having clitic argument-marking pronouns and of not allowing null objects. We will have more to say below about the very restricted null-object constructions of Italian (and also Spanish, Portuguese, and French) whose theoretical implications were first raised in Rizzi (1986).

(13)   senatus   haec,   intellegit,
         senate-NOMSG this-NEUT-ACCPL understand-3SG-PRES
         consul   Ø, videt
         consul.NOMSG   see-3SG-PRES
         'The Senate understands these things, the consul sees them.'
         (Cicero, *In Catilinam* 1.2)

(14)   milites,   imperat;   Ø, mittunt
         soldier-ACCPL call-for-3SG-PRES send-3PL-PRES
         'He calls for soldiers; they send them/some.'
         (Caesar, *Bellum Civile* 1.15)

(15)   'vinum'   inquit   'si non placet   Ø, mutabo'
         wine-NOMSG say-3SG-PRES if not please-3SG-PRES change-1SG-
         FUT
         'He said: "if the wine does not please (you) I will change it.'
         (Petronius, *Cena Trimalchionis* 48.1)

The translation of (13)–(15) into any Romance language would require an explicit object in the second clause just as in the English rendering given here. We will suggest that emergence of clitics and the loss of object *pro* are related effects to be explained through a change in constraint priority. In particular once a clitic system develops, object *pro* is automatically lost.[19]

In the light of Cole's (1987) typology of null objects, it is important to establish whether Latin null objects are genuine pronominals or variables. Van der Wurff (1993) argues that they must be analysed as variables or as null resumptive pronouns, observing that the classic test for genuine object *pro*, namely null object in a strong cross-over context, does not go through. Looked at from another perspective, we can say that Latin has null objects in contexts of high topic continuity (Pieroni 1999). This is the context in which Italian, for example, allows null subjects (Samek-Lodovici 1996) but crucially does not allow null objects.[20] We thus get the following change (the categories refer to

[19] Tolli Eyþórsson points out that Icelandic seems to have undergone a similar shift in that Old Icelandic has null objects and the modern language does not, yet there is no emergent clitic system in Icelandic. However, note first that Old Icelandic has genuine null pronominals (Sigurðsson 1993) so that the change is of a rather different kind from that which we have described for Latin and Romance. Second, our claim is that *if* a clitic system emerges, as it manifestly does in Romance, it will necessarily provide a better way to mark null objects, and thus will override the Latin state of affairs. This does not of course preclude that in the absence of a clitic system other changes might conspire to eliminate the possibility of null objects. One option for change that is excluded is the loss of null subjects and the preservation of null objects since this would violate the hierarchy established in (12′). It is of interest therefore that universally no such languages are attested (Huang 1995, Speas 1997). On the other hand, an entirely possible direction of change is the one pointed out to me by a referee as taking place in Brazilian Portuguese, namely the extension of null objects in the wake of the loss of clitic pronouns.

[20] Note that the null-object constructions in Italian analysed in Rizzi's (1986) classic paper are a very specialized subset in which the null object is interpreted as arbitrary in reference. A definite object in Italian is not freely omissible, as for instance is possible in some varieties of modern

Bresnan's pronominal scale and 'Romance' stands for the early stages of all Romance languages):

(16)   Latin   Romance
        Subject topics   bound   >   bound
        Object topics   zero   >   clitic

This is the first change that we will seek to model.

2.6.2. *Null subjects of non-finite forms*

A standard result in modern syntactic theory is that subjects of infinitives are necessarily covert—'big PRO'—unless special factors intervene to license an overt subject. It is hardly surprising therefore that both Latin and the Romance languages have control constructions. There are nonetheless a number of significant differences in the syntax of infinitivals that need to be accounted for. First, Latin allowed an infinitive to take an overt subject in the accusative case. This AcI construction, which cannot be treated as a kind of Exceptional Case Marking since it occurs as the complement of adjectival and nominal predicates, disappears in the Romance languages except in learned syntax (Skytte 1978, Pountain 1998). Second control infinitives in Romance are introduced by a new class of overt infinitival complementizers. Third, a number of Romance languages exhibit overt nominative subjects in so-called personal or inflected infinitive constructions, that is to say in contexts in which the infinitive may/must bear an overt person/number inflection.[21] It is this third aspect which will be our principal concern here.

We display in (17) the paradigms of a number of these inflected infinitives in different Romance languages.

(17)   *Old Neapolitan*   *Portuguese*

       SINGULAR   PLURAL   SINGULAR   PLURAL

   1   perdere   perderemo   comprar   comprarmos
   2   perdere   perderevo   comprares   comprardes
   3   perdere   perdereno   comprar   comprarem

Portuguese (Farrell 1990) and in Quiteño Spanish (Suñer 1988). In fact the Quiteño Spanish data reported by Suñer were brought to my attention by a referee as a possible counter-example since this language also has clitics. However, what these data suggest is rather a refinement of the idea contained in this chapter, in so far as Quiteño Spanish has lost an independent series of direct object clitics, merging them with the indirect object form *le(s)*, an extreme case of so-called *leísmo*. Thus, the rise of null objects is correlated with the loss of distinct object clitics, the converse of the development discussed in the main text (cf. also the changes in Brazilian Portuguese alluded to in note 19).

[21] Details of the construction in the individual languages may be found: for Portuguese in Maurer (1968), Raposo (1987), and Martins (1999); for Galician in Gondar (1978); for Sardinian in Jones (1993: 278–82); for Neapolitan in Loporcaro (1986) and Vincent (1996); for elsewhere in Italy in Cresti (1994), Cuneo (1997), and Ledgeway (1998).

Sardinian		Galician	
SINGULAR	PLURAL	SINGULAR	PLURAL
1 cantarepo	cantaremus	andar	andarmos
2 cantares	cantaredzis	andares	andardes
3 cantaret	cantaren	andar	andaren

The fact that Old Neapolitan (to which we can assimilate sporadic attestations in other Southern Italian dialects), Sardinian, and Portuguese/Galician involve different patterns of morphological marking, both as regards distribution and form of the suffixes, suggests that these are independent innovations. At the same time, distributional similarities across the languages argue for a common original syntactic template. In particular, in all languages the inflected infinitive is not possible with complements of modals, causatives, perception verbs,[22] and subject-to-subject raising verbs.

To see the contexts in which the inflected infinitive does occur consider the Sardinian examples (from Jones 1993) set out in (18):

(18) (*a*) Juanne nos at   natu   a   colàremus
John us have-3SG-PRES tell-PSTPR COMP call-INF-1PL
'John told us to call by.'

(*b*) Keljo   cantare una canthone prima de
want-1SG-PRES sing-INF a   song   before COMP
sink'andaren
go away-INF-3PL
'I want to sing a song before they go away.'

(*c*) Non keljo   a   bi vénneres   tue/*te
not want-1SG-PRES COMP here come-INF-2SG you-NOM/*ACC
'I don't want you to come.'

Note that the construction is always a CP, as shown by the introductory infinitival complementizers *a* and *de*; that the subject of the infinitival clause may differ from that of the main clause, and that an overt subject does not have to be present but that if it is, then it must be nominative and not accusative.[23]

The examples in (19) from Portuguese (Raposo 1987) exhibit the same patterns:

---

[22] In fact perception verbs are more complex since they typically display both a pattern of complementation parallel to causatives and an alternative one with the infinitive preceded rather than followed by its subject. It is only in the former that the inflected infinitive is barred (Vincent 1996: 401–2).

[23] A referee reminds me that the assumption of CP status is not uncontroversial. For some recent discussion of the status of *de* and *a*, see Kayne (1999), who on balance accepts their CP status. It may well be, as the referee suggests, that a more refined analysis along the lines of Grimshaw (1997) would accord infinitivals variable IP/CP status (cf. also the conclusions in Thráinsson 1993 and Bošković 1996). Constraints of time and space require me to leave the exploration of this interesting idea for future research.

(19) (a) Eles   aprovarem   a proposta será   difícil
        they-NOM approve-INF-3PL the proposal be-3SG-FUT hard
        'It will be hard for them to approve the proposal.'

     (b) Eles   estão   ansiosos   de/por votarem
        they-NOM be-3PL-PRES anxious-PL COMP vote-INF-3PL
        a   proposta
        the proposal
        'They are anxious to vote on the proposal.'

     (c) A Mara entrou   em casa sem   os meninos/eles
        the Mary enter-3SG-PST in house without the children/they-NOM
        ouvirem
        hear-INF-3PL
        'Maria entered the house without the children hearing.'

These constructions have no direct precursor in Latin but are a Romance innovation. The question which has divided scholars is: which emerges first, the inflection or the overt nominative subject? The traditional answer is that the inflection came first since these forms derive from a finite series, namely the Latin imperfect subjunctive.[24] This would also seem to be the answer most consistent with a licensing view of the function of agreement; you need the licenser before you can have the licensee. The objections to this view are however that it does not explain the contexts in which the inflected infinitive occurs in the modern languages, that there is some historical evidence for the overt subject being attested before the inflected infinitival forms (Maurer 1968), that a number of areas have overt subjects with infinitives that do not have inflections (Cresti 1994, Lipski 1991, Jones 1993: 282 on the Sardinian dialect of Campidanese),[25] and that there are also attested inflected gerunds and participles, which cannot possibly derive from Latin subjunctives. As examples of this latter category, consider (20). The (a) example is from Old Neapolitan (Vincent 1998) and the (b) example from Algarve Portuguese (Coelho da Mota 1997: 342):

(20) (a) vendene*no*   li Grieci tanta copia de cavalieri
        see-GER-3PL the Greeks such quantity of knights
        armati . . . fortemente se maraviglyaro de la multetudene loro
        armed   greatly   wonder-PST-3PL of the multitude   them
        'When the Greeks saw so many armed knights, they (= the Greeks) were truly amazed at the multitude thereof.'

---

[24] See Martins (1999) for an attempt to revive the traditional analysis.

[25] One referee objects that this argument would only hold if the inflected infinitive and the uninflected infinitive with overt nominative subject had identical distribution. However, given the historical time depth and hence the time available for inter-/intra-linguistic differences to develop, total overlap of distributions would be surprising. What is significant is the range of shared contexts for the two constructions. Jones's (1993) comparison of two varieties of Sardinian seems to me a telling argument in this regard. Vincent (to appear) shows that the same comparison can be made for the inflected gerund in Old Neapolitan and the uninflected gerund in Old Tuscan.

(b) tu   querendos,   podemos   namorar
     you-NOM want-GER-2SG can-3PL-PST court-INF
     'If you want, we can go out together.'

Given the fact that the geographical distribution of the inflected gerund as exemplified in (20) is more restricted than that of the inflected infinitive, and is only attested in dialects which also have the latter, we shall conclude that the spread of the person endings to the gerund is later than to the infinitive (cf. already Loporcaro 1986 for this same view). There thus appears to be an analogical generalization of the person inflections first from the finite forms to the infinitive and thence to the gerund.[26]

2.7. MODELLING THE CHANGES

2.7.1. *The diachrony of object pronominals from Latin to Romance*

Recall that null objects in Latin are topical (Pieroni 1999). Thus to describe the Latin situation we need to provide a constraint ranking such that the input [PRO, TOP] is expressed by zero (since there is no object agreement morphology of any kind). The required ranking is set out in Tableau IV.

TABLEAU IV

Input	[PRO, TOP, OBJ]	HARM	*af [PRO]	FAITH	*Ø [PRO]
☞ Zero:	[PRO, TOP]				*
Bound:	[PRO, TOP, AGR]		*!		
Pronoun:	[PRO, AGR]			*!	

Latin null objects are like Italian (and Latin) null subjects except that the structural markedness constraint that falls below FAITH is the one which forbids zero being associated with pronominal content. In other words, Latin is prepared to envisage a violation of the iconicity constraint (4b). The situation in Italian and other Romance languages requires instead the constraint ranking established in Tableau V.

TABLEAU V

Input	[PRO, TOP, OBJ]	HARM	*Ø ~ af [PRO] ICONICITY	FAITH	*cl [PRO] ALLOTAXY
Zero:	[PRO, TOP]		*!		
☞ Bound:	[PRO, TOP, AGR]				*
Pronoun:	[PRO, AGR]			*!	

---

[26] Old Neapolitan in fact also attests inflected present and past participles, but the examples are so few and far between that it is difficult to come to any satisfactory concusion about them. We leave them out of account in what follows.

Italian objects are like Italian subjects; they have to be encoded and this is done by a clitic pronoun. Assuming clitics are different from affixes, this means the downgrading of a different member of the set of STRUCT constraints to a position below FAITH. In this instance, the iconicity constraints are respected but the allotaxy ones are violated.[27]

The foregoing analysis works within the system proposed in Bresnan (1998*b*). However a comparison of Tableau IV with Tableau II reveals that the constraints *Ø[PRO] and *af [PRO] have been reversed in their priority. It is exactly this kind of reversal which is outlawed in the hierarchical approach to constraint ranking developed by Aissen (1998) and Artstein (1998), and discussed briefly in §2.5 (cf. also note 17). We must leave it for the moment as an open question whether these data are a counter-example to such an approach or, as seems more probable, further research will find a way of reconciling the two. Under either approach, change is modelled as a shifting in constraint rankings, and more specifically in those drawn from the set defined in (4) above as structural markedness constraints. This is all well and good but still leaves open the question as to why such a reranking should occur. What drives this change? Our answer is the independent development of a clitic pronoun system in Romance (Vincent 1997). This means that when it comes to encoding a particular content—in the present instance that of pronominal object topic—there is a better, more iconic in the sense of (4) above, candidate available in the Romance languages than there was in Latin.

2.7.2. *A role for grammaticalization*

If we assume with Bresnan a universal initial state with the ranking HARMONY ≫ STRUCTURE ≫ FAITHFULNESS, then alternative rankings must be driven by exposure to data. How could this arise? Note that the hierarchy of markedness above reflects the universal patterns attested in studies of grammaticalization (Hopper and Traugott 1993: chapter 6). Let us assume that these patterns of grammaticalization reflect universal semantic potentials definable in terms of a cognitive space which encompasses grammaticizable domains like tense, number, pronominality, definiteness, etc. There is an analogy here with the way sound changes reflect universal phonetic potentials definable over the parameters that govern the working of the vocal tract. We can then postulate a potential for semantic drift external to the grammatical system leading to a grammatical change just as phonetic drift leads to phonological change (Ohala 1993). Hence just as the operation of a sound change may obscure a previously motivated phonological alternation—the creation of new phonemes out of the originally

---

[27] There is an unresolved problem here in that Latin object marking is genuinely zero whereas both subject marking and prepositional object marking are overt (affixal and pronominal respectively). This seems to go against the natural prediction that degree of marking parallels degree of obliqueness (cf. Bresnan 1998*b*: 18 and Siewierska 1999).

allophonic products of German umlaut is the textbook example—so the effect of a morphophonemic change, namely the emergence of clitics, may inadvertently as it were remove the availability of a previously available structure: a kind of diachronic emergence of the unmarked. The mechanisms of grammar, that is to say the constraint rankings, then encode the outcome of these changes for the next generation.

If a scenario of this kind is on the right lines, it provides an interesting alternative to a commonly held view of change in generative grammar. Consider the following remark by Longobardi (1996: 2): 'outside phonological change, linguistic systems are in principle diachronically inert, unless some specifically motivated conditions apply.' There is a remarkable similarity between this view and the Neogrammarian insistence on the 'blindness' of sound change, which has long been known to oversimplify, indeed falsify, the relation between phonological and grammatical change (see Harris 1978 for an effective diagnosis of the problem). The model of change as constraint reranking that we have adumbrated here offers an alternative approach. I would rather adapt Longobardi's remark by saying 'outside phonetic and semantic change', subsuming grammaticalization under the latter but not treating it as a substitute for a formal syntactic theory, here modelled as a set of OT-style constraints. Research in grammaticalization would then be a contribution to mapping out the space within which grammars of particular languages can be stated, but it would not obviate the need for such grammars (*pace* Bybee *et al.* 1994: 1). This would also be consistent with the view expressed by Aissen (1998: 11):

The ranking of constraints in a subhierarchy is universally fixed, and expresses the universal markedness relations in this domain. Language-particular variation can be described through the interpolation of other constraints among those in a subhierarchy, but not through differences in ranking within the subhierarchy itself.

We turn now to our second change which will show a role within OT for that other classic weapon from the nineteenth-century armoury, namely analogy.

2.7.3. *The diachrony of the personal infinitive/gerund*

Following the discussion in §2.6.2, we will assume that the right historical chronology is that first overt subjects are possible in infinitival and gerundival constructions and second that the inflectional morphology extends its domain to encode that fact.[28] We can achieve this end by refining our account of the Structural Markedness Constraint labelled in §2.4 *af* [PRO], whose effect was to ban structures in which pronominality was encoded via affixes as a violation of

---

[28] We leave open the question of exactly how overt NPs are licensed as the subject of infinitives. Pressure of space also forces us to omit consideration of the proper analysis of control patterns. We envisage a treatment roughly along the lines of Speas (1997), but adapted naturally to the theory of pronominals used in this chapter.

iconicity. Instead of taking this as a single constraint we will treat it as a family of constraints applying to the whole range of possible verb forms. If the direction of spread is as in (21) then we will need the constraint hierarchy in (22):

(21)   finite forms > infinitive   > gerund

(22) $*af[\text{PRO}]_{ger} \gg *af[\text{PRO}]_{inf} \gg *af[\text{PRO}]_{fin}$

Thus, (22) says that a violation of the ban on affixes attached to gerunds is worse than violating the ban on infinitival inflection which in turn is worse than violating the ban on finite inflection. Tableau II above, which permitted bound inflection to express pronominality—the classic *pro*-drop effect—in Latin, should in this more refined system be replaced by Tableau II′:

TABLEAU II′

Input [PRO, TOP]	HARM	*∅ [PRO]	FAITH	$*af[\text{PRO}]_{fin}$
Zero: [PRO, TOP]		*!		
☞ Bound: [PRO, TOP, AGR]				*
Pronoun: [PRO, AGR]			*!	

The grammar of an innovating language such as Portuguese or Sardinian can then be represented as in Tableau II″, where both the infinitival and finite members of the family have fallen below the FAITH.[29]

TABLEAU II″

Input [PRO, TOP]	HARM	*∅ [PRO]	FAITH	$*af[\text{PRO}]_{f/i}$
Zero: [PRO, TOP]		*!		
☞ Bound: [PRO, TOP, AGR]				*
Pronoun: [PRO, AGR]			*!	

In the extreme case, where all the members of the *af [PRO] constraint family have fallen below FAITH, the grammar will then license the full portfolio of

---

[29] This account oversimplifies in one important respect. As a referee points out, in certain contexts the inflected and uninflected infinitives are optional alternants. Thus:

(i) Eles sairam para irem   ao   cinema
    they left   to   go-INFL-INF-3PL to-the cinema
(ii) Eles sairam para ir   ao   cinema
    they left   to   go-INF to-the cinema

The issue here is the larger one of how to deal with optionality in OT. I refer the reader to the discussion in Kager (1999: 404–7) and to Bakovic (1997).

inflected forms and their pronominal arguments found in Old Neapolitan and some Algarve dialects of modern Portuguese. Thus:

TABLEAU II‴

Input	[PRO, TOP]	HARM	*Ø [PRO]	FAITH	*af [PRO]$_{f/i/g}$
Zero:	[PRO, TOP]		*!		
☞ Bound:	[PRO, TOP, AGR]				*
Pronoun:	[PRO, AGR]			*!	

Notice once again that this account makes a quite clear prediction, namely that one will not find languages with an inflected gerund and inflected finite forms but no inflected infinitives. There are thus constraints on the constraints (Grimshaw 1998), namely that they must not violate the universally definable and hierachically organized space of possible grammars. It is not a consequence of OT that anything in the world can count as a constraint, despite persistent malicious and ill-informed gossip to the contrary!

2.7.4. *A role for analogy*

Just as in accounting for the replacement of null objects by clitics we found a role for the traditional concept of grammaticalization, so the use of an ordered progression through the members of a family of constraints may be thought of as the OT analogue of the traditional concept of 'analogical extension'. Thus, once again the constraint hierarchy models the structure of the domain, in the present instance the cline from finite to infinitive, and the reranking of the constraints reflects the direction of the analogical shifts. In this sense, the model proposed here follows the logic of Kuryłowicz's (1949) classic intervention, suggesting that the directionality of analogical change is (at least in part) predictable from considerations of markedness. Like him, we do not propose a predictive account of when analogy may take place, but only of the direction in which it will move if it occurs. We may also recall Meillet's (1912: 131) observation that analogy and grammaticalization exhaust the possible types of morphosyntactic change. What the present account seeks to do is to use OT as a way of conceptualizing the relation between analogy, grammaticalization, and the internal mechanisms of grammar.

2.8. LESSONS FOR A THEORY OF SYNTACTIC CHANGE

In this section we reflect on the theoretical lessons that can be learned from the account of the Latin-Romance data presented above. There we have emphasized two general concepts: competition and correspondence. Let us consider the diachronic implications of each in turn.

2.8.1. *Why a competition-based account is superior to an absolutist one*

The intuition behind a competition-based model of a synchronic system is that the grammaticality of a given structure is precarious: it is always potentially threatened by the other universally available competitors, which are only kept at bay by the language-particular constraint-ranking operative at that point in time and space. Any change in that ranking would force a different solution to the ever-present problem that languages (and language users) face: how to match form and content to express the intended meaning within the resources available. Historical linguists, of course, have always emphasized the notion of competition between forms as the basis of change. For instance, Hopper and Traugott (1993: 123) write: 'Rather than replace a lost or almost lost distinction, newly innovated forms compete with older ones . . . this competition allows, even encourages the recession or loss of older forms.' The same point is also made by Kroch (1992: 113): 'Languages at any synchronic moment of their existence may be seen as systems of competing forms'; he goes on to note that 'quite abstract linguistic subsystems, not just isolated forms, may be the elements in competition.' Standard derivational frameworks model this sort of scenario rather badly; they frequently provide neat and elegant accounts of given synchronic states expressed as the interaction of universal principles and the individual values of particular parameters (Lightfoot 1991; Roberts 1993*a*). They do not however readily extend to include in the picture the notion of alternative solutions waiting, so to speak, in the grammatical wings. Kroch's original answer to this was to envisage the speaker's competence as containing internally competing grammars (Kroch 1989*b*). The problem with this approach is that every time a new set of competing forms are identified within a language, a new set of parallel grammars will have to be postulated. Such proliferation of grammars involves taking a very powerful hammer to crack the variationist nut. More recently, Kroch (1994) has suggested that the competition is between alternative functional heads. Following up this line of argument, Pintzuk (1998: 123) observes: 'If we characterize the difference between OV and VO languages in terms of features of grammatical formatives, the source of the variation is not the order within the VP but rather the directionality feature of some functional head. Contra our original assumptions, this entails that all non-finite verbs move out of the VP to the head of a higher functional projection, one that is distinct from I or its components, and that the directionality feature of this functional head is undergoing change.' Proliferation of grammars is replaced by proliferation of functional heads. However, whereas many functional heads have both overt form and morphosyntactic content, and are indeed the result of processes of grammaticalization (Vincent 1993), the heads being postulated here are empty and distinct from the items with grammatical content ('I and its components'); they are simply a way of encoding word order variation into a syntactic configuration. Word order and word order changes are not reduced to independently available functional heads as proposed for example in Roberts (1997), but are restated in terms of specially invented and otherwise unmotivated new heads. These heads are the Last Resort solution, as envisaged under the Minimalist Programme (Chomsky 1995, Lasnik 1999: chapter 6), to the derivation of the required structure, while still respecting the universal requirement of Economy (Chomsky 1995: chapter 2). With no restriction on the number and type of functional heads, however, this approach runs a clear risk of unfalsifiability (Börjars, Payne, and Chisarik 1999).

The insight that functional heads are the end product of processes of grammaticalization (Vincent 1993) certainly seems worth preserving. At the same time it is necessary to counter the standard objection to grammaticalization theory from those within the formalist tradition—and it appears to me a very substantial and forceful objection—namely, that it is conducted in an intuitionistic way with too strong a faith in a direct correlation between linguistic form and meaning and function (Croft 1995, Newmeyer 1998*a*). It does not allow enough space for functionally arbitrary synchronic structure, for the presence of language universals not driven by functional needs, and crucially it does not provide any means of modelling linguistic structure in a way that allows the consequences of particular shifts to be computed across the rest of the system. In that sense it seems wilfully to discard the achievements of more than half a century of formal linguistics, both structuralist and generativist (cf. Bybee *et al.* 1994: 1). This metaphysical stance has made it all too easy for generative theorists of language change such as Lightfoot (1991, 1999) to ignore rather than confront the evidence of grammaticalization (though see Roberts 1993*b* for an honourable exception). Yet the evidence needs to be confronted. Grammaticalization chains or paths seem to be real and recurrent phenomena in the histories of natural languages, and as such constitute a genuine empirical challenge to the stepwise, abductive, and potentially reversible view of change that typifies work in the generative tradition. They are the diachronic counterpart of the morphosyntactic hierarchies discussed above.

In the present chapter I have sought to argue that an OT-inspired interpretation of grammatical change provides the means to achieve a much needed reconciliation of the two approaches: we can model, as precisely and computably as necessary, both the structural properties of individual systems and their interaction with universally available and hierarchically organized (hence potentially directional) dimensions of change. In particular, by requiring that constraints be grounded in finite systems of independently definable grammatical primitives, we can avoid the charge that OT simply replaces an infinite set of functional heads with an infinite set of constraints. The difference is that, as I have tried to show here, a finite constraint domain plus the notion of reranking can capture the required effects, whereas a derivational movement-based model seems doomed to spawn potentially limitless numbers of functional heads to achieve the same ends.

2.8.2. *Why a correspondence model is preferable to a derivational one*

The last section sketches an argument for the correctness of the competition-based account of change that the OT vision imposes. At the same time, in the data we have discussed and the model we have adopted, another concept has been fundamental, namely that the relation between linguistic form and content should be based on correspondence and not on derivation. What is the justification for this assumption? As we have noted, correspondence depends on the idea that the structure of subdomains of the linguistic system reflects the natural categories and primitives of the domain in question; there is no *a priori* reason to believe that the form of representation most appropriate to phonology, for example, will generalize to syntax, or that what is natural in semantics is equally natural in morphology. In particular, morphological structure does not have to be 'syntacticized' and represented as an X-bar tree, and empty categories or zeros (whether morphological or syntactic) do not have to be postulated simply in order to ensure that form corresponds to content. Historically this means that the input can be the same—in the material discussed here constellations of [PRO, TOP, AGR]—even when its realization can vary over time from morphological to syntactic and back again.

2.9. CONCLUSION

In this chapter I hope to have shown three things. First, and most directly, I have demonstrated that the OT-inspired account of pronominals and their cross-linguistic markedness relations offered in Bresnan (1998*b*) can be applied in a simple and elegant way to the diachronic data presented by some of the changes in the patterns of argument marking between Latin and Romance. Second, I have argued that such an account provides answers to puzzles that had previously eluded solution, and to that extent offers a genuine conceptual advance over— and not just a simple reformulation of—earlier treatments, both those which were philological and those which were theoretical-linguistic in inspiration. Third, I have sought to show that the best account of the data in question crucially involves *both* the notions of competition and correspondence. In addition, via the parallel correspondence type of architecture linked to competition, we have a way to incorporate the insights of grammaticalization, which—*pace* Lightfoot (1999) and Newmeyer (1998)—are real and important, without forsaking formalizability or incurring the penalty of teleology. To the extent that all these notions only converge in an LFG type of architecture under an OT interpretation as developed by Bresnan (1997, 1998*a*, *b*), I believe I have in turn provided a further and original line of argumentation in favour of this approach to linguistic inquiry in general, whether synchronic or diachronic.

3

Jespersen's Cycle Revisited:
Formal Properties of Grammaticalization

ANS VAN KEMENADE

In this chapter I present a description and analysis of the rise and fall of multiple sentential negation in English. The cyclic development identified by Jespersen (1917), in essence a case of grammaticalization, can be traced in detail, with the proviso that in English multiple sentential negation is attested rather earlier than has been generally assumed.

I analyse the development from a theoretical perspective, making crucial use, for reasons explicated below, of the current generative practice of projecting grammatical categories such as Tense, Mood, Negation as syntactic constituents, each according to the standard phrase structure format. With respect to negation, this entails postulating the NegP introduced by Pollock (1989). This perspective allows a very precise and insightful account of the historical development, which in turn shows the relevance of structure. This is important when we consider the historical development from the point of view of a typology of change: Jespersen's negative cycle could count as a schoolbook case of grammaticalization: the semantic and morphosyntactic weakening of an erstwhile independent constituent and its subsequent entrenchment in a system of grammatical marking, as in Meillet's original definition (1912). Grammaticalization theorists such as Hopper and Traugott (1993) generally regard this type of change as a long-term, diachronic, and semantically motivated process. The account here, on the other hand, implies that grammaticalization is primarily a morphosyntactic change, and shows that the long-term development is necessarily punctuated by synchronic shifts. We will see that the history of English negation is shaped by a delicate interplay between various negation positions and strategies.

The material in this article, in whole or in part, has been presented at a workshop on Indo-European with NELS 26, Harvard, October 1995; a workshop on Indo-European, Manchester, August 1997; Ninth Wuppertaler Linguistisches Kolloquium, Wuppertal 1997; the Fifth Diachronic Generative Syntax Conference, York 1998. I thank the audiences on these occasions. I am grateful to Frank Beths, Bettelou Los, and to the editors of this volume for their comments on an earlier version.

3.1. THEORETICAL UNDERPINNINGS

I adopt the current generative mode of representing (inflectional) morphology as a syntactic constituent, in which pieces of morphology like Agreement, Tense, Mood, Negation constitute separate projections according to the standard constituent format. In this approach, Negation is represented as a NegP (for Negation Phrase) as in (1*b*), according to the general phrase structure format as in (1*a*):

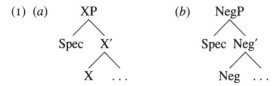

A syntactic tree in this perspective consists crucially of a number of lexical projections that are dominated by functional projections for Tense, Mood, Negation, and so on, which define the functional/morphological properties of lexical elements in a syntactic tree. In the minimalist approach of Chomsky (1995), lexical elements are generated fully inflected; inflectional morphology is 'checked' against functional properties, either by moving the inflected element to a functional position in the syntax, or by doing this at the postsyntactic level of Logical Form. Movement dependencies then always reflect the syntactic displacement of a lexical element (or constituent) to a functional position. Since functional positions reflect grammatical categories that often find a morphological expression, many movement strategies are said to be motivated by morphological considerations.

The interdependency between inflectional morphology and syntax as mediated by functional constituents in a syntactic tree has become a firm property of the Principles and Parameters approach to syntactic theory. It is this interdependency that has recently yielded a spate of work on morphosyntactic change. The reader is referred for example to Roberts (1993*a*), the papers in van Kemenade and Hulk (1993), Battye and Roberts (1995), and van Kemenade and Vincent (1997). A typical (simplified) scenario of change in this perspective is that, where at some stage A the presence of a comparatively rich system of inflection licenses certain movement dependencies, these are lost when the system of inflection is in demise. Such change is abrupt, at least at the level of the speaker's internalized grammar. In Kroch (1989*b*), Roberts (1993*a*), Lightfoot (1997), and Warner (1997), a number of variations on this theme are found with respect to the loss of finite verb movement to the inflectional position I in the history of English, a prime example of a parametric change. What is important is that the connection between changes in inflection and their results in the syntax can be expressed in a direct and insightful way. Much of the effort in this type of work on morphosyntactic change is therefore devoted to giving theoretical and empirical content to the traditional observation that loss of inflection results in rigidification of word order.

Another type of change in which functional constituents may play an important role is grammaticalization. Here, however, the scene is dominated by a quite different approach, which we may call grammaticalization theory. In their many case studies of how grammatical morphemes arise out of erstwhile lexical elements, grammaticalization theorists emphasize that this type of change is a gradual and long-term one, whose driving forces are primarily semantic and/or pragmatic. Such change is said to go hand in hand with syntactic fixing and morphological impoverishment, but the semantic development is seen as primary.

At this point it is worth emphasizing the fundamental differences between the two approaches mentioned above. Perhaps the most important difference is in the object of research. Grammarians working from a *Principles and Parameters* perspective are concerned with recovering from the historical material those properties that reflect grammar in a Chomskyan sense: the system internalized by the speaker that underlies the actual surface diffuseness found in language as reflected in historical texts. Grammaticalization theorists, on the other hand, make no such distinction between grammar and language; indeed they would feel it is a fundamentally wrong one to make. Grammar for them, to the extent that they recognize so discrete a notion, arises out of discourse and other aspects of communicative competence. Some of the further differences between the approaches follow from this one pervasive difference: while a generative grammar is organized modularly, the language of the grammaticalization theorist is organized in terms of interrelated clines; where a generative grammar is organized along the binary dimensions of parametrization, the grammaticalization theorist sees prototypes with marginal, fuzzy areas in between. Another important difference is between a synchronic and a diachronic viewpoint. Grammaticalization theorists see a case of grammaticalization as a diachronic phenomenon, which, once set in motion, cannot be reversed. Any synchronic step in this process makes sense to them only if viewed against the background of the larger diachronic picture. For the generative grammarian, on the other hand, the synchronic viewpoint is primary, since the emphasis is on how grammars change in the process of grammar acquisition by each new (generation of) speaker(s). From such a perspective, a diachronic process cannot exist because each learner constructs a new grammar. In view of these differences in approach, it would seem that we have to consider grammaticalization phenomena as a type of change that can be profitably approached from vastly different angles. It will be clear from the above that a generative perspective will put an interpretation on the nature of this type of change that is rather different from that of grammaticalization theorists. The functional constituents mentioned above play an important role in this interpretation, as they do in other types of (morphosyntactic) change.

In the work done so far on grammaticalization from a generative perspective, the analysis crucially revolves around functional constituents. For a survey of some cases, the reader is referred to Roberts and Roussou (1999), who also give an interpretation in minimalist terms. An explicit treatment of the history of English modals, building on much earlier work by other scholars, is Beths (1999). In the case of the modals, we are looking at the gradual development of syntactically fixed free morphemes marking modality, out of a class of verbs that at an earlier stage had at least a number of lexical properties (like a limited range of complementations), and which itself took part in a system of tense, mood, person, and number marking. Some important conditioning factors in this chain of development were the loss of inflection marking the subjunctive mood, person, and number, beside the loss of complementation. The reader is referred to Warner (1993) for a thorough and subtle treatment. In a framework which expresses grammatical categories in terms of functional constituents in a phrasal projection, we can model this complex of developments as follows: Mood is projected as a separate constituent. In a grammatical system with transparent mood marking, the finite verb checks for mood against the head of MoodP (see (2)).

(2)

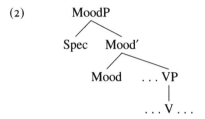

In Old English, this checking is very often done overtly,[1] in which case it is visible as syntactic movement to Mood, subject to the usual constraints on head movement. As long as this movement dependency is recognizable as such, modal verbs are interpreted as V-heads that undergo syntactic movement to check for Mood. Warner (1993) makes it clear that what happened to the verb system in the course of the Old and Middle English periods (and beyond) was an ever increasing divergence between lexical verbs on the one hand, and the later auxiliaries on the other. Following on the loss of certain main verb properties and, crucially, morphology marking the subjunctive mood (cf. Plank 1984), modals were no longer recognized as part of the paradigmatic class of verbs, and instead became frozen in the Mood position, ending up as free morphemes with a fixed syntax, marking modality.

This account can easily be extended to a number of other well-known cases, as in Roberts and Roussou (1999): the emergence of determiners out of erstwhile demonstrative pronouns (see Abraham 1997, Philippi 1997 for Germanic, Vincent 1997, and Batllori and Roca, in this volume, for Romance) can be thought of naturally as the reanalysis from demonstrative pronoun to a head D, following

---

[1] I refrain from discussion of the proper analysis of the position of the finite verb in Old English. The reader is referred to chapter 4 of Fischer, van Kemenade, Koopman, and van der Wurff (2000) for a discussion of the issues.

on a long period of movement to that position. A further case in point is Roberts' (1993*b*) treatment of the Romance future ending—*a* as in French *chantera*, Spanish *cantarà*, Italian *canterà* 'will sing'. Numerous other cases can be mentioned, but I will leave it here.

There is an important implication of this approach which has not been made sufficiently explicit in the literature, namely that grammaticalization is to an important extent a morphosyntactic change, contrary to the grammaticalization theorists' contention that its driving forces are primarily semantic/pragmatic. This is in fact a central claim of this chapter: grammaticalization is primarily a morphosyntactic change. The approach in terms of functional projections yields a very insightful way of analysing grammaticalization as a type of morphosyntactic change: the creation of new morphology. Above, I quoted recent work in which the emphasis is on the syntactic effects of the loss of case morphology, verb morphology, etc. Let us consider for a moment how this type of change is related to grammaticalization as viewed from our perspective.

In the type of work concentrating on the effects of the loss of inflectional morphology, the typical analysis says that, as a result of the loss of case morphology, NPs that were formerly case-marked and as a result enjoyed greater positional freedom became syntactically fixed (e.g. Allen 1995, Weerman 1997); verbs which lost their inflections ceased to undergo movement (recalling the discussion on the loss of V-to-I in English as summarized and discussed in Warner 1997). The question then becomes why some elements continue life as lexical elements that are syntactically more fixed than they previously were (NPs, lexical verbs, etc.), and other elements are reanalysed as functional heads (demonstrative pronouns, modal verbs, negative elements, personal pronouns becoming clitics/ agreement markers and so on). I believe we can go some way towards an answer to this question. First, NPs and lexical verbs, among the examples of cases that do not typically undergo grammaticalization, are by their very nature lexical: they have lexical meaning and the full panoply of related grammatical trappings. On the other hand, the elements that typically undergo grammaticalization seem to have in common that even at the onset of the grammaticalization story their lexical meaning is underspecified, their overall meaning strongly context-dependent. This, I contend, makes them more prone to the addition of constructional meaning added by the functional level, thus promoting the further loss of what lexical meaning they had to begin with, after the loss of morphology. A second point is made by Postma (1995), who argues that the existence of a movement dependency itself is the first step in a grammaticalization story. According to Postma, movement of an element to a functional position has the effect that lexical meaning is overlaid with functional meaning. This feeds into my remarks above: if that element happens to have weak lexical meaning to begin with, it is more prone to grammaticalize than a fully-fledged lexical element. This idea extends the onset of grammaticalization to a historical stage with a movement strategy, and, by implication, to the rise of a movement strategy.

If the approach outlined here has anything of interest to offer, we would expect that there is more to grammaticalization than the big long-term diachronic process in grammaticalization theory in which 'tout se tient'. In particular, we would expect that it is possible to isolate synchronic steps in a grammaticalization process, and that we can see that a structured grammar plays an important role in such steps. If grammaticalization is primarily a morphosyntactic change, we would further expect to be able to find evidence that morphosyntactic change can demonstrably precede semantic change. In the next section I will therefore consider in detail the history of negation in English, showing that these expectations are borne out.

3.2. THE HISTORICAL DEVELOPMENT OF NEGATION

3.2.1. *Jespersen's cycle*

In his 1917 work *Negation in English and Other Languages*, Otto Jespersen made his seminal observations on the cyclical development of systems of sentential negation. His negative cycle can be summarized as follows:

(3) Stage 1: negation is expressed by one negative marker
      Stage 2: negation is expressed by a negative marker in combination with a negative adverb or noun phrase
      Stage 3: the second element in stage 2 takes on the function of expressing negation by itself; the original negative marker becomes optional
      Stage 4: the original negative marker becomes extinct

Jespersen's negative cycle looks like a schoolbook case of grammaticalization: negative adverbs are depleted of lexical meaning and they undergo phonological and morphosyntactic reduction to a bound morpheme prefixed to the finite verb, up to a point where a new negative adverb is introduced, apparently because the old form is worn out as a linguistic sign. Once this new, initially free, morpheme is introduced, the old one disappears altogether, upon which the new sign shows the first traces of weakening, and so on. In the next sections, Jespersen's cycle will be discussed and illustrated in detail for English. From the point of view of the theoretical issues surrounding grammaticalization as discussed in the previous section, it is of particular interest to look at negation. The fact that the lexical meaning of negative adverbs themselves is fairly straightforward allows for relatively tight control over the role of semantic change. This will allow a sharper focus on the substantial role of syntax and morphology, which I will show to be amenable to precise analysis.

The sentential structure recently introduced in the Principles and Parameters framework, in which negation is represented as a phrase conforming to the phrase structure format discussed above, yields a particularly insightful account of this sequence of change. A precise analysis in these terms will enable us to see the history of sentential negation in English as a pure case of morphosyntactic change. Viewed broadly, this development goes hand in hand with depletion of lexical content, but I will show that at some synchronic stages, the morphosyntactic impoverishment is more advanced than the semantic development. In addition, I will show that the syntactic configuration in which negation figures is of crucial importance in structuring this sequence of change through a millennium of historical development.

Let me spell out the structural assumptions I make about the clausal architecture of Old English. To start with, I will repeat for convenience the NegP format mentioned above. In the Old English found in the prose texts of the ninth and tenth centuries, sentential negation is dominantly expressed by the negative marker *ne*, which immediately precedes and is often procliticized to the finite verb, whatever the position of the latter. This is illustrated in (4):

(4) (*a*) *ne* sende se deofol ða fyr of heofenum, þeah þe hit
       not sent the devil then fire from heaven, though that it
       ufan   come
       from-above came
       'The devil sent not fire from heaven, though it came from above.'
       (Ælfric, *Catholic Homilies* i.6.13)

     (*b*) Nolde   se Hælend for his bene swaþeah hym fram gewitan
         not-wanted the Lord   for his prayer however him from depart
         'However, the Lord did not want to depart from him because of his
         prayer.'   (Ælfric, *Homilies*, Pope XIV.199)

This is sufficient motivation for regarding *ne* as the (incorporating) head of NegP, allowing us to see the positional covariance of *ne* with the finite verb as an instance of head incorporation.

(5)   NegP

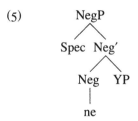

The NegP format advocated here allows a principled view of the relative strength and weakness of negative adverbs. The notion of strength I employ here should be understood as a morphosyntactic one: specifier elements are in general full constituents, whereas the head elements of non-lexical projections generally correspond with inflectional morphemes which, whether free or bound, are syntactically dependent. We will see in the material discussed below that negative adverbs 'enter' Jespersen's negative cycle as independent constituents that come to be checked against a specifier feature in Spec,NegP, or Spec,CP. The weaker of the negative markers, Old English *ne*, is an incorporating head, i.e. a bound morpheme, as just observed. If an element hosted by the specifier of a functional projection then develops into a functional head element, this can be reasonably viewed as weakening in the sense of an increase in morphosyntactic dependence.

One way of modelling Jespersen's cycle in theoretical terms is as follows: in the development of negation systems, independent constituents that are checked in Spec,NegP are weakened morphosyntactically to negative head status, after which a new specifier element is introduced. In the early Old English period and in the early Modern English period, there are facts that suggest that incorporation with the finite verb plays an important role in the transition from specifier element to head element. Anticipating discussion of this below, I will therefore formulate the following theoretical recasting of Jespersen's cycle:

(6)　　　Jespersen's cycle recast:
　　　　　Negative adverbs grammaticalize to negative head status through incorporation resulting from verb movement

Let us now consider in some detail the relevant facts from the history of English, beginning with Old English (for general discussion of negation in Old English, the reader is referred to Mourek 1903, Einenkel 1912, and Mitchell 1985: §§1596 ff.). Old English is a negative concord language, which means that a logically negative sentence can contain more than one negative marker. As we saw above, the finite verb in negative sentences is always preceded by *ne*, which we assume is a negative head. I distinguish sentential negation from constituent negation, as in van Kemenade (1999: 148–9). This narrows down our cases to those instances in which no constituent reading is available. This is straightforward in the standard case where sentential negation is predominantly marked by *ne* alone, as in (4) above. We will see below that there is also a minority pattern with multiple sentential negation in Old English.

3.2.2. *Early Old English*

I start off with the earliest Old English. An extensive poetic text from this period is the heroic poem *Beowulf*, written in alliterative four-stress lines. Although the only manuscript we have of the poem was written somewhere around AD 1000, there is some consensus that the version we have must have been composed in the course of the eighth century.[2] This puts the poem rather earlier than any of

---

[2] By 'some consensus', I mean that the dating of *Beowulf* is still controversial. The arguments for dating it to the eighth century are based on the content of the poem as well as its linguistic features. There is a marked Christian element in the poem, which indicates that it was composed after the christianization of England, putting it no earlier than about 700. Moreover, it is thoroughly Scandinavian in subject matter, in a way so sympathetic to Danish affairs that it must have been composed before the Scandinavians became the enemies of the English at the end of the eighth century. The morphological and phonological characteristics of the language are consistent with this rough date of composition.

the large prose texts we have. Moreover, it was presumably composed and written up in the form we know after centuries of oral transmission, which makes it likely that archaic linguistic features have been preserved in it. Against this background, it is tempting to consider as archaic those syntactic patterns that are different from the norm apparent in the ninth- and tenth-century prose texts. Before I go on to consider such a pattern, let us briefly consider how sentential negation in general is manifested in *Beowulf*.

With respect to negation, there is an interesting asymmetry between root clauses and non-root clauses. In root clauses, the dominant negation strategy is to prepose a negative adverb, and this is optionally accompanied by fronting of the finite verb. I will discuss this pattern and its implications in more detail below. In non-root clauses, negative elements are found somewhere in the body of the clause. In two cases, the negative adverb is *no*; in the remaining sixty-six cases, it is *ne*. Of the two cases with *no*, one has *no* separated from the finite verb (example (8)). *Ne* is always on the immediate left of the finite verb. The negative element in non-root clauses is therefore dominantly found in a low position, since the word order of non-root clauses in *Beowulf* is more strictly verb-last than in the later prose texts (Pintzuk and Kroch 1989).[3] Some examples are the following:

(7)   . . . þæt ic me   ænigne / under swegles begong gesacan   ne
                  that I myself any   under sky's   compass adversary not
            tealde
            counted
            'so that I thought I had no enemy under the stretch of the sky'
                (*Beowulf* 1772–3)

(8)   . . ., þæt hie   seoððan   no geseon moston, / modige
                  that they (each other) afterwards not see   might,   brave
            on meþle
            in council
            'that they might never meet again, brave in council'
                (*Beowulf* 1875–6)

While it seems reasonable to say for (8) that *no* is a full negative adverb in some position low in the clause, perhaps in Spec,NegP, the status of *ne* in the far more dominant pattern exemplified by (7) is less clear. Is *ne* here likewise an adverb in a low position in the clause preceding a non-preposed finite verb, or a prefix checked against the head of NegP as is well-motivated for later Old English? If

---

[3] Of the sixty-eight examples of negated non-root clauses in *Beowulf*, sixty-four have the negative adverb + finite verb in a low position in the clause, i.e. negative adverb + finite verb is preceded by a variety of constituents. In the remaining four examples, negative adverb + finite verb are in a position following a pronominal subject and preceding a further OV word order. This position is consistent with one of the standard patterns in later Old English.

we postulate a NegP for this stage by theoretical assumption, it seems impossible to find evidence for its position in the clausal architecture, since there is no multiple sentential negation of the kind that could guide us to the position of a second sentential negator (although there are three examples with double sentential negation in Spec,CP, as discussed below). I will nevertheless assume a NegP for this stage of the language, for the following reasons: first, there is the fact that in its reduced form, the negative element *ne* is always left-adjacent to the finite verb. This is not only the case in those non-root clauses in which the verb is in a low position, but also in the four examples in *Beowulf* which we need to analyse as having the negated finite verb preposed to a high position, as in (9):

(9)   þæt he ne mehte on þæm meðelstede / wig Hengeste   wiht
       that he not could on the   battlefield   fight to-Hengest in-any-way
       gefeohtan
       offer
       'so that he could in no way offer fight to Hengest on the battle field'
          (*Beowulf* 1082–3)

The negated finite verb *ne mehte* has been preposed to a position to the right of the pronominal subject. This pattern is consistent with one that occurs at higher frequency in later Old English, as analysed in van Kemenade (1999), and Pintzuk (1991) has shown that it involves verb movement in non-root clauses. The four examples with V-movement in *Beowulf*, amounting to about 6%, show that *ne* in non-root clauses is already positionally covariant with the finite verb. This means that we should assume, at least for the cases that involve movement of the negated finite verb, that *ne* is an incorporating negative head, which in turn implies the presence of NegP. Example (8), alone of its kind, with *no* separated from the finite verb, may represent an earlier stage at which the negative adverb has not yet undergone morphosyntactic weakening. The discussion below of negative-initial root clauses in *Beowulf* reveals the same type of phenomenon with a good deal more robustness. One further point should be noted here: a reanalysis of this sort, in a position low in the clause, would seem to suggest that we need to postulate a position for NegP that is low, i.e. to the right of objects in an O . . . V order. We have no independent evidence for this.

Let us now turn to negated root clauses. It was mentioned above that a standard strategy in *Beowulf* is to front a negative adverb to clause-initial position.[4] The counterpart of this construction in later Old English is the extremely frequent pattern with a negated finite verb in clause-initial position, which was exemplified above by (4). The pattern as in (4) is found in *Beowulf* as well and is exemplified in (10), but there is also an alternative pattern as in (11).

---

[4] This is not the only negation pattern in root clauses, although it is the clearly dominant one, amounting to about 85% of the cases. Other patterns are consistent with those of single sentential negation in later Old English.

(10)   Nolde   eorla   hleo   ænige þinga / þone cwealmcuman
       not-wanted of-earls protector any   thing   the   kill-comer
       cwicne forlætan
       alive   release
       'The protector of earls was minded in no wise to release the deadly
       visitant alive.'   (*Beowulf* 791–2)

(11) (*a*)   No he wiht fram me / flodyþum feor fleotan meahte, hraþor
            not he thing from me on waves far   swim   could, quicker
            on holme; no ic fram him wolde
            in water; not I from him wanted
            'In no way could he swim far from me on the waves of the flood,
            more quickly on the sea; I would not consent to leave him.'
            (*Beowulf* 541–3)

    (*b*)   no ic me   an herewæsmun hnagran talige, / guþgeweorca, þonne
           not I myself in war-strength inferior count,   battledeeds,   than
           Grendel hine
           Grendel himself
           'I do not count myself less in war-strength, in battle deeds, than
           Grendel does himself.'
           (*Beowulf* 677–8)

There are 124 negative-initial clauses in *Beowulf*, 73 of which conform to the pattern (10), and 51 to pattern (11). That is, 59% of the negative-initial root clauses have a preposed finite verb.

There are several points of note about the data in (11). First, the sentences are negative-initial, like the standard Old English ones in (4); second, the initial negative element is not reduced to *ne* or procliticized as *n-*, but has a distinctive vowel; third, the initial negative element is not incorporated with the finite verb: while *no* is in first position, the finite verb, *meahte* in (11*a*), *talige* in (11*b*), does not seem to have been moved at all. A final observation is that the patterns in (10) and (11) are in complementary distribution: an unreduced form like *no* (but also *n-*, *næfre*) does not go together with movement of the finite verb, but the reduced form *ne* or the procliticized form does.[5]

We are looking here at an interesting asymmetry between root clauses and non-root clauses, which partially goes hand in hand with V-movement: *ne* is positionally covariant with the finite verb; *no* is not, since it occurs separated

---

[5] There are three 'counter-examples' to this, all three a combination of the *no*-initial pattern and
. . . *ne* Vf, like (i):

(i) . . . / no þu ymb mines ne þearft / lices   feorme lenge sorgian.
       not you about my   not need   body's disposal long worry
    'in which case you will not need to trouble long over the disposal of my body'
       (*Beowulf* 450–1)

from the finite verb in a rather large number of root clauses (41%), and in one of the two examples in non-root clauses. This is a point of similarity between the patterns, which I will explore further below. But there are also important differences: while it seems reasonable to interpret the facts in non-root clauses in terms of NegP, the facts in negative-initial root clauses can have little to do with NegP, since the pattern (11) appears to reflect fronting of a negative adverb to Spec,CP, alternating with the pattern in (10), which is robust throughout the Old English period and is standardly assumed to reflect V-to-C movement. I will therefore regard them as separate developments, which share as a common trait the phonological weakening of the negative constituent *no* to the bound morpheme *ne*. In root clauses this takes place in the CP domain in about 85% of the cases; in the remaining root clauses and in non-root clauses this takes place in NegP. I now return to root negation as in (11).

Given the fact that the pattern (11) without V-movement has largely died out by the ninth-century prose texts, it is tempting to see the alternation between the two root negation patterns in *Beowulf* as the result of a change in progress: the rise of V-movement in negative-initial sentences, a grammatical environment, beside questions, in which English throughout its history has had V-movement to C. There are pieces of circumstantial evidence for this idea, in the absence of earlier texts. The first of these is that the putatively early pattern without movement (11) is found with any frequency only in older texts, specifically in the oldest poetry: examples can be found, for instance, in *Widsith, Genesis A, Daniel*. This might lead us to think that it is a pattern of poetry rather than prose, but this is not the case: the oldest poems have it in varying degrees, but the one poem which we know is late, *The Battle of Maldon*, written up close to its late tenth-century composition date, soon after the battle it relates (991), does not have a single example of the pattern (11).

There is also some cross-linguistic evidence in that Latin (as in Adams 1994) and Gothic (as in Ferraresi 1991) have known a similar rise of V-movement triggered by negative constituents. I will therefore conclude that we are looking at the rise of V-movement here. This hypothesis has several very interesting implications: the first of these is important from the point of view of grammaticalization. It seems reasonable to analyse the initial negative element in root clauses in early Old English as a Spec,CP element, and to say that the finite verb, when moved, is in C. The motivation for the rise of this V-movement strategy could then plausibly come from a condition of Universal Grammar, stating that an (operator) element in Spec,CP must be licensed by a lexically filled C. This kind of condition is well known in the theoretical literature; one appropriate way of formulating it for English past and present is Rizzi's *Wh*-criterion (Rizzi 1990), and his adaptation of Haegeman's analogous *Neg*-criterion (Haegeman 1995). The only element that can satisfy this condition without violating the usual conditions on head movement is V, as pointed out in Lightfoot (1998: 152–3). A further important implication is the following:

The alternation between the two root-negation patterns in *Beowulf* suggests that V-movement and the grammaticalization of the negative element to *ne* or proclitic *n-* are crucially related, and more particularly that movement of the verb to a functional head whose specifier hosts *no* entails phonological weakening of *no* to *ne*, with the possibility of *ne* being proclitic phonologically but not syntactically. This argues for the following formalized representation of the two root negation patterns in *Beowulf*, which I suggest are successive stages overlapping at the time of the early poetry:

(12)   Eighth-century English
      The non-V-movement pattern:
      $[_{\text{Spec,CP}}$ no [. . . finite verb . . .]]

(13)   Early and later Old English
      The V-movement pattern:
      $[_{\text{Spec,CP}}$ ne $[_{\text{C}}$ finite verb [. . .]]]
             cliticization

(12) represents the 'oldest' pattern. Root sentential negation is dominantly expressed by moving *no* to Spec,CP. The finite verb is not moved. In (13), there is again a negative constituent in Spec,CP, but now the finite verb has been moved to C.

It seems that V-movement to C, with the negative element in Spec,CP, entails that *no* is reduced/procliticized to the finite verb. I hypothesize that at the stage represented in (13), this cliticization is phonological, which means that, although *ne* is a prefix/proclitic, it does represent a constituent in Spec,CP syntactically. I will come back to this below, as we will see that this yields a plausible account for the fact that the construction in (12) and (13) resists topicalization throughout the Old English period.

At the stage of the language represented by *Beowulf*, the negative element seems to be undergoing a reanalysis from an independent constituent, an adverb as far as we can tell, to becoming a functional head incorporated with the finite verb. This transition is a good deal more advanced in non-root clauses (only two cases of unreduced *no* against sixty-six of *ne*, i.e. 3% *no*) than in root clauses (41% *no*). This discrepancy, and the fact that the standard strategies for negation are so different between root and non-root clauses, suggests that they are separate developments, which share as a common trait the reanalysis to functional head status, in the CP domain in root clauses; in NegP in non-root clauses. By the time of the extensive prose texts of the ninth and tenth centuries, *ne* is firmly in place as a negative head.

3.2.3. *Classical Old English*

In later Old English, sentential negation is dominantly expressed by *ne* alone. In the vast majority of cases, such sentences are negative-initial, as in (4) above.

This in itself gives us evidence for the existence of a negative head, but it gives no independent distributional evidence for locating NegP in the clausal architecture. There is also sentential negation with more than one negative marker in Old English, contrary to what is often said. The standard story, implicit in Jespersen (1917) and explicit in Jack (1978*a–c*), is that multiple sentential negation is first attested in Middle English. But there is, on a limited scale, multiple sentential negation in Old English: the most common second negator in such cases is the constituent negator *na/no*.[6]

(14) (*a*) Ne het   he us *na* leornian heofonas to wyrcenne
             not ordered he us not learn   heavens to make
             'He did not order us to learn to make the heavens.'
             (Ælfric, *Lives of Saints* XVI.127)

      (*b*) Ne sæde *na* ure Drihten þæt he mid cynehelme oððe mid purpuran
             not said not our Lord   that he with diadem   or   with purple
             gescryd, cuman wolde to us
             clothed, come   wanted to us
             'Our Lord did not say that he wanted to come to us with a diadam
             or clothed in purple.' (Ælfric, *Lives of Saints* XXXI.762)

Note that these are instances of sentential negation with *na*: a constituent negation reading is not available: (14*a*) cannot mean 'he ordered us not to learn . . .', nor can (14*b*) mean 'it was not our Lord who said . . .'. Rather, they mean: 'it is not the case that he ordered us . . .' and 'it is not the case that our Lord said . . .'. The pattern (14) with two sentential negators is a minority pattern: while the pattern (4) with one negator is attested several times over on any page of Old English prose, I have found some 330 examples of the pattern (14).[7] The two examples in (14) are representative of this minority pattern, and they show up a striking distributional contrast between pronominal subjects on the one hand (14*a*) and DP subjects on the other (14*b*), as discussed in more detail in van Kemenade (1999). It allows us to establish the relative distribution of subjects and negation: pronominal subjects (as well as pronominal objects) appear on the

---

[6] There are also some instances where the precursor of present-day English *not*, *nawiht/nowiht*, is used as a second sentence negator. But *nawiht/nowiht* is somewhat variable in its behaviour; it can be used as a negated noun, as an emphatic negator, meaning something like 'not at all', and as a non-emphatic second negator. Rissanen (1999) presents figures from the Helsinki Corpus on all three, which confirm the picture in van Kemenade (1999)

[7] The corpus consists of: *The Old English Orosius*, ed. Bately; *King Alfred's Version of St Augustine's Soliloquies*, ed. Carnicelli; *King Alfred's Old English Version of Boethius' 'De Consolatione Philosophiae'*, ed. Sedgefield; *King Alfred's West-Saxon Version of Gregory's Pastoral Care*, ed. Sweet; the early part of the Parker MS of the *Anglo-Saxon Chronicle*, from *Two of the Saxon Chronicles Parallel*, ed. Plummer; volume I of the *Homilies of Ælfric*, ed. Thorpe; both volumes of *Ælfric's Lives of Saints*, ed. Skeat; both volumes of the *Homilies of Ælfric*, ed. Pope; the *Homilies of Wulfstan*, ed. Bethurum; the later part of the Parker MS of the *Anglo-Saxon Chronicle*, ed. Plummer. The texts were searched exhaustively in the machine-readable version of the Toronto text corpus.

left of the reinforcing negator; DP subjects on the right of it. This affords clear evidence for locating NegP in the clausal architecture. Recall that in early Old English, this evidence is lacking because *ne* co-varies with the finite verb, and there is no reinforcing negator other than three examples of root negation in CP. On the basis of the distribution of multiple sentential negation, van Kemenade (1999) argues that the functional structure of ninth- and tenth-century Old English includes the following projections, in this order:

(15) CP FP NegP TP ____VP

By way of illustration, let us consider a run-of-the-mill sentence in Classical Old English, and identify the syntactic surface positions in the sentential structure (15).

(16) þonne ne miht þu *na* þæt mot ut ateon of ðæs mannes eagan
      then not could you not the speck out draw of the man's eye
      'then you could not draw the speck out of the man's eye'
      (Ælfric, *Homilies*, Pope XIII.153)

(17)

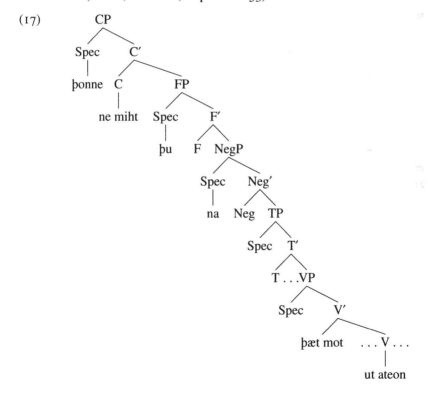

Although I refer informally to *ne* as the head of NegP in later Old English, more strictly this head is the negative feature required to check *ne*, which is an inflectional prefix since it is never separated from the finite verb. It is checked against the negative head, overtly in clauses with syntactic V-movement, covertly in others. (14) has syntactic V-movement: *ne miht* is base-generated as the head of the VP, and is moved overtly, to T, Neg, F, and C (recall that negative-initial sentences have V-to-C movement). Personal pronouns are checked in Spec,FP, cf. van Kemenade (1999); I have not further specified the precise checking position for *þæt mot ut*, my suggestion is to treat it as a resultative small clause. The element *na* in Spec,NegP is the reinforcing sentential negator. We are at stage 2 of Jespersen's cycle here: the original negative marker *ne* has been weakened to negative head status, and a second negative adverb *na* in introduced. This second negative adverb has a fixed position because it is overtly licensed in Spec,NegP. Its fixed position illuminates the positions of different types of subject: the DP subject appears on the right of *na*, in Spec,TP, which we therefore assume is the position where nominative case is checked; the pronominal subject, and other non-nominative personal pronouns as well, occur on the left of *na*. At this stage, we thus have distributional evidence for NegP: the fixed position of the negative adverb *na* or some variant thereof, with a fixed syntactic position, Spec,NegP. It should be noted that the position of the reinforcing negator *na/no* is not restricted to negative elements; other adverbs have the same kind of distribution, as discussed in Haeberli (in this volume) and in more detail in van Kemenade (forthcoming). Observe that this does not weaken the case for NegP in Old English: what distinguishes negative adverbs from others is that we have clear evidence for a specifier element as well as a head element.

3.2.4. *The development of the negative-initial position*

Let us now take a closer look at the development of the initial negative element in root clauses, as discussed above for early Old English. It was argued in the motivation for (12) and (13) that the initial negative element in both early and classical Old English is syntactically a topic. This allows an account for the well-known fact that Old English root clauses with the negated finite verb in C, as exemplified by (4), (10), and (16) above seem to resist topicalization: (18) is one of the extremely rare examples:[8]

(18)   ðinra   synna ne weorðe ic gemunende, ac gemun   ðu hiora.
        of-your sins not become I mindful,   but remember you of-them
        'I will not remember thy sins, but do thou remember them.'
        (*Cura Pastoralis* 53.413.20)

At a later stage, however, topics occur freely in this construction, as we will see below. If the preposed negative adverb is in Spec,CP, we can account for this

---

[8] The number does not qualify as 'extremely rare' if we count examples with initial adverbs, for which we anyway have to countenance the possibility that they may be in a higher, CP-adjoined, position. Of examples like (18), with an object topic and single sentential negation, I have found only two.

on the assumption that the standard position of topics is Spec,CP in Old English: if the negative adverb counts syntactically as a topic, no further topic can be hosted in Spec,CP, as argued in van Kemenade (1997a). By the same account, the fact that at a later stage a topic is readily tolerated in this construction is accounted for by assuming that the constituent status of *ne* in Spec,CP is weakening, and that therefore it ceases to be interpreted syntactically as a topic. A crucial intermediate step in this weakening process is the introduction of a reinforcing negator in Spec,NegP, which supposedly marks the weakening of the original negator. If this line of argument is correct, the next synchronic step may be formalized as follows:

(19)   classical Old English and Early Middle English
         The topic-*ne*-finite verb pattern, multiple sentential negation with
         ne . . . na
         [$_{\text{Spec,CP}}$ topic [$_\text{C}$ ne + finite verb [. . . [$_{\text{NegP}}$ na . . .] . . .]]]

(19), in conjunction with earlier stages as formalized in (12) and (13), represents a hypothesis about the historical development which should correlate with the facts in the following ways: first, since in early Old English sentence-initial *no* is syntactically a topic in Spec,CP, we expect that topicalization is incompatible with *no* in Spec,CP. Second, since in early as well as late Old English, *ne* followed by the finite verb in CP counts as a topic, we expect that this construction does not tolerate topicalization, but there might be some leakage leading to the odd example. Third, in the classical Old English and Middle English pattern in which there is a second sentential negator, indicating that *ne* is now becoming syntactically weak as well, we expect that it no longer counts as a syntactic topic, and that topicalization thus begins to occur more frequently. These expectations are borne out: first, *no* in *Beowulf* is never preceded by a topic. With respect to the second prediction, we can say that, while there are 124 negative-initial clauses in *Beowulf*, there is only one example of a topic preceding *ne* + finite verb:

(20)   Hreðsigora   ne gealp goldwine Geata;   guðbill
         of-famous victories not boasted gold-friend of-Geats; war-sword
         geswac, nacod æt niðe,   swa hyt no sceolde, iren ærgod.
         failed, naked at battle, as   it   not should, iron long-famous.
         'The gold-friend of the Geats boasted not of famous victories; the war-sword, naked in battle, failed, as it should not have done, the long-famous brand.'   (*Beowulf* 2583–6)

It was already noted above that in late Old English topicalization is similarly rare.[9] The third expectation is also borne out: topicalization in negative clauses

---

[9] I do not discuss the position of clause-initial subjects here. There is good evidence that initial DP subjects in root clauses are, like topics, in Spec,CP, and this may be true for pronominal subjects as well. Initial DP subjects in negated clauses are at least as rare as topics (this fact is noted in Traugott 1992: 268). Space does not permit my going into the complex distributional evidence.

with V-to-C movement becomes more frequent from the onset of multiple sentential negation. While such topicalization is rare in single sentential negation, it is attested with some frequency in the Old English multiple sentential negation pattern: there are thirty-two examples in the pattern with multiple sentential negation, which amounts to 10%. (21) is an example:

(21)   þeah ða   his lufe ne sece he no for him selfum, þylæs . . .
             yet   then his love not seek he not for himself,   lest . . .
             'yet he must not seek popularity for himself, lest . . .'
                 (*Cura Pastoralis* 147.15)

We will see in the following section that topic-initial negative clauses become quite common in Middle English. I conclude therefore, that the three synchronic stages formalized in (12), (13) and (19) represent historical stages whose structure can be formalized. This is an interesting result in that it shows that at each stage, the syntactic structure is of precise relevance.

   The stage formalized in (13) is of particular interest from the point of view of grammaticalization. Note that, while the element *ne* in Spec,CP is morphophonologically weak, it is syntactically a constituent, which is evident from the fact that it counts as a topic. This implies that the morphophonological weakening at this stage is further advanced than the syntactic and semantic weakening, which in turn suggests that this process is not semantically driven, as grammaticalization theorists contend about grammaticalization in general.

3.2.5. *Middle English and Early Modern English*

The development in the Middle English period is characterized primarily by the ongoing weakening of *ne*, in line with the discussion in the previous section. In the Middle English period, the reinforcing negator is no longer *na/no*, which becomes restricted to marking constituent negation, for reasons that are not really clear. The reinforcing negator is now some spelling variant of *not* (*noht*, *noȝt*, *nauht*, *nawht*, etc.), the descendant of Old English *nawiht/nowiht*, which in Old English was used as a negated noun or an emphatic negative adverb. *Not* is clearly a semantically bleached version of its Old English precursor, and is now used as a negative adverb with rapidly increasing frequency, as described in detail in Jack (1978*a*–*c*). But *not* is deployed in exactly the same syntactic environments as *na/no* in Old English in its use as a sentence negator, as is evident from the fact that its distribution continues the pattern attested in Old English: the subject pronoun precedes *not*, the nominal subject follows it.

(22) (*a*)   þet ne seide he noht
              that not said   he not
              'That he did not say.'
                  (*Kentish Sermons* 214.25)

(*b*) nule   nawt þi leofmon þoli   na leas þing ta lihe   þe
       not-will not   your beloved tolerate no false thing to deceive you
       longe
       long
       'Your beloved will not allow any false thing to deceive you long.'
       (*St Juliana* 33.332)

(23) (*a*)   yet ne wolde he nat answare sodeynly   (Chaucer, *Melibee* 2222)
      (*b*)   also ne accordeth nat the poeple to that   (Chaucer, *Melibee* 2132)

It seems reasonable to assume, therefore, that *not* replaces *na/no* as the negative adverb in Spec,NegP in the transition from Old English to Middle English.

Negated preposed verbs now frequently occur with topics preceding them:

(24) (*a*)   þer   ne þerf he habben kare of ʒefe ne of ʒelde
              there not need he have   care of gifts nor of rewards
              'There he needn't be worried about gifts or rewards.'
              (*Poema Morale* 163.45)

      (*b*)   for of al his strengðe ne drede we nawiht
              for of all his strength not dread we not
              'For of all his strength we don't have any dread.'
              (*Sawles Warde* 255.8)

      (*c*)   þis ne habbe ic nauht ofearned
              this not have I not   earned
              'This I have not earned.'   (*Vices and Virtues* 17.9)

As already noted, this syntactic behaviour seems to reflect the ongoing weakening of *ne*. *Ne* is beginning now to be dropped altogether, which takes us to stage 3 of Jespersen's cycle: *not* is fast increasing in frequency, and the original negative marker *ne* becomes optional. Indeed, at the close of the Middle English period, it has to a large extent disappeared, as discussed in Jack (1978*a–c*). This takes us to stage 4 of Jespersen's cycle: the original negative marker becomes extinct.

As soon as *ne* has disappeared, the reinforcing negative adverb *not* in Spec,NegP begins to show signs of morphophonological weakening, and there is clear evidence that it is becoming a negative head. To see this, we will first look at the relative ordering of subjects and *not* during the Middle English period. Recall that the pattern inherited from Old English is one in which *not* has a fixed position, with pronominal subjects preceding it, DP subjects following it. This was the very evidence that we took to motivate an analysis of *na/not* as a Spec,NegP element. On the other hand, *ne* behaves as an incorporating head, co-varying positionally with the finite verb. Following hard on the heels of the disappearance of *ne*, *not* is beginning to show evidence of being a negative head: it moves along with the finite verb when the latter is moved to C, for instance in negative questions. This is illustrated by (25).

(25) dyd not I send unto yow one Mowntayne that was both a traytor and a
herytyke, . . .?   (Mowntayne 210)

(25)

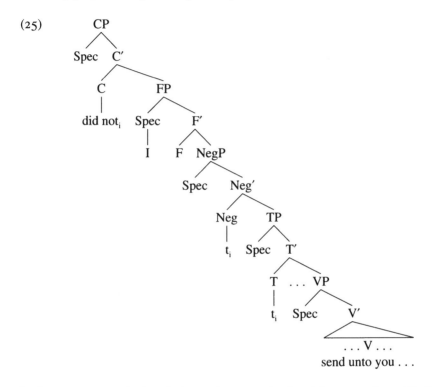

In the grammar producing (25), *not* is a negative head incorporating with the
finite verb *did*, which is moved to C in the syntax. The innovation is that a new
generation of learners is constructing grammars in which *not* is no longer an
AdverbP in Spec,NegP, but a negative head. What triggers this innovation? There
is no shift in the positional evidence: the position of *not* was always fixed. The
trigger therefore seems to be the loss of *ne*. Again, we see that, upon the loss of
the head *ne*, the negative adverb in the specifier is incorporated as a negative
head with the finite verb. This reconfirms the interpretation of Jespersen's
cycle (6).

There is independent evidence for this account from the facts in Table 3.1,
which gives the results of a quantitative examination of the Middle English section of the Helsinki Corpus. Observe that the new pattern with the pronominal
subject following *not* (column 2), which we analyse as movement of the new
negative head *not* with the finite verb to C, is first attested when *ne* has disappeared: the pattern does not occur at all in those instances when *ne* is still
around. This makes sense on the assumption that as long as *ne* was around, *not*
was interpreted by the learner as a specifier element. Once *ne* has disappeared,

TABLE 3.1. *The relative position of subject and* not *in negative subject–verb inversion sentences in Middle English*

	Spro + not	not + Spro	SNP + not[10]	not + SNP
ne + not, have/be/modal	68	0	6	11
ne + not, main verb	82	0	1	4
not, have/be/modal	68	5	3	12
not, main verb	51	1	2	4

learners construct grammars in which *not* is a head, moving with the finite verb, which at this stage could be a lexical finite verb, auxiliary, or *DO*. We are at the last stage of Jespersen's cycle, where the cycle comes full circle: in Jespersen's terms, the original negative marker (*ne*) becomes extinct, upon which the new negative marker begins to show the first signs of weakening. Weakening is again narrowly structurally circumscribed: a strong, positionally invariant, negative specifier is reinterpreted as a negative head, and incorporates with the finite verb as a clitic, moving with the finite verb to the C-position. Weakening of the negative element is seen immediately as incorporation with the finite verb. This syntactic cliticization must crucially involve head incorporation with the finite verb: in the tree diagram (25), the finite verb incorporates with the negative head on its way to C, moving together past the pronominal subject. If this movement does not take place, *did* and *not* would not be adjacent. This can therefore not be a case of phonological cliticization under adjacency.

There are some relics of the old pattern in the present-day language: according to Quirk *et al.* (1985: 11.7) there is, beside the familiar pattern with negative contraction in negative questions as in (26), an uncontracted, more formal usage as in (27), in which the old pattern handed down from Old English times is retained. In this pattern, the pronominal subject precedes *not*, while the nominal subject follows it.[11]

(26) (*a*)   Didn't they warn you?
     (*b*)   Isn't history a social science?

(27) (*a*)   Did they not warn you?
     (*b*)   Is not history a social science?

The new pattern emerging in Table 3.1, with the pronominal subject following *not*, should then be identified as the rise of negative contraction (this insight is due to Rissanen 1994, 1999, who also presents quantitative evidence through the history of English), resulting from the emergence of *not* as a negative head, hard on the heels of the loss of *ne*.

---

[10] These can often be interpreted as constituent negation; also the subject is often *mon/men*, which in its syntactic behaviour straddles the divide between DPs and pronouns.

[11] A note of caution: the pattern in the uncontracted variant (27*a*–*b*) is not confirmed by judgements of a number of native speakers.

To summarize the discussion so far, we have seen two distinct developments with respect to sentential negation: the development of a negative-initial pattern involving the CP-domain; and a development in the body of the clause. At the stage of *Beowulf*, the position for NegP is most plausibly low, though the evidence as we have considered it so far is not clear. In later Old English and through to the early Modern period, the position for NegP as we have seen it is high, within the domain where various types of subjects are licensed.

In the course of the Middle English period, a further negation pattern emerges with some clarity, whose syntax is distinct from those discussed so far: a negation position that is bound to be considerably lower. (28) gives some examples:

(28) (a)   And freeten hym, for that they knewe hym naught
             (Chaucer, *Knight's Tale* 2068)

      (b)   if you knew them not   (John Lyly 1580)

      (c)   I woot right wel, thou darst it nat withseyn
             (Chaucer, *Knight's Tale* 1140)

      (d)   so slyly that the preest it nat espide
             (Chaucer, *Canon Yeoman's tale* 1230)

Examples (28c–d) make it particularly clear that the position of *not* is a low one, considering that in (28c) it is preceded by a pronominal subject, finite verb and pronominal object, in (28d) by both a DP subject and a personal pronoun object. Since object pronouns from the early Middle English period onward no longer occur in the high pronoun position that we saw above for Old English (cf. van Kemenade 1987), we are in (28c) looking at a negation position lower than Spec,TP (the position for DP subjects) and the position for an object pronoun in what looks like a late OV word order. Late OV orders are discussed in van der Wurff (1997); I follow van der Wurff's proposal that the pronominal object is in a licensing position for objects: Spec,AgrOP. It seems reasonable to treat (28a–b) as variants of the word order in (28c): supposing that the pronominal object is in the same position in all three examples, (28a–b) distinguish themselves from (28c) by movement of the finite verb to a functional head position, most likely T. This is in fact the analysis proposed by Roberts (1995) for this pattern.[12] This analysis depends, however, on the assumption of a low negation position.

The fact that this low negation position crops up once again in Middle English raises interesting questions, and space will not permit me to discuss them in any detail. I will, however, give a brief sketch of the issues and provide a perspective towards an answer that must at this stage remain speculative. The primary

---

[12] Roberts (1995) puts this pattern on a par with Holmberg's Generalization, according to which in the Scandinavian languages the object moves leftwards only if the verb moves to a higher position. This is problematic with respect to (28c) which has no V-movement. Space prevents my going into this further here.

question is whether we can indeed distinguish two negation positions in the history of English, and if so, how they develop.

At this point, it is useful to consider work on negation in closely related languages: Holmberg (1993) argues explicitly for two distinct adverb positions (including negation) in Mainland Scandinavian, whose positional properties agree closely with those of the positions identified here. Furthermore, the typology of negation positions in Zanuttini (1997) likewise subsumes two relevant positions: her NegP1 and NegP4. NegP4 in this typology, the lowest position, is one for negative elements that may have primary stress. This is consistent with the default low negation position in Dutch from the work of Klooster (1994).

I assume that the evidence for the high NegP is robust from late Old English onward, as discussed above, and I have identified its location in the clausal architecture with some precision. The low NegP is one that I have assumed somewhat tentatively for early Old English above, but in early Old English there is little independent evidence. There is one example in *Beowulf* involving a low negation position in which the negative adverb is not reduced, and in which it has primary stress, as is evident from the fact that it alliterates:

(29)   Hreðsigora   ne gealp goldwine Geata;   guðbill
        of-famous victories not boasted gold-friend of Geats; war-sword
        geswac, *nacod æt niðe*, *swa hyt no sceolde*, iren ærgod.
        failed, *naked at battle, as it   not should*, iron long-famous.
        'The gold-friend of the Geats boasted not of famous victories; the war-sword, naked in battle, failed, as it should not have done, the long-famous brand.'   (*Beowulf* 2583–6)

There is little evidence in late Old English for a low position. Recall that multiple sentential negation is itself not frequent in Old English. The 330 examples I have include many cases of the high position, quite a few examples that are ambiguous, and only one example in which we can be certain that the reinforcing negative is on the left of the non-finite verb.

The Middle English evidence was quoted in (28), and the evidence I have so far is consistent with primary stress: it is clear in all three cases from Chaucer in (28) that the negative coincides with an arsis position. In (28a) moreover, the final negative element rhymes, another sure guide to primary stress. A computerized search through *The Canterbury Tales* suggests that this observation holds up. I will pursue this matter in future research. The pattern as in (28) did not die out before the end of the early Modern period: examples of it are found as late as the last subperiod of the early Modern period in the Helsinki Corpus.

A further property that distinguishes the low position from the high position is that a low negative can be stranded in sentence-final position, as the first two examples in (28) testify. This is another property shared by Dutch, and is in sharp contrast to the high position, for which I have no single example from

Old or Middle English in which the negative element is stranded in sentence-final position.

While the evidence for a low position needs to be further pursued, it would be consistent with the low position identified by Holmberg (1993), Klooster (1994), and Zanuttini (1997), which means that the low NegP selects VP:

(31)   . . . NegP VP

If it is correct to postulate two NegPs beside the CP-level invoked for the negative-initial pattern that is quite robust throughout the history of English, it would seem that the history of negation is shaped by a delicate interplay between the high and the low negation position: low in early Old English; high in late Old English and early Middle English; low again in late Middle English and early Modern English. There may be a cycle here as well.

3.3. CONCLUDING DISCUSSION

In this chapter, I have brought together two strands of work: I have analysed in some detail the history of sentential negation in English, tracing Jespersen's cycle from early Old English to early Modern English. I have analysed this historical development from the perspective of the Principles and Parameters approach, making use of two instantiations of the functional projection NegP. I have argued that the weakening of negative constituents that is part and parcel of Jespersen's cycle, whether in NegP or in CP, is primarily morphosyntactic, and shows up as the reanalysis of a functional specifier element to a functional head element incorporating with the finite verb. Functional projections like NegP allow an insightful way of modelling morphosyntactic change: on the one hand they allow an appropriate formalization of the syntactic consequences of the loss of inflectional morphology, as apparent in much recent work. On the other hand they show up grammaticalization as the creation of new inflectional morphology. This history of sentential negation that I have argued for here shows at each stage the synchronic relevance of syntactic and morphological structure, which argues against the idea that grammaticalization is a diachronic process that is semantically driven.

4

Evolutionary Perspectives on Diachronic Syntax

TED BRISCOE

The main purpose of this chapter is to argue the merits of 'population thinking' in gaining insight into linguistic and, in particular, syntactic change. Population-level thinking and modelling can shed new light on many issues in the study of language acquisition and language change, and leads directly to a precise and useful characterization of E-language, something which is lacking in current generative linguistics. Moreover, this way of thinking is fully compatible with the major insights of the latter, and integrates them into a framework in which language variation and change are inherent and inevitable, rather than peripheral and/or accidental, properties of language. I will argue that (E-)languages are best modelled as particular kinds of *dynamical systems*; namely, *complex adaptive systems* (where these terms are used in technical senses made precise below).

The chapter both introduces some relevant ideas and techniques from modern evolutionary theory, and from the mathematical and computational study of dynamical systems, and also offers a critique and review of some recent work on syntactic change in this emerging framework, arguing that a useful population model needs to support overlapping generations of language users and learners and to allow quite detailed modelling of differing demographic scenarios. I utilize simple linguistic scenarios based on constituent order changes to illustrate the ideas and techniques clearly. I abstract away from the sociolinguistic detail of the actuation and diffusion of changes, and also from much of the linguistic detail of attested changes. However, the chapter also contains extensive references both to further background material and to more specific and detailed work within the general framework exemplified here.[1]

I would like to thank the DIGS-5 audience for insightful feedback which helped shape this chapter as well as Jim Hurford, Simon Kirby, Susan Pintzuk, George Tsoulas, and Anthony Warner for very helpful comments on earlier drafts of this chapter. The remaining errors, infelicities, and opinions are entirely my responsibility.

[1] McMahon (1994: ch. 12) is a brief account of the chequered history of evolutionary ideas and terminology in linguistic theory. Keller (1994) provides a detailed critique of Müller and Schleicher's theories of language and goes on to argue for a similar view of (E-)language to that taken here. My fundamental argument is that, despite this chequered history, it is worth a second try as the neo-Darwinian synthesis and subsequent analytic and algorithmic thinking about evolution and dynamical systems makes available a panoply of new perspectives and techniques that were not available to

4.1. THE BASIC MODEL

A formal model achieves greatest generality, and thus validity, by making as few assumptions as necessary and by omitting as much extraneous detail as possible. It is a matter of judgement, of course, deciding what is extraneous and what essential. Chomsky (1965) defined grammatical competence in terms of the language of (i.e. stringset generated by) an ideal speaker-hearer at a single instant in time, abstracting away from working memory limitations, errors of performance, and so forth. The generative research programme has been very successful, but one legacy of the idealization to a single speaker at a single instant has been the side-lining of variation and change. My model will embody similar assumptions: language users will, in essence, be Chomskyan ideal speaker-hearers (and learners), their linguistic interactions will be very simplified, and so forth. An assumption I will make here, in common with most work in diachronic generative syntax, is that language acquisition is the fundamental factor in significant syntactic change, and that there is a critical period for, at least, syntactic acquisition, after which no major change to the acquired adult grammar takes place (e.g. Lightfoot 1979, 1999).

4.1.1. *A language agent*

We want to model language users and learners in a manner which abstracts away from many details potentially relevant to their behaviour, but which preserves what we think is essential for a model of language learning and use. A language agent can learn, produce, and interpret a language, defined as a well-formed set of strings with associated logical forms, by acquiring and using a generative grammar according to precisely specified procedures.[2] We can think of language agents as embodying a model of the language acquisition device (i.e. a universal grammar, *UG*, a parsing procedure, *P*, and a grammar learning procedure, *LP*) with the addition of a simple generating procedure, *G*.

I will define *UG* to be the space of classical Categorial Grammar (i.e. AB CG, e.g. Wood 1993: 7–14) with atomic categories S, N, and NP, other (complex) categories formed by left-associative combination of categories with slash or backslash (e.g. S\NP, 'English intransitive verb'; (S\NP)/NP, 'English transitive verb'), and the two directional variants of function-argument application defined below (where X and Y are variables over distinct tokens of (sub)categories and X' and Y' denote the semantic values of these (sub)categories):

---

nineteenth-century or even nineteen-sixties linguists. For accessible introductions to this new intellectual landscape see e.g. Cziko (1995), Dennett (1995), Kauffman (1993), Peak and Frame (1994), Sigmund (1993).

[2] I borrow the term 'agent(s)' from computer science for this idealization to emphasize both their autonomy and their artificiality, and because they are going to form part of a decentralized, distributed system.

Forward Application (FA):
$$X/Y \ Y \Rightarrow X \quad \lambda \ Y' \ [X' \ (Y')] \ (Y') \Rightarrow X' \ (Y')$$
Backward Application (BA):
$$Y \ X\backslash Y \Rightarrow X \quad \lambda \ Y' \ [X' \ (Y')] \ (Y') \Rightarrow X' \ (Y')$$

Application combines a complex functor category with an argument category to form a derived category (with one less (back)slashed argument category). So, for example, the category associated with an English intransitive verb encodes the fact that it can combine with a subject NP to its left to form a sentence. Grammatical constraints of order and agreement are captured by only allowing directed application to adjacent matching categories. Application is paired with a corresponding determinate semantic operation, shown here in terms of the lambda calculus, which compositionally builds a logical form from the basic meanings associated with lexical items.[3] A simple derivation is shown in Figure 4.1. A trigger sentence is defined as a surface form (SF), a string of words, with an associated logical form (LF), a possibly underspecified formula of the lambda calculus: $t_i = \{<w_1, w_2, \ldots w_n>, LF_i\}$. In the case of the example in Figure 4.1 these are (1a) and (1b), respectively.

Kim	loves	Sandy
NP	(S\NP)/NP	NP
kim'	λ y,x [love' (x y)]	sandy'
	—————————————— FA	
	S\NP	
	λ x [love' (x sandy')]	
—————————————— BA		
S		
love' (kim' sandy')		

FIGURE 4.1. CG Derivation for *Kim loves Sandy*

(1) (*a*)   Kim loves Sandy
    (*b*)   love' (kim' sandy')
    (*c*)   Kim:NP loves:S\NP$_S$/NP$_O$ Sandy:NP

A valid category assignment to a trigger ($VCA(t_i)$) is defined as a pairing of a lexical syntactic category with each word in the SF of t_i, $<w_1:c_1, w_2:c_2, \ldots w_n:c_n>$ such that the parse derivation, d_i for this sequence of categories yields LF$_i$, as in

---

[3] Thus, I adopt a deterministic syntax-driven compositional LF construction framework in common with Montague Grammar and most work with CGs (see e.g. Dowty, Wall, and Peters 1981, Wood 1993: 29–33). However, the details are not essential to an understanding of what follows, beyond the fact that the LF is determined by the derivation and, given a derivation, a LF is recovered.

(1c).[4] Given $VCA(t)$, the parse derivation in CG (and thus the LF) will be unique, so the parsing algorithm, P, can be defined precisely and deterministically in terms of a simple shift-reduce parser that orders reduction via forward/backward application before shifting new words onto the analysis stack.[5]

The generation procedure, G, selects a trigger (i.e. an SF:LF pairing) given the agent's grammar and lexicon. A trigger is defined as any one of the finite proper subset of strings generated by a grammar and lexicon which involves at most one level of recursive application, in terms of a single recursive category or a chain of categories involving recursive application.[6] I will assume a highly skewed distribution over such degree-0 and degree-1 triggers so that a learning agent has a very high probability of being exposed to a fair and effective sample of them for any given target grammar and lexicon. Given a space of possible grammars, UG, and a learning procedure, LP, a fair and effective sample of triggers, $t_1 \ldots t_n$, from the language defined by a target grammar, $L(g')$, will allow a learner to converge on g' with high probability (i.e. $p > 1 - \varepsilon$—where ε denotes a small error probability), because it will contain enough information to select the target grammar uniquely from others in UG using LP:[7]

$$p[LP(UG, t_1 \ldots t_n \in L(g')) = g'] > 1 - \varepsilon$$

The acquisition procedure, LP, is error-driven and incremental. A learning agent begins with an empty lexicon and empty category set and incrementally hypothesizes new category types and/or word:category associations. On each trigger presentation, LP finds a $VCA(t)$ yielding the appropriate LF. If this can be done using word:category associations available in the current lexicon, then no change takes place. Otherwise, new word:category associations are hypothesized and retained if these lead to successful recovery of the appropriate LF. For

---

[4] I will write SVO for S(ubject), O(bject), etc. to informally indicate relevant aspects of both SF and LF. I will also use the same abbreviations to indicate the LF associated with particular CG categories where it is convenient to suppress details of the semantic framework employed.

[5] Briscoe (1997, 1998) gives a more detailed and precise definition of such a parsing algorithm. In fact, the correct fully-specified and determinate LF cannot always be recovered from $VCA(t)$. For example, if this includes a sequence like: *almost*: (S\NP)/(S\NP) *smiled*: S\NP *deliberately*: (S\NP)\ (S\NP), the parsing algorithm outlined yields the left-branching derivation and interpretation where the second adverb has wide scope. Such complications are not relevant here.

[6] Thus, triggers will not involve derivations such as N/N N/N N $\Rightarrow$ N or NP/S NP/S S S\NP $\Rightarrow$ NP. This restriction is in accord with psycholinguistic evidence that children are exposed to a preponderance of unembedded (degree-0) triggers with about 16% of child-directed utterances involving one level of (degree-1) embedding (e.g. Newport 1977). Restricting possible triggers to a finite proper subset of sentences generated by a given grammar also facilitates modelling.

[7] This formal setting and associated assumptions concerning models of language acquisition is based on recent work on formal learnability—see, for example, Niyogi (1996) for a particularly thorough treatment—though its antecedents go back at least to Wexler and Culicover (1980). The assumption that the learner has access to a fair and effective sample circumvents most of the substantive issues of language acquisition. However, our focus here is not on these issues but rather on how the process of acquisition influences language change.

concreteness, I will assume *LP* only hypothesizes one new word:category association per trigger, tries existing category types before creating new ones, and never deletes an association.[8] For example, a learning agent presented with the trigger in (2*a,b*), with the word:category associations in (2*c*) as well as, say: *tall*:N/N might hypothesize and retain *red*:N/N.

(2) (*a*) give me the red sock

  (*b*) give' (me' x) ∧ red' (sock' (x))

  (*c*) give:(S/NP)/NP me:NP the:NP/N red:? sock:N

On the other hand, an agent without any instance of N/N would need to hypothesize this new category type in the grammar before being able to add the appropriate word:category association to the lexicon. Thus, *LP* incrementally expands the lexicon and, if necessary, the category set to find the smallest grammar and lexicon (i.e. that containing the least number of category types and word:category associations) compatible with the analysable subset of the trigger sequence seen so far. The current $g \in UG$ hypothesized by a learning agent is entirely defined by the category set (and lexicon) since *UG* specifies forward/backward application as the only means of grammatical combination.

Though learning agents may be exposed to different triggers in different orders, given *LP* a learning agent must be exposed to a (not necessarily continuous) sequence of triggers in which the addition of one new word:category association per trigger leads to g'. This implies that such incremental trigger sequences must be fairly common in the more likely subsets of triggers which will be sampled for $g \in UG$ otherwise *LP* will not be able to converge with high probability on exposure to a finite specific sequence, t_n. This requirement follows directly from the twin requirements that *one* hypothesized word:category association must yield the *complete* correct LF for a trigger.[9]

LP, as outlined, has no way of guaranteeing that the correct *VCA(t)* will be recovered for each trigger. Even given the correct LF, there is still ambiguity in the assignment of *VCA(t)* given arbitrary sequences of triggers. A well-known example (e.g. Clark 1992) is the ambiguity of SVO triggers when *UG* includes V2 grammars. *LP* could 'prematurely' learn categories like $S\backslash NP_S/NP_O$ for such sequences, although g' might be a V2 grammar and also generate OV triggers. With CG there will always be indeterminacy concerning the form of the new category that should be hypothesized. For example, a learner could infer a type-raised category like (NP/N)\(NP/N) with semantics λP λx NP/N' [(NP/N)\ (NP/N)' P(x)]] for *red* in (2*a, b*) yielding the same LF (e.g. Wood 1993: 42–6).

---

[8] The restriction to a single word:category association per trigger entails that the learner must acquire a lexicon of names, N(P), before acquiring some one-place predicates, S\N(P).

[9] Gibson and Wexler (1994), following earlier work on formal learnability, incorporate both these requirements into the Trigger Learning Algorithm. However, Niyogi and Berwick (1996), Frank and Kapur (1996), Dresher (1999), and Fodor (1998) have all questioned one or both and made alternative proposals.

Again the assumption that the learner infers the simplest category (i.e. the one requiring the least number of atomic categories and (back)slash operators) would often suffice for this type of indeterminacy. Since we are not currently concerned with how the learner resolves such indeterminacies, I will assume (unrealistically) that a trigger comes labelled with the correct (partial) $VCA(t)$, as in (2c) above, and that the learner always determines the correct new category.

LP, as defined, is a lexically conservative learner because variant category assignments to a word token will not be generalized to other words of the same type. For example, if a learning agent has acquired the word:category associations: *nicely*:(S\NP)|(S\NP) and *quickly*:(S\NP)/(S\NP) (where | is a variable which can be instantiated as slash or backslash), then *LP* will not generalize the association for *quickly*. I will assume that *LP* includes lexical (redundancy) rules of the general form: $Cat \Rightarrow Cat$ which get hypothesized appropriately. This assumption allows us to abstract away from lexical issues and the lexical content of triggers, which are also not our primary concern.[10]

This completes the linguistic part of our definition of a language agent. I extend this definition with an age, between 1 and 10, and a communicative success ratio (CSR), between 0 and 1, for reasons which will become clear in the next section. So, to summarize, a language agent has the following components:

$$
\begin{aligned}
&\text{LAgt:} \\
&LP(UG,t) \;= g \\
&P(g,t) \qquad = LF \\
&G(g,LF) \quad = t \\
&Age: \qquad\; [1\text{–}10] \\
&CSR: \qquad [0\text{–}1]
\end{aligned}
$$

Of course, there is much that is questionable about this simple model, the choice of *UG*, *LP*, and so forth. However, my intention is to explore what happens when such relatively simple and comprehensible models of language learners and users form speech communities, and then show how these predictions can be used to refine the model of a language agent.

4.1.2. *Populations of language agents*

A population is simply a set of language agents. However, we want this set to change over time as new agents are added ('born') and old agents are removed ('die'). One way of achieving this is to disallow generations of learning and adult agents to overlap; that is, to remove all adult agents from the population

---

[10] Of course, the issue of when to hypothesize a (potentially semi-productive) lexical rule and how to determine its range of application is complex (e.g. Pinker 1989, Schütze 1997, Briscoe and Copestake 1999). They are also relevant to diachronic syntax, since most accounts of lexical rule induction will predict initially slow lexical diffusion, followed by more rapid syntactic change when triggering data licenses induction of the rule, rather than just induction of specific word:category associations.

once the learning period is finished, declare the learners the adults, and add a new batch of learners. This makes the population dynamics simple but unrealistic. My model supports overlapping generations because demographic dynamics, for example altering the proportion of learners to adults, may well be a factor in some types of language change (see e.g. §4.4 below).

The constitution of the population changes over time according to some prespecified rules; agents are usually removed at age 10, and two distinct adult (age ≥ 4) agents 'reproduce' one and only one new (age 1) learning agent during each of their adult ages (so agents can help create up to seven offspring). We have already effectively defined a dynamical system; that is, a system which changes over time in a manner determined by the previous state. The system has a set of states, corresponding to distinct agent ages, and an update rule which determines the state of the system at time $t+1$ in terms of its state at t:

$$s^{t+1} = Update(s^t)$$

Update will update the age of the agents at each time step of the system, remove any over age 10, and reproduce new agents from the set of adults. To see how the system behaves, suppose that we start in s^0 with four agents all aged 4. Table 4.1 shows the behaviour of the system through the first 20 states. Each row shows the state number, the total population size, the number of learners

TABLE 4.1. *Growth and composition of a population of agents*

State	Population size	Learners	Non-learners	Ratio
0	4	4	0	∞
1	6	2	4	0.5
2	8	4	4	1.0
3	10	6	4	1.5
4	12	8	4	2.0
5	15	9	6	1.5
6	19	11	8	1.375
7	18	12	6	2.0
8	22	14	8	1.75
9	27	16	11	1.454
10	34	19	15	1.266
11	40	24	16	1.5
12	47	29	18	1.611
13	55	34	21	1.619
14	66	40	26	1.538
15	78	47	31	1.516
16	92	56	36	1.555
17	110	67	43	1.55
18	132	80	52	1.53
19	158	96	62	1.54
20	187	114	73	1.56

(aged 1–4), the number of non-learners (aged 5–10), and the ratio of learners over non-learners.

From s^1 to s^4, *Update* simply adds two new agents reproduced by the four original adults. At s^5 and s^6, three and then four new agents are added. At s^7 the total number of agents drops because the original four agents have reached age 10 and are removed. At this point learners outnumber non-learners two to one. The population continues to expand exponentially. However, the ratio of learners over non-learners lies between 1.51 and 1.57 from s^{14} onwards. Thus, these few apparently simple linear rules have some quite surprising and unintuitive properties, highlighting both the need for simulation and/or mathematical analysis in order to understand the behaviour of even very simple dynamical systems, and the need to keep the model as simple as is consonant with our modelling purposes.

The *Update* rule above is unrealistic because there is no bound on population growth. Real populations compete for finite resources and, therefore, typically show approximately logistic or S-shaped growth (e.g. Maynard-Smith 1998: 15–18; Peak and Frame 1994: 132–9). We can impose a limit (crudely) by specifying an upper bound to the total number of agents that can be reproduced in a single time step. If we do this then we place an upper bound on the size of the population defined by the age of death multiplied by this limit. Furthermore the maximum number of learners is defined by this limit multiplied by the age at which learning ceases (i.e. the end of the critical period). From these two upper bounds we can derive the ratio of learners to non-learners once the population has converged to these upper bounds. For example, if we set an upper bound of ten new agents per time step, then the example above will converge to a population of a hundred, forty of whom are learners, giving a learner–non-learner ratio of 0.66. These two linear components of *Update* now define a non-linear dynamical system.

The first plot in Figure 4.2 shows the composition of a population constructed as described, starting from two age 4 agents. Superimposed on this plot of total population size across time is an S-shaped curve constructed using the logistic map. This represents an approximation of the actual population growth; for example, it does not model the drop in population which occurs when the original agents die. The number of learners and non-learners is shown in the second plot. As can be seen there is fluctuation in the ratio until the population settles into its steady state.

The choices I have made here are different from those taken by Niyogi and Berwick (1997) in which a speech community is modelled using non-overlapping generations in a population of fixed size. These and other abstractions enable them to simulate the behaviour of the model in terms of update rules which reduce to quadratic or higher polynomial maps, and thus prove analytically properties of the resulting dynamics. In effect, they simulate the *average* behaviour of a learner at each time step of the system given the probability distribution of triggers predicted from the adult population. If we simply took the logistic map as a correct model of population growth, then we could abstract away from the

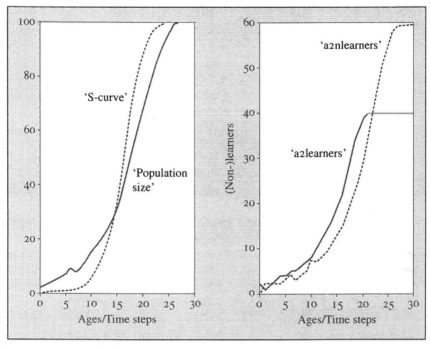

FIGURE 4.2. Population dynamics

specific rules of birth, death, and reproduction presented in this section and model the population dynamics abstractly. However, we would lose the flexibility and low-level variation inherent in the 'microscopic' rules introduced above. Below we will see that this flexibility is important for modelling some types of language change.[11]

In all versions of the model, agents in the population attempt to interact with each other a prespecified number of times during each time step of the system; therefore, the time steps will be called interaction cycles. The *Update* rule then maps the population to the next state, and another interaction cycle commences. Note that a generation, defined as the time between birth and reproductive age, is four interaction cycles. The number of times agents interact during an interaction cycle is set so that, with high probability, each learning agent will be

---

[11] Maynard-Smith (1998: 15–18) discusses the difference between modelling at the microscopic and the macroscopic level with respect to population dynamics. As modelling at the macroscopic level inevitably builds in more (perhaps unwarranted) assumptions and abstraction, I prefer the microscopic approach. In the long run derivation of mathematical laws of language change may, though, warrant macroscopic modelling. In the short run, we need microscopic modelling to discover the appropriate (if any) macroscopic model(s). In fact, the dynamics of the *Update* rule I have adopted here are probably better modelled macroscopically by the tent map (see Peak and Frame 1994) for discussion and a general accessible introduction to non-linear dynamical systems).

exposed to enough triggers to acquire any $g \in UG$ during the critical period. Thus if it takes one hundred triggers to guarantee convergence to the 'hardest' grammar with $p > 0.99$, then the number of interactions might be set to a mean of seventy-five per agent per cycle, giving a mean of three hundred interactions per learner during the critical period. In a mean hundred and fifty of these interactions, a learning agent will be the listening/parsing agent. Therefore, with high probability, learners will be given adequate triggering data to converge accurately to an adult grammar.[12]

The precise number of interactions per cycle depends on population size, so is calculated after each time step of the model. For each interaction, two distinct agents are randomly chosen from the population and one is randomly selected to be the speaking agent, the other the listening agent.[13] The speaking agent generates a trigger given its current grammar (if any) and the listening agent attempts to parse it. If the listening agent is able to recover the same LF from the trigger that the speaking agent associates with it, the interaction is successful. If not, and the listening agent is still learning, then it attempts to modify its grammar and reparse the trigger. If this results in recovery of the right LF, then the interaction is successful, otherwise it fails. A population of agents constitutes a speech community if $> 90\%$ of interactions between adult agents are successful. This is a fairly arbitrary cut-off, but nevertheless some such definition is needed to distinguish a population with no language or not much (shared) language from a speech community. The communicative success of an agent is just the ratio of successful to all interactions in which it has participated, regardless of whether it was the parsing or generating agent. The CSR is recalculated after each interaction cycle for each agent. For the moment, the only role that this ratio will play is to track whether a population constitutes a speech community.

For now, I will assume that reproduction simply creates a new agent with identical properties to all the other agents in the population. That is, the population of agents changes, and the ratio of learners to non-learners can vary, along with factors such as age of reproduction, death, and so forth. However, the population does not *evolve* at the genetic level because all agents have the same *UG*,

---

[12] We could try to characterize this probability more precisely via a probabilistic analysis in terms of the (normal) distribution and standard deviation on triggers. However, it is also straightforward to find values which yield a stable model empirically.

[13] By random here and below, I mean randomly sampled with uniform probability, so that any two distinct agents have an equal chance of interacting during every interaction and each interacting agent has an equal chance of being the speaker or listener. Randomly sampling with respect to a uniform distribution is tantamount to making the weakest assumptions; in this case, about who talks to whom. We could, for example, assume that learners talk more to their parents and siblings or that populations are structured into subgroups with greater interactions within rather than across such groups. However, though these moves would make the model more concrete, they would also potentially make it less general if such assumptions do not hold in every situation. Niyogi (2000) contrasts the dynamics which result if learners are exposed to triggers just from their parents, from the entire adult community, or according to a spatial distribution of adults.

LP, *G*, and *P*. In this case, it is irrelevant which agents reproduce new agents. Nevertheless, I define reproduction in terms of two parent agents to facilitate extension to a model in which agents' language faculties do evolve. Figure 4.3 summarizes the main properties of the model introduced in §§4.1.1 and 4.1.2.

LAgt:	
$LP(UG,t)$	$- g$
$P(g,t)$	$= LF$
$G(g,LF)$	$= t$
Age:	$[1-10]$
CSR:	$[0-1]$
Pop:	
POP_n:	$\{LAgt_1, LAgt_2, \ldots LAgt_n\}$
INT:	$Gen\,(LAgt_i, LF_k), Parse\,(LAgt_j, t_k), i \neq j,$
SUCC-INT:	$Gen\,(LAgt_i, LF_k) = t_k \wedge Parse\,(LAgt_j, t_k) = LF_k$
REPRO:	$Create\text{-}LAgt\,(LAgt_i, LAgt_j), i \neq j$

FIGURE 4.3. The basic model

4.1.3. *A simple example of language change*

Before we begin to study language change, it is important to consider under what conditions a speech community will be maintained, and under what conditions a language will *not* change. In general, speech communities do not seem to undergo such fundamental language change that communication breaks down significantly, even if during periods of major change there may be a small degree of intergenerational miscommunication (e.g. Lightfoot 1999: 7–9). An intuitive requirement for maintenance of a speech community is that if there is no initial linguistic variation in that community and learners are presented with enough triggers, then they should converge to g'. However, this is not necessary to maintain a speech community, nor sufficient to preclude language change in our model. It is possible for most learning agents in several overlapping generations to 'misconverge' to g' and still maintain >90% successful interactions when adults. For example, a community in which learning agents outnumber adults may fixate on a proper subset grammar of g', because a high proportion of the triggers the learners are exposed to come from the 'intermediate' subset grammars of other learners.[14] Thus, linguistic stasis requires not only a high probability of convergence to g' during learning—which, in turn, requires little or no variation in triggers—but also population stability too. We will begin by considering stable models, in which the ratio of learning agents to adults will not

[14] Briscoe (1998) discusses change via contraction of this type in more detail and argues that a realistic model of a language agent must incorporate a counteracting pressure for expressivity to prevent communities fixating on easily learnable but more restrictive subset languages.

significantly skew the distribution of triggers, and where the size of the population means that very occasional misconvergence by a single learner, typically to a subset language, will not skew the subsequent distribution of triggers to further learners enough to cause a chain reaction. In this situation, both the speech community and a homogeneous language will be maintained if there is little or no initial linguistic variation.[15]

As a first example, consider the following scenario. Initially there are sixty adult agents, of whom half have acquired grammar, g^1, and half g^2, in equal proportions. These grammars are identical except that g^1 generates nominal postmodifiers by associating them with category N\N, and verbal postmodifiers (S\NP)\(S\NP), while g^2 generates nominal and verbal premodifiers by replacing the (highest-level) backslash operator with slash for these categories. The model is set up to be stable so that a learning agent exposed to triggers exclusively from g^1 (or g^2) would converge to that grammar with very high probability; so, in the absence of variation, linguistic homogeneity would be maintained within the speech community. However, once the variation is introduced (perhaps through contact between previously isolated communities) the situation is very different. A learner will, on average, be exposed to equal numbers of variant triggers, such as (3*a*) and (3*b*) with the same logical form (3*c*) but variant *VCA*s (3*d*) or (3*e*).

(3) (*a*) Daddy gave you the sock red nicely
  (*b*) Daddy nicely gave you the red sock
  (*c*) nicely′ (give′ (daddy′ you′ x) ∧ red′ (sock′ (x)))
  (*d*) daddy:NP gave:((S\NP)/NP)/NP you:NP the:NP/N sock:N
    red:N\N nicely:(S\NP)\(S\NP)
  (*e*) daddy:NP nicely:(S\NP)/(S\NP) gave:((S\NP)/NP)/NP you:NP
    the:NP/N red:N/N sock:N

For example, if we assume that $1/12$ of triggers generated from g^1 (or g^2) exemplify the variation, then a learning agent has, on average, a $1/24$ chance of seeing data distinguishing g^1 from g^2 every time it is exposed to a trigger (since, on average, half the triggers will be generated by agents who have acquired g^1). If the mean number of triggers the learning agent is exposed to is one hundred, then it will be exposed to both variations one or more times with probability $p = 0.971$.[16]

---

[15] Briscoe (1998, 2000) discusses the conditions required for linguistic stasis in more detail within a very similar model. Taking a stable model of this form as the starting point for the study of change represents a rather different philosophy from that of Niyogi and Berwick (1997) in which, given the learning procedure and conditions they model, a population initially speaking a –V2 language always fixates on +V2 grammars. See also Robert Clark (1996) for further discussion.

[16] We think of the triggering data as one hundred Bernoulli trials in which success, i.e. a variant trigger, has probability 1/24 for each trial. Then by the binomial theorem, the probability that the learner will see one or more variants from g^1 (equivalently g^2):

LP, as defined in §4.1.1, will acquire both variants if it sees each at least once during the learning period, so learning agents will almost certainly converge to a grammar, g^3, capable of generating triggers like (4) as well as all the original variant triggers in (3).[17]

(4) (*a*)   Daddy nicely gave you the sock red

    (*b*)   nicely' (give' (daddy' you' x) ∧ red' (sock' (x)))

    (*c*)   daddy:NP nicely:(S\NP)/(S\NP) gave:((S\NP)/NP)/NP you:NP
        the:NP/N sock:N red:N\N

The introduction of g^3 into the community represents language change in two ways. Firstly, (4*a*) is a new type of potential trigger; previously it was not possible for a single speaker to combine pre/postmodifiers. Secondly and consequently, the distribution of trigger types will change because the distribution of grammars amongst agents in the community has changed. Once grammar, g^3, has entered this community, the overall proportion of triggers exhibiting pre/postmodifier variation will rise. Subsequent learners will be exposed to triggers like (3) from the original adult agents and to triggers like (3) and (4) from new adults who have acquired g^3. This creates a chain reaction, that is, positive feedback, so that, unless further variation is introduced, the community will soon fixate on g^3 (in the sense that all adult agents will have acquired g^3). The first generation of learners will each acquire g^3 with $p = 0.971$. The joint probability that all will acquire g^3, assuming ten learners, is $p = 0.745$. The probability that more than half will is $p = 0.999$. Subsequent generations of learners, exposed to g^1, g^2, and increasingly g^3, will converge to g^3 with increasingly higher probability. Then the original adult population of g^1 and g^2 agents will begin to die, so the proportion of g^3 agents will increase further. If no learner acquires a subset grammar, or g^1 or g^2, then the community can fixate on g^3 within six interaction cycles.[18]

$$P(X>0) = (1 - P(X) = 0)$$
$$= 1 - \binom{100}{0} (1/24)^0 (1 - 1/24)^{100}$$
$$= 1 - (23/24)^{100}$$
$$= 0.985$$

So the probability of seeing both variants one or more times is 0.985 multiplied by itself. (See for example McColl (1995) for a straightforward introduction to probability theory, Bernoulli experiments, and the binomial theorem.)

[17] Notice that an assumption that either appropriate lexical rules are induced or the triggering data is sufficiently lexically uniform is critical to maintenance of the speech community in this case. Otherwise different learning agents exposed to different triggers may acquire incompatible word: category associations for the same nominal and verbal modifiers. That is, one agent may only be exposed to *nicely* as a postmodifier and another as a premodifier during the learning period. As adults these agents would not be able to interact successfully using any sentence containing *nicely*.

[18] Analytically characterizing the exact behaviour of the model given such scenarios is very complex because of the use of overlapping generations and 'horizontal' (learner→learner) as well as 'vertical' (adult→learner) interactions. However, in this fairly clear-cut case the lower bound on fixation within six cycles is $p \approx 0.994$.

Now consider what happens if we start with fifty-nine adult agents with g^1 and one agent with g^2. The initial generation of learning agents each has a 1/60 times 1/12 chance of being exposed to the variant triggers in g^2 so the probability of this happening during the learning period is $p = 0.130$. Assuming ten new learners again, the probability of half or more of them being exposed to the g^2 variant is $p = 0.005$, so the probability of subsequent generations of learners acquiring the g^2 variant is lower not higher, as the relative frequency of the variant trigger(s) will decline as long as more than half of the new agents acquire g^1. Thus, it is very unlikely that a variant seen this infrequently during acquisition would ever spread through the community. Another way of saying this is that the community (as defined by the model) is unlikely to acquire variations based on individual innovations. However, in this community if 1/12 of the adult agents (i.e. five) generate a variant trigger with a 1/12 chance, a new grammar is quite likely to be acquired by subsequent generations of learners; that is, the probability that more than half of the first generation of learners will acquire a grammar covering the variant is $p > 0.6$, so the positive feedback dynamics have a reasonable chance of getting started. This type of analysis allows us to characterize more precisely the degree of variation that a stable model, maintaining linguistic stasis, will tolerate, given *LP* and the population dynamics.

To close this section, let us consider what happens if we introduce a sequence of variations into such a speech community. Suppose that every sixteen interaction cycles the current adult population is increased by around 1/3 new adult agents who have acquired a grammar with variant trigger(s) exemplified in their output 1/12 of the time. I will call such events migrations and introduce ongoing variation into the model via such 'population movements'. Each of these successive variant triggers has a good chance of being incorporated into a new grammar acquired by subsequent learners. If the variant grammars are otherwise close, it is very likely that the speech community will be maintained; such migrations model contact between dialects, rather than mutually incomprehensible languages. Nevertheless, language change will be characterized by the acquisition of increasingly large 'covering grammars' which successively incorporate more and more variation and allow successively greater interactions between variants originally localized in earlier smaller grammars. This is a profoundly unrealistic dynamic for grammatical change, and probably much lexical change too. It implies that as languages change, grammars will tend to incorporate more and more of the possibilities defined by *UG*. There is no evidence that grammars grow monotonically in this fashion, incorporating ever increasing variation and optionality (e.g. Lightfoot 1999: 77–92). Yet there is abundant evidence that linguistic heterogeneity rather than homogeneity is the norm during language acquisition.

4.2. DATA-SELECTIVE LEARNING PROCEDURES

A fundamental principle of change and variation is that most variation is mutually exclusive; that is, grammars or linguistic variants tend to compete rather than coexist as optional variants (e.g. Kroch 1989*b*, Lightfoot 1999: 92–101). A grammar-learning procedure which selects between variants rather than acquiring them all (at least by default) will model this aspect of language change better. There are several ways in which agents could be modified to yield data-selective learners. Firstly, *UG* could be parameterized so that the sets of categories defining full grammars was disjoint. For example, at the moment there is nothing to prevent a learning agent acquiring both categories, $(S/NP_S)/NP_o$ and $(S\backslash NP_S)/NP_o$ either for overlapping or disjoint sets of transitive verbs, thus acquiring I-languages with mixed VOS or SVO clause orders. However, if the set of categories available is parameterized so that once the order of subjects is determined for one (verbal) category all other (verbal) categories must conform to this ordering, then *UG* will not include grammars with mixed subject ordering in canonical clauses, and thus *LP* will not be able to acquire them. Secondly, *LP* could be modified so that there is data-driven competition between variant categories. For example, *LP* might count the instances in which variant categories (i.e. ones generating the same LF up to lexical variation) occur, and G might select the current most frequent one for trigger generation.

These alternatives would lead to different outcomes assuming once again the scenario of §4.1.3. Given a *UG* which parameterized cross-categorially for head-initial/final modification, then a learning agent could acquire g^1 or g^2, but not g^3.[19] If we assume that *LP* sets such parameters deterministically, never altering a parameter once it has been set via triggering data (e.g. Briscoe 1997), then the first variant trigger a learning agent is exposed to will determine the relevant part of the category set available thereafter. Thus, learning agents will each select g^1 or g^2 solely on the basis of the specific sequence of triggers they are exposed to. Agents of the initial generation each have an equal chance of seeing a postmodifier or premodifier first, so on average learners have an equal chance of selecting g^1 or g^2. However, the actual probability of exactly half the learning agents acquiring g^1 is only $p = 0.246$, so the probability that the first generation of learners will alter the subsequent distribution of triggers in favour of either g^1 or g^2 is $p = 0.754$ (rising to $p = 0.999$ by the fifth generation). Similarly, if, following Gibson and Wexler (1994) and others, we assume that parameters are continuously reset on parse failure (i.e. that the learning procedure is 'memoryless' and free to revisit previous hypotheses), then the dynamics remain identical but the grammar selected is now dependent on the last variant trigger seen. We could also posit a different parameterization in conjunction with either

---

[19] Once we posit parameterization of *UG* or, more generally, a data-selective learner, then it may no longer be possible to characterize the E-language of the community in terms of any I-language grammar which can be acquired by an individual learning agent. Lightfoot (1999: 81–2), for example, argues that 'social grammars' are, at best, fictitious linguistic constructs and will probably have to embody very different properties from 'biological grammars' generating I-languages. This section amplifies this point and demonstrates how either properties of *UG* and its parameterization *or* of *LP* may make it true. However, 'social grammars' might still turn out to be useful constructs for modelling triggering data succinctly.

of these models of *LP*, such as one that licensed, say, verbal postmodifiers and nominal premodifiers but not both types of modifier for one type of head: then learning agents could acquire one of four possible grammars. However, the dynamics of which grammar the community fixated on would remain essentially the same. The model of language change developed by Niyogi and Berwick (1997) and Niyogi (2000) is of the type just outlined. Learners select between variants (i.e. set a parameter) on the basis of the last relevant trigger they see before the learning period ends. This accounts for the (unrealistic) preference for +V2 over –V2 languages in their simulations, because in the *UG* fragment developed by Gibson and Wexler (1994) +V2 languages have more determinate +V2 triggers than –V2 languages have determinate –V2 triggers. Therefore, a learner is more likely to see +V2 triggers, on average, if +V2 grammars are present in the adult population and trigger generation is random.

Learners of this type predict that a speech community will drift randomly between variant grammars until one or other variant reaches fixation. Even though there will be positive feedback favouring any variant which is slightly better exemplified in the learner's data, random effects, such as the particular sequences of triggers seen by individual learners, may override an incipient trend towards one variant. However, at some point, one or other variant will become dominant enough to fixate with virtual certainty. This pattern is well known and well studied in population genetics and evolutionary theory as (random) *genetic drift* (e.g. Maynard-Smith 1998: 24–6). Eventual fixation on one variant is inevitable in finite populations, so we would typically expect to see a longish period of random fluctuations followed by an exponential increase in the frequency of one variant, leading to fixation. Notice that this pattern is very different from S-shaped logistic growth. As far as I know, this pattern of 'grammatical drift' has not been attested.[20]

The alternative approach of modifying *LP* to track the frequency with which variant categories are exemplified in the learning data will yield different dynamics again. Consider first a non-parameterized learner as defined in §4.1.1 with a modified version of *LP* which records the number of times each word:category association hypothesized is used in a successful parse of a trigger. At any given point, the learning agent generates using only the most frequent word:category association when there are variant alternatives generating the same LF. At the end of the learning period, the agent stops counting, so the most frequent word:category associations at that point are the ones which define the acquired grammar. This 'statistical' learning procedure will acquire the 'majority grammar' which incorporates the most frequent variants from potentially multiple source grammars. For the pre/postmodification example, four grammars would be avail-

---

[20] The notion of drift being employed here is, of course, very different from that introduced into (historical) linguistics by Sapir (1921: 150), who used this term to designate stereotypical and thus apparently 'directed' processes, such as loss of case marking leading to increased periphrasis.

able to the learning agent representing the possible combinations of pre/postmodification with nominal/verbal heads. Thus, superficially this approach resembles the weaker parameterization discussed above. However, the dynamics of language change will now depend much more closely on the frequency with which variants are exemplified across the whole learning period, and thus on the true frequency of the variants in the community. If initially variants are equally represented in the community, then the grammar acquired by a learner will depend on random fluctuations in triggering data. However, as soon as one variant is incorporated into more than half of the grammars, learners will tend more consistently to acquire that variant, because their final hypothesis will be much less sensitive to the particular sequence of triggers they were exposed to. Thus the amount of random drift will decrease and patterns of change should, other things being equal, show less fluctuation and proceed more consistently towards fixation on one variant.

The differences between these dynamics are illustrated graphically in Figure 4.4 which shows the spread of a single variant grammar through a stable population of one hundred agents, forty of whom are learners (see §4.1.2). The *y*-axis of the left-hand graph indicates the proportion of all agents who have acquired the variant; that of the right-hand graph, the proportion of learning agents acquiring the variant in the same simulation run. The S-Learner curve shows the spread of the variant when learning agents use the statistical version of *LP* described above. R-Learner1 models this spread when *LP* acquires the

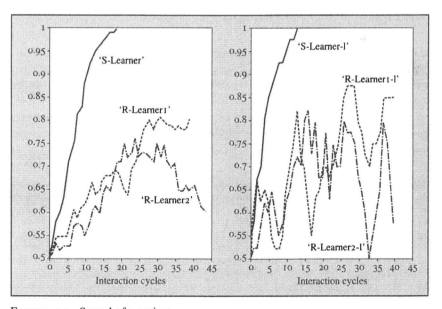

FIGURE 4.4. Spread of a variant

variant determined by the first (or last) relevant trigger, and R-Learner2 represents the effect of *LP* selecting a grammar as a probabilistic function of the proportion of agents who have acquired each variant grammar at that point. The simulations were initialized with equal proportions of adult agents with g^1 and g^2. In each of the three runs selected, representing the three different variants of *LP*, g^1 spreads at the expense of g^2 and the *y*-axis starts at 0.5.

The statistical version of *LP* shows steep, though still logistic spread of g^1 until all learners are acquiring this variant (by interaction cycle 13 on the right hand graph). Fixation in the adult population is slower (as indicated in the left hand graph) because once all new learners are reliably acquiring g^1, the remaining g^2 adult population must die out. This slope can be made more gradual by increasing the age of death relative to the critical period or by increasing the proportion of adults to learners. The dynamics of the spread of g^1 with the other versions of *LP* are more random, with downward as well as upward fluctuations and no fixation within the time scale plotted, as predicted by the analysis above. Niyogi and Berwick (1997) argue that logistic spread follows from but is not 'built into' the model of language change they develop. Robert Clark (1996) shows that in many situations their model actually produces exponential rather than logistic growth. These microscopic simulations suggest that their framework, and in particular the Trigger Learning Algorithm, will also frequently predict random grammatical drift. The particular derivation of logistic spread proposed here follows from a more realistic modelling of the composition of the population (with overlapping generations and variant proportions of learners to non-learners).[21]

The statistical version of *LP* is quite compatible with (any) parameterization of *UG*. For example, if, as before, we posit a head-initial/final parameter which selects for pre/postmodifiers cross-categorially, then the learning agent will simply select between two rather than four grammars on the basis of the frequency with which pre/postmodification is exemplified cross-categorially in the triggering data. In general, parameterization will yield a more efficient *LP* which explores a smaller hypothesis space and thus more robustly selects a final grammar on the basis of a smaller number of associated cues in triggering data (e.g. Dresher 1999). Therefore, there are independent reasons for expecting *UG* to be

---

[21] Whether this is a correct account of any particular case of syntactic change remains to be seen. Kroch (1989*b*) demonstrates that logistic change via competition between grammatical subsystems occurs, but is not explicit about whether this competition is between grammars internalized by single speakers, across speakers, or a mixture of both. This account does not address the bilingual or diglossic scenario. However, diglossia is much easier to account for if learners track parameters of variation rather than utilizing a 'memoryless' *LP* because it is straightforward to augment the statistical version of *LP* so that the evidence for alternative settings of each parameter is recorded. Simon Kirby (p.c.) points out that logistic change would also be expected if learners acquired both variants but produced one in preference to the other. Hurford (2000) discusses such 'production bottlenecks' in the context of a detailed comparison of the various ways in which language changes have been modelled computationally.

parameterized, apart from data-selectivity. Nevertheless, parameterized or not, a *LP* which selects between grammars using single trigger instances predicts very random dynamics in language change. These have not been observed to my knowledge, and certainly would not lead us to generally expect logistic patterns of change.[22]

4.3. LEARNING PROCEDURES WITH INDUCTIVE BIAS

So far we have explored the interaction of population dynamics and *LP* in determining the dynamics of selection or absorption of linguistic variants exemplified in a speech community, assuming that *LP* has no preferences concerning the grammars it learns. That is, that within the space defined by *UG*, there is no inductive bias favouring some grammars over others. Formal learnability work on language acquisition has tended, at least implicitly, to take the position that there is no such bias, by assuming that the starting point for learning is arbitrary or random (e.g. Gold 1967, Gibson and Wexler 1994) and by defining learnability in terms of reachability of any $g \in UG$ (given triggers from g) from any such starting point.[23] More substantively oriented work on parameters has tended to assume that some, perhaps most, parameters will have unmarked or default values (e.g. Chomsky 1981: 7–11, Hyams 1986, Wexler and Manzini 1987). Such an assumption is a form of inductive bias, or soft constraint, over and above the hard constraints determined by *UG*, as it creates a preference ordering on the acquisition of $g \in UG$ by *LP*. For example, if we assume that there is a V2 parameter which has an initial unmarked or default –V2 value, we are saying that –V2 grammars will be ordered higher and considered before +V2 grammars within the space of possible grammars defined by *UG*. So a learner must be exposed to robust positive evidence to reset this parameter to the non-default or marked value. The unmarked default value, however, will dictate the shape of the acquired grammar in the absence of (robust enough) evidence.

Inductive bias can also be introduced by assuming that parameters of *UG* are set in a particular order and that the effects of parameters are partly dependent on the settings of others (e.g. Briscoe 1997, 1998, Dresher 1999). For example,

---

[22] A statistical learning procedure of the type outlined can also account for robust acquisition in the face of indeterminacies of parameter expression (e.g. Clark 1992), such as the ambiguity of SVO triggers given V2 grammars discussed in §4.1.1 (see Briscoe 1999). Deterministic and/or local parameter setting procedures of the type described by Gibson and Wexler (1994), Niyogi and Berwick (1996), Dresher (1999), and Briscoe (1997, 1998) suffer from possible 'premature' and irrecoverable convergence to an incorrect grammar in the face of such indeterminacies.

[23] In fact, an assumption of inductive bias is the norm rather than the exception in learning theory; for example Cosmides and Tooby (1996) and Staddon (1988) argue that evolution equips organisms with specialized domain-specific learning mechanisms incorporating inductive bias assimilated from the environment of adaptation for the learning mechanism. More statistically oriented approaches to language learnability also often rely on an assumption of 'closeness' or informativeness of prior knowledge in proofs of learnability or high probability convergence (e.g. Muggleton 1996).

if the effects of a head-initial/final parameter, having been (re)set, can be partly
overridden by the setting of a more specific parameter which determines the
order of heads and arguments for a specific category, then *LP* will first consider
'harmonic' head-initial/final grammars, but adopt 'mixed' grammars on the basis
of positive evidence of specific categorial exceptions.[24] Similarly, a statistical
approach to the setting of parameters (or choice between variants) can naturally
be extended to incorporate inductive bias by positing a Bayesian approach to
learning in which the final (posterior) setting (or choice) rests on the interplay
between a prior probability of a setting (or choice) and its probability given the
triggering data (e.g. Briscoe 1999). For example, if a head-initial/final parameter
has a prior probability of 2/3 for the value head-initial (and thus a prior probability of 1/3, i.e. 1−2/3, for head-final), then we can quantify precisely the degree
of evidence required for *LP* to reset the parameter from its default value using
Bayes theorem. In this case, the probability derived from the triggering data must
be >2/3 for the posterior probability to favour the marked setting.[25]

If *LP/UG* includes inductive bias, then the dynamics of language change will
no longer be determined so directly by properties of the triggering data (within
the overall space defined by *UG*). Instead the relative frequency with which a
variant is exemplified in triggering data will interact with the bias inherent in *LP*,

---

[24] Briscoe (1997, 1998) details how *UG* can be modelled using a default inheritance hierarchy
describing possible categories of a CG. In this model, the setting of more general cross-categorial
parameters, by default, sets more specific parameters, so that the learner predicts harmonic grammars
and only revises such predictions if subsequent triggers force this.

[25] We assume that 'relevant' triggers provide positive evidence for head-final or positive evidence
for head-initial. Therefore the so-called likelihood probability (derived from the triggering data) for
head-final is given by:

$$P_l(X = final) = \frac{f(t_{final})}{f(t_{final/initial})}$$

where f denotes frequency counts (i.e. the maximum likelihood estimate over the relevant triggers).
The posterior probability is given by:

$$P_{po}(X = final \mid t_n) = \frac{P_{pr}(X = final) \, P_l(X = final)}{P(t_{final/initial})}$$

(i.e. by Bayes theorem). The probability of the relevant triggers, $P(t_{final/initial})$, is a constant normalizing
factor which can be ignored. We need only compare the unnormalized posterior for head-final to that
for head-initial and choose the highest. As the prior, P_{pr}, is multiplied by the likelihood, P_l, the
unnormalized posterior for head-final will only exceed that for head-initial (when $P_{pr}(X = final) =$
1/3) if the associated likelihood probability is >2/3. For example, if five out of six relevant triggers
are head-final, then the two unnormalized posteriors are computed as follows:

$P_{po}(X = final \mid t_n) = 1/3 \times 5/6 = 10/36$
$P_{po}(X = initial \mid t_n) = 2/3 \times 1/6 = 4/36$

Briscoe (1999, 2000*a*) develops a Bayesian approach to parameter setting in greater detail. Sivia
(1996) provides a good introduction to Bayesian data analysis.

as well as, of course, the population dynamics. Returning to the example of pre/postmodification, if we assume, as is natural in CG, that the same *UG* parameter also selects between head-final/initial modifiers, that head-initial is the default unmarked value, and that this default has a relatively strong prior of 4/5, then in a community fixated on g^1, a premodifier grammar would need to be swamped by migrating agents generating postmodifiers so that the triggering data to the next generation contained >4/5 triggers exemplifying postmodification. Thus, the Bayesian approach is one way of making concrete and precise Kiparsky's (1996) proposal that change results from the interplay of triggering data with internal preferences created by *LP/UG*.

To address the question of how likely it is that the language faculty incorporates inductive bias, the population model introduced in §4.1.2 can be modified to incorporate natural selection for language agents by using the CSR as a measure of fitness and making reproductive success relative to fitness. For this to be meaningful there must be variation in the language faculty with which language agents are initially endowed. In Briscoe (1997, 1998) I describe in detail an encoding of *UG* which allows the 'starting point' for learning to be varied, in terms of what counts as a principle or parameter and which parameters have default or unset values. Mutation and crossover operators are defined over this encoding so that the creation of new agents can both introduce and spread (the analogue of) genetic variants. Thus, we modify the basic population model with a more evolutionarily realistic version of reproduction (see Figure 4.3 above for comparison):

REPRO: Create-LAgt(Mutate(Crossover(LAgt$_i$,LAgt$_j$))), $i \neq j$, CSR$_i$ ∧ CSR$_j$ > Mean-CSR

The cross-over operator combines the encoding of *UG* randomly from the two higher than average fitness 'parent' agents, while the mutate operator with equal and low probability converts a parameter to a principle, or vice versa, flips the value of a default parameter, or converts a default to an unset parameter. Once such genetic variation is introduced, it is essential to posit natural selection for language agents on the basis of their CSR, otherwise populations inevitably cease to learn and communicate after a few hundred cycles, as random variation in language faculties builds up. However, with natural selection, the population evolves to a (local) optimum in the predefined space of *UG*s, determined in part by the range of grammars/languages sampled before they cluster around such an optimum. For example, if the languages sampled during a significant period during adaptation are OV, then the population is likely to genetically assimilate an unmarked OV parameter setting, since this speeds up learning.

This is an example of genetic assimilation (e.g. Waddington 1942), or the so-called Baldwin Effect (Baldwin, 1896), in which changes in a species' behaviour (the advent of language) create new selection pressures (the need to learn language efficiently).[26] When language change is as rapid as is consonant with maintenance of a speech community during adaptation, genetic assimilation results in around twice as many soft constraints (inductive bias) as hard constraints (incorporation of principles into *UG*); as the former have a less fatal effect on successful learning if subsequent change renders an assimilated principle incorrect. Additionally, genetic assimilation slows and ultimately ceases once a near optimal balance between learning speed and the speed of linguistic change has been found; in this model, when around half of the possible parameters in the predefined space of *UG*s have been converted to principles or default-valued parameters. Without continuous linguistic change, there is no reason why the process of genetic assimilation should not proceed until the need for (grammatical) learning is eradicated (*pace* Pinker and Bloom 1990). However, with constant linguistic change, too much constraint on learning becomes maladaptive.

These simulations cannot, of course, *prove* that the language faculty incorporates inductive bias via genetic assimilation, but they do help to clarify the (prehistoric) conditions under which this would have been likely. In particular, the relative speed of language change compared to biological evolution and the size of the relevant population during the period of adaptation are unlikely to have been critical factors (*pace* Deacon 1997: 328–40), and the possibility that the language faculty arose *de novo* via a single macromutation or exaption (e.g. Berwick 1998, Bickerton 1998) does not affect the argument because organs which arise via exaptions of spandrels or by macromutations are still susceptible to *subsequent* modification by natural selection (e.g. Ridley 1990, Lieberman 1991, Kirby 1998). Indeed in these simulations, language agents do begin with language faculties (either random or converged) and these are merely refined by subsequent evolution. However, the current model does assume a one to one correlation between changes to the genetic encoding and phenotypic changes to *LP/UG*. Such a close correlation would be unlikely in nature, and has the effect of speeding up genetic assimilation effects (e.g. Mayley 1996). Until we know more about the genetic encoding and neurological basis of the language faculty, it is impossible to quantify how long it might actually have taken for assimilation to occur.

If we accept that there is inductive bias in language acquisition, as I think we should, given both the evidence from the simulation work and from empirical studies of language acquisition (e.g. Wanner and Gleitman 1982) and general considerations of learning theory (e.g. Cosmides and Tooby 1996), how does this affect our view of language change?[27]

---

[26] Waddington (1975) and Pinker and Bloom (1990) both propose that genetic assimilation played a role in the formation of the language faculty. Kirby and Hurford (1997) and Briscoe (1997, 1998, 2000*b*) develop detailed models of this process and provide a more thorough discussion of the effect and its likely relevance.

[27] Lightfoot (e.g. 1999: 165–7) criticizes some specific arguments for inductive bias as an explanation of grammatical change and also makes the general point that if a bias explains how a variant was eradicated, we also need an account of how the variant can arise. I address the more general point

4.4. LANGUAGES AS ADAPTIVE SYSTEMS

So far I have argued that (E-)languages are dynamical systems, the aggregate output of a set of grammars which change over time as the membership of a speech community changes. However, if grammar learning is data-selective and biased, then languages are better seen as *adaptive* systems which will inevitably evolve to fit their unique ecological niche—the human language faculty and wider cognitive system. Under this view, languages are evolving on a *historical* rather than biological timescale, and the primary source of *linguistic selection* is the language acquisition 'bottleneck' through which successful grammatical variants must pass repeatedly with each new generation of language learners. Evolution and selection are not being used here metaphorically, but in their technical 'universal Darwinist' sense (e.g. Cziko 1995, Dawkins 1983, Dennett 1995: 343) of (random) variation, selection amongst variants, and thus differential inheritance. These terms are potentially applicable to any dynamical system, whether that system is 'implemented' in biological organisms, silicon, or cognitive linguistic representations.[28]

Returning to the example of pre/post-modification and the Bayesian parameter setting learner outlined in the previous section, assume again that *LP/UG* incorporates a cross-categorial head-initial/final parameter with a bias for head-initial and also category-specific parameters which, by default, pick up their value from the more general cross-categorial parameter, but can be reset by positive evidence in triggering data. This creates a bias for harmonic head-initial grammars. Change in (E-)languages can now be seen in terms of selection amongst grammatical variants which are more or less 'natural' with respect to *LP/UG*. There will clearly be an asymmetry in terms of the dynamics of change as non-harmonic and head-final grammatical variants will need to be exemplified in the triggering data frequently enough to overcome the bias in *LP* and to force the resetting of more specific parameters. Thus, the competition between grammatical variants is biased. Assuming, as in §4.3, that the prior bias for head-initial is 4/5 and this bias is inherited by all the more specific parameters, yielding harmonic head-initial settings, then a community fixated on a (partially) disharmonic or head-final grammar can begin shifting to a more harmonic head-initial one if variant triggers are exemplified with >1/5 likelihood probability to any given learner. That is, there is differential linguistic selection in favour of

---

in §4.5. The detail of the specific arguments are beyond the scope of this paper, but I also agree with Lightfoot (1999: 218–20) that if there is bias, this must interact with triggering data in explaining change. The Bayesian model of *LP* allows us to quantify precisely the interplay of data and bias.

[28] As far as I am aware, Hurford (1987) is the earliest expression of this view from a syntactician, though the argument is presented much more clearly in Hurford (1999) and Kirby (1998, 1999). Lindblom (1998) and colleagues have developed a similar approach to the evolution of phonological systems. Others who have adopted similar viewpoints include Batali (1998), Deacon (1997), and Steels (1998).

head-initial harmonic grammars as a consequence of *LP/UG*, so (E-)languages are highly likely to adapt to *LP/UG* over time, given some continuing source of (random) variation.

There is no requirement that the bias, or process of change, is 'functional' in any deeper sense. For example, if *LP/UG* incorporates such a bias, this may rest on nothing more fundamental than the fact that the languages sampled during the period of adaptation for the *language faculty* were mostly harmonic and head-initial (see §4.3). Alternatively, 'harmonic' languages may have been preferred initially because they facilitate language processing (see §4.5 below), so the bias assimilated into *LP/UG* would rest ultimately not (entirely) on (pre)historical accident but on wider aspects of human cognitive capacities and limitations. Either way, (E-)languages can be said to have adapted to their niche via linguistic selection.

Superficially, characterizing (E-)language changes as an adaptive evolutionary process may not seem to add much to the view that languages change or, more specifically, that languages can be modelled as non-linear dynamical systems. However, it does commit us to the claim that language change is a process of differential selection amongst variants, so it rules out scenarios in which language acquisition is not data-selective and biased, and also ones which involve a significant amount of 'invention'; that is, going beyond the data. Perhaps, more importantly, modern population genetics provides a battery of tools to analyse the situations under which a variant with a small selective advantage manifested by a single individual, or small minority of individuals, can spread through a population. These tools can be adapted to the study of linguistic change straightforwardly once we have precise enough theories of language acquisition and processing. In particular, the move from a random drift, 'neutral' theory of change to an adaptive account may be a necessary prerequisite to an understanding of how some changes can spread from very small beginnings.[29]

Creolization has been characterized by Bickerton (1984: 173) as a process of 'invention' in terms of the learner's innate bioprogram; first language learners exposed exclusively to an impoverished pidgin subset language acquire a super-set creole grammar. If this view is correct, then it would undermine the claim that significant language change can be modelled as an evolutionary process. However, Lightfoot (1991: 178–80; 1999: 167–74), while accepting the abruptness of creolization, challenges the idea that it requires a special account of language acquisition, arguing that properties of the pidgin triggering data lead to reanalysis and consequent parameter resetting across generations. Roberts (1998) argues that some features of Hawaiian creole took two generations to emerge, which also supports the hypothesis that creolization is very fast language change,

---

[29] Kirby (1997, 1999) is one example of a detailed and carefully worked-out account of linguistic change based on adaptation to language acquisition.

rather than the result of a special process of consistent invention by each first language learner.

I have simulated creolization, especially the situation in Hawaii, in as much linguistic and demographic detail as is practical, given the limits of the model of *LP/UG* developed in Briscoe (1999) and what is known about the demographic factors. Creoles emerge when first language learners are born to a diverse community of indentured workers or slaves with an impoverished pidgin as their *lingua franca*. In Hawaii the proportion of such learners by the end of the first generation (i.e. twenty years) constituted about 35% of this community and was increasing throughout this period. In other cases of plantation creolization this proportion may have been lower, but was probably increasing throughout the early (overlapping) generations of first language learners.[30]

The demographic situation is modelled by introducing six new learning agents per interaction cycle into a community of sixty-four adults who are not changed during the simulation run. Agents learn for four interaction cycles and can reproduce thereafter. The proportion of learners reaches a maximum of 28% at the sixth interaction cycle and then tails off gradually to a stable 15%. We are interested in the proportion of learners converging to a creole grammar across interaction cycles, bearing in mind that four interaction cycles is equivalent to one generation (i.e. twenty years).

The statistical version of *LP*, outlined in §4.3, was integrated with a version of *UG* which contains fifteen parameters which determine the number and type of CG categories in an acquired grammar. These categories can be divided into those that determine ordering of arguments to functor categories and those which determine the availability of specific functor categories. For example, one parameter controls the availability of a functor category which licenses relative clause modifiers of nominal heads. However, whether the *wh*-element precedes or follows the relative clause and whether this is pre/postnominal depends on potentially interdependent but distinct ordering parameters. The bias assumed in *LP* is based on Bickerton's (1984) account of Saramaccan, as the prototypical creole grammar, and models a preference for simple SVO right-branching grammars.

---

[30] The estimate of 35% is based on census figures for 1890, 1900, and 1910 kindly supplied by Derek Bickerton. These are incomplete in some areas but indicate an under-fifteen population of at least 20% by 1900 and 35% by 1910, assuming a similarly high birthrate amongst Hawaiians as amongst Portuguese immigrants (44% by 1910). (This assumption is in turn supported by school attendance records of 5–14 year olds.) Bickerton suggests that creoles emerge when the proportion of under-twelves was between 15% and 25%. The speed of spread of the creole through the learner and total population will both be increased if the proportion of learners is greater and the increase in this proportion is steeper. Therefore, it is possible that (features of) Hawaiian creole spread more rapidly (within two generations, according to Roberts 1998) because the birth rate was high. Only further demographic and linguistic work on other pidgin–creole transitions will tell, but the model predicts such speed differences.

Such learners, exposed exclusively to pidgin data, modelled as clauses with a verb and single word subjects and objects appearing in random orders, tend to acquire a grammar generating a SVO subset language with similar clauses. That is, they do not generalize the pidgin data and invent a creole superset grammar but they do converge to SVO order. Furthermore, by around the sixth interaction cycle (i.e. within two generations) all learners in these simulation runs are converging to SVO grammars. This result can be understood in terms of the interplay of the triggering data and *LP* in conjunction with the increase in SVO triggers as the population of learners grows. Faced with conflicting and equivocal evidence for basic constituent order, *LP* will tend to set parameters in terms of prior biases. However, trigger sampling variation will mean that some early learners may not acquire a SVO grammar, or may hypothesize non-SVO grammars at intermediate stages in acquisition. Nevertheless, if the majority of learners do (eventually) acquire SVO grammars, then the incidence of SVO triggers will increase causing the familiar positive feedback dynamics to take over. Thus, the inductive bias for SVO is enough to kick the system in the right direction, but it is only as the population gains SVO speakers that the chances of learners acquiring non-SVO grammars declines to negligible levels. Thus, this account is purely selectionist and predicts that the birthrate will be a factor in the speed of creolization, but as yet does not explain how first language learners can acquire a superset creole grammar.

Bickerton (1981, 1984, 1988) has argued that superstratum and substratum languages play no role in the acquisition of the creole. The evidence for this comes from the lack of a consistent grammatical relationship between the creole and these potential sources, as well as the similarities of unrelated creoles (e.g. Roberts 1998). Bickerton (e.g. 1984: 182–8) recognizes that in many cases, including Hawaii, learners would be exposed to a small proportion of superstratum and substratum utterances but downplays their role as triggers on the basis of their relative infrequency and, in the case of substratum utterances, mutual inconsistency. Nevertheless, if the triggering data to the statistical *LP/UG* model is enhanced to include a small proportion of more complex superstratum triggers, with or without a further small proportion of random substratum language triggers, exemplifying multiword phrases and subordination, learners converge to and fixate on a SVO right-branching superset grammar with essentially the same dynamic and timecourse as that discussed above.

Briscoe (2000a) discusses these simulations and their interpretation in further detail. While they are by no means conclusive and rest on rather sketchy demographic information and consequent assumptions about the nature of the triggering input, they nevertheless add weight to the argument that creolization should be seen as a case of rapid language change caused by the interaction of ordinary language acquisition with radical demographic changes. Though creolization poses the most obvious challenge to a selectionist account of language change in terms of inductive bias in language acquisition, there are other difficulties which require us to adopt a more sophisticated model of the evolutionary process which incorporates conflicting and interacting selection pressures on language change stemming from wider cognitive capacities and limitations.

4.5. LANGUAGES AS COMPLEX ADAPTIVE SYSTEMS

If languages adapt solely to innate preferences during language acquisition, we would expect the history of languages to show nearly inexorable development towards an optimal or most natural grammar. Presumably, we would expect all speech communities to fixate ultimately on creole-like grammars if these represent the most natural optimal or default solutions with respect to *LP*. Chance factors might temporarily move a language away from such a solution but, over time, constant and universal selection pressure should (re)assert itself. While supporters of grammaticalization have argued for a (prototypical) unidirectionality in change (e.g. Hopper and Traugott 1993: chapter 5) and there is evidence of skewing in the distribution of attested languages with respect to the range of possible grammars most theories of *UG* license (e.g. Hawkins 1994), no-one would argue that language change is this deterministic.

Lightfoot (1999: 213–18) uses similar arguments to criticize accounts of language change which rely on innate preferences or inductive bias, asking how the relevant variation might have arisen in the first place if bias is the explanation for the selection of a particular variant. He, in fact, goes on to endorse models, such as that of Kiparsky (1996), which explain change in terms of the interplay of acquisition preferences and changes in triggering data (as does the Bayesian version of *LP* outlined in §4.3). Surprisingly, he also accepts the argument of Niyogi and Berwick (1997) that historical tendencies in language change may result from dynamic trajectories caused by learners misconverging. However, Kiparsky's position and that of Niyogi and Berwick are quite different. As we noted in §4.1.2, Niyogi and Berwick explore a model in which change is inevitable even without initial 'external' perturbation of triggering data. Given a speech community fixated on a –V2 grammar some learners will misconverge, initiating a process of change. This is essentially because the Trigger Learning Algorithm will not converge, or will converge with very low probability, given a random starting point and the theory of *UG* they consider (Niyogi and Berwick 1996). Thus, the model is unstable and predicts inexorable change towards some fixed point. Robert Clark (1996) illustrates the instability of their model very clearly in a series of replicated simulations which explore the behaviour of the model when learners are given between 8 and 256 triggers. This account, then, is really an extreme version of the accounts of language change being driven by internal preferences (or failings) during acquisition. However, even accounts which predict stability under conditions of homogeneity, and require changes in triggering data as well as acquisition preferences in order for change to occur, still require some account of how apparently suboptimal variants ever arise in speech communities.

The idea that there are competing motivations or conflicting pressures deriving from the exigencies of production, comprehension and acquisition has been developed by linguists working from many different perspectives (e.g. Langacker 1977, Fodor 1981, Croft 1990: 192–202). In linguistics little progress has been made in quantifying these pressures or exploring their interaction, except in the area of phonology where Lindblom (e.g. 1998) has adopted a similar evolutionary model to that advocated here. Evolution is *not* a process of steady improvement along a single trajectory leading to a single optimal solution. Sewall Wright (1931) introduced into evolutionary theory the idea of adaptive or fitness landscapes with multiple local optima or peaks, and this idea has been considerably refined since (e.g. Kauffman 1993: 33–45). The modern picture of (co)evolution is of a process of local search or hill climbing towards a local optimum or peak in a fitness landscape which itself inevitably changes. Conflicting selection pressures will cause the fitness landscape to contain many locally optimal solutions, and thus the evolutionary pathways will be more complex and the space of near optimal solutions more varied (Kauffman 1993: 44).

A simple and well-attested example of conflicting selection pressures from biology is the case of 'runaway' sexual selection for a non-functional marker such as the peacock's tail, counterbalanced by natural selection for efficient movement (e.g. Dawkins 1989: 158f.). A simple linguistic example is given in Briscoe (1998). There are (as in §4.4) seventeen parameters to be set during learning, and only setting a subset of these parameters yields a subset language. Given some degree of linguistic variation, the speech community will tend to fixate on a subset language, optimizing learnability at the expense of expressivity. Regardless of whether there is natural selection for agents on the basis of communicative success, optimizing learnability at the expense of expressivity is highly likely. To counteract such a tendency, we can either posit that *LP* requires all parameters to be set (somehow), or that there is a counteracting pressure for expressivity. This could be introduced into the model by positing some range of logical forms that must be realizable (possibly 'economically') and penalizing agents' communicative success whenever their current grammar does not allow this. Introducing such a conflicting or competing pressure (suitably weighted) prevents unconstrained optimization for learnability. Now variants which are adaptive must improve learnability and maintain expressivity (or vice versa).

Another and perhaps better understood pressure on the evolution of grammatical systems derives from parsability (e.g. Gibson 1998, Hawkins 1994, Miller and Chomsky 1963, Rambow and Joshi 1994). A number of metrics of the relative parsability of different constructions have been proposed, both as accounts of the relative psychological complexity of sentence processing and of the relative prevalence of different construction types in attested languages. A metric of this type can be incorporated into an evolutionary linguistic model in a number of ways. Kirby (1999) argues, for example, that parsability equates to learnability, as triggers must be parsed before they can be used by a learner to acquire a grammar. By contrast, Hawkins (1994: 83–95) argues that parsability may influence generation so that more parsable variants will be used more frequently than less parsable ones (within the space of possibilities defined by a given grammar), and presents evidence concerning the relative frequency of constructions from several languages in support of this position. This would entail that less parsable constructions would be less frequent in potential triggering data, in any case. Briscoe (1998) demonstrates that either approach, alone or in combination, can account for linguistic selection in favour of more parsable variants.

One type of common non-argument against the view that languages are adaptive is that languages exhibit dysfunctional or maladaptive properties. For example, many languages peripherally exhibit multiple centre- and self-embedding constructions (e.g. De Roeck *et al.* 1982, Hudson 1995). Yet such constructions are known to cause parsing problems (e.g. Miller and Chomsky 1963, Gibson 1998). If languages are (complex) adaptive systems why have such constructions survived? It is easy to devise models in which their survival is a mystery. For example, Kirby's (1999) equation of parsability with learnability predicts that relatively less parsable constructions will be less likely to function as triggers. As his learning model does not involve predictive generalization, it is inevitable that a less parsable construction will be replaced by a more parsable variant. However, a more complex and adequate model of grammar learning, such as that of Kirby (2000), may make very different predictions. For example, if learning involves setting parameters on the basis of degree-0 triggers (e.g. Lightfoot 1991), then embedded constructions will be learnt indirectly as a predictive consequence of simpler triggers, and thus will continue to be 'inherited' by subsequent generations if the interaction of parameter settings generates centre- and/or self-embedded constructions, even though their acceptability in the arena of language use may well be marginal in view of the desire for communicative success. The models of *LP/UG* discussed in this paper are all potentially of this type since the interaction of functor categories acquired from degree-0 or degree-1 triggers will generate such constructions. Putative examples of dysfunctional or maladaptive features are not in themselves counter-evidence to the view of (E-)languages as complex adaptive systems, any more than unanalysed strings are evidence for or against a specific syntactic theory.

Once we recognize that there are conflicting selection pressures, it is easier to see why language change does not move inexorably (and unidirectionally) towards a unique global optimum. No such optimum may exist, and in any case, change will always be relative to and local with respect to the current 'position' in the current fitness landscape. For instance, a canonical SOV grammar might evolve increasingly frequent extraposition because SOV clauses with long or 'heavy' object phrases are relatively unparsable (e.g. Hawkins 1994: 196–210). However, SVO grammars will be less likely to do so since long object phrases will mostly occur postverbally anyway and will not create analogous parsing problems. Once such a change has spread, it may in turn create further parsability (or expressivity or learnability) issues, altering the fitness landscape; for example, by creating greater structural ambiguity, resulting perhaps in evolution of obligatory extraposition. (It is this locality or blindness in the search for good solutions that makes the evolutionary process more like tinkering than engineering.) In the framework advocated here, we can recognize that such historical pathways can be stereotypical responses to similar pressures arising in unrelated languages, in much the same way that eyes and wings have evolved independently in different lineages many times, without the need to posit a substantive theory of such changes or see them as deterministic (see e.g. Lightfoot 1999: 261–8).[31]

4.6. CONCLUSION

Models of non-linear dynamical systems can play several useful roles in the study of language change: to characterize population dynamics during a change, to characterize the dynamics of the linguistic change within the population, and to characterize the interaction of the population and linguistic dynamics. For instance, it is clear that creolization is a type of rapid linguistic change which is also dependent on radical demographic changes. The model developed here allows characterization of the linguistic change in the context of the demographic changes. The speed of linguistic change (i.e. the spread of the variant through the relevant part of the speech community) can then be seen to be faster in this case than in the case of a more stable population. This perspective supports an account of creolization as rapid but otherwise normal selective linguistic change.

Characterizing (E-)languages as adaptive systems undergoing differential linguistic selection enriches and constrains their modelling as non-linear dynamical systems. Adaptive systems are a subset of possible dynamical systems, so this step is only justified if we can demonstrate clear selection pressure as opposed to (random) drift. Logistic growth is predicted by selection rather than by random drift. Adaptive systems which change on the basis of interactions between conflicting selection pressures in unpredictable ways, involving positive or negative feedback, with no centralized control are increasingly termed

---

[31] Lightfoot (1999: 239–49) argues that *UG* may be maladaptive because it incorporates a constraint against extraction of subjects from tensed clauses, while speakers/languages have developed idiosyncratic means to circumvent the constraint to fulfil expressive needs. He concludes: 'if maladaptive elements evolve, then we need something other than natural selection to drive evolutionary developments' (1999: 248). However, as he points out, the constraint against extraction of subjects from tensed clauses may be adaptive with respect to parsability, reducing ambiguity over the location of traces. If it is maladaptive with respect to expressivity, this is only an argument against a simplistic 'one-dimensional optimization' view of evolution. Given the framework developed here, it is quite possible that such a constraint evolved in one or more languages (and either was or was not ultimately assimilated into *UG*) as a local step in evolutionary space, which in turn created expressivity problems requiring further local adaptations of a possibly idiosyncratic and language specific nature.

complex adaptive systems. Viewing (E-)languages as complex adaptive systems promises new insights into old issues, such as prototypical unidirectionality, competing motivations, or internally motivated change, ones which do not involve teleology or a substantive theory of linguistic change *per se*.

Serious exploration of this framework is only just beginning because the requisite understanding of dynamical systems and of the tools to study them are very recent developments. It would be unfortunate if old prejudices, or misunderstanding of modern evolutionary theory, precluded the full and proper exploration of languages as complex adaptive systems.

PART II

The Comparative Basis of Diachronic Syntax

5

Adjuncts and the Syntax of Subjects in Old and Middle English

ERIC HAEBERLI

Old English shows characteristic properties of a Verb Second (V2) language. However, certain phenomena can be found in Old English which suggest that V2 in this language cannot be dealt with in terms of analyses that have been proposed for the Modern Germanic V2 languages. Different alternative analyses have therefore been explored in the recent literature which account for the distinct properties of Old English. Although there seems to be a general consensus on the central points, the different analyses vary with respect to several issues. In this chapter, some of these issues will be addressed and it will be argued that important evidence can be obtained from a comparative analysis of Old English, later stages in the history of English, and the Modern Germanic languages with respect to phenomena concerning the distribution of adjuncts and subjects. In addition, it will be shown not only that the comparative evidence used provides information for the analysis of Old English, but also that the Old English data contribute to a more detailed understanding of a general Germanic word-order phenomenon.

5.1. INTRODUCTION: V2 AND THE SYNTAX OF SUBJECTS IN OLD ENGLISH

Apart from Modern English, all the Modern Germanic languages exhibit what has been called the Verb Second (V2) phenomenon, at least in main clauses. The characteristic property of this phenomenon is that any type of constituent can get fronted to the beginning of the clause and the verb immediately follows this constituent. At first sight, Old English seems to share this property with the Modern Germanic languages (example from van Kemenade 1987: 17).

Parts of the material discussed in this chapter have been presented at the Fifth Diachronic Generative Syntax Conference, University of York (June 1998), and at the Tenth International Conference on English Historical Linguistics, University of Manchester (August 1998). I would like to thank the audiences at these conferences and in particular the editors of this volume for valuable comments and suggestions. All remaining errors are of course my own.

(1)   [Eall ðis] *aredað* se reccere swiðe ryhte
         all   this arranges the ruler   very   rightly
         'The ruler arranges all this very rightly.'
         (*Cura Pastoralis* 169.3)

In (1), an object is fronted and it is immediately followed by the finite verb, in line with the V2 constraint.

However, there is one aspect of the syntax of V2 in Old English which cannot be found in the Modern Germanic languages and which suggests that V2 in Old English cannot be analysed in exactly the same way as V2 in the Modern Germanic languages. In Old English, pronominal subjects generally precede the finite verb even when another constituent has been moved to the front (cf. e.g. van Kemenade 1987: 109ff., Pintzuk 1991: 133ff., 201ff., 1993). This is illustrated in (2) (example from Pintzuk 1991: 202).

(2)   [hiora untrymnesse] [he] *sceal* ðrowian on his heortan
         their weakness   he shall atone   in his heart
         'He shall atone in his heart for their weakness.'
         (*Cura Pastoralis* 60.17)

The example in (2) is parallel to that in (1) in that an object is fronted. But in (2), the subject and the finite verb are not inverted, and instead the pronominal subject also precedes the finite verb, giving rise to a V3 order.

Yet, there is a restricted context in which subject pronouns do follow the finite verb, namely in interrogative clauses, negative clauses, verb-initial clauses and clauses introduced by some adverbs like *þa* ('then') (cf. van Kemenade 1987, Pintzuk 1991, 1993). One of these contexts is illustrated in (3).

(3)   [hwi] *sceole* we oþres   mannes niman
         why should we another man's   take
         'Why should we take those of another man?'
         (Ælfric, *Lives of Saints* 24.188)

In (3), subject–verb inversion applies although the subject is pronominal.

On the basis of the word-order patterns in (1) to (3), it has been concluded in the recent literature that V2 in Old English cannot be analysed simply along the lines generally proposed for the Modern Germanic languages, i.e. in terms of XP-movement to [Spec,CP] and verb movement to C. Instead, the standard analysis within most recent work is that (1) to (3) can be accounted for under the assumption that different types of subjects occur in different structural positions (pronouns, being clitics or weak pronouns, in a higher position than non-pronominal subjects) and that V-fronting in Old English targets two possible positions, C in some contexts (cf. (3)) and a lower inflectional head, which I will label X for the moment, in cases of topicalization of other elements (cf. Cardinaletti and

Roberts 1991, Hulk and van Kemenade 1997, van Kemenade 1998, Kroch and Taylor 1997, Pintzuk 1991, 1993). Schematically, this analysis can be represented as follows (+pro = pronominal; −pro = non-pronominal):

(4) $[_{CP}$ C $[_{XP}$ SU$_1$(+pro) **X** $[_{YP}$ SU$_2$(−pro) . . .]]]

C and X in (4) are two head-positions for verb fronting which are used according to the type of element that gets moved to [Spec,CP]. SU$_1$ and SU$_2$ are two subject positions which are used by different types of subjects. In terms of (4), (1) is the result of topic fronting, V-movement to X and the occurrence of the subject in position SU$_2$. In (2), a topic is fronted again and V moves to X but the subject now occurs in position SU$_1$. In (3) finally, the verb moves to C and therefore all types of subjects occur postverbally.

Despite the agreement of several authors with respect to the analysis of Old English along the lines of (4), there are certain theoretical issues for which there is no general consensus. Three main issues are listed in (5).[1]

(5)   (I)   The nature of the lower landing site of V-movement (X in (4) above: Infl in Pintzuk 1991, 1993; F in Hulk and van Kemenade 1997; Agr1 in Cardinaletti and Roberts 1991; AgrS suggested by Kroch and Taylor 1997).

      (II) The status of the lower subject position ([Spec,YP] in (4) above: [Spec,VP] in Pintzuk 1991, 1993; [Spec,TP] in Hulk and van Kemenade 1997; [Spec,Agr2P] in Cardinaletti and Roberts 1991).

      (III) The position of the topic in (1) and (2) ([Spec,CP] in Hulk and van Kemenade 1997, Kroch and Taylor 1997; [Spec,IP] in Pintzuk 1991, 1993; [Spec,Agr1P] in Cardinaletti and Roberts 1991).

In this chapter, I will argue that by considering the distribution of subjects with respect to adjuncts in Old English and Middle English, we can shed some light on the issues in (I) to (III). Furthermore, I will show that a contrast which corresponds basically to that in (4) can also be found in the Modern Germanic languages, but that the contrast in Old English/Middle English provides additional information for the syntactic analysis which cannot be obtained from the Modern Germanic languages.

The remainder of the chapter is organized as follows. In Section 2, the word-order phenomenon that I will focus on in this chapter will be introduced on the basis of the Modern Germanic languages, and its relevance for Old English will

---

[1] An additional important issue is the question as to why a non-pronominal subject does not have to move to the subject position occupied by pronouns, i.e. to [Spec,XP] in the structure in (4) or also for example in (7c) below. Again different proposals can be found in the literature, but for our purposes a detailed analysis of this issue will not be central. I will therefore leave this point aside here. But cf. Haeberli 1999: chs. 7 and 8 for discussion.

be discussed. Section 3 deals with the properties of Old English with respect to this word-order option. Section 4 then introduces data from later stages of the history of English and Section 5 summarizes the chapter.

5.2. ADJACENCY OF THE FINITE VERB AND SUBJECTS IN V2 CLAUSES

5.2.1. *A source of cross-linguistic variation* . . .

The starting point for my discussion is an aspect of the syntax of the Modern Germanic V2 languages, and more precisely the variation which can be found with respect to the occurrence of adjuncts in a position immediately preceding subjects. In some languages, we can find word orders of the type 'XP–subject', whereas such orders are impossible in some other languages. This variation is illustrated in (6) with a temporal adverb (but other types of adverbs or adjunct PPs exhibit the same variation; cf. Haeberli (1999: chapter 4), Vikner (1995) for more details).

(6) (*a*)   Wahrscheinlich *wird* (später) *Hans* dieselbe Uhr kaufen   (*German*)
     (*b*)   Misschien *goa* (*loater) *Jan* tzelfste orloge kuopen   (*W. Flemish*)
     (*c*)   Waarschijnlijk *zal* (%later) *Jan* hetzelfde horloge gaan kopen (*Dutch*)
     (*d*)   Wierskynlik *wol* (letter) *Jan* itselde horloazje keapje   (*Frisian*)
     (*e*)   Waarskynlik *sal* (*later) *Jan* dieselfde oorlosie gaan koop
             probably will (later) John the-same watch (go) buy   (*Afrikaans*)
             'Probably, John will buy the same watch (later).'
     (*f*)   Minastam *vet* (shpeter) *Moyshe* koyfn dem zelbikn zeyger (*Yiddish*)
     (*g*)   Sennilega *mun* (*seinna) *Jón* kaupa sama úrið   (*Icelandic*)
             probably will (later) John/M. buy the same watch
             'Probably, John will buy the same watch later.'
     (*h*)   Dette ur *vil* (*senere) *min far* købe   (*Danish*)
     (*i*)   Den här klockan *hade* (senare) *min gamle far* köpt   (*Swedish*)
     (*j*)   Denne klokka *hadde* (seinere) *min gamle far* kjøpt   (*Norwegian*)
             this watch will/had (later) my (old) dad buy/bought
             'This watch my dad will buy/had bought later.'

In German, Dutch, Frisian, Yiddish, Swedish, and Norwegian an adjunct can intervene between a fronted verb and a definite subject, whereas this option is not available in West Flemish, Afrikaans, Icelandic, and Danish.[2]

At first sight, it is surprising that a distributional option for adjuncts which occurs in certain languages cannot be found in some other, very closely related languages. The question that arises therefore is how the cross-linguistic variation with respect to V-subject (non-)adjacency can be accounted for. One possibility

---

[2] Note that a similar phenomenon can also be found in Modern English in contexts of 'residual V2':

(i) *Will* (*later) *John* buy the same watch?

would be to relate this variation to variation with respect to the placement of adjuncts. Thus, we could assume that the languages which allow 'XP–subject' orders license adjunction to, say, IP whereas in the more restrictive languages such adjunction is banned (cf. e.g. Holmberg (1993), Vikner (1995) for proposals along these lines).

But such an analysis would raise two important problems. The first problem is an acquisitional one which concerns the languages in which 'XP–subject' orders are ungrammatical. Given that, in terms of such an approach, IP-adjunction would be legitimate in principle and given that negative (i.e. ungrammatical) evidence is not part of the language learner's input, it would not be clear how in some languages a ban on IP-adjunction could be acquired on the basis of the overt evidence available to the language learner. In other words, we would have what has been referred to as a 'poverty of stimulus' problem because there is no overt evidence for the ungrammaticality of 'XP–subject' orders in the input of learners who acquire the more restrictive languages. Apart from this acquisitional problem, an adjunction analysis would also raise another problem. If the data in (6) simply illustrated a variation with respect to the availability of IP-adjunction, then the choice made by each language basically seems arbitrary and the way in which the Germanic V2 languages are divided into two groups would therefore be random. In other words, no genuine explanation could be provided for the cross-linguistic pattern found in (6).

In order to account for the variation in (6) and its acquisition, it therefore seems necessary to derive it from factors which are independent of properties of adjunct placement. An analysis along these lines is proposed in Haeberli (1999: chapter 4). The two main hypotheses made there and adopted here are: (*a*) adjunction to maximal projections is highly restricted universally, and in particular adjunction to functional projections such as IP or, within a richer clause structure, AgrSP and TP is ruled out; and (*b*) contrasts as shown in (6) are obtained through differences with respect to the syntax of subjects; more precisely, there are (at least) two structural positions available for subjects, and adjacency between the finite verb and the subject occurs when the subject has to occupy the highest structural subject position whereas non-adjacency is possible when the subject can remain in a lower subject position in the overt syntax. This variation is illustrated in (7) (e = empty position).

(7) (*a*) $[_{CP}$ ZP V $[_{XP}$ SU$_1$ ... $[_{YP}$ SU$_2$ ...]]]
   (*b*) $[_{CP}$ ZP V $[_{XP}$ **SU** ...]] (V-subject adjacency)
   (*c*) $[_{CP}$ ZP V $[_{XP}$ e ... $[_{YP}$ **SU** ...]]] (V-subject non-adjacency)

One question that remains in terms of (7*c*) is what position an adjunct occupies when it occurs between a fronted finite verb and a subject. Given that adjunction to a maximal projection is restricted by hypothesis (cf. hypothesis (a) above), two main options are available. First, the adjunct could occupy the specifier position of an independent functional projection (FP), in line with proposals made by Alexiadou (1997), Cinque (1999), Kayne (1994). The second option is that the adjunct is X'-adjoined, an option which is assumed to be available for example by Chomsky (1995: 235). These options are summarized in (8).

(8) (a) [$_{CP}$ ZP V [$_{XP}$ e X [$_{FP}$ *adjunct* F [$_{YP}$ **SU** . . .]]]]
   (b) [$_{CP}$ ZP V [$_{XP}$ e [$_{X'}$ *adjunct* [$_{X'}$ X [$_{YP}$ **SU** . . .]]]]]

The main difference between the two theoretical options in (8) is that in (8a) the adjunct follows the head X whereas in (8b) it precedes this head. But given that the verb moves on to C in the Modern Germanic V2 languages and that X is therefore not overtly filled, there is no clear empirical evidence from the Modern Germanic languages for choosing between the two options in (8).

Assuming that adjuncts can occur in one of the two positions shown in (8), the variation with respect to 'XP–subject' orders among the Germanic languages can be analysed in terms of the structures in (7) and hence in terms of variation with respect to the syntax of subjects. Languages of the type (7b) show adjacency effects whereas languages of the type (7c) allow V-subject non-adjacency. As argued in Haeberli (1999: chapter 4), this structural variation provides the basis for deriving the variation in (6) to a large extent from independent properties of the grammars of the different languages, such as the status of verbal agreement morphology or the licensing of non-overt expletives. For reasons of space, the analyses of the different Modern Germanic languages cannot be discussed here, and I refer the reader to the references cited above for more details. What will be central for our discussion, however, is the structural analysis in (7) and (8) and the observation that this structural analysis provides the basis for an analysis of a word-order variation among the Modern Germanic languages.

5.2.2. . . . and its relevance for Old English

Given the variation in (6), it would already be of interest from a purely typological point of view to consider what the status of Old English is in this respect, in particular since Old English has a relatively peculiar status with respect to the syntax of V2 (cf. §5.1). However, the data in (6) are also immediately relevant for another reason. In the Modern Germanic languages, there is one important additional restriction with respect to 'XP–subject' orders. As observed for example by Vikner (1995: 103 ff.), pronominal subjects (weak pronouns) generally have to occur in a position which is adjacent to the finite verb even in languages like German which license 'XP–subject' orders with non-pronominal subjects. This property of subject pronouns is shown in (9a) which should be compared to (6a), repeated here in (9b).

(9) (a) Wahrscheinlich *wird* (*später) *er* dieselbe Uhr kaufen.   (*German*)
       probably will (later) he the-same watch buy

(*b*)   Wahrscheinlich *wird* (später) *Hans* dieselbe Uhr kaufen
probably will (later) John the-same watch buy

The contrast between (9*a*) and (9*b*) can be analysed by assuming that weak subject pronouns have to occupy the highest subject position even in languages like German ([Spec,XP] in (7*c*) and (8)). This means that we get exactly the same kind of contrast in the Modern Germanic languages as the contrast shown in (4) for Old English. The only difference is that the presence of two subject positions is not determined on the basis of a head position between the two subject positions as in Old English when the verb does not move to C but on the basis of the presence of an adjunct position. This parallelism is illustrated in (10), where (10*a*) represents the Old English contrast based on the data in (1) and (2) and (10*b*) represents the Modern Germanic contrast based on data such as (9*a*) and (9*b*) for German.

(10)   (*a*) $[_{CP} \ldots \quad [_{XP} SU_1(+pro) \quad \mathbf{V} \quad [_{YP} SU_2(-pro) \ldots]]]$
(*Old English*)

(*b*) $[_{CP} \ldots \mathbf{V} [_{XP} SU_1(+pro) \ \mathbf{adjunct} \ [_{YP} SU_2(-pro) \ldots]]]$
(*Modern Germanic*)

Thus, the Old English variation with respect to pronominal vs. non-pronominal subjects has a very close equivalent in the Modern Germanic languages. But note now that Old English can provide additional evidence for the analysis of the Modern Germanic languages and more particularly for the open issue concerning the placement of adjuncts shown in example (8), repeated below.

(8)   (*a*) $[_{CP} ZP \ \mathbf{V} \ [_{XP} e \ X \ [_{FP} adjunct \ F \ [_{YP} \mathbf{SU} \ldots]]]]$
(*b*) $[_{CP} ZP \ \mathbf{V} \ [_{XP} e \ [_{X'} adjunct \ [_{X'} X \ [_{YP} \mathbf{SU} \ldots]]]]]$

In (8), two options for adjunct placement are presented. One of the two options involves a maximal projection between XP and YP (8*a*), and the second option involves adjunction to X′ (8*b*). These two options make different predictions for Old English now. As mentioned above, Old English has V-fronting to two distinct positions, C (in interrogative clauses etc.; cf. (3)) and the functional head X which occurs right below C (in all other types of clauses, cf. examples (1), (2), and the structure in (10*a*)). This means now that if a pre-subject adjunct could only occur in an X′-adjoined position (cf. (8*b*)), then V-subject non-adjacency could only occur in cases in which the verb moves to C. In all other contexts in which the verb only moves to X, V-subject non-adjacency would not be possible because a constituent adjoined to X′ would precede rather than follow the verb. In terms of a functional projection between X and YP however (cf. (8*a*)), V-subject non-adjacency should be possible regardless of whether the verb moves to C or to X. Old English therefore allows us to test at least one of the two hypotheses shown in (8).

Thus, we have seen two initial motivations for considering the status of Old English with respect to the variation shown in (6). First, the question arises as to where Old English is situated in this typological split and, secondly, Old English can provide evidence for the structural analysis of this variation. However, we will see that several additional results can be obtained on the basis of an investigation of V-subject (non-)adjacency in Old English (and Middle English), in particular results which are relevant for the open issues raised in (5) above.

5.3. V-SUBJECT NON-ADJACENCY IN OLD ENGLISH[3]

Let us start by considering the typological issue, i.e. the question whether Old English is a language in which verb fronting leads to adjacency between the verb and a non-pronominal subject or whether Old English belongs to the group of Germanic languages which allow 'XP–subject' orders after a fronted finite verb.

5.3.1. *Some preliminary remarks*

A brief look at the Old English data shows that subjects do not need to be adjacent to fronted finite verbs. However, not all data are of equal importance for the cross-linguistic issues raised in §5.2. I will distinguish three main types of constructions in which a subject is not directly right-adjacent to the finite verb:

A. Another predicative element intervenes between the finite verbal form and the subject (generally the participle in passives as in (11), but sometimes also other non-finite verb forms, adjectives, or particles).

(11)   þy ilcan geare *wæs* **gecoren** *Æþelheard abbud* to biscepe
         the same year was chosen   Æþelheard abbot to bishop
         'In the same year, the abbot Æthelhard was chosen as bishop.'
             (CHROA2,54.790.1)

B. An argument (generally a pronoun) occurs between the finite verb and the subject.

(12)   þonne *mot* **hine** *se hlaford* gefreogean
         then   may him   the master liberate
         'Then, the master may liberate him.'
             (LAW2,120.74.1)

C. The subject follows an adjunct.

(13)   þa *blon* **micelre tiide** *se biscopdom*
         then ceased much   time the bishopric
         'Then, the bishopric was vacant for a long time.'
             (BEDE,252.7)

---

[3] If not mentioned otherwise, the Old English data are taken from the 1998 version of the Brooklyn–Geneva–Amsterdam–Helsinki Parsed Corpus of Old English, a syntactically parsed and morphologically tagged corpus of Old English, and follow the referencing conventions of that corpus.

For our comparative analysis of the syntax of subjects in Old English, only Type C is crucial. As for Type A, it presumably involves a different position from the [Spec,YP] subject position in the structures in (4) or (10). For example in the passive construction in (11), it can be argued that the subject occupies an underlying object position if we assume (as e.g. Roberts 1997, Pintzuk 1998) that Old English allows VO base orders. As for Type B, its occurrence may not be related to the syntax of subjects but rather to distributional properties of pronouns. This observation is based on the fact that in languages like Icelandic and West Flemish which generally require V-subject adjacency (cf. examples (6*b*) and (6*g*)) object pronouns nevertheless can intervene between a fronted verb and a subject (cf. e.g. Hellan and Platzack 1995: 59 for Icelandic, Haegeman 1996: 142 for West Flemish). The most plausible analysis for these two languages is that, since V-subject non-adjacency is restricted to contexts involving pronouns, the properties of subjects create an adjacency configuration but that pronominal objects have properties which allow them to intervene between the verb and the subject, possibly as the result of head movement. Given these cross-linguistic observations, data of Type B may not be central for determining the syntax of subjects.

Given these observations, I will consider neither Type A nor Type B constructions here in my discussion of the syntax of subjects in Old English (but cf. Haeberli 1998 for additional observations concerning these constructions). Instead, I will focus on Type C constructions. But since, as discussed in §5.1, V-fronting targets two positions in Old English, we have to distinguish two contexts with respect to V-subject (non-)adjacency, namely V-to-C movement contexts and contexts involving V-movement to the projection below CP (cf. structure (4)). The next section deals with the former context.

5.3.2. *V-subject non-adjacency with V-movement to C*

V-movement to C occurs in interrogative, negative and V1 clauses and in clauses introduced by adverbs like *þa*. That subjects do not have to be adjacent to the fronted verb in these contexts has already been observed sometimes in the literature. Pintzuk (1991: 214) and Koopman (1996) for example point out that adverbs can intervene between a verb in C and the subject. This option is shown in (14).

(14) (*a*) Ne *dorste* **swa þeah** *se mæssepreost* þone bisceop geaxian
        not dared however the mass-priest the bishop ask
        for hwan . . .
        why . . .
        'However, the priest did not dare to ask the bishop why . . .'
        (GREGD3,22.58.3)

    (*b*) *gielden* **syððan** *his mægas* þone wer
        pay afterwards his male-kinsmen the man's-legal-value
        'Afterwards, his relatives should pay the man's legal value.'
        (LAW2,120.74.1)

PP adjuncts can also occur in this position (cf. also (13) for a DP adjunct):

(15) (a)   &   ðonne *wyrð* **þurh**   **Godes mihte sona** *deofol* swyðe
         and then   gets   through God's power soon devil   very-much
         geyrged
         terrified
         'Then, soon, the devil is very much terrified through God's power.'
            (WULF3,176.28)

     (b)   þa   *wæs* **in þa tid**   *Uitalius papa* þæs apostolican seðles
         then was in that time Vitalius pope the apostolic   see's
         aldorbiscop
         high-priest
         'At that time, Vitalius was chief bishop of the apostolic see.'
            (BEDE,1.252.1)

5.3.3. *V-subject non-adjacency with V-movement to the head below C (X)*

Having considered V-subject non-adjacency in V-to-C contexts, let us now turn to contexts in which the verb only moves to the head below C. As the following examples show, adverbs and PP adjuncts can occur between the fronted verb and the subject even in these contexts in Old English.

(16) (a)   Him *geaf* **ða**   *se cyngc* twa hund   gildenra pænega
         him gave then the king   two hundred golden   coins
         'Then, the king gave him two hundred golden coins.'
            (APOLLO,42.51.20)

     (b)   &   hine *hæfde* **ær**   *Offa Miercna cyning* & *Beorhtric*
         and him had   before Offa Mercians king   and Beorhtric
         Wesseaxna cyning afliemed iii   gear . . .
         West-Saxons king   expelled three years
         'Offa, the Mercian king, and Beorhtric, the West-Saxon king, had expelled him for three years.'
            (CHROA2,62.836.1)

     (c)   Ac mycel *geþolode* **ðurh**   **his mildheortnesse** *Crist* for ure
         but much suffered   through his loving-kindness Christ for our
         þearfe
         need
         'But through his kindness, Christ suffered much for us.'
            (WULF3,227.34)

     (d)   In ða tid   *wæs* **in Mercna mægðe** *Wulfhere* cyning
         in that time was in Mercians' country Wulfhere king
         'At that time, Wulfhere was king in Mercia.'
            (BEDE,3.260.22)

In (16a–b) an object is fronted and the verb therefore only moves to the inflectional head below C (cf. §5.1). Finally, in (16c–d), adjuncts are fronted which do not trigger V-movement to C, either. We can therefore conclude that 'XP–subject' orders are possible when the verb moves to the head below C.

In summary, the data in (14) to (16) show that 'XP–subject' orders occur in Old English regardless of the position to which the finite verb moves. Old English thus clearly patterns with the more permissive Germanic languages in (6) which do not require adjacency between a fronted verb and the subject.[4]

5.3.4. *A theoretical consequence: the placement of adjuncts*

As discussed in §5.2.2, both Old English and the Modern Germanic languages show evidence for two subject positions in the overt syntax, one occupied by pronominal subjects and one occupied by non-pronominal subjects. But the diagnostics for the presence of these two subject positions are not the same. In Old English, the distributional contrast can be identified on the basis of the position of the finite verb, whereas in the Modern Germanic languages, it is the placement of adjuncts which allows us to distinguish the two subject positions. This contrast is repeated here in (17) (cf. (10)).

(17) (a) $[_{CP}$ $[_{XP}$ $SU_1(+pro)$ V $[_{YP}$ $SU_2(-pro)$ . . .]]]   (*Old English*)

 (b) $[_{CP}$ V $[_{XP}$ $SU_1(+pro)$ **adjunct** $[_{YP}$ $SU_2(-pro)$ . . .]]] (*Modern Germanic*)

As discussed in §5.2.1, the Modern Germanic languages do not provide clear evidence for establishing the position occupied by the adjunct in (17b). Given that the cross-linguistic variation with respect to V-subject non-adjacency may

---

[4] For some of the Old English examples of V-subject non-adjacency, it could be argued that they do not illustrate the syntactic structure shown in (10b) for the Modern Germanic languages but that they are obtained as the result of rightward movement of the subject. Such a conclusion certainly would be plausible for clause-final heavy subjects as for example in (i).

(i) Mycele mede *geearnað* **æt þam ælmihtigan Gode**, *se þe   him clænlice þenað æt his*
    Great reward earns   at the almighty   God he who him purely serves at his
    clænume weofode.
    clean   altar
    'He who purely serves the almighty God at his altar earns a great reward with God.'
       (ÆLET3,174.74)

(i) could be argued to involve movement of the heavy subject to the right edge of the clause, and such an example would therefore not provide any relevant information concerning the placement of the adjunct.

If we assume that such a postposition process is available for subjects, it may not always be entirely clear whether V-subject non-adjacency is the result of the structure (10b) proposed for the Modern Germanic languages or of postposition of the subject. However, I will assume here that rightward movement is restricted to a large extent to heavy subjects. Most of the examples given in (14) to (16) therefore do not seem to be plausible candidates for postposition analyses, and the conclusion reached in the text, i.e. that Old English allows V-subject non-adjacency of the Modern Germanic type, can be maintained. The same observations also hold for the examples discussed in (21) and (22) below.

best be analysed in terms of a restrictive system of adjunction, i.e. a system in which adjunction to XP and YP in (17b) is ruled out, there are two remaining options for the placement of the adjunct in (17b): Either it is adjoined to X′ or it occupies a specifier position of an independent functional projection between XP and YP (cf. example (8)). As pointed out already in §5.2.2, Old English can shed some light on this issue.

As the data in (16) show, the order 'XP–subject' is possible in Old English even if the verb only moves to X and not to C. This means that the adjunct in pre-subject position cannot occur in an X′-adjoined position but must occur in an independent projection between X and YP.[5] Thus, we obtain the following structure for 'XP–subject' orders with V-movement to X:

(18) . . . [$_{XP}$ e **V** [$_{FP}$ *adjunct* F [$_{YP}$ **SU** . . .]]]]

The structure in (18) corresponds to the option shown in (8a) above. The Old English data thus show that an adjunct in pre-subject position must be able to occupy an independent functional projection between XP and YP. Old English therefore provides evidence for the details of the structural analysis of adjuncts which cannot be obtained from the Modern Germanic languages. The reason why Old English allows us to draw more precise conclusions is that in Old English we can combine the distribution of adjuncts with the distribution of a head, given that Old English has V-movement into the domain which is relevant for our purposes. Old English thus contributes to a more detailed understanding of a general word-order phenomenon found in the Germanic languages.[6]

---

[5] The fact that PPs can precede the subject (cf. (16c–d)) suggests that a pre-subject adjunct also cannot simply be an element which has been cliticized to the verb, for example. Cf. also Vikner (1995: 106) for arguments against treating pre-subject adjuncts as clitics in the Modern Germanic languages.

[6] There may be some additional data which are relevant for the issues discussed here, however. The observations made in the text show that option (8a), i.e. adjunct placement in a projection between X and YP, must be available, but they of course do not mean that option (8b), i.e. X′-adjunction, must be ruled out. X′-adjunction cases could indeed be argued to exist in Old English. Consider the following example.

(i) [mid py] [**ða**] [*ongon*] [*firenlust*]   weaxan
    with that then   began   riotous-living increase
    'With that, riotous living then began to increase.'
    (Bede 48.27; Pintzuk 1991: 213)

In (i), the adverb *þa* occurs between a topic and a fronted finite verb. Assuming that the verb is in X and that, as argued in the following subsection, the topic occurs in [Spec,CP], we could say that the adverb is adjoined to X′ in such examples. The conclusion thus would not be that one of the two options for adjunct placement shown in (8) is not available in the grammar but that both options occur.

However, there may be an alternative analysis for (i) which does not depend on X′-adjunction of the second adjunct. It could be argued that the topic position in the CP domain is not a unique position but that multiple topics are possible (cf. e.g. Rizzi 1997: 290–1, 295 ff. on recursive topic positions in the CP domain). Hence, both adjuncts in (i) occupy topic positions, i.e. specifier positions in the CP domain, and (i) would therefore not provide evidence for X′-adjunction.

5.3.5. *An additional observation: pronominal subjects and topics*

In the previous section, I showed that V-subject non-adjacency in Old English provides evidence for the analysis of a more general Germanic word-order phenomenon. In this section, I will argue that the Old English data concerning V-subject non-adjacency are also relevant for one of the issues raised in (5) which are specific to Old English, i.e. the question as to what position topics occupy.

One of the observations that we can make with respect to V-subject non-adjacency in Old English is that in cases where (weak) pronominal subjects occur postverbally (i.e. in V-to-C contexts) the subject pronoun is always adjacent to V. I have not found a single example in my corpus in which a constituent intervenes between the finite verb and a postverbal pronominal subject. Thus, it seems that the following restriction holds even in contexts where V occupies C.

(19)   *V(**finite**)–*adjunct*–**pronominal subject**

This observation is relevant for issue (5 III) which concerns the position occupied by topics in Old English as for example in (1) above, repeated here in (20).

(20)   [Eall ðis] **aredað** se reccere swiðe ryhte
          All this arranges the ruler   very   rightly
          (*Cura Pastoralis* 169.3)

One option that has been proposed, on the basis of analyses of languages like Icelandic and Yiddish, is that topics occupy a position below CP in Old English ([Spec,XP] in the structures used so far, [Spec,IP] in Pintzuk's 1991, 1993 analysis, and [Spec,Agr1P] in Cardinaletti and Roberts 1991). Thus, [Spec,XP] in (20) is an A'-position. Furthermore, in order to obtain the order *Topic–pronominal subject–V* (cf. (2) above), it has to be assumed that the pronominal subject somehow can occur between the specifier and the head X. Pintzuk (1991, 1993) and Cardinaletti and Roberts (1991) therefore argue that subject pronouns can cliticize to a position between [Spec,XP] and the verb in X. However, such an assumption is problematic for deriving (19). (19) should be possible as the result of: (*a*) placement of an adjunct in [Spec,XP] given that [Spec,XP] is an A'-position; (*b*) cliticization of the subject pronoun to the right of the element in [Spec,XP]; (*c*) movement of the verb to C. Given these possible derivational steps, it seems to be difficult to rule out the word-order pattern shown in (19).[7]

The point made in the text does not depend on the status of (i), however. Old English provides evidence for the option of inserting an adjunct in a specifier position between XP and YP and such evidence cannot be found among the Modern Germanic languages. As for the status of X'-adjunction and hence of data like (i), I will leave it open for future research.

[7] Some cases of (19) could possibly be ruled out as Relativized Minimality violations. For example a *wh*-element generally cannot move past a topic (cf. e.g. Vikner 1995: 73 ff.). However, for V-initial cases, such an approach is more difficult to motivate. If V1 is analysed in terms of an empty

In terms of an alternative analysis of topicalization in Old English, however, i.e. in terms of topicalization to [Spec,CP], the adjacency requirement between the verb in C and a pronominal subject can be accounted for straightforwardly in terms of a restrictive system of adjunction to maximal projections. Assuming still that adjunction to XP is restricted (cf. §5.2.1), the adjacency required by (19) is obtained through movement of the pronominal subject to [Spec,XP] (i.e. position SU_1 in example (4), which is repeated below) and movement of the verb to C.

(4) $[_{CP}$ **C** $[_{XP} SU_1 (+\text{pro})$ **X** $[_{YP} SU_2 (-\text{pro}) \ldots]]]$

In summary, the distribution of adjuncts and pronominal subjects supports an analysis of topicalization in Old English in terms of movement to CP.

5.4. V-SUBJECT NON-ADJACENCY IN MIDDLE ENGLISH AND DIALECT VARIATION[8]

Having considered the status of Old English with respect to 'XP–subject' orders, let us now turn to the distribution of adjuncts and subjects in Middle English. I will focus here mainly on the two Middle English dialects that Kroch and Taylor (1997) have identified on the basis of the syntax of V2, and I will show that the two dialects also seem to vary with respect to the phenomena discussed here, i.e. with respect to the occurrence of adjuncts between a fronted verb and the subject. Furthermore, I will argue that the Middle English data also provide evidence for dealing with the issues (I) and (II) raised in (5) above.

5.4.1. *The southern dialects*

Kroch and Taylor (1997) show that the V2 syntax of Old English as illustrated in (1) to (4) is maintained to a large extent in the Early Middle English of the West Midlands and the South. Pronominal subjects still follow the finite verb in the contexts shown in (3) (interrogatives etc.) but they precede the finite verb in all other contexts. Non-pronominal subjects generally follow the fronted verb in both contexts. Thus, southern Early Middle English can still be analysed in terms of V-movement to C or to X and in terms of different positions for pronominal and non-pronominal subjects (cf. (4)).

---

operator in [Spec,CP] (e.g. an interrogative operator in yes/no questions or different types of operators in declarative and negative V1), the most straightforward assumption would be that this empty operator is generated in [Spec,CP] (in the same way that even certain *wh*-elements seem to be generated in CP, cf. Vikner 1995: 75–6 on *how*). Thus, it would not be clear why and from where empty operators would have to move past the topic for ruling out (19).

[8] The Middle English data are all taken from the first edition of the Penn–Helsinki Parsed Corpus of Middle English, a syntactically parsed corpus of Middle English, and follow the referencing conventions of that corpus (cf. http://www.ling.upenn.edu/mideng).

If we now consider the distribution of adjuncts and subjects, we can again observe that southern Early Middle English patterns like Old English. Adjuncts can still occur in a position between the finite verb and a postverbal non-pronominal subject, and again this word-order option can be found in contexts of V-movement to C as well as in contexts of V-movement to X. This is shown in (21) (V-to-C) and (22) (V-to-X).

(21) (*a*)   *Wende* **þa**   *porphire* to freinen þis meiden
           turned then Porphire to question this maiden
           'Then Porphire turned to question this maiden.'
               (Kathe 39.328)

   (*b*)   Ne *don* **swa** *ðe heðene*?
           not do   so   the heathens
           'Do not the heathens do so?'
               (Vices1 77.338)

(22) (*a*)   þis *singeð* **þenne** *iweddede*
           this sing   then   wedded
           'The wedded sing this then.'
               (Hali 142.221)

   (*b*)   Forði   us *menegeð*   **allre ðinge arst** *ure laurde* of ðesre eadi
           for-this us admonishes all   things first our lord   of this   blessed
           mihte
           virtue
           'Therefore, our lord admonishes us of this blessed virtue first of all things.'
               (Vices1 121.544)

   (*c*)   Se þicke *is* **þrinne** *þe þosternesse* þt . . .
           so thick is therein the darkness   that . . .
           'The darkness is so thick in there that . . .'
               (Sawles 171.80)

5.4.2. *The northern dialect*

Considering the *Northern Prose Rule of St Benet*, a text from around 1400 which is the oldest surviving prose document from the North, Kroch and Taylor (1997) argue that the northern dialect of Middle English differs significantly from the southern dialects with respect to the syntax of V-movement. The Benet text exhibits basically a regular V2 syntax as found in the Modern Germanic languages, instead of the complex V2 pattern found in Old English and southern Early Middle English. Thus, when some constituent is fronted in the Benet text, subject–verb inversion applies regardless of whether the subject is a pronoun or a full DP. The Old English/southern Early Middle English contrast between subject pronouns (no inversion except in certain syntactic contexts) and

non-pronominal subjects (generally inversion) therefore cannot be found in the
northern dialect.[9]

As Kroch and Taylor (1997: 314) point out, the categorical subject–verb
inversion pattern of the northern dialect can best be accounted for by assuming
that the verb always moves to C in this dialect, as it has been proposed for
Modern Germanic V2 languages. The difference between the southern and the
northern dialect would therefore be that while in the southern dialect (and Old
English) the verb can occur in two distinct positions when it is fronted (C or
X), V-fronting always targets C in the northern dialect.

What is interesting for our purposes now is that the dialect variation described
by Kroch and Taylor (1997) also seems to be reflected in the distribution of
adjuncts and subjects. As discussed in §5.4.1, the southern dialect behaves like
Old English with respect to this issue, since adjuncts can still occur in a position
between the finite verb and a postverbal non-pronominal subject in contexts of
V-movement to C as well as in contexts of V-movement to X. In the northern
text, however, the situation is substantially different. Within the entire text, not
a single instance of the word-order pattern *V–adjunct–subject* can be found. The
only examples in which a subject is non-adjacent to a fronted finite verb are
cases which I classified as Type A and Type B in §5.3.1, i.e. cases with
passivized verbs and with intervening pronouns. Illustrations of these two constructions are given in (23).

(23) (a)   And eftir   *sal* **be redde** *þe lescun of þapostils*   wid gude
           And afterwards shall be read   the lesson of the apostles with good
           deuocion
           devotion
           'And afterwards, the lesson of the apostles shall be read with devo-
           tion.'   (Benrul 16.441)

     (b)   In þis first sentence *bidis*   **us** *sain   benet* . . .
           In this first sentence commands us Saint Benet
           'In this first sentence, Saint Benet commands us . . .'
           (Benrul 1.7)

As discussed in §5.3.1, (23a) can be argued to involve a subject in its underlying
object position, whereas (23b) may not be related to properties of subjects but

---

[9] As Warner (1997: 389–90) points out, there may be an alternative to Kroch and Taylor's (1997)
conclusion, however. Since Kroch and Taylor's claim is based on a single text, it could be argued
that Benet is simply a stylistically marked text rather than a text representing the grammar of a
different dialect. Yet, the points discussed below may provide some support for analysing the Benet
text as a text with a different grammar. As we will see, the distinct behaviour of the Benet text with
respect to V2 seems to coincide with another syntactic peculiarity, namely the absence of
'XP–subject' orders. In terms of a stylistic interpretation of the V2 pattern in the Benet text, the
co-occurrence of the two phenomena would seem accidental. However, as I will argue below, an
analysis of the Benet text in terms of a distinctive grammatical property allows us to link the two
phenomena to a common underlying source. I will therefore continue using Kroch and Taylor's
distinction between different dialects.

rather to the syntax of pronominal elements. Hence, neither of the two cases in (23) are genuine cases of V-subject non-adjacency as discussed in the earlier sections (i.e. 'XP–subject', Type C). As for Type C non-adjacency, it is entirely absent from the Benet text.

The question that arises then is how to interpret the absence of Type C examples in the Benet text. In particular, we may wonder whether the absence of 'XP–subject' orders in the northern dialect is the manifestation of an underlying grammatical property which bans such orders (as for example in West Flemish, Afrikaans, Danish, or Icelandic, cf. example (6)) or whether the absence of 'XP–subject' orders is simply due to a gap in the corpus, possibly because the corpus is not large enough. Based on statistical evidence, I will argue here that the latter option is not very likely.

In order to test whether the absence of 'XP–subject' orders in the Benet text is simply due to the size of the corpus, I compared the northern text to several Old English and southern Early Middle English text samples with respect to the frequencies of V-subject non-adjacency. More precisely, for each text, I counted the number of examples in which the subject follows the finite verb and an 'XP–subject' order therefore could have occurred, and the actual occurrences of such orders. The relevant numbers are given in Tables 5.1 to 5.3. Four different figures are given in these tables. The first figure represents all the cases in which V-subject non-adjacency could have occurred because a non-pronominal subject follows the finite verb (listed under 'Total V-SU' in the tables).[10] Then,

TABLE 5.1. *V-subject non-adjacency in some Old English texts*

	Total V-SU	Type A		Type B		Type C	
ÆLet	91	7	7.7%	2	2.2%	16	17.6%
ÆLS	97	6	6.2%	1	1.0%	11	11.3%
ApT	99	2	2.0%	4	4.0%	6	6.1%
Bede	92	4	4.3%	9	9.8%	19	20.7%
Boethius	78	2	2.6%	1	1.3%	5	6.4%
ChronA	364	15	4.1%	4	1.1%	16	4.4%
GDC	37	2	5.4%	1	2.7%	2	5.4%
GDH	48	6	12.5%	4	8.3%	11	22.9%
Laws	144	1	0.7%	11	7.6%	19	13.2%
Orosius	95	8	8.4%	4	4.2%	7	7.4%
WHom	144	5	3.5%	0	0.0%	19	13.2%
average %[11]			5.2%		3.8%		11.7%

[10] Thus, VS orders with pronominal subjects are not included in my counts. Clauses containing the indefinite element *man* ('one') are also not included in the totals of VS orders, since this element seems to have pronoun-like syntactic properties (cf. van Bergen 1998).

[11] The average percentage is calculated purely on the basis of the percentages obtained for the individual texts and not on the basis of the total number of the examples in all texts. The aim of calculating the percentages this way is to give each text sample the same weight, independently of its size. If the percentages were calculated on the basis of the total number of examples in the entire Old English corpus, the figures would be slightly lower: Total V-SU: 1289; Total Type A: 58 (= 4.5%); Total Type B: 41 (= 3.2%); Total Type C: 131 (= 10.2%).

I counted the number of occurrences of the three types of V-subject non-adjacency among the 'V-SU' cases (Type A, B, and C). As mentioned above, the crucial pattern is Type C, but I added Types A and B for comparative purposes. Apart from the absolute numbers for the different types of V-subject non-adjacency, I have also given their frequencies in each text, calculated on the basis of the total number of 'V-SU' orders. Table 5.1 shows the results for the Old English period, Table 5.2 the results for southern Early Middle English and Table 5.3 the results for the northern Middle English Benet text.

TABLE 5.2. *V-subject non-adjacency in some southern Early Middle English texts*

	Total V-SU	Type A		Type B		Type C	
AncRiw	42	3	7.1%	1	2.4%	3	7.1%
Hali	63	4	6.3%	2	3.2%	12	19.0%
Kathe	49	5	10.2%	6	12.2%	9	18.4%
Lambeth	118	2	1.7%	3	2.5%	7	5.9%
Sawles	28	1	3.6%	2	7.1%	7	25.0%
Trinity	48	2	4.2%	1	2.1%	2	4.2%
Vices	110	4	3.6%	3	2.7%	7	6.4%
average %[12]			5.2%		4.6%		12.3%

TABLE 5.3. *V-subject non-adjacency in the* Northern Prose Rule of St Benet

	Total V-SU	Type A		Type B		Type C	
St Benet	126	6	4.8%	3	2.4%	0	0.0%

Tables 5.1 to 5.3 show that, compared to the other text samples, the number of contexts in which 'XP–subject' orders could occur (cf. 'Total V-SU') is relatively high in the Benet text. Several other texts have considerably lower figures for 'V-SU' orders but they nevertheless all contain at least two examples of Type C, in contrast to the Benet text which does not contain a single example of this type.

The contrast between the Benet text and the other texts can also be illustrated by calculating the expected number of occurrences of the different word-order patterns for the Benet text on the basis of the average frequencies found in the other texts. As shown in Table 5.1, the average frequency for Type A is 5.2%, for B 3.8% and for C 11.7% in Old English. For southern Early Middle English, the averages are 5.2% (A), 4.6% (B) and 12.3% (C) (cf. Table 5.2). For both

---

[12] In terms of the total numbers of occurrences in all Early Middle English text samples together, the percentages would again be slightly lower (cf. also note 11 for Old English): Total V-SU: 458; Total Type A: 21 (= 4.6%); Total Type B: 18 (= 3.9%); Total Type C: 47 (= 10.3%).

Old English and southern Early Middle English, this gives average frequencies of 5.2% (A), 4.1% (B) and 11.9% (C). On the basis of these frequencies, we would expect the following numbers of occurrences in the Benet text.[13, 14]

TABLE 5.4. *Expected and observed occurrences in St Benet based on all V-SU clauses*

	Total V-SU	Type A	Type B	Type C
Expected	126	6.6	5.2	15.0
Observed	126	6	3	0

While the numbers for Type A and Type B constructions are very close to the expected numbers, there is a considerable discrepancy with respect to Type C constructions. Instead of the expected fifteen examples showing 'XP–subject' orders, we do not find a single example of this type.

However, there is one additional aspect which should be considered at this point. A closer investigation of the St Benet data shows that many 'V-SU' clauses are characterized by the fact that they contain a fronted constituent, the verb and the argument(s) but no additional adjunct(s) which could intervene between the

---

[13] Here, the question may arise however as to whether Tables 5.1–2 and Table 5.3 are entirely comparable. As discussed earlier, 'V-SU' orders in Old English and southern Early Middle English can be the result of V-movement to X or to C. In northern Middle English however, the verb always moves to C in 'V-SU' orders according to Kroch and Taylor's (1997) analysis. Thus, one may wonder whether the inclusion of V-to-X contexts in the Old English/Early Middle English data has undesirable effects for the comparison with northern Middle English since northern Middle English only has V-to-C.

If we distinguish between V-to-C contexts and V-to-X contexts in the Old English and southern Early Middle English text samples studied here, we obtain the following results with respect to Type C orders. In Old English, the likelihood of Type C is almost equally high in V-to-X contexts as in V-to-C contexts. In southern Early Middle English, however, there is a slight contrast between the two V-movement landing sites. 'XP–subject' is found more frequently in V-to-C contexts than in V-to-X contexts (roughly 15% vs. 10%). Thus, if V-to-X movement contexts were eliminated from the Old English/Early Middle English data, the expected number in northern Middle English for Type C would be slightly higher than shown in Table 5.4 (17.3 expected examples of Type C rather than 15.0). The distinction between V-to-X and V-to-C contexts would thus reinforce the point made in the text below, since the gap between the expected number of 'XP–subject' orders in northern Middle English and the observed number would be even bigger.

However, given the fact that a contrast between V-to-C and V-to-X can only be identified clearly in the Early Middle English data but not in Old English, and given that the contrast in Early Middle English is relatively small, I tentatively conclude here that the contrast between V-to-C and V-to-X contexts is not a substantial general factor determining the status of 'XP–subject' orders, and I will therefore base my quantitative data for Old English and Early Middle English on both V-to-C and V-to-X contexts.

[14] In terms of total numbers for the Old English and Early Middle English texts (cf. notes 11 and 12), the expected figures would be slightly lower. Among the 1747 'V-SU' examples in the Old English and Early Middle English text samples studied, 79 are of Type A (4.5%), 59 of Type B (3.4%) and 178 of Type C (10.2%). The expected numbers for northern Middle English would therefore be as follows: Type A: 5.7; Type B: 4.3; Type C: 12.9.

finite verb and the subject. Thus, many clauses contain no additional adjunct(s) at all or they only contain heavy adjuncts like adjunct clauses or adjuncts modified by an entire clause which generally do not occupy the XP-position in 'XP–subject' orders in Old English/Early Middle English. Leaving aside such heavy adjuncts, we can observe that in the Benet text only 31 out of the 126 'V-SU' clauses or 24.6% contain an adjunct in a position following the finite verb, and hence that in terms of the elements which are available in the clause, only 24.6% of the 'V-SU' clauses could have given rise to a Type C order.

The question that arises then is whether the absence of 'XP–subject' orders in the Benet text is a consequence of the general low frequency of adjuncts in postverbal position. The answer to this question seems to be negative. A comparison with Old English and southern Early Middle English text samples shows that the low frequency of postverbal adjuncts among 'V-SU' orders cannot be identified as a clear factor determining the absence of Type C orders in the Benet text. Two observations are relevant here. First of all, although the frequency of postverbal adjuncts is indeed lower in the Benet text than in the Old English/Early Middle English text samples studied here (24.6% vs. 43.0%), the Benet text is by no means exceptional in terms of absolute numbers. Three Old English and five Early Middle English text samples contain fewer instances of 'V-SU' order with a postverbal (non-heavy) adjunct than the Benet text (Boethius 29 examples; GDC 13; GDH 27; Ancriw 14; Kathe 20; Sawles 16; Trinit 13; Vices 21). Furthermore, three Old English and two Early Middle English text samples show similar numbers as Benet (ÆLS 38; ApT 34; Bede 39; Hali 33; Lambeth 37). Finally, there are only five Old English text samples which show considerably higher numbers of 'V-SU' orders with postverbal adjuncts (ÆLet 52; ChronA 147; Laws 77; Orosius 47; WHom 66). Hence, most Old English/Early Middle English text samples have comparable or lower numbers of postverbal adjuncts in V-SU structures. On the basis of the absolute numbers, it would therefore not be expected that the Benet text is the only text among those considered here which does not contain any Type C orders.

The conclusion that the low frequency of 'V-SU' orders with postverbal adjuncts does not seem to be a clear source of the absence of Type C orders in the Benet text is supported by a calculation of the expected number of Type C orders on the basis of the Old English/Early Middle English data. For each Old English/Early Middle English text, I calculated the percentage of Type C orders among those cases of 'V-SU' which contain all the necessary elements for potentially giving rise to Type C orders (i.e. cases which contain at least one non-heavy adjunct following the finite verb). I then calculated the average percentages for Old English, Early Middle English and Old English/Early Middle English together. The results are as follows. Among the Old English text samples, the average percentage for Type C orders among the 'V-SU' clauses containing a postverbal adjunct is 25.6%. For Early Middle English, the average percentage is 29.5% and for Old English/Early Middle English together 27.1%.

On the basis of the Old English/Early Middle English figure, we obtain the following expected and observed numbers of Type C orders in the Benet text.[15]

TABLE 5.5. *Expected and observed occurrences of Type C in St Benet based on V-SU clauses containing a postverbal adjunct*

	Total V-SU with a postverbal adjunct	Type C
Expected	31	8.4
Observed	31	0

Although the discrepancy between the expected and the observed figures is smaller in Table 5.5 than in Table 5.4, the difference is still considerable.

In summary, the Old English and Early Middle English data studied here would lead us to expect 15 or, calculated in a more restrictive way, 8.4 examples of Type C in the Benet text (cf. Tables 5.4 and 5.5). Instead, we do not find a single instance of such an order. Although it is not possible to determine the ungrammaticality of a construction conclusively on the basis of positive evidence as found in corpus data, the difference between the expected and observed numbers of Type C is high enough to suggest that the absence of 'XP–subject' orders in the Benet text is not simply an accidental gap in the data, but that it is the result of a restriction on such orders in the grammar of the northern dialect of Middle English.

The conclusion thus is that the only Old English or Middle English text studied here which shows a clearly distinct V2 syntax (cf. Kroch and Taylor 1997) also shows a clearly distinct behaviour with respect to V-subject non-adjacency. The question that arises now is whether the two phenomena are related. In the remainder of this section, I will argue that a uniform account of the two phenomena is indeed possible on the basis of Kroch and Taylor's (1997) proposals and the assumptions made so far.

One important property of northern Middle English is that, compared to Old English and southern Middle English, it has a very impoverished verbal agreement system. The only morphological ending that remains in the Benet text is an -(e)s ending in the present tense of the second and third person singular and of the third person plural. In the past tense, no agreement distinctions are made in this text (cf. Kock 1902: xlvii §120, Haeberli 1999: 391). Kroch and Taylor (1997: 317 ff.) propose that the fact that the Benet text only exhibits V-movement to C but no V-movement to the position below C (i.e. X in structure (4)) can be

---

[15] In terms of the alternative methods of calculation discussed in notes 11 to 13, the figures would again be slightly different. First, if we use percentages based on the total numbers of Old English and Early Middle English examples rather than average percentages (cf. notes 11 and 12), the expected number of occurrences of Type C in Benet would be slightly lower, namely 7.6. However, if only V-to-C movement contexts are taken into account in the Old English/Early Middle English text samples (cf. note 13), the expected number would be 9.4.

related to the impoverished agreement system of the northern dialect. Such a correlation is possible under the assumption that the lower V-fronting position in Old English (i.e. X) is AgrS and that weak agreement does not trigger V-movement to AgrS any more. As a consequence, V-fronting can only be obtained through V-movement to C in the northern dialect. This dialect therefore does not exhibit the characteristic properties of Old English illustrated in (1) to (4) because these properties depend on the availability of two landing sites for V-fronting.

I will pursue Kroch and Taylor's (1997) proposal here, but I will adapt it to Thráinsson's (1996) system according to which impoverishment or absence of verbal agreement can mean the absence of the AgrSP level (cf. also Bobaljik 1995, Bobaljik and Thráinsson 1998). Assuming again that XP in (4) corresponds to AgrSP, the absence of AgrSP means that one of the two V-fronting options found in Old English have disappeared from the syntax of the northern dialect, in line with Kroch and Taylor's (1997) analysis. However, the absence of AgrSP also has a second consequence. Reconsider first the structure (4) (repeated in (24a)) and the same structure in (24b) under the assumption that XP is AgrSP and hence that YP is presumably TP (cf. also e.g. Bobaljik and Jonas 1996 for analysing AgrSP and TP as distinct subject positions).

(24) (a) $[_{CP}$ C $[_{XP}$ SU$_1$ (+ pro) X $[_{YP}$ SU$_2$ (– pro) . . .]]]
     (b) $[_{CP}$ C $[_{AgrSP}$ SU$_1$ (+ pro) X $[_{TP}$ SU$_2$ (– pro) . . .]]]

Recall furthermore that I have been assuming that 'XP–subject' orders occur when the subject occurs in the lower one of the two subject positions in (24) (cf. examples (8) and (18)). What is crucial now is that once AgrSP disappears, we also lose a subject position. The lower subject position in (24) therefore becomes the highest subject position and, assuming still that adjunction is restricted (cf. §5.2.1), this position then becomes a position which is adjacent to V.

The change described above is illustrated in (25).

(25) (a) $[_{CP}$ ZP V $[_{AgrSP}$ SU$_1$ V $[_{TP}$ SU$_2$ . . .]]]
                                           (*Old English/Middle English* (*South*))
   ⇒ (b) $[_{CP}$ ZP V $[_{TP}$ SU . . .]]]   (*Middle English* (*North*))

Once AgrSP is lost in the North, we not only lose a position for V-fronting but we also lose the higher subject position. V-fronting therefore has to target C and the subject in TP is now adjacent to V in C.

The phenomenon of V-subject (non-)adjacency and in particular its development within Middle English thus provides evidence for the analysis of issues (5 I) and (5 II), i.e. for the question of what the nature of the projections below CP is in the structure in (4) (i.e. (24a)). By identifying XP as AgrSP and YP as TP, the specific syntactic properties of the northern dialect can be directly linked to its morphological properties, and the contrast to Old English and southern Middle English can be accounted for.

One additional point remains to be addressed, however. V-subject adjacency in (25*b*) means that FP, which occurs above TP and hosts adjuncts (cf. (8*a*) or (18)), has to disappear together with AgrSP. I propose that this result can be obtained in terms of an analysis of AgrSP as a 'proxy category' (cf. Nash and Rouveret 1997), i.e. a category which has no features of its own but is created in the course of a derivation for the purposes of feature checking. More precisely, I propose that FP in (8*a*) or (18) is a proxy category which is created for AgrS checking but which can be occupied 'parasitically' by an adjunct due to the lack of intrinsic features of proxy categories. Hence, once no AgrS checking is necessary, no proxy categories above TP get created, and FP therefore disappears together with AgrSP (cf. Haeberli 1999: chapter 4 for a more detailed discussion of this point).

5.5. SUMMARY

In this chapter, I have considered the status of Old English and Middle English with respect to a word-order pattern which gives rise to considerable variation among the Modern Germanic V2 languages, i.e. the occurrence of adjuncts between a fronted finite verb and a subject ('XP–subject'). I showed that Old English and southern Early Middle English allow 'XP–subject' orders regardless of the position to which the finite verb moves. The northern dialect of Middle English, however, seems to be more restrictive in this respect, and 'XP–subject' orders cannot be found in this dialect. This dialect variation coincides with a dialect variation identified by Kroch and Taylor (1997) with respect to the syntax of V2.

I have argued that the data related to V-subject (non-)adjacency provide evidence for several theoretical issues related to the analysis of Old English and to the more general structural analysis of adjuncts in pre-subject position. First, I argued that the absence of 'XP–subject' orders with pronominal subjects can be used as an argument in favour of analysing topics as occupying a position in the CP-domain in Old English rather than a position in the inflectional domain, as has sometimes been proposed for symmetric V2 languages such as Icelandic or Yiddish. And secondly, on the basis of the dialect variation in Middle English, I proposed that the projection below CP in Old English and southern Early Middle English should be identified as AgrSP, because such a clause structure allows us to relate the peculiar syntactic properties of the northern dialect of Middle English directly to the impoverished agreement morphology in this dialect. Finally, the Old English data also provided evidence for the analysis of pre-subject adjuncts as occupying a specifier position of an independent projection, and I showed that this type of evidence can only be obtained from Old English but not from the Modern Germanic languages. Hence, a comparative study of V-subject (non-)adjacency in the history of English not only provides evidence for the analysis of Old English, but also contributes to a better understanding of a more general word-order phenomenon found in the Germanic languages.

6

Verb–Object Order in Early Middle English

ANTHONY KROCH and ANN TAYLOR

6.1. INTRODUCTION

In the standard account (Canale 1978, van Kemenade 1987, Lightfoot 1991), there is a sharp divide in word order between Old and Middle English. Old English is INFL-final and OV while Middle English is INFL-medial and VO. Indeed, Lightfoot gives an account of the transition from Old to Middle English based on a catastrophic reanalysis in the twelfth century (Lightfoot 1991, 1999) and, viewed from a certain distance, this story has considerable plausibility. Thus, up until the entry for 1122 CE, the syntax of the Peterborough version of the *Anglo-Saxon Chronicle*, the manuscript which extends furthest into the twelfth century, is that of standard literary Old English. The brief continuations, which end in 1154, are hard to interpret but are not revolutionary in their syntax. These are the last documents of Old English. Then in the first quarter of the next century, several prose texts of West Midlands provenance appear, the *Ancrene Riwle* and the Katherine Group of saints' lives, whose word order is considerably more modern. INFL-final word order seems absent and surface OV word order becomes a minority pattern. Nevertheless, there is reason to doubt the standard account. Pintzuk (1991, 1993, 1995) has shown that the transition from INFL-final to INFL-medial word order was a long-term trend characterizing the entire Old English period, so that its disappearance in Early Middle English can be taken as a continuation of Old English development rather than a break with it, though the paucity of material in the twelfth century has made it difficult to tell whether this is the case. Moreover, recent work by Haeberli (1999), W. Koopman (1990), and Pintzuk (1997) has uncovered evidence that underlying VO word order already occurs in late Old English texts, further suggesting continuity

We would like to thank the following colleagues and friends for much helpful discussion and for their own work on the issues we tackle in this chapter: Robin Clark, Eric Haeberli, Chunghye Han, Johannes Gísli Jónsson, Ans van Kemenade, Paul Kiparsky, Willem Koopman, David Lightfoot, Susan Pintzuk, Don Ringe, Eiríkur Rögnvaldsson, Beatrice Santorini, Carola Trips, Sten Vikner, Anthony Warner, Alexander Williams, and Wim van der Wurff. Thanks also to Beth Randall for CorpusSearch, the search utility that makes the PPCME2 usable.

between Old and Middle English. In this chapter, we will present additional evidence, derived from the grammatical and statistical analysis of five Early Middle English texts, for such continuity. Specifically, we will show that these texts exhibit all three of the base orders that have been proposed for Old English: INFL-final with an OV verb phrase, INFL-medial with an OV verb phrase, and the modern order—INFL-medial with a VO verb phrase. In addition, we will give evidence for the leftward scrambling of complement noun phrases and we will show that although there are quantitative differences between the texts of the two dialect areas from which our texts come (the South-east and the West Midlands), the range of possibilities in the two dialects is the same. From this, we conclude that the more innovative West Midlands texts are further along in the transition from Old to Modern English syntax than the more conservative South-east Midlands ones but that both dialects are following the same trajectory. This conclusion represents a change in emphasis from our views of the relationship among the Early Middle English texts in earlier, unpublished work (Kroch and Taylor 1994*a*). In the earlier work, we emphasized the differences between the South-east Midlands and West Midlands texts, claiming that the former were essentially INFL-medial and OV while the latter were essentially INFL-medial and VO. Under our present view, the differences between the texts do not justify drawing a sharp distinction between the grammars of the texts from the two groups. Rather the differences are of frequency in the use of the available options.

6.1.1. *Structural assumptions and notational conventions*

For the purposes of this discussion, we will adopt the phrase structure of *Barriers* (Chomsky 1986*a*); that is, the structure of the clause will be assumed to follow the schema in (1).

(1)

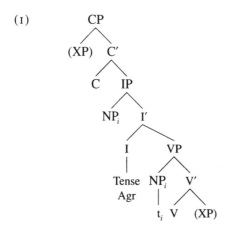

We will further assume that INFL-final IPs and verb-final VPs differ from their head-initial counterparts only in linear order and not in structure. In other words, we are adopting neither the 'exploded INFL' hypothesis of Pollock (1989) nor the 'antisymmetry' hypothesis of Kayne (1994). We want to emphasize, however, that in making these notational decisions, we are not expressing a theoretical commitment but simply adopting the minimally complex structural descriptions needed for our purposes in this chapter. Indeed, other work (for example, Han in this volume) gives evidence for an exploded INFL in Middle English, and further investigation may show the antisymmetry hypothesis to be useful in the analysis of the language. We hope to explore this latter possibility in future work, but the results we report here do not bear on the question.

We assume that the tensed verb, in both matrix declarative and tensed subordinate clauses, is located in INFL rather than in COMP. Here we follow Pintzuk's (1991, 1993) analysis of Old English and our own previous work (Kroch and Taylor 1997). The crucial point for current purposes is that in Early Middle English INFL-medial clauses, scrambled pronouns commonly appear between the XP in first position and the tensed verb, as they do in Old English. Most often, of course, this initial XP is the subject of the clause, especially in subordinate clauses; but since Middle English is a verb-second language, it may also be a topic. The two possibilities are illustrated by the italicized pronouns in the following examples.

(2) (a)   ac ȝif min lauerd godd *me* wolde swingen mid ani swinge . . .
           but if my Lord God me would scourge with any scourge
           'but if my Lord God would scourge me with any scourge'
                (CMVICES1,13.145)

   (b)   &   swuch swettnesse *þu*   schalt ifinden in his luue &   in his seruise
          and such   sweetness thou shalt find   in his love and in his service
          'And such sweetness thou shalt find in his love and in his service.'
               (CMHALI,131.48)

   (c)   hwat so we beseceð at gode, *he us* wile sone teiþin
          what so we beseech at God he us will soon grant
          'Whatever we ask of God, he will soon grant us.'
               (CMVICES1,141.1746)

It is not clear what position the scrambled pronouns occupy in these examples and we will not pursue the question here. It is sufficient for our purposes that the pronouns are to the left of INFL and so must have moved out of VP.

The single most prominent issue in the syntax of Early Middle English is that of the transition from OV to VO word order, and this chapter is largely devoted to illuminating the problem. The primary descriptive difficulty we face is the high degree of structural ambiguity present in Middle English. To begin with, clauses with a single tensed verb, the most common clause type, generally tell us little about underlying order. As we will see, Early Middle English texts, though they contain a remnant of INFL-final word order, are overwhelmingly INFL-medial in both main and subordinate clauses; and, as is well known, verb-raising to INFL is categorical in the language. It follows, therefore, that if an Early Middle English clause contains only a single tensed verb, we cannot determine whether its verb phrase is head-initial or head-final. The verb, having moved to INFL, will in any case precede its complements. Hence, we will analyse primarily clauses that contain both an auxiliary and a main verb. In such cases, we can assume that the main verb is in its underlying position and we can, therefore, hope to determine the direction of VP-headedness from these cases. Still, there are further complicating factors that must be controlled for. We know that Old English allowed both leftward scrambling and rightward extraposition of complements and adjuncts (van Kemenade 1987, Pintzuk and Kroch 1989) and these movements obscure underlying order even in the absence of verb movement (Pintzuk 1991). Only to the extent that such movements are subject to observable constraints limiting their application will we be able to work out the underlying structure of the VP. As we will see, these constraints are quite complex; and in order to keep our study within manageable bounds, we limit the discussion presented here largely to the cases of noun phrase and pronoun complements, leaving to future work the study of the behaviour of prepositional phrases and adverbs, whose positional licensing follows quite different principles.

Schematically, an INFL-medial clause can be divided into three regions: the region to the left of the tensed verb, the region between the tensed and the untensed verb, and the region to the right of the untensed verb. We will refer to these regions as the PRE-INFL, the POST-INFL, and the POST-VERB regions, respectively, as indicated by the XPs in the following schema.

(3) $\ldots \text{XP}_1 \ldots \text{I}^0 \ldots \text{XP}_2 \ldots \text{V}^0 \ldots \text{XP}_3 \ldots$

Unsurprisingly, our three regions correspond directly to the 'Vorfeld', 'Mittelfeld', and 'Nachfeld' into which German verb-second clauses have traditionally been divided. Unlike traditional grammarians, however, we will not be satisfied to note or tabulate the occurrences of constituents in the three surface positions of the schema. Rather we will be looking for grammatical patterns in the sorts of constituents that can occur in each of the positions, with the aim of using these patterns to work out the underlying structures and transformational movements that give rise to the observed surface word orders.

6.1.2. *The texts*

Our analysis will be based primarily on five Early Middle English prose texts from the early thirteenth century. Three are from the West Midlands area and two from the South-east Midlands. The three texts from the West Midlands are the *Lambeth Homilies* (MS Lambeth 487), the *Ancrene Riwle* (MS Cotton Cleopatra C vi) and the Katherine Group (MS Bodley 34), which is comprised of five short texts: *Hali Meiðhad, St Julian, St Katherine, St Margaret,* and the *Sawles Warde.* The latter two manuscripts date to the first quarter of the thirteenth century and seem to be copies of originals written not many years earlier. The manuscript of the *Lambeth Homilies* is copied from two exemplars with different orthographies, both of the twelfth century but one probably earlier than the other (Sisam 1951). The earlier exemplar is a compilation of older documents from the eleventh century which have been transliterated into Middle English. Homilies ix and x are transliterations of two of Ælfric's homilies of the same title. Homily xi includes a passage from Ælfric (pp. 121–2 in Morris's edition (Morris 1969)), and Homily ii includes most of Wulfstan's *Be Godcundre Warnunge.* The source of the remainder is unknown. The other exemplar, in Sisam's view, did not contain any Old English material. Five of the *Lambeth Homilies* also appear in the *Trinity Homilies.* The Katherine Group is written in the AB language centred on the border of Herefordshire and Shropshire (Tolkien 1929, Dobson 1972, 1976). The Corpus manuscript of the *Ancrene Wisse* (MS Corpus Christi College, Cambridge, 402) is also in this dialect. The Cleopatra manuscript, which we use here, is, according to Dobson, from the eastern periphery of the AB area, perhaps Worcestershire. While there are differences in orthography and morphology between the two manuscripts, the syntax is very similar. The *Lambeth Homilies* have been localized to the same West Midlands area by M. L. Samuels (quoted in Laing 1993).

The South-east Midlands texts are the *Trinity Homilies,* a series of homilies found in MS Trinity 335 (B.14.52) (Trinity College, Cambridge) and *Vices and Virtues,* a dialogue found only in MS Stowe 34 (British Library). The manuscript is dated to 1200–25, but according to Utley (1972) the date of composition is perhaps as early as 1175. The general conservatism of the text and inclusion of Old English forms is considered by Hall (1920), however, to indicate a scribe versed in the older language rather than an Old English exemplar. The *Trinity Homilies* manuscript dates from before 1225 and may be based on Old English exemplars. Four of the five *Trinity Homilies* that also appear in the Lambeth manuscript, however, are from the part of Lambeth based on the later, non-Old English exemplar (see above). Samuels (again quoted in Laing 1993) considers the language of *Vices and Virtues* representative of Essex, while the language of the *Trinity Homilies* is London 'influenced by immigration, perhaps from East Anglia' (Samuels quoted in Hill 1977).

The data in this chapter are drawn from the texts of these works as they appear in the second edition of the Penn–Helsinki Parsed Corpus of Middle English (PPCME2) (Kroch and Taylor 2000). Examples cited from the corpus are identified with a decimal number, the integral part giving the page in the book from which the sample comes and the decimal part giving the token number assigned to the example in the electronic corpus. The current edition of the corpus contains exhaustive samples of all of the texts except the *Ancrene Riwle,* from which a 50,000-word sample was drawn. Sample sizes are as follows:

Ancrene Riwle: 50,926 words, 3,560 sentences
Katherine Group: 38,445 words, 2,539 sentences
Lambeth Homilies (E): 20,882 words, 1,409 sentences
Lambeth Homilies (L): 6,549 words, 525 sentences
Trinity Homilies: 41,874 words, 3,075 sentences
Vices and Virtues: 28,358 words, 1,894 sentences

6.2. INFL-FINAL WORD ORDER IN EARLY MIDDLE ENGLISH

It is sometimes thought that INFL-final word order had disappeared entirely from English by the beginning of the Middle English period, but this is an oversimplification. A small number of INFL-final clauses can be found in all our Early Middle English texts.[1]

As in Old English, the INFL-final clauses in our corpus come in two variants, one in which the tensed auxiliary follows a non-finite main verb (the German order), as in (4),

(4) (*a*)   er þanne þe heuene oðer eorðe *shapen were*
         before   that heaven or   earth created were
         'before heaven and earth were created'
         (CMTRINIT,133.1776)

    (*b*)   for ði   ðat godd *isæd hadde* to Adame: Morte morieris!
         because that God said had   to Adam Morte morieris
         'because God had said to Adam "Morte morieris!"'
         (CMVICES1,105.1276)

and one in which the tensed auxiliary precedes the untensed verb (the Dutch or verb-raising order) as in (5).

(5) (*a*)   þat þurh   soð scrifte synnes *ben forgeuene*
         that through true shrift sins   are forgiven
         'that through true shrift sins are forgiven'
         (CMTRINIT,23.304)

    (*b*)   þen ei wel itohe   muð for scheome *mahe seggen*
         than any well disciplined mouth for shame   may say
         'than any well-disciplined mouth for shame may say'
         (CMHALI,146.262)

Although INFL-final word order was already very rare in main clauses by the

---

[1] It is not clear whether these cases are imitations or copies of Old English or low-frequency but productive forms of Middle English. For our purposes, it is not necessary to distinguish these possibilities since the same can be said for every other clause in the corpus. Our first goal must be to characterize the corpus accurately as a step towards understanding the underlying linguistic competence of the texts' authors.

late Old English period (Pintzuk 1996a: 247), we still find one such case in our
most archaic text, *Vices and Virtues*, which we give in (6).

(6)   Ne   dieuel ne mann none mihte ne none strengþe *habben ne*
         neither devil nor man no   power nor no   strength have   NEG
         muӡen ouer oðren, bute . . .
         may   over others, except . . .
         'Neither devil nor man may have power or strength over others,
         except . . .' (CMVICES1,107.1292)

In evaluating the distance between Old and Middle English syntax, it would
be useful to have a quantitative estimate of the frequency of INFL-final word
order. Such an estimate can be constructed for the subordinate-clause context,
where the number of examples, though low, is not vanishingly small, as it is in
the main-clause context. Column 1 of Table 6.1 gives the number of superficially
INFL-final subordinate clauses in our texts.

TABLE 6.1. *Subordinate INFL-final clauses with an auxiliary verb*

	Surface INFL-final	Subject gap cases removed	Pronoun subjects removed	Number of subordinate clauses	% necessarily INFL-final
Ancrene Riwle	12	10	3	560	0.5%
Katherine Group	54	41	3	416	0.7%
Lambeth Homilies (L)	11	11	1	98	1.0%
Lambeth Homilies (E)	26	23	10	275	3.5%
Trinity Homilies	65	55	10	362	2.7%
Vices and Virtues	44	31	13	487	2.6%
TOTAL	212	171	40	2,198	1.8%

This number, however, cannot be used directly to estimate the frequency of
INFL-final word order because superficially INFL-final clauses often have another possible analysis; that is, they can also be analysed as instances of stylistic
fronting of the main verb. In a stylistic fronting clause, a participle, infinitive,[2]
or adverb is moved to the position immediately before the tensed verb. This
order is possible only when the subject does not occupy its canonical preverbal
position (the so-called 'subject gap' condition, Maling 1990). When the stylistically fronted element is the untensed verb of a clause with a single auxiliary, the
resultant string word order is not distinguishable from INFL-final order. Among

---

[2] The fronting of infinitives is not as much discussed in the literature on stylistic fronting as the
fronting of participles, but it is possible in both Old and Modern Icelandic (Eiríkur Rögnvaldsson,
personal communication). However, the stylistic fronting of infinitives is limited to cases where the
infinitival marker *að*, more or less equivalent to English infinitival *to*, is absent (see Jónsson 1991
and the references cited there). In Early Middle English, *to*-less infinitives are common and appear
to behave just like participles with respect to stylistic fronting.

the modern North Germanic languages, stylistic fronting is found only in Icelandic, but it was found in all of the attested medieval Scandinavian dialects. An
example from Icelandic is given in (7).

(7)   Honum mætti standa á   sama, hvað *sagt* væri um   hann
        him   might stand on same what said was about him
        'It might be all the same to him what was said about him.'
        (Example (5) in Maling 1990)

Although stylistic fronting is characteristic of North rather than West Germanic, the possibility that apparently INFL-final clauses are actually instances of
stylistic fronting cannot be ignored in Middle English texts, due to the substantial
Scandinavian influence on English that resulted from the Viking invasions and
settlements of the ninth and tenth centuries. Trips (1999) gives evidence that
stylistic fronting occurred in the Ormulum, a late twelfth-century northern poetic
text with a considerable Scandinavian element in its vocabulary and other signs
of Scandinavian influence. This result considerably increases the likelihood that
stylistic fronting occurred generally in Early Middle English and makes it clear
that we cannot take the surface word-order numbers in Table 6.1 at face value.
Indeed, there are a certain number of examples in our texts, many of them in the
Vices text, that are clear instances of stylistic fronting. These are clauses with
an INFL-medial tensed auxiliary, a following non-finite verb, and a subject gap,
in which a third non-finite main verb or the adjectival complement of a verb
appears before the tensed auxiliary, as in the following example.

(8)   auriche manne ðe *i-boreȝen* scal bien
        every   man   that saved   shall be
        'every man who shall be saved'   (CMVICES1,63.695)

We have found five such examples in the *Vices* text and one in the *Ancrene
Riwle*. The case for treating these clauses as instances of stylistic fronting is
strengthened by the fact that neither *Vices* nor the other texts contain any instance of such fronting in the clear absence of a subject gap. The *Vices* text also
contains the following example, in which the negative adverb *noht* appears before the tensed auxiliary and its following main verb. This is another common
type of stylistic fronting in Scandinavian.[3]

(9)   and he besohte at gode þat *naht* ne   scolde reinin
        and he sought of God that not NEG should rain . . .
        'And he asked of God that it should not rain.'
        (CMVICES1,143.1787)

---

[3] There is one sort of stylistic fronting in Icelandic that we have not attempted to find in our Early
Middle English texts; that is, the fronting of adverbs. Because adverb placement is very variable in
English, we have not so far found it possible to define contexts where the stylistic fronting of ad-
verbs can be unambiguously identified.

Platzack (1988) argues that in Medieval Scandinavian stylistic fronting was not limited to clauses with subject gaps of the modern Icelandic type. In particular, he claims that Medieval Swedish texts exhibit stylistic fronting in subordinate clauses with pronoun subjects. According to Platzack, this was possible because the subject pronoun could cliticize onto the complementizer to its left, leaving a gap to license stylistic fronting.[4] The same environment appears to license stylistic fronting in Early Middle English. The following clauses exhibit the fronting of adjectives and negation with pronoun subjects in the same syntactic contexts as the previous examples with undoubted subject gaps.

(10) (*a*)   þah   ich *cwic* beo forbearnd baðe lim & lið
            though I   alive be burned   both limb and joint
            'though I be entirely burned alive'
                (CMJULIA,99.62)

(*b*)   ha *nawhit* ne   þearf of oðer þing þenchen
        she not   NEG   must of other thing think
        'She must not think of anything else.'
            (CMHALI,130.32)

We have found four such examples in our texts, two with fronted adjectives and two with fronted *not*. None of the pronoun subject examples with two verbs and a third fronted element involves participle fronting.

   Given the strong possibility that English borrowed the stylistic fronting construction from Scandinavian, we cannot be sure that Early Middle English examples like those in (11) are structurally INFL-final.

(11) (*a*)   Cumeð children, ðe *liernien* willeð
            come children that learn   will
            'Come children who want to learn.'
                (CMVICES1,59.653)

---

[4] We should note that Falk (1993*a*) argues against Platzack's extension of stylistic fronting to clauses with pronoun subjects in Medieval Swedish. She gives two grounds for doubting Platzack's proposal. First, the surface word order of stylistic fronting examples with fronted adverbs is not distinguishable from that of clauses in which V-to-I raising has failed to apply; and second, the surface word order of examples with fronted non-finite verbs is not distinguishable from INFL-final word order. Hence, she believes that there is no convincing evidence for the existence of stylistic fronting in clauses with pronoun subjects. In our opinion, however, the Early Middle English facts undermine both of Falk's arguments against Platzack. Firstly, perhaps unlike Medieval Scandinavian, Early Middle English is clearly a categorical V-to-I raising language, so that the potential ambiguity with adverbs is not relevant in the English case. Secondly, the quantitative analysis we present below argues against treating as INFL-final all of the clauses with pronoun subjects that are ambiguously cases of INFL-final order or stylistic fronting.

(b) & hef hire heorte up to þe hehe healant þe *iheret* is in
and raised her heart up to the high saviour that praised is in
heouene
heaven
'And [she] raised her heart up to the high saviour who praised is in
heaven.' (CMKATHE,21.43)

If all subject-gap clauses with surface INFL-final word order are removed from
consideration, the result is Column 2 in Table 6.1. If, following Platzack's analysis, we count clauses with pronoun subjects as potential stylistic fronting contexts
and remove them from our data, we are left with very few cases of necessarily
INFL-final word order. The numbers of these remaining instances are given in
the third column of Table 6.1.[5] These remaining examples have either an NP
subject, as in (12a), or an empty/pronoun subject and a heavy constituent before
the untensed verb, as in (12b–c).

(12) (a) er þanne þe *heuene oðer eorðe* shapen were
before that heaven or earth created were
'before heaven or earth were created'
     (CMTRINIT,133.1776)

(b) ʒef ʒe þus *godes heste*   halden wulleð
if you thus God's commandment keep will
'if you will thus keep God's commandment'
     (CMANCRIW,II.141.1889)

(c) þe on þisse liue her *hare scrift* enden   nalden
that in this life here their shrift complete NEG-would
'who in this life here would not complete their shrift'
     (CMLAMBX1,43.544)

Note that the frequency of INFL-final word order we are left with does not
directly give an estimate of the frequency of such clauses. We have no way of
knowing, at least at present, how many of the possible cases of stylistic fronting
are actual instances of that construction. The fewer the cases of stylistic fronting,
the higher the frequency of INFL-final word order. If, contrary to appearances,
stylistic fronting was not borrowed into Middle English at all or occurred at a
very low rate, then the average frequency of INFL-final word order in our texts
would be on the order of 10%, about five times higher than the frequency of

[5] To obtain the figures in column 3 of Table 6.1 we removed all examples where no heavy element intervenes between the complementizer and the untensed verb. Pronouns and light adverbs in
that position are treated as potential clitics on COMP and so as compatible with stylistic fronting of
the untensed verb. A pronoun is defined as a single, unmodified personal pronoun, and a light adverb
as a one-syllable adverb or *ever/never* in any form.

necessarily INFL-final cases. This would imply a much greater continuity with Old English than is generally assumed; and in our opinion, it is implausibly high, especially for the West Midlands texts, whose syntax is otherwise quite modern.

We can find another sort of necessarily INFL-final example in our data among those subordinate clauses with only a single tensed verb. Here we follow Pintzuk (1991) and take any clause in which the tensed verb is preceded by at least two heavy constituents to reflect underlying INFL-final word order. Examples are given in (13).

(13) (*a*)   and wel þeaʒh þanne þat folc godes word ʒierneliche listede
            and well throve when that folk God's word earnestly   heard
            'and [it] throve well when that folk earnestly heard God's word'
            (CMTRINIT,163.2185)

      (*b*)   hwen ameiden ure muchele ouergant þus auealleð
             when a-maiden our great   arrogance thus casts-down
             'when a maiden thus casts down our great arrogance'
             (CMMARGA,81.408)

The frequency of such INFL-final cases is given in Table 6.2, which includes all subordinate clauses with a transitive verb in which one of the heavy constituents before the verb is the object.

TABLE 6.2. *Subordinate INFL-final clauses with one transitive verb*

	Number INFL-final	Number of subordinate clauses	% necessarily INFL-final
Ancrene Riwle	10	514	1.9%
Katherine Group	11	278	3.9%
Lambeth Homilies (L)	6	152	3.9%
Lambeth Homilies (E)	11	232	4.7%
Trinity Homilies	27	569	4.7%
Vices and Virtues	23	393	5.9%
TOTAL	88	2,138	4.1%

The frequencies obtained by this method are, on average, about twice as high as those in Table 6.1, but are still quite low. Once again, the total against which the necessarily INFL-final cases are being compared contains an unknown number of ambiguous clauses,[6] so that we cannot consider the frequency calculated here to be an unbiased estimate of the frequency of INFL-final word order either. As with the frequencies in Table 6.1, the frequencies in Table 6.2 are only a lower bound. There is no reason, moreover, to expect the size of the underestimate here to be the same as in Table 6.1.

---

[6] All SVO clauses are ambiguous since underlyingly they could be either SVO or INFL-final with extraposition of the object.

We can obtain an unbiased estimate of the rate of INFL-final word order at the expense of reducing our sample size (hence increasing sampling error) if we consider only clauses with a full NP subject in preverbal position and an auxiliary verb. In such clauses, illustrated in (14), surface word order is a sure guide to underlying order, given our structural assumptions. Because a full NP subject cannot be a clitic on COMP, these clauses cannot be cases of stylistic fronting.

(14)   þt neauer mi sawle ne   isuled beo in sunne
       that never my soul NEG defiled be in sin
       'that my soul may never be defiled in sin'
          (CMMARGA,57.36)

Table 6.3 gives the results for these data. The numbers are, as expected, somewhat higher than the uncorrected ones in Table 6.1, which are also based on clauses with auxiliary verbs. The fact that this unbiased estimate is lower than the frequencies in Table 6.2 is unexpected, but the unbiased subsample is so small that the differences between the frequencies based on it and the other two calculations are not statistically significant.

TABLE 6.3. *Subordinate INFL-final clauses with an NP subject and auxiliary verb*

	Number INFL-final	Number of subordinate clauses	% INFL-final (unbiased)
Ancrene Riwle	I	95	1.1%
Katherine Group	I	84	1.2%
Lambeth Homilies (L)	I	26	3.8%
Lambeth Homilies (E)	I	60	1.7%
Trinity Homilies	6	76	7.9%
Vices and Virtues	3	84	3.6%
TOTAL	13	425	3.1%

Three conclusions can be drawn from the data on INFL-final word order in the texts. First, all of the texts contain some INFL-final clauses. Second, the South-east Midlands texts exhibit more INFL-final word order on every measure than do the West Midlands texts, indicating that the South-eastern dialect was syntactically more conservative than the West Midlands one, a conclusion that will be reinforced as we examine more data. Because the rate of INFL-final word order is very low, it can be treated as a non-productive remnant of Old English. On the other hand, the fact that the word order occurs even in the West Midlands texts, which are known not to be derived from Old English originals, suggests that INFL-final word order was still somewhat productive in the writing practices of the Early Middle English period. Third, in addition to the specific examples we have cited from the texts, we have quantitative evidence that Early

Middle English allowed stylistic fronting. We noted above that if we assume the contrary, the rate of INFL-final word order is implausibly high. We can also give a more precise quantitative argument. Consider the data in Table 6.4. We can see from the last row in this table that our small unbiased subsample of subordinate clauses with auxiliary verbs shows somewhat less than twice as much INFL-final word order as there are necessarily INFL-final clauses in the whole sample (3.1% vs. 1.8%). This means that some of the clauses that are ambiguous between INFL-final word order and stylistic fronting are likely to be INFL-final. If, however, we suppose that *all* of the ambiguous cases are INFL-final (that is, there is no stylistic fronting), then the rate of INFL-final is 9.6% and the unbiased estimate (3.1%) is three times too low, an unlikely result ($p < .001$).

TABLE 6.4. *Estimates of INFL-final order in clauses with auxiliary verbs*

	% INFL-final unbiased	% necessarily INFL-final	Ratio unbiased/ necessarily	% surface INFL-final	Ratio surface/ unbiased
Ancrene Riwle	1.1%	0.5%	2.20	2.1%	1.91
Katherine Group	1.2%	0.7%	1.71	13.0%	10.8
Lambeth Homilies (L)	3.8%	1.0%	3.80	11.2%	2.95
Lambeth Homilies (E)	1.7%	3.5%	0.486	9.5%	5.59
Trinity Homilies	7.9%	2.7%	2.93	18.0%	2.28
Vices and Virtues	3.6%	2.6%	1.38	9.0%	2.50
ALL DATA	3.1%	1.8%	1.72	9.6%	3.1

6.3. VO WORD ORDER IN EARLY MIDDLE ENGLISH

6.3.1. *Diagnostic environments for VO phrase structure*

There is considerable superficial VO word order in all Early Middle English texts; but, as we have mentioned, the existence of rightward extraposition processes in Germanic, including Old English, renders surface VO word order unreliable as a guide to underlying position. There are instances of surface VO order, however, where extraposition is grammatically excluded, so that surface and underlying order should coincide. In general, prosodically light elements do not extrapose to the right in West Germanic; and in clauses with auxiliaries, we can conclude from the presence of such a light element following the untensed verb that the underlying word order of the clause is VO. We have found three types of light elements that can be used as word-order diagnostics in this way: pronouns, verbal particles, and stranded prepositions.

The examples in (15) illustrate that in INFL-medial clauses with auxiliary verbs in our texts, pronouns are found in all three of the regions defined by verb position: PRE-INFL, POST-INFL, and POST-VERB.

(15) (*a*) Halie alde ancres   *hit* maȝe don summes weis
        holy old anchoresses it may do some   ways
        'Holy old anchoresses may do it in a certain way.'
        (CMANCRIW,II.58.565)

(*b*) Sara þu   hauest *me* ouercumen
      Sarah thou hast   me overcome
      'Sarah, thou·hast overcome me.'
      (CMANCRIW,II.173.2409)

(*c*) oðet he habbe iȝetted *ou* al þet ȝe wulleð
      until he has   granted you all that you desire
      'until he has granted you all that you desire'
      (CMANCRIW,I.68.229)

When the pronoun occurs to the right of the untensed verb, as in (15*c*), we have evidence for underlying VO word order.[7] It is necessary for the clause to contain an auxiliary verb, of course, because in clauses without an auxiliary the word order finite verb > pronoun is ambiguous between an underlying postverbal pronoun and underlying post-INFL pronoun with verb movement to INFL. Table 6.5 shows that by the pronoun position diagnostic all the texts have some VO order, but the West Midlands texts appear to be considerably more VO than the Southeastern ones. The Lambeth text is an exception to this generalization and we will return to the significance of its behaviour below (see §6.4.2). Because the larger part of the *Lambeth Homilies* is apparently derived from an eleventh-century original (see §6.1.2 above) and because the homilies are to some extent based on Old English originals, we do not include the data from it in our West Midlands totals. The designation 'Total West Midlands' in the table below and in subsequent tables, therefore, is an abbreviation for the totals from the locally composed twelfth-century West Midlands works—the *Ancrene Riwle* and Katherine Group manuscripts.

Our second diagnostic for VO word order is the position of particles, which like pronouns are light elements and therefore do not move rightwards. Again we must examine clauses with an auxiliary verb to avoid the interfering effect of verb movement to INFL. Table 6.6 gives the distribution of particles in our texts. Particles do not generally appear in the pre-INFL position, with the following single exception from the *Vices* text.

(16)   þat non godes word *upp* ne   mai springen
      that no god's word up NEG may spring
      'that no word of God's may spring up'
      (CMVICES1,69.778)

---

[7] Since the failure of pronouns to extrapose is a consequence of their prosodic weakness, they should be extraposable when stressed. We are ignoring this possibility because the frequency in texts of pronouns whose discourse function (primarily contrast) would support stress is very low.

TABLE 6.5. *Position of pronouns in clauses with an auxiliary verb*

		Pre-I	Post-I	Post-V	% Post-V
WEST MIDLANDS					
Ancrene Riwle	main	10	7	36	68%
	subordinate	23	15	36	49%
	total	33	22	72	57%
Katherine Group	main	13	10	49	68%
	subordinate	29	17	32	41%
	total	42	27	81	54%
TOTAL WEST MIDLANDS	main	23	17	85	68%
	subordinate	52	32	68	45%
	total	75	49	153	55%
Lambeth Homilies (L)	main	6	3	0	0%
	subordinate	6	1	1	13%
	total	12	4	1	6%
Lambeth Homilies (E)	main	28	15	3	7%
	subordinate	20	13	4	11%
	total	48	28	7	8%
SOUTH-EAST MIDLANDS					
Trinity Homilies	main	13	12	8	24%
	subordinate	29	14	8	16%
	total	42	26	16	19%
Vices and Virtues	main	31	11	1	2%
	subordinate	59	19	5	6%
	total	90	30	6	5%
TOTAL SOUTH-EAST MIDLANDS	main	44	23	9	12%
	subordinate	88	33	13	9%
	total	132	56	22	10%

The particle data show the same tendency and incline us to the same interpretation as the pronoun data; however, the data here are very sparse and thus not
very reliable. As is well known (Spasov 1966), verbal particles are much rarer
in Early Middle English than in either Old English or Modern English, for reasons that have yet to be elucidated. To the extent that the data are sufficient to
allow interpretation, it seems that they show the same relationship among the
dialect areas as the pronoun data. Unfortunately, the data from Lambeth are

TABLE 6.6. *Position of particles in clauses with an auxiliary verb*

DIALECT	Post-INFL	Post-VERB	% Post-VERB
West Midlands	2	12	86%
Lambeth Homilies	0	2	100%
South-east Midlands	3	1	25%

entirely too sparse for us to be able to determine how that text is behaving relative to the others in this context.

Our final diagnostic for VO order is the position of prepositions that are stranded when their objects move to the left, as illustrated in (17).

(17) hel mi blodi   saule of al þe blodi   sunnen þet ha is *wið* iwundet
     heal my bloody soul of all the bloody sins   that she is with wounded
     þurh   mine fif wittes;
     through my   five senses
     'Heal my bloody soul of all the bloody sins that it is wounded with through my five senses.'
       (CMANCRIW,I.62.202)

Leaving aside certain cases that are irrelevant for our purposes, like extraction from noun phrases, it is generally assumed that stranded prepositions, in languages that allow them, must be lexically governed by the main verb of their clause. If we further assume, as in Kayne (1984), that this government must be in the direction canonical for the language, then we will expect the pre- or postverbal position of stranded prepositions to be diagnostic of underlying verb–complement word order. Of course, if stranded prepositions can scramble to the left and/or extrapose to the right, or if they can be stranded after such movements, then their surface position will not reliably correspond to their underlying order. Consider in this light the data in Table 6.7.[8] These data, though based on many fewer cases, are similar to the pronoun data in Table 6.5. As in the earlier table, moreover, the Lambeth text here behaves like the South-eastern texts rather than like its geographical neighbours from the West Midlands, reinforcing

TABLE 6.7. *Stranded prepositions in subordinate clauses with an auxiliary*

	Pre-INFL	Post-INFL	Post-VERB	% Post-VERB
WEST MIDLANDS				
Ancrene Riwle	0	9	9	50%
Katherine Group	0	11	10	48%
TOTAL WEST MIDLANDS	0	20	19	49%
Lambeth Homilies (L)	0	3	0	0%
Lambeth Homilies (E)	0	3	1	25%
SOUTH-EAST MIDLANDS				
Trinity Homilies	(2)	10	1	8%
Vices and Virtues	(5)	1	0	0%
TOTAL SOUTH-EAST MIDLANDS	(7)	11	1	5%

[8] The data in Table 6.7 is limited to subordinate clauses because there are only two main-clause examples of preposition stranding in our dataset. This is not surprising as most of the stranded prepositions are stranded by *wh*-movement and the overwhelming majority of instances of *wh*-movement in the corpus occur in relative clauses and indirect questions.

the notion that there is a systematic difference between it and the other texts. On another point, the similarity between the stranded preposition data and the pronoun data suggests that preposition stranding in Early Middle English is incompatible with extraposition. If it were not, we would expect to find more stranded prepositions in postverbal position than pronouns, since pronouns do not extrapose. Since the frequency of postverbal stranded prepositions is, if anything, slightly lower than the frequency of postverbal pronouns, this expectation is directly contradicted. In this regard, Early Middle English seems to resemble Modern English, which also seems to disallow the combination of preposition stranding and extraposition, as illustrated in the examples in (18).

(18)   Who$_i$ did you give books to t$_i$ yesterday?
          *Who$_i$ did you give books yesterday to t$_i$?

6.3.2. *Scrambling and VO word order*

If we took the data of the three tables in §6.3.1 at face value we would be inclined to say that the West Midlands texts exhibit a robust competition between OV and VO word order while the South-east Midlands texts and the *Lambeth Homilies* are still largely OV. This conclusion would, however, be premature. Although postverbal pronouns and other light elements are diagnostic of VO word order, preverbal placement of these elements is *not* diagnostic of OV word order. The reason for this asymmetry is that, while light elements do not extrapose to the right, they are known to scramble leftwards in the Germanic languages. Hence, surface OV word order could reflect leftward scrambling from an underlyingly VO structure. We must, therefore, investigate the extent of leftward scrambling in our texts if we are to establish the true extent of VO word order.

To begin with, the frequency with which pronouns appear in the pre-INFL position, as in (2) above, tells us that pronoun scrambling was productive in Middle English. Whenever a non-subject pronoun appears to the left of an auxiliary verb, we can be sure that it has moved from its base position; and since the topic position in these cases is filled by another phrase, the movement is due either to cliticization or to scrambling, which we take to be closely related processes in Germanic. The scrambling of noun phrases to the pre-INFL position is not possible in Middle English INFL-medial clauses, perhaps on account of the verb-second constraint; but both noun phrases and pronouns can be shown to scramble leftwards when they appear to the left of a VP-adjoined adverb, as in the following examples.

(19) (*a*) þet heo ne   schal *þene stude* neauer mare changin bute for nede
            that she NEG shall the   abode never more change but for need
            ane
            alone
            'that she shall never again change her abode except when necessary'
            (CMANCRIW,I.46.52)

(*b*) þach   god ne   cunne *him* neauer þonc of his sonde
      though God NEG can   him never thank of his sending
      'though God can never thank him for sending it'
      (CMANCRIW,II.102.1233)

Such scrambling is inherited from Old English, as illustrated by the following examples of direct objects scrambling across VP-adjoined adverbs.

(20) (*a*) &   *æghwæþer operne* oftrædlice utdræfde
        and every-one other   frequently out-drove
        'and each of them frequently drove the other away'
        (CHROA2,80.10 (887); Haeberli 1999: 356, example (39*c*))

   (*b*) he sæde Bedan þæt se cyning Ecfrid *him* oft   behete   mycel on
        he said Bede that the king   Ecfrid him often promised much on
        lande and on feo
        land and on property
        'He said to Bede that King Ecfrid often promised him much land
        and property' (Ælfric, *Lives of Saints* B1.3.21)

The word order of these Old English examples is underlyingly OV and one might suppose that leftward scrambling is limited to OV structures in Germanic. The Middle English examples in (19) show that Germanic scrambling occurs in INFL-medial clauses but the examples would be consistent with a constraint limiting scrambling to underlyingly head-final verb phrases. Certainly, scrambling is common in German and Dutch, both OV languages, and impossible in Modern English, a VO language.

However, leftward scrambling is possible in some VO Germanic languages. In Modern Icelandic, clearly VO in base order, there is productive leftward scrambling of negative and quantified noun phrases (Rögnvaldsson 1987), a phenomenon we discuss in more detail below; and in modern Yiddish, generally taken to be VO in underlying order, scrambling is very productive. Thus, Yiddish pronouns, when unstressed,[9] usually, though not always, appear to the left of the untensed verb, as illustrated in (21).

(21) (*a*) Hot der yingl dos gevizn dem tatn   un hot *im* gezogt . . .
        has the boy that shown the father and has him said . . .
        'So the boy showed that to his father and said to him . . .'
            (Olsvanger 1947: 4)

   (*b*) Farvos host du *mikh* damols geshmisn?
        why   have you me   then hit
        'Why did you hit me then?' (Olsvanger 1947: 4)

---

   [9] In her corpus of Yiddish texts, Beatrice Santorini reports that focused (therefore, stressed) pronouns in Modern Yiddish normally occur in postverbal position, as expected in a VO Germanic language (Santorini, personal communication).

(*c*) Mit dem posik hot *zikh*   undzer rov   gemakht a shem.
with the   verse has REFL our   rabbi made   a name
'With that judgement, our rabbi made a name for himself.'
(Olsvanger 1947: 168)

Note that in examples (21*b*) and (21*c*) the pronoun is not only preverbal but has scrambled past another preverbal constituent. The scrambling of noun phrases is also possible in Yiddish, though much less frequent. The examples in (22) illustrate this possibility.

(22) (*a*)   Un er ken *di mayse* beser dertseyln.
and he can the story   better tell
'And he can tell the story better.'
(Olsvanger 1947: 3)

      (*b*)   Men zol   *dem yidn* araynlozn tsun im.
one   should the Jew in-let   to   him
'They should let the Jew see him.'
(Olsvanger 1947: 75)

Given the widespread occurrence of leftward scrambling in Germanic and the fact that it seems to occur in VO languages, the Early Middle English data we have seen so far can only be interpreted as giving a lower bound on the amount of underlying VO word order in the texts. Indeed, at this point in our discussion, the data are compatible with uniform underlying VO word order in all INFL-medial clauses combined with different rates of leftward scrambling in the different texts. To determine whether there actually is leftward scrambling in Early Middle English INFL-medial clauses, however, we need undoubted examples of underlying VO word order in which a potentially scrambled element occurs. In other words, we must look for clauses that contain a diagnostic element in postverbal position and another element which might scramble to the left. If this

TABLE 6.8. *Position of the remaining object in double-object clauses*

	NP-V-pro	V-pro-NP
WEST MIDLANDS		
Ancrene Riwle	5	9
Katherine Group	3	13
TOTAL WEST MIDLANDS	8	22
Lambeth Homilies (E)	0	1
SOUTH-EAST MIDLANDS		
Trinity Homilies	0	4
Vices and Virtues	0	2
TOTAL SOUTH-EAST MIDLANDS	0	6
ALL TEXTS	8	29

potentially scrambling element never actually appears preverbally and if our sample of possible occurrences is large enough, then we have evidence that scrambling is impossible in the language of our texts. If, on the other hand, we find cases of preverbal placement of the relevant element, we can conclude that scrambling is allowed. The most common diagnostic environment in our texts is the clause with a double-object verb, with one object a pronominal in postverbal position. The other object will then appear in preverbal position if and only if it has scrambled to the left. As Table 6.8 shows, scrambling clearly does occur.

The scrambled noun phrase in this environment may be either a pronoun or a full noun phrase. We give examples of each type, by way of illustration.

(23) (a) & he *hit* wule ȝelde þe as his treowe feire
         and he it will yield thee as his true company
         'and he will yield it to you as his true company'
         (CMANCRIW,II.91.1090)

    (b) For alle þeo þe habbeð *ani good* idon me
         for all those that have any good done me
         'for everyone who has done me any good'
         (CMANCRIW,I.64.212)

The evidence for scrambling that we see in Table 6.8 is limited to the West Midlands texts, excluding once again the *Lambeth Homilies*. This fact, however, does not allow us to conclude that scrambling is limited to the West Midlands. The reason is that postverbal pronouns are very rare in the South-eastern texts and Lambeth. As a result, our diagnostic environment arises so rarely that the absence of scrambling is unsurprising and uninformative.

Since, in addition to postverbal pronouns, we treat postverbal particles and stranded prepositions as diagnostic of VO order, we should expect to find instances of scrambling in clauses containing these elements. Unfortunately, there are only a handful of clauses in our texts that contain these diagnostic elements along with a direct object. In all but one of these, the direct object is also postverbal. The single instance of scrambling is, however, from a South-eastern text. Example (24) from the *Trinity Homilies* has a stranded preposition to the right of the untensed verb and a pronoun to its left.

(24)   Vnderstondeð get an <þing> þat ich *giu* wile warnie *fore*.
        understand yet one thing that I you will warn of
        'Understand yet one thing that I will warn you of.'
          (CMTRINIT,57.774)

If we are correct in treating postverbal stranded prepositions as diagnostic of underlying VO order, then this example is evidence of the scrambling of a pronoun.

In his study of double-object clauses in Old English, W. Koopman (1990) found several instances of postverbal pronouns with scrambled second noun phrases, one of which we give below.

(25)   Hwi noldest   ðu   *hyt* secgan *me*
         why NEG-wanted thou it   say   me
         'Why didn't you want to say it to me?'
              (Gen 31.27; W. Koopman 1990: 170, example (108))

We take examples like this to show that underlying VO order was possible in Old English, as argued by Pintzuk (1997), and also that underlying VO order coexisted with scrambling in Old English. Based on Koopman's Old English data and our example from the Trinity text, we think it most plausible to assume that scrambling was possible in the South-eastern dialect of Early Middle English as well as in the West Midlands. This conclusion is supported by the fact that the South-eastern texts are conservative relative to the West Midlands ones with respect to the frequency of INFL-final word order, since such conservatism implies that the South-eastern texts should be, if anything, more like Old English than the West Midlands texts are. Indeed, we will give evidence below that the rate of scrambling in the South-eastern dialect is quite high, at least for pronouns, and that this high rate of pronoun scrambling is actually responsible for the shortage of diagnostic clauses in the South-eastern texts.

   In addition to the evidence for NP scrambling in VO clauses, there is one bit of evidence in our texts that stranded prepositions also scramble leftwards across the verb. In particular, we have found the example in (26), in which a pronoun appears to the right of the untensed verb and a stranded preposition has been scrambled leftwards.

(26)   þt   he schulde *in* huden *him* ʒef he walde libben.
          that he should in hide him if he would live
          'that he should hide himself in if he would live'
               (CMANCRIW,II.132.1744)

The existence of preposition scrambling in Early Middle English is not surprising given that something similar seems to have been possible in Old English. While we have not found examples of scrambled stranded prepositions in the secondary literature on Old English, the examples in (27) from W. Koopman (1990) do seem to be instances of particle scrambling, arguably a similar phenomenon.

(27) (*a*)   þonne hi ðe *forð* mid him to ðam ecan   forwyrde gelædon
             when she thee forth mid them to the eternal damnation led
             'when she led you forth with them to the eternal damnation'
                  (Ælfric, *Catholic Homilies* i.516.18; W. Koopman 1990: 31,
                  example (34))

     (*b*)   þæt ða tanas   *up* æppla bæron
             that the branches up apples bore

'so that the branches bore apples'
(*Sat* 479; W. Koopman 1990: 31, example (36))

Of course, in Old English, the assumption has always been that scrambling was occurring from an OV verb phrase but the example in (25) above indicates that this assumption is unwarranted as a general rule, though we have not so far encountered a demonstrably verb-initial verb phrase with scrambling of a particle or prepositional phrase.

6.4. OV WORD ORDER IN EARLY MIDDLE ENGLISH

Given the evidence for the scrambling of pronouns and other light elements, the possibility exists, as noted above, that Early Middle English INFL-medial clauses are all underlyingly VO. We do not, however, believe this to be the case. In all of the Germanic languages that move from INFL-final OV word order to INFL-medial VO word order, there is a period when INFL-medial OV surface order is frequent. It seems plausible that learners would posit this order as an underlying possibility at some point in the course of the transition, unless Universal Grammar precluded it; but, as we know, INFL-medial OV languages do exist, for example the West African language Vata, described in H. Koopman (1984). The plausibility of the underlying OV hypothesis is increased by the fact that Early Middle English continues to manifest INFL-final OV order. The language, therefore, has both OV and VO verb phrases, as well as both INFL-final and INFL-medial clauses. It is natural then to expect that the INFL-medial and OV options would combine. Of course, it is true that INFL-final and VO do not combine, but this failure seems to be due to some property of UG (Kiparsky 1996).

Our problem with INFL-medial OV word order is a methodological one. To decide with certainty whether it is a possible underlying order, we must find diagnostics that distinguish underlying INFL-medial OV from the same order when it is produced by scrambling. In addition, there are statistical facts that could potentially bear on the question. In what follows, we attempt to establish a relevant diagnostic and to present associated statistical evidence in support of the hypothesis that there were INFL-medial clauses with underlying OV word order in all of the Early Middle English texts. As we will see, however, the matter is a difficult one to resolve in a definitive way.

There is certainly a great deal of superficial OV word order in all Early Middle English texts, as illustrated below.

(28) (*a*)   ear   he hefde his ranceun fulleliche ipaiȝet
           before he had his ransom fully   paid
           'before he had fully paid his ransom'
           (CMANCRIW,II.101.1218)

     (*b*)   for þat hie nedden here synnes er   bet
           for that they NEG-had their sins before atoned-for

'because they had not atoned for their sins before'
(CMTRINIT,69.950)

(c)   ðanne hie   willeð here ibede   to godde bidden
      when they will   their prayer to God   pray
      'when they will pray their prayer to God'
      (CMVICES1,143.1773)

None of these illustrative examples, however, is a certain case of INFL-medial OV underlying order, since the objects and prepositional complements could have scrambled leftwards across the verb. In the examples in (28), the position of the direct object to the left of the adverb indicates, in fact, that scrambling has occurred, but we do not know whether the original position of the scrambled object was pre- or postverbal. The fact that we commonly find examples like (28c) with all arguments of the verb in preverbal position, may indicate that underlying OV order is possible but does not demonstrate it. Consider, however, the following examples.

(29) (a)   þeos ne   schulen neauer *song* singen in heouene
           these NEG shall   never   song sing   in heaven
           'These shall never sing songs in heaven.'
              (CMHALI,142.222)

     (b)   þat ne   haue noht *here sinnes* forleten
           who NEG have not   their sins   forsake
           'who have not forsaken their sins'
              (CMTRINIT,67.934)

     (c)   and makede him fleme þere   he hadde er   *louerd* iben
           and made   him outcast where he had   before lord   been
           'and made him an outcast where he had earlier been a lord'
              (CMTRINIT,61.822)

Here we find direct objects to the right of adverbs that they sometimes scramble across. In the INFL-final/OV West Germanic languages, this order is ordinarily taken to indicate that scrambling has not applied. If this interpretation is correct, then these examples are cases of underlying INFL-medial OV order. Unfortunately, the standard interpretation depends on the assumption that the adverbs are attached low enough in the clause that any leftward scrambling of the object will move it across the adverb. In Middle English, however, this is probably not the case, as the following example shows.

(30)   Þv qð ha keiser   nauest   nawt *þis strif* rihtwisliche idealet
          thou said she emperor NEG-have not   this strife rightly   settled
          ' "Thou, Emperor," she said, "hast not rightly settled this dispute" '
             (CMKATHE,30.184)

Here the direct object appears to have scrambled across one adverb but still to be to the right of a second adverb, indicating that the leftmost adverb is attached too high in the clause to serve as a diagnostic for scrambling.

6.4.1. *A constraint on the scrambling of noun phrases*

In a recent paper, van der Wurff (1999) describes a construction in Late Middle English in which a quantified noun phrase appears immediately before the untensed verb. He suggests this construction is related to the Modern Icelandic possibility of placing a negative or quantified object in the same position. This word order is also found to a limited extent in present-day Norwegian and was more widespread in that language in the last century (Christensen 1986, 1987). Examples from Icelandic and Middle English are given below.

(31) (*a*)   Jón   hefur fáar bækur lesið.
 John has   few books read
 'John has read few books.'
    (Van der Wurff 1999: 5, example (7))

(*b*)   he haþ on vs mercy, for he may al þynge do
 'He has mercy on us, for he can do everything'
    (*Barlam* 2740; Van der Wurff 1999: 8, example (19))

Van der Wurff points out that only quantified, especially negatively quantified, noun phrases can appear in this position in Late Middle English and Scandinavian, and we might expect the same construction also to be possible in Early Middle English. If it were the case that the scrambling of non-pronominal noun phrases were limited to quantified ones, then we would have evidence for underlying INFL-medial OV word order, since most preverbal noun phrases in our texts are not quantificational. Again, clauses with two objects, one of which is a postverbal pronoun and the other a non-pronominal noun phrase, are diagnostic.[10] If the non-pronominal noun phrases that appear preverbally all prove to be quantificational, we have evidence that the Late Middle English limitation on scrambling also held in Early Middle English. If we remove the cases with two pronominal objects from Table 6.8 and separate the noun phrases into quantificational and non-quantificational types, we obtain the results presented in Table 6.9.

The numbers here are, of course, very small, and while they lean toward the hypothesis, the following exceptional case occurs in the *Ancrene Riwle*.

(32)   <Me schal> leoue sustren þeose storien tellen eft   ou
 one shall   dear sisters these stories tell   afterwards to-you
 'One shall, dear sisters, these stories tell afterwards/later to you'
    (CMANCRIW,II.122.1552)

This instance of a postverbal pronoun not immediately following the verb is

---

[10] In addition, there are two examples in our corpus (although not in the sample being considered in this chapter) with a postverbal particle and a preverbal noun-phrase object. In both cases the preverbal noun phrase is quantified (CMAYENBI,109.2100, CMPETERB,58.571).

TABLE 6.9. *Position of quantified and non-quantified NP objects in clauses with a postverbal pronoun object*

	NP-V-*pro*		V-*pro*-NP	
	Quant. NP	Non-quant. NP	Quant. NP	Non-quant. NP
WEST MIDLANDS				
Ancrene Riwle	2	1	2	7
Katherine Group	2	0	4	8
TOTAL WEST MIDLANDS	4	1	6	15
Lambeth Homilies (E)	0	0	1	0
SOUTH-EAST MIDLANDS				
Trinity Homilies	0	0	1	3
Vices and Virtues	0	0	1	1
TOTAL SOUTH-EAST MIDLANDS	0	0	2	4
ALL TEXTS	4	1	9	19

unique in our dataset. The fact that the pronoun occurs after an adverb suggests that it is extraposed, although from the context it does not appear to be stressed. No other manuscript of this text has exactly this order, but the other manuscripts do not help us to decide what to make of the example. Two (Royal, and Gonville and Caius) lack this sentence entirely and two (Titus and Corpus) have the same order with the adverb absent. The remaining manuscript (Nero) has the noun phrase also in postverbal position (*tellen ou þeos storie*).

If we dismiss the exceptional example as an OV clause with an extraposed pronoun, then we can take the position that non-quantificational noun phrases do not prepose in Early Middle English. In other words, noun-phrase scrambling in Early Middle English obeys the same constraints as in Late Middle English. If instead we take this example as an instance of the scrambling of a non-quantified noun phrase, then we can perhaps make use of the large difference in the rates of scrambling for quantified and non-quantified noun phrases. From Table 6.9 we would estimate the rate for quantified noun phrases to be about one-third while it would be about 5% for non-quantified noun phrases. Table 6.10 shows that the average rate of surface OV word order with non-quantified objects in our texts is 30%, a frequency which is too high to be accounted for by leftward scrambling.

If the rate of underlying OV word order is the same for quantified and non-quantified objects, then the surface frequency of preverbal position for quantified objects will be higher than that for non-quantified objects as a result of the difference in frequency of leftward scrambling of quantified as opposed to non-quantified noun phrases. As Table 6.11 shows, this is indeed the case.

Given the assumption that the frequency of underlying OV word order is independent of whether the object is quantified or not, the figures in this table allow

TABLE 6.10. *The distribution of non-quantified noun phrases in clauses with an auxiliary verb*

		Post-INFL	Post-VERB	% Post-INFL
WEST MIDLANDS				
Ancrene Riwle	main	18	75	19%
	subordinate	25	80	24%
	total	43	155	22%
Katherine Group	main	15	51	23%
	subordinate	25	49	34%
	total	40	100	29%
TOTAL WEST MIDLANDS	main	33	126	21%
	subordinate	50	129	28%
	total	83	255	25%
Lambeth Homilies (L)	main	2	14	13%
	subordinate	19	7	73%
	total	21	21	50%
Lambeth Homilies (E)	main	9	42	18%
	subordinate	20	63	24%
	total	29	105	22%
SOUTH-EAST MIDLANDS				
Trinity Homilies	main	18	49	27%
	subordinate	45	36	56%
	total	63	85	43%
Vices and Virtues	main	11	45	20%
	subordinate	37	54	41%
	total	48	99	33%
TOTAL SOUTH-EAST MIDLANDS	main	29	94	24%
	subordinate	82	90	48%
	total	111	184	38%
ALL TEXTS	total	244	565	30%

us to calculate an estimate of the rate of scrambling for quantified noun phrases that is independent of the estimate we obtained from the sparse double-object data in Table 6.9. The estimate relies on an auxiliary estimate of the frequency of underlying OV word order in clauses with non-quantificational noun phrases. This auxiliary estimate, which is based on the surface frequency of preverbal non-quantificational noun phrases from Table 6.11 (30%) and the rate of scrambling for this noun phrase type from Table 6.9 (5%), comes out to be 26%,[11]

---

[11] We arrive at 26% on the basis of the following reasoning. The surface frequency of preverbal non-quantificational noun phrases from Table 6.11 (30%) includes instances of both underlying OV word order and of leftward scrambling from underlying VO word order. If we let x stand for the

Table 6.11. *The distribution of quantified noun phrases in clauses with an auxiliary verb*

		Post-I	Post-V	% Post-I QNP	% Post-I Non-QNP
WEST MIDLANDS					
Ancrene Riwle	main	2	10	17%	19%
	subordinate	6	12	33%	24%
	total	8	22	27%	22%
Katherine Group	main	5	8	38%	23%
	subordinate	4	6	40%	34%
	total	9	14	39%	29%
TOTAL WEST MIDLANDS	main	10	27	28%	21%
	subordinate	18	26	36%	28%
	total	28	53	32%	25%
Lambeth Homilies (L)	main	0	1	0%	13%
	subordinate	1	1	50%	73%
	total	1	2	33%	50%
Lambeth Homilies (E)	main	3	8	25%	18%
	subordinate	7	7	50%	24%
	total	10	15	40%	22%
SOUTH-EAST MIDLANDS					
Trinity Homilies	main	4	10	29%	27%
	subordinate	10	5	67%	56%
	total	14	15	48%	43%
Vices and Virtues	main	9	10	47%	20%
	subordinate	9	7	56%	41%
	total	18	17	51%	33%
TOTAL SOUTH-EAST MIDLANDS	main	13	20	39%	24%
	subordinate	19	12	61%	48%
	total	32	32	50%	38%
ALL TEXTS	total	60	85	41%	30%

with a corresponding frequency of underlying VO word order of 74%. Turning now to quantified noun phrases, the surface frequency of OV word order in our texts is 41%. Since the difference of 15% between this figure and the frequency of underlying OV word order must be due to scrambling from a VO verb phrase, we obtain an estimated rate of scrambling for quantified noun phrases of 20% (15%/74%). If we assume, on the other hand, that non-quantificational noun phrases do not scramble at all, then the frequency of preverbal non-quanti-

frequency of underlying OV word order, then the frequency of scrambling is the product of the frequency of VO word order $(1-x)$ and the assumed scrambling rate. Solving the following equation for x yields 26%: $0.30 = x + (1-x)*0.05$.

ficational noun phrases in Table 6.11 directly reflects the frequency of underlying OV word order, and we obtain an estimated rate of scrambling for quantified noun phrases of 16%.[12] In sum, then, the estimated rate of scrambling for quantified noun phrases ranges between approximately 15% and 20%.[13]

It is of interest to compare quantitatively the pattern of surface OV word order in Early Middle English to that described by van der Wurff for Late Middle English. Table 6.12 gives the frequencies of surface OV word order for quantified and non-quantified objects in the Late Middle English texts of the second edition of the PPCME.[14]

TABLE 6.12. *The distribution of quantified and non-quantified noun phrases in clauses with an auxiliary verb in Late Middle English*

	Post-INFL		Post-VERB		% Post-INFL	
	QNP	non-QNP	QNP	non-QNP	QNP	non-QNP
Main	28	13	289	1,694	9%	1%
Subordinate	42	34	305	2,367	12%	1%
TOTAL	70	47	594	4,061	11%	1%

As expected, there is a substantial frequency of OV order with quantified objects but almost no OV word order with non-quantified objects. If we assume that Late Middle English is uniformly VO in underlying word order, then these data give evidence for a measurable but very low rate of leftward scrambling of non-quantified object noun phrases. Of course, the other possibility is that the OV word order with non-quantified noun phrases represents a last remnant of underlying OV order. In either case, the data support our conclusion that leftward scrambling of non-quantified objects is too rare to account for the frequencies of OV word order in our Early Middle English sample. Note that the

[12] Under the assumption that non-quantificational noun phrases do not scramble, the frequency of preverbal quantificational noun phrases that must be derived by scrambling is 11% (41%–30%), the frequency of underlying VO word order is 70% (100%–30%), and the rate of scrambling is the quotient of the two.

[13] The calculations we have given ignore the effect of the extraposition of noun-phrase objects from an underlying OV position to a surface postverbal position, as we currently have no way of estimating the frequency of that process. So long as that movement occurs at the same rate for quantified and non-quantified noun phrases, ignoring it will not distort our conclusions. Unfortunately, we cannot at this stage demonstrate that the assumption of a single rate of noun-phrase extraposition is justified.

[14] Table 6.12 is based on the following texts (the designations are those of the PPCME): CMAELR3, CMROLLEP, CMROLLTR, CMASTRO, CMBENRUL, CMBOETH, CMCLOUD, CMCTMELI, CMCTPARS, CMEDTHOR, CMEDVERN, CMEQUATO, CMGAYTRY, CMHILTON, CMHORSES, CMJULNOR, CMMANDEV, CMMIRK, CMNTEST, CMOTEST, CMPOLYCH, CMPURVEY, CMROYAL, CMVICES4, CMWYCSER, CMAELR4, CMCAPCHR, CMCAPSER, CMEDMUND, CMFITZJA, CMGREGOR, CMINNOCE, CMKEMPE, CMMALORY, CMREYNAR, CMREYNES, CMSIEGE, CMTHORN.

frequency of scrambling of quantified objects in Late Middle English is only slightly lower than the estimates we obtained above from our comparison of the overall rates of OV word order with quantified and non-quantified objects.[15] This will be true however we treat the small amount of surface OV word order with non-quantified objects in the Late Middle English data. Since both the Early Middle English and Late Middle English estimates are based on substantial amounts of data, the near agreement between them is meaningful. Hence, the Late Middle English data indirectly support our hypothesis that underlying OV word order exists in Early Middle English.[16]

6.4.2. *Pronoun scrambling*

We noted in §6.3.2 that pronouns as well as noun phrases scramble leftward in Early Middle English, and the existence of pronoun scrambling raises the issue of whether the large difference in the frequency of OV word order with pronoun objects between the West Midlands and the South-eastern texts (see Table 6.5) is due to a difference in the frequency of underlying OV word order or a difference in the frequency of pronoun scrambling. Because the data from our diagnostic double-object environment are so sparse, we have no direct way of answering this question. We can, however, address it based on the estimate of OV word-order frequency we arrived at in the preceding section. Looking once again at Table 6.11, we see that the rates of OV word order with non-quantified objects are 25% and 38% in the West Midlands and South-eastern texts, respectively. The difference is somewhat larger in subordinate clauses and nearly disappears for main clauses. If, as we have done, we take these numbers to be reasonable estimates of the rates of underlying OV word order in the texts, then it follows that the observed differences in the placement of pronouns in the two

---

[15] Given that scrambling of quantified objects is eventually lost from English, it is possible that the difference between the Early Middle English estimate of 15–20% and the Late Middle English estimate of 11% reflects the beginnings of a decline in such scrambling in the Late Middle English texts.

[16] These data also support a suggestion by Pintzuk (cited in van der Wurff 1999) that Middle English quantified noun-phrase scrambling may be historically and grammatically independent of generalized OV word order. She proposes that such scrambling may already be present as an independent process in Early Middle English and simply be hidden from the analyst's view by the prevalence of generalized OV order. When generalized OV order is lost, quantified noun-phrase scrambling remains and becomes easily observable. Van der Wurff, on the other hand, proposes that quantified noun scrambling results from a reanalysis of certain cases of word order. For some reason, not specified, learners resist the uniform postverbal placement of negative and quantified noun phrases, instead reanalysing the grammar to allow special overt movements of these elements (to Spec,NegP and via Quantifier Raising, respectively) when generalized OV order, which he treats as movement to Spec,AgrO, is lost. Van der Wurff recognizes that he has found little empirical evidence to choose between his account and Pintzuk's alternative. Pintzuk suggests that quantitative data might provide the missing evidence. Indeed, our data seem to us to provide clear support for Pintzuk's proposal since they indicate that the frequency with which quantified noun phrases are scrambled leftwards is constant from Early to Late Middle English. This fact is most easily interpretable if such scrambling is grammatically independent of generalized OV word order.

groups of texts cannot be due entirely to differences in the rate of underlying OV word order. As Table 6.5 shows, the frequency of OV pronoun placement is 45% and 90% respectively; and the difference is found in both main and subordinate clauses. Hence, we can conclude that, in addition to a modest difference in the frequency of underlying OV word order between the West Midlands and South-eastern texts, there was a large difference in the rate of pronoun scrambling in the two groups of texts. Assuming no scrambling of non-quantified objects, the rate of pronoun scrambling in the West Midlands texts is 27% and the rate in the South-eastern texts is 84%. The fact that we are led to postulate a difference in the rate of pronoun scrambling in our two text groups helps us to make sense of the behaviour of the *Lambeth Homilies* data. The text, although from the West Midlands, behaves like the South-eastern texts in the placement of pronoun objects and stranded prepositions (see Tables 6.5 and 6.7 above). On the other hand, it behaves more like a West Midlands text in the placement of noun-phrase objects. Since the *Lambeth Homilies* text is both somewhat earlier than our other West Midlands texts and probably more influenced by Old English, this pattern leads us to propose that while both OV word order and pronoun scrambling decline earlier in the West Midlands than in the South-east, the decline of the former predates the decline of the latter. The parallelism between the behaviour of pronouns and of stranded prepositions provides, in addition, a little more support for our tentative claim in §6.3.2 that stranded prepositions scramble. Hence, like pronouns, they can be diagnostics for underlying VO word order in post-verbal position but are not diagnostic of OV order in preverbal position. Further evidence for decoupling the rate of pronoun scrambling from the rate of underlying OV word order can be found in the word-order patterns of the *Ayenbite of Inwit*, a Kentish text from the fourteenth century that we have discussed elsewhere in connection with the verb-second constraint in Middle English (Kroch and Taylor 1997, Kroch, Taylor, and Ringe 2000). With regard to the verb-second constraint, this text is very conservative. At a time when the constraint is being lost everywhere else in England, it is largely intact and in the Old English form in the *Ayenbite*. With regard to object position, the text distinguishes pronouns from noun-phrase objects in just the expected way. While the latter are largely postverbal (85%), the former are almost entirely preverbal (97%); that is, the *Ayenbite* looks here like the *Lambeth Homilies*; largely VO in underlying order but with consistent pronoun scrambling.[17]

We end this section by pointing out that Table 6.13 shows that pronoun object scrambling has largely disappeared from Late Middle English at a time when the

---

[17] There is a difficulty in the interpretation of the *Ayenbite* data which weakens the point we are making. It is a translation from the French, and a poorly constructed word-for-word translation at that. It is possible, therefore, that the placement of pronouns in the text has been influenced by the French original, where the object pronouns are verbal clitics. Detailed comparative work on the *Ayenbite* and the French original might shed light on the likelihood that syntactic calquing is distorting the data.

scrambling of quantified noun phrase objects was still productive.

TABLE 6.13. *The distribution of pronouns in clauses with an auxiliary verb in Late Middle English*

	Pre-INFL	Post-INFL	Post-VERB	% Post-VERB
Main	2	10	868	99%
Subordinate	10	33	1,208	97%
TOTAL	12	43	2,076	97%

6.4.3. *Summary*

It is difficult to find unambiguous evidence for underlying INFL-medial OV word order in Early Middle English but our double-object data do seem to indicate that non-quantificational objects scramble leftwards at only a very low rate, if at all. Assuming these data, though sparse, to be representative leads to three consequences. First of all, about one-third of Early Middle English INFL-medial clauses become underlyingly OV, with a somewhat higher frequency in the South-eastern texts and a somewhat lower one in the West Midlands texts. As in the case of INFL-final word order, the South-eastern texts appear to be modestly more conservative than the West Midlands ones. Second, if we assume that the rate of underlying OV word order is the same for quantified and non-quantified objects, then our Early Middle English data and comparable data from Late Middle English agree on an estimate of 10%–20% for the leftward scrambling of quantified objects. Third, not only is there evidence from double-object clauses that pronouns scramble across the untensed verb in Early Middle English but there are also too many preverbal pronouns for them all to reflect underlying OV order. Furthermore, the South-eastern and West Midlands texts exhibit different rates of pronoun scrambling. The *Lambeth Homilies*, while similar to the other West Midlands texts in their rate of underlying OV word order, behave like the South-eastern texts in their rate of pronoun scrambling.

6.5. CONCLUSIONS

This chapter reports the first extensive quantitative analysis of Middle English syntax using the second edition of the Penn–Helsinki Parsed Corpus of Middle English. Using a combination of the methods of modern comparative syntax and of quantitative analysis, we have attempted to work out the underlying positions of noun phrase and pronominal objects in Early Middle English as well as the transformational movements that such objects undergo. Because transformational movements like scrambling and extraposition can produce surface word orders that are indistinguishable from those that reflect untransformed underlying orders, our project has been a difficult one. Nevertheless, we believe that we have uncovered solid evidence for the following conclusions. First, all Early Middle

English texts exhibit a small remnant of INFL-final word order, suggesting continuity with Late Old English. The South-eastern texts are more conservative in this and other regards than the West Midlands ones. However, the apparent rate of INFL-final word order is much higher than the actual rate due to the interfering effect of stylistic fronting, which mimics INFL-final word order when the fronted element is an untensed verb. Second, there is leftward scrambling of both pronouns and full noun phrases across the untensed verb in VO clauses with auxiliary verbs. This scrambling mimics underlying OV word order and makes it difficult to determine whether such underlying word order exists at all. Third, despite the empirical difficulties, we have found good evidence for the existence of underlying OV order due to the difference in the behaviour of quantified and non-quantified objects. The former appear to scramble productively, as in the Scandinavian languages, but the latter either do not scramble leftwards at all or do so at a very low rate. Since the rate of surface OV order is quite high (nearly one-third of clauses with non-quantified noun-phrase objects), there is reason to admit OV word order underlyingly. Fourth, the frequency of preverbal pronouns in all of our texts is too high to be entirely accounted for as a reflex of underlying OV order, leading to the conclusion that pronoun scrambling was very productive in Early Middle English, as in Modern Yiddish. Comparison of the texts, furthermore, shows that the rate of pronoun scrambling varied independently of the rate of underlying OV word order and that the latter declined more broadly and quickly than the former. Finally, it may be useful to point out a broader implication of our study. We have assumed that variation in underlying word order is possible within texts and, based on that assumption, have been able to account for both categorical and frequentistic aspects of Early Middle English word-order patterning. The ability of our analysis to account for the facts in detail provides, we believe, solid support for the hypothesis, for a time controversial but now perhaps more widely accepted, that grammar competition is a fundamental feature of the texts of languages undergoing syntactic change.

7

Null Subjects in Middle English Existentials

ALEXANDER WILLIAMS

7.1. INTRODUCTION

In Early Middle English (1150–1250) as in Old English (850–1150), the expletive pronoun *there* (*þer*, *þear*, etc.) is often missing from existential sentences in which it could grammatically occur, as it is missing from (1). (2) comes from the same text as (1), but here the expletive is pronounced.

(1) Nis   buten an godd, as ich ear   seide, þt al þe world wrahte
     not-is but one god as I   before said   that all the world wrought
     'There is but one god, as I said before, that wrought all the world'
           (*St Katherine* 24.87, *c.*1225)

(2) Ah þer   nis   buten an godd þurh   hwam witerliche ha   all
     but EXPL not-is but   one god through whom certainly they all
     weren iwrahte
     were wrought
     'But there is just one God, through whom certainly they all were
     made'   (*St Katherine* 22.61, *c.*1225)

After 1250, however, both the frequency and the structural variety of existentials without an overt expletive decrease radically.

§7.3 reports results from a study, described in §7.2, of fifty-two Middle English texts from the Penn–Helsinki corpus. In Early Middle English roughly seven in every ten sentences intuitively classed as existential lack *there*, but after 1250 the proportion drops to about one in five. Certain of these existentials without *there*, I subsequently argue, do not have a silent expletive subject either. Eliminating these from the count, we find that three in five existential expletives in the hundred years before 1250 were unpronounced. Immediately afterwards, the number plummets to around one in thirty.

Thanks to Anthony Kroch, Chunghye Han, Jeff Lidz, Ann Taylor, and Don Ringe for their help, as well as to the very friendly editors and reviewers of this volume. Special gratitude is due to Anthony Kroch for reading this chapter at the University of York while I was in Kazakhstan.

These facts prompt two questions, which I aim to solve in §§7.4 and 7.5. First, how were silent expletives possible at all in the grammar of Early Middle English? And second, why was their loss so sudden and so extreme?

The first question depends on certain generalizations about the syntax of Early Middle English and the distribution of silent expletives in Germanic which should be put forward immediately.

As in Old English, full NP subjects in Early Middle English obey the regular V2 pattern, following the finite verb (Vf) when another phrase fills the clause-initial 'topic' position; but pronominal subjects do not (Pintzuk 1991, van Kemenade 1987, Kroch and Taylor 1997). In so-called *canonical* declarative clauses, pronominal subjects precede the finite verb, even when another phrase is fronted, as in (3).

(3) (*a*) And alle hire sinnen he forȝaf
          and all her sins   he forgave
          'And he forgave all her sins.'
             (*Vices and Virtues* 111.431, *c*.1225)

    (*b*) His louerd he dede arst michel harm
          his lord   he did first much harm
          'He did much harm first to his lord.'
             (*Vices and Virtues* 115.486, *c*.1225)

Just so, expletive subjects will precede Vf in canonical declaratives.

I will make two crucial assumptions, (4) and (5).

(4)   Subject pronouns in Early Middle English that precede Vf are not c-commanded by Vf (that is, are not within the sister of Vf), even when another constituent occupies the clause-initial topic position.

(5)   Unpronounced pronouns in Early Middle English distribute just like pronounced pronouns in the syntax, and not like full NPs.

(4) is a corollary of the theories in Pintzuk (1991, 1996*b*) and Kroch and Taylor (1997), which supply the background for this chapter. Both Pintzuk and Kroch and Taylor take the normal position of Vf in Old English and Early Middle English to be I°. Non-topic subject pronouns Pintzuk puts in a clitic position adjoined to Spec,IP, and Kroch and Taylor at 'the CP–IP boundary'. Either way, they are not in the sister of I°, and (4) follows. (5) is supported by the claim in Pintzuk (1996*b*) and van Kemenade (1987) that non-topic pronouns in Old English are 'syntactic clitics', as are the weak pronouns in modern Germanic (Cardinaletti and Starke 1994). This means that the positional difference between nominal and pronominal non-topic subjects is established already in the syntax, and is not just an effect of phonology. Assuming the same for Early Middle English, we derive (5), since the pronunciation of the Early Middle English expletive should not affect its distribution in the syntax.

The pattern of silent expletives (pro_X) in Germanic is arguably described by the licensing principle in (6). (6) allows the surface structure in (7) and rules out that in (8).[1]

(6)   An expletive may be silent only if its surface position is within the sister of F, where F is a feature generated in the position of the finite verb in declarative main clauses.

(7)   (8)

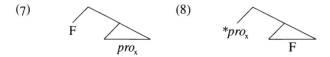

In German, main clause Vfs are in C°, so F is in C°. Thus German forbids pro_X above C° and allows it below, whether C° hosts a verb or a complementizer. Main clause Vfs in Yiddish are generally below C°, let us say in I° (Diesing 1988, Iatridou and Kroch 1992, Santorini 1992, 1994). So long as Vf remains in I°, no expletive above I° can be silenced; Yiddish does not allow pro_X following a complementizer. But if Vf moves onward to C°, as it does in questions, F is carried along and pro_X is thereby licensed in Spec,IP. Assuming that the crucial dependency between F and pro_X consists not in their linear order, but in a hierarchical structural relation, (6) follows. Similar observations can be made for the other Germanic languages, modern and historical, if sometimes with subtlety.[2] I will therefore assume (6) is correct, and will expect any adequate syntax of Middle English to abide by it. The converse of (6), importantly, does not hold: nearly all Germanic languages pronounce existential expletives below F sometimes, if not always.

The conjunction of (4–6) implies that silent expletives could not possibly be licensed in canonical Early Middle English declaratives, where pronouns are not in the c-command domain of F. Yet pro_X is abundantly attested in the Early Middle English texts.

The resolution of this apparent paradox, I will show in §7.4, emerges from a proper taxonomy of the facts. Before 1250, most of the existentials without *there* are not canonical clauses. They are of exceptional types where Vf inverts with subject pronouns. In the resulting configuration, the expletive is c-commanded by F, and its silence is licensed. The remaining minority, as well as the vast majority of the few cases after 1250, consists largely of locative inversions and existentials of the shape 'NP be'. I argue in §§7.4.2–3 that these sentence types

---

[1] See Falk 1993*a*, Hulk and van Kemenade 1993, Platzack 1987, Platzack and Holmberg 1989, Rizzi 1986, Roberts 1993*a*, Rögnavaldsson and Thráinsson 1990, Safir 1985, Santorini 1992, and Vikner 1995 for relevant data and, in most cases, an equivalent generalization.

[2] One language which demands a subtle treatment is Icelandic; see Maling 1990, Rögnvaldsson and Thráinsson 1990, Sigurðsson 1990, and Vikner 1994. It is not difficult to argue that most of the apparently discordant data from Icelandic in fact comply with (6); but there is a small and obscure residue (see Santorini 1994: 93–4).

are best analysed as not containing an expletive subject at all, and so there is no question of licensing a silent one. In the end, then, I will have shown two things. First, the Early Middle English data are consistent with the principle in (6), even assuming (4) and (5). And second, the data argue against any theory which denies either (4) or (5)—for instance, that of van Kemenade (1987, 1997*a*)—since without these we do not predict that silent expletives will occur only in so-called non-canonical clauses.

My analysis will also permit insight into the diachrony of the expletive. There is evidence that the capacity to silence an expletive, when the condition in (6) is met, was still fairly active *circa* 1400. The sudden loss of silent expletives, therefore, could not have resulted entirely from erosion of this capacity. The more significant cause, I will propose in §7.5, was a severe decrease in the frequency of the licensing configuration, precipitated by a loss in the productivity of verb-first (V1) order in simple indicatives. As this loss is concomitant with a bundle of changes which appear in the textual record with notorious suddenness, the abrupt disappearance of silent expletives will receive some explanation.

7.2. THE STUDY

The data I discuss come from fifty-two Middle English texts as excerpted and parsed in the first edition of the Penn–Helsinki Parsed Corpus of Middle English (Kroch and Taylor 1994*b*). A complete list, with dates, appears in an appendix. I follow the divisions used in the corpus, given in (9). By Early Middle English, I will mean the language(s) of the Period One texts.

(9)   Period One: 1150–1250 (5,153 sentence tokens)
        Period Two: 1250–1350 (4,228 sentence tokens)
        Period Three: 1350–1420 (9,060 sentence tokens)
        Period Four: 1420–1500 (7,477 sentence tokens)

Seven of the texts outside Period One have manuscripts dated in a period other than their period of composition. Whether these are grouped in the period of the manuscript or the period of the composition, it turns out, does not make much difference to the tabulations in this chapter. I chose to class them by their date of composition.

The texts were searched for existential sentences. What counted as an existential sentence was of course up to me, but I regard my decisions as having been conventional, and minimally committed on points of theory. Essentially, I counted those sentences which should or must be glossed with the overt expletive *there* in Modern English, and could or were in the source language as well. Necessarily, these interpretive criteria selected sentences whose non-expletive, 'logical' subjects were indefinite. Generally, the sentences had as their main verb *be*, or sometimes a verb like *come* or *appear*. And, with a small class of exceptions to be mentioned presently, the logical subject followed the verb.

There are certain sentence-types without an overt expletive, but still plausibly regarded as existential, that the parsers of the corpus did not consistently treat as having a silent dummy subject. (10) and (11) identify the types I have in mind, which I call NP-*be* Existentials (NPBEs) and Existential Locative Inversions (ELIs), respectively.

(10)　　*NP-be Existentials*
　　　　Moni cunne riwlen　beoð
　　　　many kinds of-rules are
　　　　'There are many kinds of rules.'　(*Ancrene Riwle* I.42.5)

(11)　　*Existential Locative Inversions*
　　　　In euch an　beoð fif　uers
　　　　in each one are　five verses
　　　　'In each one are five verses.'　(*Ancrene Riwle* I.68.264)

Sentences like (10) are certainly existential in spirit, and since their modern translations require an overt expletive, one must at least entertain the hypothesis that they include covert expletives in earlier English. ELIs like (11), on the other hand, are still possible today without the addition of an overt expletive. Yet given the existence in all periods of English of very similar sentences which overtly have expletive subjects, for example (12) and (13), it is certainly possible that (11) does contain a null subject.

(12)　　In Egipt þere ben v prouynces
　　　　'In Egypt there are five provinces.'
　　　　　(*Mandeville* 29.28)

(13)　　[U]nder the cercle of Cancer ben there 12 divisouns
　　　　'Under the circle of Cancer there are 12 divisions'
　　　　　(Chaucer, *Treatise on the Astrolabe* 667.CI.115)

ELIs cannot be excluded a priori from the tally of sentences which might contain a silent expletive, therefore, whatever our eventual conclusions about whether or not they do. I will discuss NPBEs and ELIs in detail below.

Entirely excluded from the study were clauses with extraction or relativization of the logical subject, as well as any string naturally interpreted (from the perspective of modern English) as an eventive passive.[3]

---

[3] In a language with silent expletives, extraction of the logical subject in an existential will in general produce a string that is ambiguous between an existential and a simple predicative reading. One could not straightforwardly decide whether a sentence like (ia) has the surface structure in (b) or the one in (c). Hence I excluded such cases from the count.

(i)　(a)　What is in Philadelphia?
　　(b)　What$_i$ is$_j$ *pro*$_x$ t$_j$ t$_i$ in Philadelphia?
　　(c)　What$_i$ is$_j$ t$_i$ t$_j$ in Philadelphia?

7.3. THE PRIMARY NUMBERS

Table 7.1 shows that the large majority of existential sentences in Period One, 71%, do not include an overt expletive. The numbers are roughly reversed in all subsequent periods. Expletive *there* is absent in only 15% of Period Two, 25% of Period Three,[4] and 17% of Period Four existentials. (Breivik 1989 reports very similar numbers, despite very different methodology.) Not much changes if we eliminate from the count sentences with verbs other than *be*, as in Table 7.2.

TABLE 7.1. *Existentials with vs. without expletive* there, *for all verbs*

Period	*there*	no *there*	% without *there*
1 (1150–1250)	28	70	71%
2 (1250–1350)	41	7	15%
3 (1350–1420)	179	60	25%
4 (1420–1500)	154	32	17%

TABLE 7.2. *Existentials with vs. without expletive* there, *for just the verb* be

Period	*there*	no *there*	% without *there*
1 (1150–1250)	23	52	69%
2 (1250–1350)	39	7	15%
3 (1350–1420)	162	38	19%
4 (1420–1500)	121	17	12%

Dividing these numbers up by dialect group, or sorting them into main versus subordinate clauses, turns up little of robust significance, as far as I have been able to tell. The basic patterns are simply recapitulated in finer counts, and space prevents me from discussing details. Two aspects of the data are salient and impressive. First, *there*-less existentials are quite common in Period One. Second, they become much less common immediately after 1250, and remain stably

---

My reasons for excluding sentences that read like eventive passives were similar. Many such sentences do include an overt expletive *there* (as in *There was a pig roasted*). But I was uncomfortable with regarding as existential, rather than eventive, cases that do not, much less with postulating for these a null expletive subject, even provisionally. To give any analysis for a string like (ii) (an artificial example with modern words, for simplicity's sake) would have involved me in issues of Middle English participles and proto-passives which I was not prepared to handle.

(ii) yesterday was a crook hanged in the town square

An ideal study would handle these issues. But their avoidance is at worst a venial convenience, since it discounts just a small number of tokens, relative to the size of the database.

   [4] The anomalous size of this number has to do with a large group of NP-*be* Existentials found in the two versions of *The Mirror of St Edmund*. Without these, the Period 3 number falls to 18%, in line with Periods 2 and 4.

so through the later periods, where there is little change. I aim to explain the first fact in §7.4 and the second in §7.5.

7.4. ACCOUNTING FOR *THERE*-LESS EXISTENTIALS IN EARLY MIDDLE ENGLISH

7.4.1. *Exceptional inversion and the silent expletive*

How could Early Middle English allow silent expletives when pronominal subjects are generally not c-commanded by the finite verb? A close look at the data reveals that the silent expletives occur exactly and only in those cases where the canonical order of pronouns and Vf is reversed.

In Old English and Early Middle English, certain environments exhibit a non-canonical word order where Vf precedes all pronouns, topic or not. Pintzuk (1991) and van Kemenade (1987) describe four such environments: non-subject *wh*-questions (14*a*); sentences introduced by discourse sequencing adverbs like *then*, *now*, *thus*, or *yet* (14*b*); sentences with subjunctive, imperative, or negative verbs, a category I illustrate with a negative verb in (14*c*); and 'certain verb-initial sentence types, principally so-called "Narrative Inversions"' (Kroch and Taylor 1997: 303), as in (14*d*).

(14) (*a*) *Non-subject* wh-*questions*

      & hwer edbrec ha ut from daue þe hali king godes prophete?
      & where broke she out from Davy the holy king God's prophet
      'And where did she break out from Davy the holy king, God's prophet?' (*Ancrene Riwle* II.40.347)

    (*b*) *Discourse Adverb Inversions*

      þa ifunden heo þer ðrittiȝ welsprunges
      then found they there (loc.)thirty well-springs
      'Then they found there thirty springs.'
      (*Holy Rood Tree* 2.23)

    (*c*) *Subjunctive, imperative, or negative verbs*

      Ant nis ha witerliche akeast & in-to þeowdom idrahen
      and not-is she truly cast into slavery drawn
      'And she is not truly cast or drawn into slavery'
      (*Hali Meiðhad* 130.30)

    (*d*) *Narrative inversions*

      Comen alle to his bode
      came all at his command
      'All came at his command.'
      (*St Katherine* 18.19)

Pintzuk (1991) treats these inversions as involving movement of Vf from I° to C°. I will say the same, though I need only commit to Vf (and F with it) moving from its usual position where it does not c-command non-topic pronouns to a higher position where it does. In C°, Vf+F will license a silent expletive at the periphery of IP, as in (15).[5]

(15)

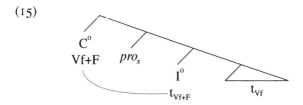

As expected, we find existentials without *there* corresponding to these inversion types, which I will call Discourse Adverb Existentials (DAEs), *Nis* Existentials (NISEs), and Existential Narrative Inversions (ENIs).

(16)   *Discourse Adverb Existentials*

Ach nu   is sum   wummon þe   nalde   for nan þing wilni
but now is some woman   who wouldn't for no thing desire
fulðe
lewdness
'But now there is some woman who wouldn't for anything desire lewdness.'   (*Ancrene Riwle* II.49.365)

(17)   Nis *Existentials*

For nis   nan sunne þet he ne con
for not-is no sin   that he not know
'For there is no sin that he doesn't know.'
     (*Lambeth Homilies* 35.260)

(18)   *Existential Narrative Inversions*

& com   a culur se briht as þah   ha bearnde of   heouene
& came a dove so bright as though it burned from heaven
'And there came a dove from heaven so bright as though it burned.'
     (*Margarete* 89.564)

---

[5] If the landing site of Vf in non-canonical clauses is in fact C°, then we do not expect to find silent expletives below complementizers, unless the embedding context is one that commonly allows recursion of CP, as do *said that* and *so that* (Iatridou and Kroch 1992, Tony Kroch, p.c.). This is arguably true, assuming that my argument in §7.4.2, that ELIs do not have expletive subjects, is correct. Most importantly, with some effort, one could make the case that all the subordinate NISEs are in environments for CP-recursion. In any case, I do not commit to the absolute position of Vf.

I did not find any interrogatives or verb-first subjunctives with obviously existential interpretation but without *there*.[6] This is unfortunate, as these were very regular environments for inversion in early English, as they are today. But it is hardly surprising when the entire pool of texts contains only two questions and one conditional with *there* (all from Period Three).[7]

The inference that the expletive lurks unpronounced below Vf in (16–18) has empirical support. We sometimes find overt expletives following the verb in these same constructions, as in (19) and (20),[8] even in texts where the variant with a silent expletive is attested. I was unable to find an ENI with postverbal *there*, but it is reasonable to assume that these pattern with DAEs like (19).

(19)   þa   com þer   an helendis Mon
         then came EXPL a   foreign man
         'Then there came a foreign man.'
         (*Lambeth Homilies* 79.496)

(20)   Ah nes   þear nan þt mahte neauer eanes wrenchen hire
         but not-was EXPL none that might never once wrench   her
         'But there was none that could ever once divert her.'
         (*St Katherine* 19.36)

Since the verb occurs above the pronounced expletive in (19) and (20), we have strong evidence that there is an unpronounced expletive in (16–18) as well, and that the verb is above it. The expletive in these sentences is *not* in a preverbal topic position. Hence the configuration described by (7) obtains in (16–18), and the silence of the expletive is licensed. Of course the contrast between (20) and (21) (=(2)) must be noted.

(21)   Ah þer nis buten an godd
         'But there is just one God.'
         (*St Katherine* 22.61)

If NISEs like (1) and (17) are to comply with the licensing condition in (6), then their underlying shape must be that of (20), not (21). I will assume that it is, and

---

[6] There is one likely candidate, however, from a Period Three text. The sentence in (i) was not parsed as having an expletive subject, but one might question this decision. In any case, this is a direct gloss of Thomas's Latin, making it likely that any syntactic oddity results from calquing.
  (i) Where is such accepte auctorite in anny prelate as was in Gregore Nazanzene?
      (*Sermons from the MS Royal*, 253.199)

[7] I should note that one does find some relative clauses with *wh*-relativization of a locative out of an apparently existential sentence, where no overt subject precedes the verb. Since there is no V-to-C raising in relative clauses, I treated these as a derived from ELIs. In §7.4.2, I argue that ELIs do not have a covert expletive subject.

[8] In judging the *þer* in (19) and *þear* in (20) to be expletive subjects, I follow the parsers of the Penn–Helsinki corpus, as usual. The parsers' judgements in turn accord with those implicit in the facing-page translations provided in the source texts. Within the contexts in which (19) and (20) occur, a locative interpretation of the *there* would be quite odd, semantically and pragmatically.

not just for theory-internal reasons. Even the pronounced expletive, *there*, is more likely to follow than to precede *nis*. Eight of the twenty-nine existentials with *nis* in Period One have an overt *there*. In six of these, *there* follows Vf, as in (20), and only twice does it come first, as in (21).[9]

Now consider the taxonomy of existentials without *there* in Table 7.3. The first three columns give the numbers for the three regular V-to-C sentence types.

TABLE 7.3. *Typology of* there-*less existentials, for all verbs*

Period	DAE	NISE	ENI	*be*-ɪ	ELI	NPBE	Other	TOTAL
ɪ (1150–1250)	15	21	5	2	17[10]	9	3	70
	21%	30%	7%	3%	24%	13%	4%	
2 (1250—1350)	0	ɪ	0	0	4	2	0	7
	—	14%	—	—	57%	29%	—	
3 (1350—1420)	3	0	0	ɪ	38	17	ɪ	60
	5%	—	—	2%	63%	29%	2%	
4 (1420—1500)	0	0	0	0	23	ɪ	8	32
	—	—	—	—	72%	3%	25%	

NISEs constitute nearly a third of all tokens without *there* in Period One, and DAEs, about a fifth. Adding the five ENIs, we discover that *at least* 59% of all the Period One existentials without *there* are V-to-C clauses, where the licensing feature F will occupy a governing position above the pronominal subject. Over half of the threatening *there*-less data, therefore, are clearly in compliance with (6).

It remains to explain the other half of the data, on the right side of Table 7.3. Among these, there are two types which are by far the most commonly attested: NP-*be* Existentials and Existential Locative Inversions, as in (10) and (11). I argue in §§7.4.2–3 that neither of these constructions includes a silent expletive subject, thereby eliminating the problem of licensing one. The other two categories, both very thinly populated, I will handle briefly here.

---

[9] In *wh*-questions and Discourse Adverb Inversions, the finite verb raises to C, but the *wh*-phrase or adverb precedes it. This implies that V-to-C raising alone is not sufficient to produce verb-first word order. There are consequently two ways to understand sentences like (21). Either *nis* has not moved to C°, in which case Vɪ is impossible and V2 is satisfied by the expletive, or *nis* has moved to C° and the Vɪ option is simply not taken, perhaps for pragmatic reasons. The latter seems to me the more elegant explanation.

[10] Two of the tokens counted as ELIs have *nis* as their main verb, and are thus also counted as NISEs. Below, in §7.4.2, I argue that ELIs do not have expletive subjects, and so eliminate them from the tally of existentials with silent expletives given in Table 7.4 of §7.4.4. These two tokens I do not eliminate, however, as they are derivationally ambiguous. They might be ELIs, and therefore lack a silent *there*; but they might also be regular *there*-existentials with a topicalized PP, where suppression of the expletive is licensed by V-to-C raising of *nis* (see note 12). I choose to regard them in the latter way, and so count them as having silent expletive subjects.

The first is Declarative *be*-1 Existentials, of which there are just three tokens in total. Example (22) is one of the two from Period One (the other is *Ancrene Riwle* I.44.52).

(22)   *Declarative* be-*1 Existentials*
         Ah is an heouenlich gast   in hire
         but is an heavenly   spirit in her
         'But there is a heavenly spirit in her.'
              (*St Katherine* 34.240, *c.*1225)

Ordinarily the affirmative copula does not invert with subject pronouns, but occasionally it does. Kroch and Taylor (1997) report pronoun–verb inversion in 33% of predicate adjective topicalizations, based on a study of seven of the ten Period One texts examined here. I propose to handle the two early *be*-1 Existentials as exceptions of this sort, still within the range of grammatical possibilities. With this exceptional raising of *be* to C°, a silent expletive is licensed.[11] The one later token, (23), requires a slightly different explanation.

(23)   My suete sisters, I saie to yu: es na sueter   uoice þan of iesu.
         my sweet sisters I say to you is no sweeter voice than of Jesus
         'My sweet sisters, I say to you: there is no sweeter voice than that of
         Jesus.'   (*The Northern Prose Rule of St Benet* 2.23, *c.*1400)

In *St Benet*, raising of Vf over even pronominal subjects is completely regular; unless the subject is itself topicalized, it inverts with the verb (Kroch and Taylor 1997: 313). Thus we need not claim that Vf in the existential clause of (23) has raised any higher than usual. We do need to stipulate, however, that this is a bona fide V1 clause, with the preverbal 'topic' position not only silent, but unoccupied. The expletive will then necessarily follow and be subordinate to Vf, satisfying the licensing condition on *pro*$_X$ in (6). One problem with this stipulation must be admitted. Indicative V1 is exceedingly rare in fourteenth- and fifteenth-century Middle English (see §7.5), so the syntax proposed for (23), which comes from a text written *circa* 1400, is in fact improbable. Nevertheless it is possible, and of course necessary if the licensing condition in (6) is correct.

Space prevents me from discussing the diverse tokens lumped under *Other* in any detail. The three from Period One use the modal construction *is neod* with a dative argument, asserting that there is a need for somebody to do or to have something. The translations of these require an expletive ('there is need'), but one could argue that in these early English tokens, the dative is the subject, and there

---

[11] This asymmetry between negative and positive *be* has a provocative parallel in modern Englishes which allow *ain't*, namely the contrast between (i) and (ii). Space forbids me speculating on the significance of this very interesting fact.

(i)   Ain't no room in the car
(ii)   *Is still room in the car

is no expletive. Otherwise, it is again possible to posit exceptional raising of *be*. The nine later tokens are less challenging. Seven, including the single 'Other' token from Period Three, are plausibly analysed as V2 sentences where a temporal adjunct occupies the 'topic' position; thus there could be no difficulty silencing an expletive subject (if there is one), since it would be below Vf+F. The final two Period Four tokens look like complex sorts of ELI, whose explanation follows.

7.4.2. *Existential Locative Inversions*

In the Period One texts, topicalization of a PP does not trigger inversion of subject pronouns. Kroch and Taylor (1997) find pronoun–verb inversion in o out of 11 cases where a complement PP is preposed to the topic position, and 2 out of 99 with a PP adjunct. Were ELIs to contain a silent pronominal subject in Early Middle English, therefore, it would not be governed by Vf, violating (6). This problem will not arise for purer V2 sublanguages of fourteenth-century Middle English, where subjects always follow Vf when another phrase is fronted. But the problem will arise in all Middle English sentences whose syntax is modern, with regular SV order. I will therefore pursue a maximally general solution, still adhering to the ideally simple principle that silent expletives are impossible unless subordinate to the feature F. I deny the assumption that produces the problem: at no stage of English do ELIs have an expletive subject.[12]

First a historical consideration. Expletives in Middle English are often pronounced even when governed by F—as often as two-thirds of the time by the fourteenth century, it seems (see §7.5 below). But the entire corpus contains just one existential sentence with a fronted PP and a pronounced postverbal expletive, namely (13). (Falk 1993*a* makes related observations for historical and modern Swedish; see especially pages 292–4.) This discrepancy is strikingly extreme if ELIs necessarily have expletive subjects. The simplest conclusion to draw is that they do not.

Next I will argue that locative inversions in Modern English do not have expletive subjects. If this is true, then it is all the more likely that ELIs in Early Middle English do not have them either.

First, there are several strong dissimilarities between locative inversions and their putative counterparts with an overt expletive—as (25) is the putative counterpart to (24)—that are difficult to explain if locative inversions have a silent form of *there* in subject position.

(24)   On the table was/stood a bust of Mao

(25)   On the table there was/stood a bust of Mao

---

[12] For rhetorical purposes, this statement is stronger than it needs to be. I do not need to exclude the possibility of a silent expletive co-occurring with a topicalized locative in a pure V2 grammar, since in that case *pro*$_X$ will perforce occur below Vf+F. (Compare the case of the two ambiguous tokens discussed in note 10.)

I will note four such differences. Others are discussed in Bresnan (1994).

1. As noticed by Milsark (1974) and others, locative inversions do not allow the range of predicates following the postverbal 'logical subject' that existentials with *there* do: witness the contrast between (26b) and (26c).

    (26) (a)   There were two Philadelphia cops murdered (right on that corner)
          (b)   Right on that corner, there were two Philadelphia cops murdered
          (c)   *Right on that corner were two Philadelphia cops murdered
          (d)   Right on that corner were two Philadelphia cops

On the supposition that (c) has an expletive subject, its ungrammaticality is completely unexpected, given that (a) and (b) are fine. This implies that the supposition is false: (c), hence (d) and locative inversions in general, do not have expletive subjects.

2. Locative inversions without an overt expletive do not show the definiteness effect. For those who believe this effect depends somehow on the inclusion of the expletive, the acceptability of (27) implies the lack of an expletive.

    (27)   On the table is the magazine John bought
    (28)   *On the table there is the magazine John bought

3. NPs that cannot be the subject of a locative predicate cannot be the logical subject of a locative inversion either (Milsark 1974): witness (29) and (30). Yet these same NPs can serve as the logical subject of an existential with *there*, as in (31).

    (29)   *Room is in the front closet
    (30)   *In the front closet is room
    (31)   In the front closet there is room

One feels that (29) and (30) are bad for the same reason, and should receive the same explanation. This explanation could not have to do with the pragmatics of the locative inversion construction, since (29) is not a locative inversion. But neither a semantic nor syntactic explanation is likely if (30) has an expletive subject, since then (29) and (30) would differ substantially in composition and structure: (29), clearly, does *not* have an expletive subject. Furthermore, were (30) to have an expletive subject, the contrast between it and (31) would be puzzling. Presumably the two sentences would be identical, at least up to the IP level, in every way but pronunciation. But (30) is bad and (31) is good. Thus the hypothesis that (30) has an expletive subject confounds our explanation of its ungrammaticality.

4. Existentials with *be* that have an overt expletive permit adverbs of temporal quantification (*always*, *usually*, etc.) (32a), even when the PP is fronted (32b). But locative inversions are unacceptable with the same adverbs in what is apparently the same position, as shown in (32c).

(32) (a) There was always a bust of Mao on the table
     (b) On the table, there was always a bust of Mao
     (c) *On the table was always a bust of Mao

One might hope that there is a good discourse-functional explanation for this, but I have not found one.[13] Hence I suspect that the grammaticality contrast between (b) and (c) diagnoses some structural difference between them. It is at least a reasonable guess that the difference subsists in the absence of an expletive subject in (c).

A second, much broader type of problem for the idea that locative inversions contain silent expletives is that silent expletives are generally forbidden in Modern English. We see this in sentences like those in (33), which are ungrammatical without the overt *there*, despite Vf being in C^o.

(33) (a) Nor were *(there) any simpler examples
     (b) Aren't *(there) better explanations?
     (c) In which department are *(there) still honest linguists?

The burden of proof is therefore on the linguist who would claim that locative inversions do contain a silent expletive. Most likely, this linguist will argue that a fronted locative argument, and only this, has a special power to silence expletives. Already this is an unattractively narrow position. It is prone to become even more so in coping with the data from (26–32). I doubt whether these contrasts between locative inversions and *there*-existentials could be explained without saying that the putative *pro*-subject of a locative inversion differs from *there* in more than just pronunciation. But then this expletive would not be *pro*$_X$, the silent *there*. It would be a new type of expletive altogether, one which apparently has no pronounced counterpart, and which is licensed exclusively by fronted locatives. At this point, the analysis forfeits all generality. And in any case, it now implies that locative inversions are irrelevant to the study of silent *there*, the same conclusion we reach if locative inversions contain no expletive whatsoever.

Further defence of my position is warranted, but it would lead us too far off the topic. Certain well-known problems having to do with the theories of Case

---

[13] My impression is that were (32c) to occur in the right narrative context, *a bust of Mao* could introduce a referent 'relatively new to the discourse', or have 'presentational focus', these being conditions on the felicity of locative inversions according to Birner and Ward (1993) and Bresnan (1994), respectively. It is not clear to me why it should matter that the object(s) newly introduced or presentationally focused are distributed across time. Certainly the unacceptability of (32c) cannot be explained by claiming that the coda of a locative inversion must introduce a single, specific referent, since (i) is perfectly acceptable. It has only a distributive reading, and would be felicitous even if all the busts could not possibly be seen simultaneously.

(i) On every model worker's desk was a bust of Mao

and subjecthood are only briefly discussed in a footnote.[14] Yet I believe it sufficient to have shown that the no-expletive analysis of locative inversion gets
things right that its alternative cannot.

7.4.3. *NP-be Existentials*

On the face of it, (34) (=(25)=(10)) could form a syntactic minimal pair with
(35), the only difference being whether the expletive is pronounced.

(34)   Moni cunne riwlen   beoð
        many kinds of-rules are
        'There are many kinds of rules.'
             (*Ancrene Riwle* I.42.5)

(35)   Nihe wordes þer   beoð
        nine hosts   there are
        'Nine hosts there are.'
             (*Sawles Warde* 180.228)

Were this true, we should have to wonder how the silent expletive putatively
present in (34) could be licensed.

Sticking to the assumptions of this chapter, there are two possibilities. Either
(34) involves exceptional raising of *be* to C°, thereby permitting a silent expletive, or it simply does not include a silent expletive. Both solutions are defens-
ible. As mentioned above, positive *be* does sometimes raise. Unfortunately, the
ideal evidence for this first hypothesis is lacking, since there are no NPBEs in
the Period One corpus with a pronounced expletive following the verb. The
second hypothesis has in its favour tokens like (36).

---

[14] The fronted PP in a locative inversion shows some signs of subjecthood. It can raise over *seems*
(Bresnan 1994), and does not trigger *do*-support when extracted (Hoekstra and Mulder 1990). But
if there is no expletive subject in a locative inversion, why does the fronted PP not have all the
properties of a subject? Why can it not invert with the verb to form a yes–no question? Why can PPs
not be the subjects of simple predicates like *is very cold* or *pleases John*? (Bresnan 1994, den Dikken
and Næss 1993, Stowell 1981.) And how does the logical subject of a locative inversion get Case
in its postverbal position? (Lasnik 1992, Chomsky 1995, *inter alia*.)

Solutions compatible with my position are available in the literature. The theory of Chomsky
(1995: 273, 287) allows subject Case and Agreement features to be checked by a postverbal nominal
so long as the phrase satisfying the EPP does not itself bear nominal φ-features. Chomsky develops
these conclusions in his discussion of expletives, which he argues lack such features. But proceeding
from the reasonable premise that PPs too lack nominal features, we can apply the idea to fronted PPs
as well (see Harley 1995). Case for the logical subject is then not a problem. In addition, we can
explain why PPs cannot be subjects (or be subject-like) outside of locative inversions. Since PPs do
not themselves have (or check) Case, a PP can occupy the Nominative position only if there is a DP
elsewhere that will check Nominative, hence only if there is a DP elsewhere that is not in the checking domain of another Case. Were a PP the subject of *is cold* or *pleases John*, this condition clearly
would not obtain: neither of these VPs includes a Caseless DP. Thus the issues traditionally related
to Case can be addressed within my framework. Finally, one can argue that Subject–Aux inversion
diagnoses not subjecthood, but the conjunction of subjecthood and NP-hood, since it also fails to
apply to sentential subjects, whose subjecthood cannot be doubted.

(36)   Þenne sum tyme was þat he was not
        then   some time was that he was not
        'Then [there] was some time during which he was not.'
        (*Mirror of St Edmund*, Vernon 258.702)

The relative clause in (36), *he was not*, has no grammatical counterpart with an overt expletive. Presumably then, it does not have a silent expletive subject either. This suggests that here, *be* has the intransitive syntax of *exist*, as it does in 'I think, therefore I am'. Now consider the matrix NPBE, *some time was . . . .* Since its subject is indefinite, this clause can be translated with an overt *there*. This facilitates an analysis of the matrix verb as a *be* of the ordinary sort, with two syntactic arguments—but it does not force it. The author of (36) has a simple intransitive use of *be* available to him; perhaps the matrix *be* is of this type as well, leaving no room for a silent expletive here either. Potentially, all NPBEs in the Middle English corpus could receive this explanation. There are, therefore, at least two plausible analyses which will bring NPBEs into accord with the licensing condition in (6).

Perhaps most likely, however, is that they are calques. Several of the Period One NPBEs, like (37), are translations of Latin quotations. Many others occur soon after these translations, and seem to mimic their style.

(37)   *tre cruces sunt de quibus hic agitur. due corporis una mentis.* þreo
        roden beoð þa ich umbe spreche. Twa licamliche; and an gastliche.
        '*Tre cruces sunt de quibus hic agitur. due corporis una mentis.*
        Three crosses [there] are that I speak about: two bodily and one
        spiritual.'   (*Lambeth Homilies* 147.717)

Seventeen of the twenty later tokens come exclusively from the two versions of *The Mirror of St. Edmund*, which are both close translations of the Latin. And thirteen of these seventeen come from the Vernon version, which is thought to be the closer rendering (Ann Taylor, p.c.). Latin of course had no existential expletive and was generally verb final. It is therefore not unlikely that sentences like those in (34) are affected imitations of the Latin, not properly reflecting the Early Middle English grammar at all. Of course such a claim cannot easily be proven. But if it is true, then NPBEs turn out to be irrelevant to the issues of this chapter. If it is not, then both of the explanations proposed in the preceding paragraph are available.

7.4.4. *Conclusions of this section*

I have argued that not all existentials without *there* include a silent expletive: ELIs and NPBEs do not. The numbers now break down as in Table 7.4.[15]

---

[15] Counted as having 'no expletive whatsoever' are existentials of those types that I have directly argued lack expletive subjects. These are the ELIs (excluding the two from Period One with *nis* (see note 10), but including the two complex cases from Period Four classified as 'Other' in Table 7.3

TABLE 7.4. *Overt expletive vs. silent expletive vs. no expletive in Middle English existentials*

Period	Overt expletive	Silent expletive	% of expletives silent	No expletive whatsoever
1 (1150–1250)	28	43	61%	27
2 (1250–1350)	41	1	2%	6
3 (1350–1420)	179	5	3%	55
4 (1420–1500)	154	6	4%	26

Outside Period One, there are almost no instances of the silent existential expletive. Within Period One, nearly two-thirds of the existentials without *there* include a null subject. In any period, when there is a null expletive, it is appropriately subordinate to (that is, c-commanded by) F. In tokens from Early Middle English, subordination obtains by means of exceptional raising of Vf+F to C°. When there is no empty expletive, there is of course no question of licensing one. Thus the problem posed at the start of this chapter is solved, and a syntax which assumes (4) and (5) has no difficulty accommodating the data.

More than that, the data can be taken as confirming (4) and (5). (4) and (5) say that Vf does not c-command a subject pronoun, pronounced or silent, in a canonical Early Middle English clause. This predicts that silent expletives will occur only in non-canonical clauses. Since this is indeed what we find, our assumptions are supported, and with them the portions of the Pintzuk–Kroch–Taylor theory from which they derive. Notice, the same point would have to hold even if ELIs did have a silent expletive. Since this particular null pronoun would be one that is licensed independently of F, its existence would be irrelevant to the distribution of the more familiar pro_X, which *is* dependent on F. We still would not predict the preponderance of NISEs and DAEs, and the near total absence of Declarative *be*-1 Existentials, unless (4) and (5) were true.

A theory which might suffer from this conclusion is that of van Kemenade (1987, 1997a). For van Kemenade, the hierarchical relation between Vf and a subject pronoun is the same in so-called canonical and non-canonical clauses. In both cases, the pronoun is syntactically clitic on Vf, and only the linear relation between them varies. Hence her theory does not anticipate the distribution of the data. Van Kemenade could respond by rephrasing the licensing condition on

(see §7.4.1)) and the NPBEs. Also included here, quite tentatively, are the three 'Other' tokens from Period One with the modal predicate *is neod* 'is need', which I provisionally regard as lacking a null subject (see §7.4.1). The remaining *there*-less existentials are counted in the 'Silent expletive' category. Mostly, this category is populated by DAEs, NISEs, and ENIs. It also includes the three *be*-1 tokens (two from Period One and one from Period Three), which I assume have expletive subjects, exceptionally inverted with Vf, as discussed in §7.4.1. And finally, it includes the seven 'Other' tokens (six from Period Four and one from Period Three) described in §7.4.1 as cases of V2 with a fronted temporal adjunct.

pro_X in terms of precedence; but this would go against a basic principle of the syntactic metatheory assumed both by van Kemenade and by this chapter.

7.5. DIACHRONY

According to Table 7.4, 61% of existential expletives in the 1150–1250 texts are silent. After 1250 the percentage drops to between 2% and 4%. What accounts for this change, and for its severity?

The probability that an expletive is silent, $p(X = pro_X)$, depends on two factors: the probability that an expletive will be silent when subordinate to the feature F, $p(X=pro_X \mid F>X)$, and the probability that an expletive will indeed be subordinate to F, $p(F>X)$. Presumably these factors are independent, such that $p(X=pro_X)$ is equal to their product: $p(X=pro_X)=p(X=pro_X \mid F >X) \times p(F>X)$. I will assume that the frequencies observed in a group of texts correctly represent an idealized grammar underlying those texts. Thus I will assume that the observed relative frequency of (. . .) is equal to $p(. . .)$.

Adapting the argot of Rizzi (1986), we can say that $p(X=pro_X \mid F >X)$ represents the strength of the capacity to 'identify' pro_X. Most probably, the ability to identify pro_X correlates with aspects of the Case system, and perhaps with subject–verb agreement as well (Allen 1995, Falk 1993*a*, Platzack 1987, Vikner 1995, among many others). Given this, one expects fourteenth-century Middle English to have retained this capacity to some significant degree, as the Case and Agreement systems had corroded only gradually since the early thirteenth century, and certain Case distinctions absent from the modern language were still active (Allen 1995). Table 7.5 gives some evidence supporting this expectation. In Period Three, expletives are silenced in around one-third of Discourse Adverb Existentials, the one regular environment for subject–verb inversion in which we find silent expletives even outside the earliest period.

TABLE 7.5. *Overt vs. silent expletives in environments of subject–verb inversion (numbers in parentheses are for just the verb* be)

Period	Clause type	Overt *there* after verb		Silent expletive		% of postverbal expletives silent	
1 (1150–1250)	DAE	1	(0)	15	(6)	94%	(100%)
	NISE	6	(6)	21	(21)	78%	(78%)
2 (1250–1350)	DAE	0	(0)	0	(0)	—	—
3 (1350–1420)	DAE	5	(5)	3	(2)	38%	(29%)
4 (1420–1500)	DAE	4	(4)	0	0	0%	0%

The composite picture here disguises enormous variation between texts, and the data are in any case sparse. But since they corroborate our expectations based on the condition of Middle English morphology, let us cautiously suppose that they do correctly depict the state of the grammar. For Period Three Middle

Diachronic Syntax

English, then, $p(X=pro_X | F>X) = 0.38$.[16] Averaging the DAE and NISE data from Period One, we have $p(X=pro_X | F>X)=0.86$ for the Early Middle English of 1150–1250. Unfortunately we have no estimate for Period Two.

I will have nothing more to say about this erosion of the capacity to identify pro_X, except to point out that it is not of the same order as the landslide drop-off in the overall frequency of silence expletives, $p(X = pro_X)$. $p(X=pro_X | F>X)$ goes from 0.86 in Period One to 0.38 in Period Three, but $p(X = pro_X)$ dives from 0.61 to just 0.03.

It follows that $p(F>X)$ must have changed as well, since $p(X=pro_X) = p(X=pro_X | F>X) \times p(F>X)$. Specifically, according to the present estimates of $p(X=pro_X | F>X)$ and $p(X = pro_X)$ in each period (from Tables 7.5 and 7.4, respectively), $p(F>X)$ is predicted to have changed from 0.71 (0.61/0.86) in Period One to 0.08 (0.03/0.38) in Period Three. This change in the frequency of the licensing environment for pro_X-drop is of significantly greater scale than the 0.86 to 0.38 decay in the capacity to identify pro_X. Thus the decline in $p(F>X)$ turns out to be the larger factor in the crash of $p(X = pro_X)$, i.e., in the loss of silent expletives.

The remainder of this section aims to illuminate the substance of this decline in $p(F>X)$. My central point will be this. The enormous historical discrepancy in $p(F>X)$ is due largely to the availability, and (comparatively) high incidence, of verb-first (V1) order for ordinary indicatives before, but not after, 1250. Since the drop in $p(F>X)$ is the larger factor in the fall-off of $p(X=pro_X)$, the loss of V1 is primarily responsible for the desuetude of silent expletives.

$p(F>X)$ is the probability that Vf c-commands the expletive subject in an existential sentence. In the corpus under study, this configuration of Vf and the expletive may occur in one of two environments. It may occur in either a V1 clause or in what I will call an XP–Vf–expl clause. In a V1 existential, no XP (except perhaps for one of the extraclausal conjunctions, such as *and*) precedes Vf, which is clause-initial. An XP–Vf–expl existential is a V2 clause with the word order XP–Vf–expletive, where XP is some constituent in the clause-initial 'topic' position.

[16] There is independent evidence that this estimate of $p(X=pro_X | F>X)$ is close to correct. A pilot study of 12 Period Three texts, performed by Rashmi Prasad (p.c.), found that, among clauses with a pronominal subject and a non-subject XP topicalized, 19% have inversion of Vf and the subject. That is, in these Period Three texts, $p(\text{inversion}|\text{topicalization})=0.19$. My data on existential sentences show non-subjects fronting in 48% of the tokens (33% if ELIs and NPBEs are excluded). So, $p(\text{topicalization})=0.48$. The product of these probabilities—$0.19 \times 0.48=0.09$—estimates the frequency of inversion for pronominal subjects, supposing that subjects invert only when a non-subject is topicalized. For Period Three, this ancillary supposition is very nearly true: the overwhelming majority of existentials where Vf c-commands the expletive have the V2 shape XP–Vf–expletive (I demonstrate this later in §7.5). Thus we predict that the probability of inversion for pronominal subjects, $p(F>X)$, should be roughly equal to the probability of XP–Vf–expletive order, namely 0.09 (as just calculated). Remarkably, the conjecture that $p(X=pro_X | F>X)=0.38$ predicts nearly the same value: given the observed 0.03 value for $p(X=pro_X)$ in Period Three (Table 7.4), we have $p(F>X)=0.08$ (0.03/0.38=0.08). Thus the conjecture receives some support.

In Period One texts, 2.2% (100/4,450) of all tensed, non-interrogative clauses (not just existentials) have an indicative verb in initial position.[17] In texts of Period Two composition, the number falls to 0.26% (3/1,162). Periods Three and Four have just 0.13% (12/9,128) and 0.11% (7/6,310), respectively. Declarative V1 thus appears to have suffered a very significant drop in productivity at the end of Early Middle English, a drop that is quite extreme in comparison to the gradual decay from Period Two onwards.

This change is expressed very dramatically in the domain of existential sentences, as before 1250 the rate of V1 in this domain is exceptionally high. In the Period One texts, verb-first indicatives make up fully 46% (33/71) of existentials with expletive subjects, or 34% (33/98) of all existential sentences generally. In the later periods, by contrast, the proportion of V1 among existentials is never higher than 2% (Period Two: 2% (1/42), Period Three: 2% (3/184), Period Four: 0% (0/160)).

The frequency of XP–Vf–expl clauses among existentials decays as well, but more gradually. Among the Period One existentials with expletives, 28% (20/71) have XP–Vf–expletive order. Period Two shows an unexpected 0% (0/42), but Periods Three and Four register 7% (13/184) and 8% (12/160), respectively.[18]

Table 7.6 summarizes these results. What we notice is that the loss of V1 dominates the overall decline in $p(F>X)$, here represented in the rightmost column by the sum of the first two columns. (Notice, these measurements of $p(F>X)$ coincide closely with those based on the estimates of $p(X=pro_X|F>X)$ in Table 7.5.) Between Period One and Period Three, the percentage of V1 among existentials with expletives drops from 46% to 2%. The decline in XP–Vf– expletive order, on the other hand, is slighter, sliding only from 28% to 7%. It is fair to say, then, that the drop in $p(F>X)$ is due primarily to the loss of V1. The decline in XP–Vf–expletive order—or rather, the implied decline in the odds

---

[17] These numbers are based on tensed, non-imperative clauses whose tensed verb was morphologically in the past, and was not a modal. The set of V1 tokens among the complementary set of clauses (those with a modal or a present-tense verb) includes a much higher proportion of non-declaratives, mainly hortatives and conditionals, to be eliminated from the count. I should also note that this search was executed over the new, *second* edition of the online Penn–Helsinki corpus (Kroch and Taylor 2000), as it stood in late August 1999.

[18] The drop from 28% to 7% in the frequency of the V2 order XP–Vf–expletive is not due to any change in the probability that some non-subject XP will be fronted in an existential sentence. This probability remains steady throughout the four historical periods at about 0.50, or about 0.33 if ELIs and NPBEs are excluded from the count. Consequently, the 28% to 7% drop directly indicates a (nearly) equivalent change in the likelihood that fronting of an arbitrary non-subject XP will trigger inversion of the expletive and the finite verb.

One should not be surprised that the frequency of XP–Vf–expletive order suffers only a minor loss between 1150 and 1420. V2 is indeed in decline as of the late 14th century (van Kemenade 1997a: 326). But expletives are pronouns, and in the Early Middle English of Period One, clauses with pronominal subjects are generally not V2 either, strictly speaking. In canonical clauses, pronouns precede Vf. Thus, importantly, we should not expect the obsolescence of V2 to have very strong effects in the domain of existential sentences.

that a fronted XP will trigger inversion of Vf and the pronominal, expletive subject (see note 18)—is secondary. And since the decrease in $p(F>X)$ is in turn the main contributor to the severe drop in $p(X=pro_X)$, we may regard the loss of VI as the most significant factor in the near disappearance of silent expletives.

TABLE 7.6. *Percentage of existentials with expletives that have VI order vs. XP–Vf–expletive order*

Period	VI (Vf–expl)		V2 (XP–Vf–expletive)		Total Vf>expletive	
1 (1150–1250)	46%	(33/71)	28%	(20/71)	75%	(53/71)
2 (1250–1350)	2%	(1/42)	0%	(0/42)	2%	(1/42)
	2%	(3/184)	7%	(13/184)	9%	(16/184)
3 (1350–1420)						
4 (1420–1500)	0%	(0/160)	8%	(12/160)	8%	(12/160)

We can now understand why the disappearance of unpronounced expletives was so sudden, when Case and Agreement weakened only gradually. They disappeared suddenly because VI did. The dimensions of the change seem catastrophic because before 1250 VI was unusually common among existentials.[19] Were VI as common among the existentials in Period Three as in Period One, the proportion of expletives silent in Period Three would be rather higher than the attested 3% (Table 7.4), perhaps as high as 20%,[20] and consequently the drop in $p(X=pro_X)$ would not be nearly so severe as it is.

What precipitated the loss of VI? Here I can only sketch a conjecture. Historically, the loss of VI seems to coincide with the shift in the relative positions of pronouns and the finite verb, manifested rather abruptly in the textual record around 1250. Before 1250, weak pronouns preceded Vf. But in the hundred and fifty or so years thereafter many texts (those of Chaucer, for example, as well as northern texts like *St Benet*) frequently show non-topic pronouns following Vf, giving a more standard V2 word order (Kroch and Taylor 1997; see also

---

[19] Not surprisingly, fully 63% of the silent expletives in Period One occur in VI sentences. This pattern was already noticed by Butler (1980), but he left it unexplained. Here I can offer at least a partial explanation. VI is the most common environment for inversion of Vf+F and the expletive in Early Middle English. Such inversion is a prerequisite for pro_X-drop. Thus pro_X-drop will most commonly happen in VI clauses.

[20] We arrive at this number, 20%, via the calculation of $p(F>X) \times p(X=pro_X | F>X)$. The first term, $p(F>X)$, should be the sum of two quantities: the observed relative frequency (hence probability, given the usual assumption) of XP–Vf–expl clauses in Period Three, viz. 0.07 (Table 7.6), and the hypothetical probability of VI clauses, viz. 0.46, which is the observed frequency of VI in Period One (Table 7.6). The second term, $p(X=pro_X | F>X)$, is estimated to be 0.38, as in Table 7.5. Thus: $(0.07 + 0.46) \times 0.38 = 0.20$, or 20%.

note 16). Kroch and Taylor (1997) analyse this as a change in the position of the verb. The older grammar had Vf in I°, and the later V2 grammar had it in C°. Now a typological observation becomes relevant. The modern Germanic languages in which declarative V1 is most productive are Icelandic and Yiddish (Sigurðsson 1990). These are also the languages for which it has been argued that Vf is generally in I°, but sometimes in C° (Diesing 1988, Iatridou and Kroch 1992, Rögnvaldsson and Thráinsson 1990, Santorini 1994). Suppose this is correct. Declarative V2 in Yiddish and Icelandic then amounts to the requirement that Vf occupy I° and some XP occupy Spec,IP. An explanation for the correlation with declarative V1 now becomes available: V1 involves exceptional movement of Vf from I° to C°, and since nothing requires lexicalization of Spec,CP, Vf in C° is free to come first. If this theory is sound, if it can be adapted to Early Middle English, and if Kroch and Taylor's (1997) theory of the change in pronoun–verb order is correct, then we might have an understanding of why V1 drops away with the disappearance of preverbal pronouns in the V2 texts of Middle English after 1250. Clearly, much further work is required to satisfy these ifs. And, more fundamentally, the original hypothesis wants confirmation. Does the loss of V1 in fact track the change in the relative position of Vf and subject pronouns? Presently I have no certain evidence either way.

7.6. CONCLUSION

This chapter has given a substantive defence of two hypotheses: (*a*) silent expletives in Germanic are licensed only in the c-command domain of a feature associated with the finite verb; (*b*) the finite verb in (Old and) Middle English c-commands pronouns it precedes, but not pronouns it follows. Thus the chapter contributes both to the general theory of expletives across Germanic, and to the ongoing debate over the clause structure of early English, where I have found reason to prefer the theory of Pintzuk (1991, 1996*b*) and Kroch and Taylor (1997) to that of van Kemenade (1987, 1997*a*). I have also brought to the foreground a correlation between the occurrence of silent existential expletives and verb-first word order, arguing that a sharp drop in the availability of V1 explains the enormous discrepancy in the frequency of silent expletives before and after 1250. The central virtue of this analysis is that it explains why pro_X did not disappear from the textual record at the same (relatively) gradual rate that the Case and Agreement systems decayed. I have said nothing about what in these systems underlies the capacity to identify pro_X, but my arguments should sharpen the focus of research into this question, since they imply that the sudden change *circa* 1250 does not correspond to a commensurate change in that capacity. Finally, in the course of defending (*a*) and (*b*), I have argued that locative inversions do not include silent expletives, a claim with extensive implications for the theory of subjects.

APPENDIX

Source texts from the Penn–Helsinki Parsed Corpus of Middle English

Title	MS date	Composition date (if thought different)	Number of sentence tokens
Period One: 1150–1250			
Ancrene Riwle	*c*.1225		620
Hali Meiðhad	1225	*c*.1200	531
Holy Rood Tree	*c*.1175	11th c.?	599
St Katherine	1225	*c*.1200	547
Lambeth Homilies	1225	Old English	734
Margarete	1225	*c*.1200	636
Peterborough Chronicles	1150		273
Sawles Warde	1225	*c*.1200	262
Trinity Homilies	1225	12th c.?	343
Vices and Virtues	1225	*c*.1200	608
Period Two: 1250–1350			
Ayenbite of Inwit	1340		491
The Earliest Prose Psalter	*c*.1350		2,770
Kentish Sermons	*c*.1250		207
Aelfred of Rievaulx's *De Institutione Inclusarum*	1400	Period Two	173
Richard Rolle's *Form of Living*	1450	1348	327
Richard Rolle's *Prose Treatises*	1440	1349	260
Period Three: 1350–1420			
Chaucer's *Treatise on the Astrolabe*	*a*.1450	*c*.1390	319
Chaucer's *Boethius*	*a*.1425	*c*.1380	501
The Northern Prose Rule of St Benet	*a*.1425		1,190
Brut	1400		540
Cloud of Unknowing	1425	1400?	726
Documents	1388–1419		380
Equatorie	*c*.1400		312
Gaytridge	1440	Period Three	173
Hilton's *Eight Chapters on Perfection*	1450	1396	215
Horses	1450	Period Three	437
Mandeville	1425	1400?	345
Mirk	1500	1415	217
Mirror of St Edmund, Thornton	late 14th c.		780
Mirror of St Edmund, Vernon	late 14th c.		843
Official Letters	1384–1425		115
Sermons from the MS Royal	1450	1415	346
Treatise on Phlebotomy	1400–1425		195
Trevisa's *Polychronicon*	1387		412

Vices and Virtues	1450	1400	343
Wycliffite Sermons	1400		886

Period Four: 1420–1500

Aelfred of Rievaulx's *De Institutione Inclusarum*	a.1450		95
Capgrave Chronicle	1464		424
Caxton's *Prologues and Epilogues*	1477–1484		206
The Cyrugie of Guy de Chauliac	1425		338
Life of St Edmund	1450	1438	300
Fitzjames's *Sermo die lune in Ebdomada*	c.1495		242
Gregory's *Chronicle*	1465		284
In Die Innocencium	1497		157
Margery Kempe	1438		589
Malory's *Morte*	1470		1,031
The Works of John Metham	1450		348
Official Letters	1425–1430		51
Private Letters	1440–1500		1,202
Caxton's *History of Reynard the Fox*	1481		733
The Commonplace Book of R. Reynes	1470–1500		535
Siege of Jerusalem	1500		727

Mechanisms of Syntactic Change

I

Features and Categories

8

Polarity Items in Romance:
Underspecification and Lexical Change

ANA MARIA MARTINS

8.1. INTRODUCTION

Features play a central role in the Minimalist version of the Principles and Parameters model of grammar. Under Minimalist assumptions, the only elements available to the computational system for human language (C_{HL}) are features and objects constructed from them, namely lexical items and syntactic objects of greater complexity formed through successive application of operations of C_{HL}. Acquiring a language, then, would involve at least constructing lexical items (by assembling in a principled way features from a presumably universal set) and refining C_{HL} in one of the possible ways (cf. Chomsky 1998). Assuming a view of grammatical change as closely related to language acquisition (see Pintzuk, Tsoulas, and Warner in this volume), we will expect grammatical change to correlate to the acquisition tasks at work in fixing a language: making a particular choice of parameter values and lexicon. The change I will be concerned with is a change in the featural make-up of a certain kind of lexical items, namely polarity items. Since features are what feed the operations of C_{HL}, this lexical change has, as expected, significant grammatical effects.

Throughout this chapter, I will be mainly looking at diachronic and geographical variation in the domain of Romance negative polarity items (§8.2 and §8.3). Variation with respect to affirmative polarity items, however, will also be examined (§8.4).

As for the gist of the analysis to be proposed, it will be shown that the observed variation can be thoroughly accounted for by motivating in syntactic

Earlier versions of this work were presented at the *11th Going Romance* (Groningen, 1997), at the *21st GLOW Colloquium* (Tilburg, 1998), and at *DIGS 5* (York, 1998). I am indebted to the audiences of these colloquia for criticism and stimulating discussion. My special thanks to Cecilia Poletto, Delia Bentley, Fernando Tato Plaza, Lăcrămioara Stroe, Simona Fulgeanu, and Ignacio Bosque for relevant data. *Fundação para a Ciência e a Tecnologia/Reitoria da Universidade de Lisboa* and *Fundação Calouste Gulbenkian* provided the financial support that enabled me to attend, respectively, the *GLOW Colloquium* and *DIGS 5*. I am grateful to Susan Powers for reading this chapter through and helping me put the final text into standard English.

terms—and elaborating on—a typology of polarity items well established in the semantics literature, the weak/strong distinction (§8.3). Underlying this approach is the view that because the computation system for human language must be conceived of as providing a set of instructions to be interpreted at the interfaces (Chomsky 1995), there must be 'semantic' instructions encoded in the feature system. The nature of such instructions is to be made precise, being a matter of empirical scrutiny.

This trend of research leads us to the inescapable question of how the system of features should be conceived. Feature theory has been paid little attention in the syntax literature. With a few exceptions, syntacticians have been working with a system of features (of the classical binary type) which has long been challenged in the domain of phonology. Yet 'the assumption that phonology and syntax share a number of fundamental formal properties is a heuristically fruitful one which may provide new insight into the nature of both modules' (van Riemsdijk 1982: 693). I intend to show that in order to deal adequately, on a syntactic basis, with the phenomenon of polarity, we need to adopt a theory of features which integrates the notion of underspecification. Only in this way will it be possible to motivate the subtleties of the context-sensitivity of polarity items (§8.3).

Additional outcomes of the analysis with respect to possible types of polarity items and to 'expletive negation' will be considered in §8.4, and the main results of this study will be pointed out in §8.5.

It will be shown that in Romance, negative words evolved from weak polarity items to strong polarity items. This is what in traditional terms has been viewed as a change from contextually negative (i.e. getting 'negative meaning' from a negative word in the relevant context) to intrinsically (or 'truly') negative.[1] Thus the set of licensing polar contexts for negative polarity items was narrowed, negative words becoming marginal and eventually unable to occur in non-negative modal environments. Affirmative polarity items followed a partially similar pattern of change, also reducing their polar versatility. Under current assumptions on the relation between syntactic change and language acquisition (in line with Lightfoot 1991, 1998), the rationale of change is located in the fact that less salient polar contexts are not able to constitute robust enough evidence for acquisition and therefore may be insufficiently learned and eventually not acquired.

8.2. NEGATIVE INDEFINITES IN ROMANCE: THE DATA

Negative indefinites of the type listed in (1) below are the kind of Romance polarity items I will be considering in this section and in the next one.

---

[1] Cf. for example Keniston (1937: 608 ff.).

(1)		'nobody', 'no (one)', 'anybody', 'any (one)'	'nothing', 'anything'
	Portuguese	ninguém, nenhum	nada
	Galician	ninguén, ningún	nada
	Spanish	nadie, ninguno	nada
	Catalan	ningú, cap	res, gens
	French	personne, aucun, nul	rien
	Italian	nessuno	niente
	Venetian	nisun	gnente
	Romanian	nimeni, niciunul	nimic

Such polarity items are commonly referred in the literature as 'n-words' (a term due to Laka 1990), and are analysed either as negative quantifiers (e.g. Zanuttini 1991, Haegeman 1995), as negative indefinites (e.g. Bosque 1980, Laka 1990, Ladusaw 1992), or as ambiguous between quantifiers and indefinites (e.g. Rizzi 1982, van der Wouden and Zwarts 1993, Herburger 1998). There has been a long and rich debate on this issue which I am unable to do justice to here. As this is not crucial for the line of enquiry I will pursue, such a review goes beyond the scope of this chapter. Nevertheless, I will implicitly adhere to the view that n-words are indefinites. Since I will not go into the arguments which support this position, I refer the reader to Acquaviva (1993), Suñer (1995), Giannakidou (1997), and Peres (1997) for insight and further references.

For sake of clarification, I should also say that I will be using the label 'Old Romance' as a convenient shorthand to refer to 'the older stages of the Romance languages'. I will use 'Modern Romance' in a similar vein. So 'Old Romance' is not meant to refer to a particular linguistic entity nor to a periodization across all the Romance languages.

As I will be dealing with several linguistic varieties, ample exemplification will be needed to support the intended descriptive generalizations and empirically motivate the analysis to be put forth. In order not to overload the text with data, however, I will use a limited number of examples and at times refer the reader to a final Appendix (§8.6) for further empirical evidence.

8.2.1. *Old Romance*

Old Romance generally shows no subject/object asymmetry with respect to the co-occurrence of negative indefinites with negation proper in negative concord constructions. Negative indefinites, either pre-verbal or post-verbal, co-occurred with the overt negative marker. Sentences (2) and (3) below and (49) to (51) in the Appendix are relevant examples taken from medieval literary sources.[2] The

---

[2] Old Romance contrasts with Classical Latin which does not display negative concord constructions. In Vulgar Latin, however, Romance-type constructions are already found. For relevant examples see Molinelli (1988: 33–40).

abbreviations 'OP', 'OS', ' OC', 'OI', and 'OF' stand for 'Old Portuguese', 'Old Spanish', 'Old Catalan', 'Old Italian', and 'Old French', respectively.

(2) (a) OS   que a myo Çid Ruy Diaz, que *nadi*   *nol*   diessen posada
    that to my Lord Ruy Diaz that nobody not-him give   lodging
    'that nobody give lodging to Mio Cid Rui Diaz'
    (*Cantar de Mio Cid* 25. Menéndez-Pidal, ed. 1946: 910)

   (b) OS   Fablo Muño Gustioz, *non* spero a   *nadi*
    spoke Muño Gustioz not waited for nobody
    'Muño Gustioz spoke, he didn't wait for anybody else to do it.'
    (*Cantar de Mio Cid* 1481. Menéndez-Pidal, ed. 1946: 953)

(3) (a) OF   *Nient* *ne* nous vaut,   vous en   venrés
    nothing not us   is-worth you of-it will-see
    'Nothing is as valuable as we are, you will see.'
    (Cf. Foulet 1930: 245)

   (b) OF   Se g' iere Deus, je feroie   / lo siecle tot altrement, / et
    if I were God I would-do the century all otherwise and
    meillor gent i   metroie, / car   cist
    better people there would-put because these
    n' i valent *neient*
    not are-worth nothing
    'If I were God, I would do this century differently, and I would put a better people in it, because these people aren't worth anything.'
    (Cf. Foulet 1930: 280)

At later stages of Old Romance (with different chronologies for different linguistic varieties) the overt negative marker becomes optional with pre-verbal negative indefinites, as shown by examples (4), from fifteenth-century Portuguese, and (5), from thirteenth-century Italian (Florentine).

(4) (a) OP   *Nenhũu nom* mostrava que era famiinto
    no-one not showed that was starving
    'Nobody showed that he/she was starving.'
    (Fernão Lopes, *Crónica de D. João I.* Freire, org. 1977: 270)

   (b) OP   *Nenhũu* podera seer emlegido a semelhante honra
    no-one can be elevated to such   honour
    'Nobody will reach such honour.'
    (Fernão Lopes, *Crónica de D. João I.* Freire, org. 1977: 373)

(5) (a) OI   Mai *nessuno* omo *non* si   può guardare
    never no   man not himself can protect
    'Nobody can ever protect himself.'
    (Chiaro Davanzati. Cf. Posner 1984: 21)

(*b*) *OI* *Nesuna* gioa creo   che 'n esto mondo sia
       no   joy I-believe that in this world might-be
      'I do not believe that there might be any joy in this world.'
      (Chiaro Davanzati. Cf. Posner 1984: 21)

Another trait of Old Romance is the frequent use of negative indefinites in non-negative contexts. These are 'non-assertive' (Milner 1979) or 'modal' (Giannakidou 1994, Bosque 1996*a*, *b*) contexts, such as questions, imperatives, conditionals, comparatives, the scope of modal verbs, the scope of words expressing prohibition, generic constructions, subjunctive clauses introduced by the temporal connective *antes que* 'before'.[3] This particular use of negative indefinites, found in examples (6) to (9) below and (52) to (57) in the Appendix, is not found in non-negative assertive contexts, that is, not in declarative clauses.

(6) *OS* ¿Que sabe *nadie* de la manera que toca Dios a cada uno?
      what knows nobody of the manner that reveals God to each one
      'What does anybody know about the way that God reveals himself
      to each one of us?'
      (Cf. Keniston 1937: 610)

(7) *OF* S' il i   a *nul*   si hardit / qui s'   esmueve de joie fere, / . . .
      if it there is no-one so brave   that himself moves   of joy doing
      il le   fera   prendre ou desfere
      he him will-make imprison or destroy
      'If there is anyone so brave as to move to show joy, he will have
      him imprisoned or killed.'
      (Cf. Foulet 1930: 245)

---

[3] These are the kind of contexts where 'modal polarity items' (Bosque 1996*a*, *b*), such as Spanish *cualquier* (*a*) and *siquiera*, are licensed. Modal polarity items are excluded from affirmative clauses without modal import. The examples below are taken from Bosque (1996*b*).

(i) (*a*) ¿Has   escrito acaso   *cualquiera* de tus ideas?
      have-you written by-chance any   of your ideas
      'Did you happen to write any of your ideas?'
  (*b*) *He   escrito *cualquiera* de mis ideas.
      I-have written any   of my ideas

(ii) (*a*) Si la vieras   *siquiera* una vez.
      if her you-might-see at-least one time
      'if you might see her at least once'
  (*b*) *Te llamó   *siquiera* una vez.
      you he-called at-least one time
      'He called you at least once.'

(iii) (*a*) Pudo entrar   por   la ventana *cualquier* ladrón.
      could come-in through the window any   thief
      'Any thief could come in through the window.'
  (*b*) *Entró por   la ventana *cualquier* ladrón.
      came-in through the window any   thief

(8) *OS* Haçedme entender   como puede *ningun* criado alcanzar tanta
           make-me understand how   can   no   servant reach   so-much
           priuanza
           intimacy
           'Make me understand how any servant can become so intimate with
           his lord.'
               (Cf. Keniston 1937: 610)

(9) *OP* E   por decreto publico foi   defeso   que *ninguem*
           and by a-decree public it-was forbidden that nobody
           navegasse
           would-navigate
           'And by a public decree it was forbidden for anybody to navigate.'
               (Cf. Ali 1931: 199)

8.2.2. *Modern Romance*

The above-mentioned features of the earliest stages of Old Romance, taken as
a cluster, were lost in Modern Romance as the result of historical change. As far
as I am aware, there is no contemporary Romance language or dialect which
displays the obligatory co-occurrence of negative indefinites with the sentential
negative marker on a par with the possibility of using negative indefinites in
non-negative modal contexts. Historical change led to the splitting of the Romance linguistic domain into four linguistic groups as far as the behaviour of
negative indefinites is concerned. Different levels of conservatism and innovation
are displayed by the modern Romance languages.

8.2.2.1. *Romanian, north-eastern Italian dialects (Venetian)*

Romanian and some north-eastern Italian dialects, such as Venetian, show similar
traits with respect to the aspects of negative indefinites under consideration.
Some varieties of Rhaetoromance might belong in this linguistic group as well.
I will only consider Romanian and Venetian, however, since I could not obtain
a complete picture of Rhaetoromance.[4]

   Negative indefinites, either pre-verbal or post-verbal, obligatorily co-occur
with the overt negative marker in Romanian (*Rom.*) and in Venetian (*Ven.*), as
exemplified by (10) and (11):

(10) *Rom.*   *Nimeni* *(*nu*)* a   venit la petrecere
               nobody   not   has come to the-party
               'Nobody came to the party.'

---

[4] The data in Posner (1984) suggest that Rhaetoromance languages behave like Romanian and
Venetian. On the other hand, the data on Western Friulan (dialect of Felettis di Palmanova) show that
this dialect behaves more like Standard Italian. I am indebted to Cecilia Poletto for the Friulan and
Venetian data; and to Lăcrŏmioara Stroe and Simona Fulgeanu for the Romanian data.

(11) *Ven.*   *Gnente* *(*no*) ghe piaze*
                 nothing   not him pleases
                 'Nothing pleases him.'

In this respect, Romanian and Venetian are conservative, displaying the same behaviour as the earliest stages of Old Romance. But Romanian and Venetian differ from Old Romance in not allowing negative indefinites in non-negative modal contexts, as illustrated by examples (12) and (13) below and (58) to (61) in the Appendix.

(12) *Rom.*   Ai   văzut **nimic*   / *ceva*?
                 have-you seen   nothing / something
                 'Did you see anything?'

(13) *Ven.*   Ze vegnuo **nisun*   / *qualchedun*?
                 is come   nobody / somebody
                 'Did anybody come?'

8.2.2.2. *Catalan*

Catalan (*Cat.*) behaves just like late Old Romance. In negative clauses, pre-verbal negative indefinites optionally co-occur with the overt negative marker. Example (14), from Modern Catalan, is to be compared with examples (4) and (5) from later stages of Old Romance.

(14) *Cat.*   *Ningú* (*no*) *m' ha vist*
                 nobody (not) me has seen
                 'Nobody saw me.'
                            (Cf. Badia Margarit 1962: 40)

As for non-negative clauses, negative indefinites are licensed in a subset of the modal contexts where licensing of negative indefinites is attested in Old Romance. Examples (15) to (17), from Modern Catalan, should be compared with examples (6) to (9) from Old Romance; cf. also (52) to (57) in the Appendix.

(15) *Cat.*   Ha vingut *ningú*   aquesta tarda?
                 has come nobody this   afternoon
                 'Did anybody come this afternoon?'
                            (Cf. Badia Margarit 1962: 41)

(16) *Cat.*   Demana-li si   en   sap   *res*
                 ask him   whether of-it he-knows nothing
                 'Ask him whether he knows anything about it.'
                            (Cf. Badia Margarit 1962: 41)

(17) *Cat.*   Si hi   trobeu   *cap* defecte, digueu- m' ho
                 if in-it you-find no defect   tell   me about-it
                 'If you find any defect, let me know.'
                            (Cf. Badia Margarit 1962: 41)

In modal contexts, negative indefinites alternate with positive indefinites, as illustrated by example (18). The choice of a negative or a positive indefinite might be driven by sociolectal factors.[5]

(18) (a) *Cat.*   Si vols   menjar *res*,   avisa 'm
                     if you-want to-eat   nothing warn me
                     'If you want to eat anything, let me know.'
                     (Cf. Vallduví 1994: 289)

      (b) *Cat.*   Si vols   menjar *alguna cosa*, avisa 'm
                     if you-want to-eat   something   warn me
                     'If you want to eat anything, let me know.'
                     (Cf. Vallduví 1994: 289)

On the other hand—as expected given what has been said about Old Romance —in Modern Catalan negative indefinites are excluded from non-negative assertive contexts, as shown in example (19). Therefore the declarative clause in (19*c*) is ungrammatical, only a positive indefinite being allowed in such an environment (cf. (19*d*)):

(19) (a) *Cat.*   T'   ha passat   *res*?
                     to-you has happened nothing
                     'Did anything happen to you?'
                     (Cf. Badia Margarit 1962: 243)

      (b) *Cat.*   T'   ha passat   *alguna cosa*?
                     to-you has happened something
                     'Did anything happen to you?'
                     (Cf. Badia Margarit 1962: 42)

      (c) *Cat.* *T'   ha passat   *res*.
                     to-you has happened nothing
                     'Something happened to you.'

      (d) *Cat.*   T'   ha passat   *alguna cosa*.
                     to-you has happened something
                     'Something happened to you.'

8.2.2.3. *Spanish, Galician, Italian, French*

Spanish (*Sp.*), Galician (*Gal.*), Italian (*It.*), and French (*Fr.*) differ from Catalan in not allowing pre-verbal negative indefinites to co-occur with negation proper in negative concord constructions, as shown by examples (20) to (24) below.

---

[5] 'The use of non-negative existentials is favoured in the speech of younger speakers' (Vallduví 1994: 288).

(20) *Sp.*　　　　　*Nada* (**no*) funciona
　　　　　　　　nothing (not) works
　　　　　　　　'Nothing works.'
　　　　　　　　(Cf. Vallduví 1994: 276)

(21) *Gal.*　　　　*Nada* (**no*) quero de　vostede
　　　　　　　　nothing (not) want from you
　　　　　　　　'I don't want anything from you.'
　　　　　　　　(Cf. Álvarez, Regueira, and Monteagudo 1986: 458)

(22) *It.*　　　　　*Niente* (**no*) gli fa　　piacere
　　　　　　　　nothing (not) him makes pleasure
　　　　　　　　'Nothing pleases him.'
　　　　　　　　(Cf. Manzotti and Rigamonti 1991: 264)

(23) (*Standard*) *Fr.*　　*Personne n'* est (**pas*) arrivé
　　　　　　　　nobody NE is NEG　arrived
　　　　　　　　'Nobody arrived.'

(24) (*Advanced*) *Fr.*　　*Personne* est (**pas*) arrivé
　　　　　　　　Nobody is NEG　arrived
　　　　　　　　'Nobody arrived.'

As for Standard French, I should say that I am taking *pas*, not *ne*, as the true propositional negator, in view of the fact that *ne*, in contrast to *pas*, cannot by itself express negation in any variety of French[6] (cf. Rizzi 1982: 175–6, Zanuttini 1994: 436).[7] Example (25), which is ungrammatical both in Standard and Advanced French, contrasts with (26), which is not allowed in Standard French but is permitted in Advanced French.

---

[6] According to Bernini and Ramat (1996), in Middle and seventeenth-century French, negative indefinites co-occurred with *ne . . . pas*. This clearly shows that French changed in just the same direction as Galician, Spanish, Catalan, and Italian. Sentences (i) and (ii) below would be ungrammatical in Modern French (*pas* not being allowed in those sentences). In Modern French, in contrast to the other above-mentioned Romance languages, negative indefinites do not co-occur with the negative marker both in pre-verbal and post-verbal position; see §8.3.1.3.

(i) *Middle French*　　⟨Pierre *n'* a　*pas* vu　*personne*⟩
　　　　　　　　Pierre NE has NEG seen nobody
　　　　　　　　'Pierre didn't see anybody.'
　　　　　　　　(Bernini and Ramat 1996: 174)
(ii) *17th-century French* *Ne* faites *pas* semblant　de *rien*
　　　　　　　　NE do　　NEG an-expression of nothing
　　　　　　　　'Act as if nothing happened.'
　　　　　　　　(Molière; Bernini and Ramat 1996: 174)
[7] Whatever the role of *ne* is in French, this role seems to be taken up by *sans* 'without' in without-clauses: in this type of clause, negative indefinites dispense with the presence of *ne* in Standard French.

(25) *Fr.*   *Jean *n*' est arrivé
                   Jean NE is   arrived

(26) (*Advanced*) *Fr.*   Jean est *pas* arrivé
                   Jean is NEG arrived
                   'Jean hasn't arrived.'

   Spanish, Galician, Italian, and French are similar to Catalan in licensing negative indefinites in non-negative modal contexts. This is illustrated by sentences
(27) to (30) below and by (62) to (65) in the Appendix. The set of modal
contexts where negative indefinites are allowed is not the same for all of the
languages under consideration, a fact I will return to in the next section.

(27) *Gal.* ¿Cuando me regalaches ti   *nada*?
         when   me gave   you nothing
         'When did you offer me anything?'[8]

(28) *Sp.*   El comandante prohibió que saliera   *nadie* del
         the commander prohibited that would-leave nobody from-the
         cuartel.
         barracks
         'The commander prohibited anybody from leaving the barracks.'
            (Cf. Bosque 1980: 74)

(29) *It.*   Si   domandava se sarebbe   venuto *nessuno*.
         herself she-asked   if would-be come   no-one
         'She wondered if anyone would come.'
            (Cf. Bernini and Ramat 1996: 37)

(30) *Fr.*   Pierre est parti avant que *personne* ait   pu   faire
         Pierre is left before that nobody   might-have been-able to-do
         aucun geste
         no   move
         'Pierre left before anyone could make a move.'
            (Cf. Milner 1979: 81)

   Spanish, Galician, Italian, and French data are also similar to Catalan with respect to competition between negative and positive indefinites in modal contexts
(see examples (31) below and (66) and (67) in the Appendix) and exclusion of negative indefinites from non-negative declarative clauses (see example (32) below).

(31) (*a*) *Sp.* Dudo   que venga   *nadie*
             I-doubt that might-come nobody
             'I doubt that anybody is coming.'
                (Cf. Vallduví 1994: 277)

---

[8] Example (27) is courtesy of Fernando Tato Plaza.

(b) *Sp.*   Dudo   que venga   *alguien*
           I-doubt that might-come somebody
           'I doubt that anybody is coming.'
           (Cf. Vallduví 1994: 277)

(32) (a) *It.*   Si   domandava se sarebbe   venuto *nessuno*
           herself she-asked   if would-be come   no-one
           'She wondered if anyone would come.'

(b) *It.*   *Sapeva   che sarebbe   venuto *nessuno*
           she-knew that would-be come   no-one
           (Cf. Bernini and Ramat 1996: 37)

8.2.2.4. *Portuguese*

In Portuguese[9] (*Port.*), pre-verbal negative indefinites are not allowed to co-occur with the negative marker. In this respect, Portuguese is similar to Spanish, Galician, Italian, and French:

(33) *Port.*   *Ninguém* (*não) sabe   o que se passa
           nobody   (not)   knows what is-happening
           'Nobody knows what is going on.'

In contrast to Spanish, Galician, Italian, and French, however, Portuguese does not license negative indefinites in the kind of non-negative contexts where they are attested in those other languages. In non-negative modal contexts only positive indefinites can occur. This is shown by examples (34) and (35) below and (68) and (69) in the Appendix. Portuguese thus appears as the most innovative Romance language with regard to the relevant aspects of negative indefinites.

(34) (a) *Port.*   *Telefonou *ninguém*?
           called   nobody
           'Did anybody call?'

(b) *Port.*   Telefonou *alguém*?
           called   somebody
           'Did anybody call?'

(35) (a) *Port.*   *Duvido que venha   *ninguém*.
           I-doubt that might-come nobody
           'I doubt that anybody will come.'

---

[9] As in all the other cases where there is no further specification, I am using the standard variety of the intended language. As for Portuguese, the facts I will be describing are valid for both Standard European Portuguese and Standard Brazilian Portuguese, although all the examples are from European Portuguese. In Brazilian Portuguese, as well as in European Portuguese, there are geographical and social dialects which display a more conservative pattern than the one described for Standard Portuguese. This applies to both the co-occurrence of negative indefinites with negation proper and also the licensing of negative indefinites in non-negative modal contexts.

(*b*) *Port.*   Duvido que venha   *alguém.*
                I-doubt that might-come somebody
                'I doubt that anybody will come.'

8.2.3. *Negative indefinites in Romance—summary*

Table 8.1 summarizes the facts about Old and Modern Romance described in §8.2, which will be accounted for in the next section.

TABLE 8.1.

	Co-occurrence of preverbal negative indefinites with negation proper	Licensing of negative indefinites in non-negative modal contexts
Old Romance (earliest stages)	OK (obligatory)	OK
Modern Romanian Venetian	OK (obligatory)	*
Old Romance (later stages) Modern Catalan	OK (optional)	OK
Modern Galician Modern Spanish Modern Italian Modern French	*	OK
Modern Portuguese	*	*

* indicates an ungrammatical option.

8.3. POLARITY FEATURES, UNDERSPECIFICATION, AND CHANGE

8.3.1. *Assumptions*

Before I proceed to present a proposal to account for variation and change in the domain of Romance polarity items, I must make clear what my assumptions are with respect to feature theory, the syntactic encoding of polarity distinctions, and the computational operations at play when negation-features (or in general polarity-features) are to be licensed.

8.3.1.1. *The feature system*

Arguing for a feature theory accessible, as a module of grammar, to both syntax and phonology, Rooryck (1994) applies the phonological notion of underspecification to syntactic features.[10] The analysis I will put forward crucially relies on Rooryck's insight on the nature of the feature system, namely the idea that features are associated with one of three possible values: specified (+), non-variable underspecified (o), and variable underspecified (α). Rooryck's feature

---

[10] On the empirical level, Rooryck's paper deals with agreement in relative clauses in various dialects of French.

system is single-valued (or 'unary') in the sense that no element is characterized by the explicit specification of the fact that it lacks a certain property.[11] The non-variable underspecified value (o) for a certain feature is a notational device that marks the absence of the property conveyed by that feature. So an element with a [o neg-feature], for example, is simply unable to enter any operation related to the expression of a negative meaning. Borrowing a metaphor from phonological work on vowel harmony, a non-variable underspecified feature can be said to be 'opaque' inasmuch as it cannot enter or trigger 'harmony' relations (i.e. agreement-like relations). In contrast, variable underspecified features can enter operations leading to the filling in of their former underspecified value: a feature-filling 'agreement' relation converts $[\alpha F]$ to $[+F]$. That is, α-features are context-sensitive; given an adequate environment, they can 'harmonize' (with it) and are therefore said to be 'transparent'.

'Nonvariable' or o-features should be thought of as 'neutral' features: they have no positive or negative value for a given feature, they simply mark the absence of a specific feature value. In terms of an Attribute–Value feature system, this means that a given feature has an Attribute specification without a Value . . . . Variable underspecified features should be thought of as 'chameleonlike' features . . . . 'Variable' or α-features do not have a value of their own: their value needs to be 'filled in' by the features of the elements surrounding them.   (Rooryck 1994: 209)

8.3.1.2. *Polarity features (the make-up of 'Pol')*

Following Laka (1990) and Zanuttini (1994, 1997), among others, I will be assuming that the structure of the clause includes a functional projection, say PolP, where polarity features are located. I take Pol always to contain the same set of features, that is, aff(irmation)-features, neg(ation)-features and mod(ality)-features—roughly corresponding to the grammatical encoding of the semantic notions of 'veridicality', 'avericality', and 'non-veridicality' respectively (cf. Zwarts 1995, Giannakidou 1997, and Espinal 1998). Different interpretations associated with different types of sentences, in what defines polarity, will depend on the particular mapping between those features and the feature values + (specified) or o (non-variable underspecified)—variable underspecification (α-features) being by assumption a property of lexical items only.[12] For example:

---

[11] Underlying the proposals for a unary feature system is the contention that the lack of a certain property (expressed by a minus value in a binary feature system) cannot be the trigger for grammatical processes (both in phonology and in syntax); cf. Rooryck (1994: 218), van der Hulst and van de Weijer (1995), and references cited there.

[12] See Déchaine and Tremblay (1998: 27) for the proposal that 'functional categories, even null ones, always make a semantic contribution' and Zanuttini (1994: 428) for the claim that 'languages express sentential negation via certain negative features that are present in the projection PolP'. A functional category with underspecified features would not make (by itself) a semantic contribution, such as expressing a certain polarity value. On the other hand, only functional heads with specified feature values can ensure compatibility among different lexical items in a syntactic structure (therefore excluding sentences built up from unfit numerations).

(36)   Pol [+aff, oneg, omod]   — John left.
        Pol [oaff, +neg, omod]   — John didn't leave.
        Pol [oaff, oneg, +mod (mod: 'interrogative')]— Did John leave?

8.3.1.3. *Licensing of negation*

I will adopt Zanuttini's (1994, 1997) conception that 'languages express
sentential negation via certain negative features that are present in the projection
PolP' (Zanuttini 1994: 428). 'The other [NegP] positions, on the other hand, are
simply positions where the negative element is generated but which do not carry
syntactic features corresponding to sentential negation' (Zanuttini 1997: 11).

Given Chomsky's checking theory (of 1993 and 1995), it thus follows that a
Pol-head specified for neg-features must have these features checked, i.e. licensed, by the relevant features of a negative lexical element. Checking (overtly)
takes place when either a negative lexical head or a negative XP moves into the
checking domain of Pol.[13]

Zanuttini accounts for the interaction between the distribution of negation
proper and the distribution of negative indefinites in Romance by assuming that
there is variation across languages with respect to the strength of the neg-features
of Pol. In languages where the neg-features of Pol are strong (e.g. Spanish and
Portuguese), checking must take place before Spell Out; in these languages either
the negative marker or another negative element, such as a negative indefinite,
will precede the verb. In languages where the neg-features of Pol are weak (e.g.
French), checking takes place at LF; in these languages a negative element will
not necessarily precede the verb.[14]

---

[13] The checking domain of a head H includes the specifier(s) of H and the head(s) or features
adjoined to H (cf. Chomsky 1995). Chomsky (1993) assumes a less restrictive version of checking
domain allowing an element adjoined to a non-minimal category X (i.e. a maximal or an intermediate
projection) to be in the checking domain of the head of X. Zanuttini (1997: 11, 156) admits that
strong neg-features might be checked by a negative constituent in a position c-commanding PolP.

[14] According to Zanuttini (1994: 437, 448; 1997: 58), raising of *ne* in French is driven by its clitic-
like nature, not by the necessity of overtly checking the [+neg] feature of Pol, this being a weak
feature. Observe the contrast between, for example, Portuguese (with strong [+neg]) and French (with
weak [+neg]). Recall that French *ne* occurs in Standard French but not in Advanced French; moreover, it does not behave as a negative marker *per se*:

(i)   (a) Port.   A   Maria *não* gosta de *ninguém*
                   the Maria not likes of nobody
                   'Maria doesn't like anybody.'
      (b) Port.   *Ninguém* gosta da   Maria
                   nobody   likes of-the Maria
                   'Nobody likes Maria.'

(ii) (a) Fr.   Marie (n') aime *personne*
                   Marie (NE) likes nobody
                   'Marie doesn't like anybody.'
      (b) Fr.   *Personne* (n') aime Marie
                   nobody   (NE) likes Marie
                   'Nobody likes Marie.'

The analysis I will put forth in the next section relies on Zanuttini's proposal.

8.3.2. *Accounting for the data*

With the above-mentioned assumptions in mind, let us hypothesize that the distinction between strong and weak negative polarity items which has been proposed in the semantics literature (Sánchez Valencia, van der Wouden, and Zwarts 1993, among others) is a matter of specified vs. α-underspecified neg-features.

Strong negative polarity items, being specified for neg-features (i.e. [+neg]), can check the [+neg] feature of Pol in negative clauses, in the terms of Zanuttini (1994, 1997). Therefore, when they get into the right position (a checking position in the domain of Pol) at the right time (before Spell Out in languages with strong neg-features), they dispense with the presence of the overt negative marker which is then, presumably for economy reasons, forbidden. Weak negative polarity items, being underspecified for neg-features, cannot check the specified neg-feature of Pol in negative clauses; the presence of the overt negative marker is therefore needed. Since α-features are 'transparent' features, though, there will be no feature clash between the underspecified neg-feature of the weak negative polarity item and the specified neg-feature of Pol. The weak negative polarity item will have its neg-feature value 'filled in' under an agreement configuration to the negative marker.

On the other hand, strong negative polarity items, being [+neg], can only be licensed in negative contexts, that is, under a checking relation to a Pol-head specified for neg-features. Weak negative polarity items, being [α neg] and potentially also [α mod], can be licensed in negative contexts and modal contexts as well. Their interpretation will depend on the feature specification of the elements with which they enter an agreement-type relation. Being [0 aff], however, they are not licensed in affirmative clauses (without modal import); since 0-features are 'opaque' features, there would be a clash between the [0 aff] feature of the polarity item and the [+aff] feature of the Pol-head.[15]

---

[15] It should be noted that under the approach I am proposing here, the occurrence of weak polarity items in syntactic islands, such as the relative clause in (i) below, is not problematic. This is because according to my analysis, licensing of the polarity item in (i) does not involve movement into the specifier position of PolP [= NegP] of the main clause; polarity licensing is always clause internal, depending on the relevant Pol-head having the right features. So in sentence (i) below, from Catalan, the embedded clause must have a [+mod] Pol. The right feature specification for an embedded Pol derives from its polarity/mood dependency with respect to the main clause. Polarity/mood dependencies are presumably mediated by certain operator-features in CP (which is selected by the main predicate), as was suggested to me by Jacqueline Guéron and is proposed by Klooster (1998).

(i) (*a*) No dire   secrets [que puguin   ofendre ningu]
        not tell-FUT-1SG secrets that can-SUBJ-3PL offend   anybody
        'I will not tell secrets that might offend anybody.'

   (*b*) *A qui₁ no em diras   secrets que puguin   ofendre t₁]
        to who not me tell-FUT-2SG secrets that can-SUBJ-3PL offend
             (Quer 1993)

In the history of Romance, negative indefinites evolved from weak polarity items to strong polarity items, therefore 'reducing' their degree of underspecification. Meanwhile, they went through a stage of lexical ambiguity, which was common to all Romance languages at a certain point and is still found in Catalan. In other languages, the lexical ambiguity between weak negative polarity items and strong negative polarity items evolved to a lexical ambiguity between modal polarity items (Bosque 1996a, b) and strong negative polarity items.[16] Modal polarity items are o-underspecified for neg-features and aff-features but specified for mod-features.[17] The relevant languages do not allow pre-verbal negative indefinites to co-occur with the negative marker, but do license negative indefinites in modal contexts.

A question arises at this point: what could have prompted negative indefinites to reduce their degree of variable underspecification, therefore becoming, over time, more restrictive with respect to their licensing contexts? The answer is to be found in the linking of grammatical change and language acquisition and in learning considerations. If children rely on strong positive empirical evidence (or on specific cues) in order to make decisions leading to a particular linguistic choice while building up their grammars, they may well not identify a less salient polar environment as a licensing context for a certain kind of polarity items. In non-negative modal contexts, both negative indefinites and positive indefinites might occur (cf. (19a–b) and (31) above), but positive indefinites are far more common than negative indefinites. Hence this kind of context is a less salient licensing environment for negative polarity items than negative contexts are.[18]

---

[16] This is viewed by Herburger (1998) as an ambiguity between 'negative polarity items (NPIs)' and 'negative quantifiers (NQs)', respectively.

[17] Leaving aside lexical ambiguity, an example of a (strong) modal polarity item is Portuguese *ao menos* 'at least', which is licensed in non-negative modal contexts only:

(i) *Port.*   Sabes   *ao menos* quem ele é?
             you-know at least   who he is
             'Do you know at least who he is?'

(ii) *Port.*   Se soubesses *ao menos* quem ele é . . .
              if you-knew at least   who he is
              'if you could at least know who he is'

(iii) *Port.* *Não sei   *ao menos* quem ele é.
              not I-know at least   who he is
              'I don't even know who he is.'

(iv) *Port.* *Ela sabe   *ao menos* quem ele é.
             she knows at least   who he is
             'At least she knows who he is.'

Similar behaviour is exhibited by *ao menos* in Spanish, as has been kindly pointed out to me by Ignacio Bosque.

[18] Yet the well-known fact that at a certain stage young children generally use the overt negation marker with negative indefinites (of all kinds) appears to be at odds with the proposed understanding of change. Apparently, at an initial stage of acquisition children favour an interpretation of negative

The results of van der Wal's (1996) study of the acquisition of negative polarity items by Dutch children support this line of reasoning. She found that weak negative polarity items are straightforwardly used in negative contexts much earlier than in non-negative modal contexts. Van der Wal (1996) demonstrates that from the outset, negative polarity items have a restricted distribution in the children's speech, making it clear that children are sensitive to the peculiar nature of such linguistic entities from early on. However, children start out with a distribution of weak negative polarity items which is confined to negative sentences, a distribution far more restricted than the one found in the grammar of adult Dutch.[19] Whereas licensing of negative polarity items by instances of classical negation is precocious and steady, acquisition of the full range of licensing environments, namely the non-negative modal ones, is a prolonged gradual process which continues until the teenage years.[20]

The late acquisition of certain licensers might explain why considerable variation between speakers in the licensing of negative polarity items in non-negative modal contexts is commonly found within one language community (cf. Vallduví 1994 and van der Wouden 1994). It might also account for the emergence of lexical ambiguity if we admit that children cannot backtrack in an unrestricted way from earlier decisions (cf. Dresher 1999). If the extreme salience of negative polar environments as licensers for negative polarity items in a certain language leads the child to posit their strong nature at an early stage of language acquisition, he/she may not be able to review this choice when confronted with other kinds of licensing environments. In this situation the child will be left with the option for lexical ambiguity and may or may not choose it.

8.3.3. *A classification of negative indefinites in (Old and Modern) Romance*

The account I have just sketched leads to a classification of negative indefinites in (Old and Modern) Romance as given in Table 8.2. Besides summarizing the

indefinites as weak polarity items, therefore allowing for variable underspecification, instead of choosing a specified value for a certain feature. However, if we adopt the proposal of Nunes (1998: 163) that 'the elements adjoined to H a priori form the most natural configuration for the checking domain of H', we can view the relevant aspect of children's syntax in a different way. Children might be using only the simpler option with respect to checking at this stage, simpler in view of the fact that 'a given element moves to enter into a checking relation with the features of H, not with the projection formed by H and its complement'; so the [+neg] feature of Pol will always be checked by a negative lexical element which is a head, not by negative XPs.

[19] In the adults' speech, the frequency of licensing by *niet* 'not' is about three times greater than the frequency of licensing by other licensers—namely modal ones. The frequency of licensing by other licensers increases in the adults' writing (cf. van der Wal 1996: 85).

[20] According to van der Wal's grammaticality judgement test, only the group of 13- and 14-year olds 'are close to the adult standard'. The judgements of 7- and 8-year olds are still 'fuzzy' for sentences with certain pseudo-licensers. 'The two middle groups in this study, the 9- and 10-year olds and the 11- and 12-year olds, demonstrate that the differences between the oldest and youngest age groups are best described as representing gradual changes' (cf. van der Wal 1996: 175).

results of the proposed analysis, Table 8.2 shows clearly how synchronic and
diachronic variation are related.

TABLE 8.2.

Old Romance (earliest stages)	WEAK NEGATIVE POLARITY ITEMS [0 aff, α neg, α mod]	
Modern Romanian Venetian	[0 aff, α neg, 0 mod]	
Old Romance (later stages) Modern Catalan	WEAK NEGATIVE POLARITY ITEMS [0 aff, α neg, α mod]	STRONG NEGATIVE POLARITY ITEMS [0 aff, +neg, 0 mod]
Modern Galician Modern Spanish Modern Italian Modern French	MODAL POLARITY ITEMS [0 aff, 0 neg, +mod]	STRONG NEGATIVE POLARITY ITEMS [0 aff, +neg, 0 mod]
Modern Portuguese	STRONG NEGATIVE POLARITY ITEMS [0 aff, +neg, 0 mod]	

With respect to modal polarity items, note that the specified value for
'modality' will consist of the specification of the actual set of modality values
('interrogative', 'imperative', 'conditional', etc.) that license modal polarity items
in a given grammar. Variation across grammars with respect to the spectrum of
licensing contexts for modality items is therefore straightforwardly derived (e.g.
the fact that Italian licenses modal polarity items in questions but not in conditionals, while Catalan licenses modal polarity items in both questions and
conditionals); see examples (37) and (38).

(37) (a) *Cat.*   Hem   vist *res*?
              have-you seen nothing
              'Did you see anything?'

     (b) *Cat.*   Si vols   menjar *res*,   avisa 'm
              if you-want to-eat   nothing tell   me
              'If you want to eat anything, let me know.'
                    (Vallduví 1994: 289)

(38) (a) *It.*   Hai   visto *niente*?
              have-you seen nothing
              'Did you see anything?'

     (b) *It.*   Se vi   ocorre *niente* / *qualcosa*, comandate
              if you need   nothing / something order
              'If you should need anything, order it.'
                    (Posner 1984: 5, 21)

Since negation can be associated to modality values ('interrogative', 'imperative', 'conditional', etc.), those values are part of the specification set for 'negation' as well as for 'modality'. In this view, the different semantics displayed by negative and non-negative questions, for example, is a function of the actual dependency relation of the category 'interrogative'. If we were to adopt a feature-geometric model[21] to account for the hierarchical organization of polarity categories/features, the terminal features 'interrogative', 'imperative', etc. would be in a configuration of double domination by higher-level features, being accessible from either the 'negation' node or the 'modality' node. This is shown in Figure 8.1, under two alternative representations.

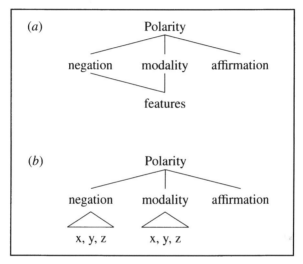

FIGURE 8.1.

8.4. EXTENDING THE ANALYSIS

8.4.1. *Types of polarity items*

The analysis that has been implemented rests on the hypothesis that, on the syntactic level, the distinction between strong and weak negative polarity items is a matter of specified vs. α-underspecified (neg-)features. Following this hypothesis, strong polarity items—negative or not—will have at least one polar feature with a specified (+) value. I hypothesize that the grammatical encoding of polarity (i.e. the geometry of features; see §8.3.3) together with semantic considerations (i.e. feature incompatibilities) derive the fact that strong polarity items have at most one specified feature value. On the other hand, following the

---

[21] See, for example, Kenstowicz (1994) and Goldsmith (1995).

same line of reasoning, weak polarity items will have at least one polar feature with a variable underspecified (α) value. Furthermore, since feature specification is assumed to be a trait of strong polarity items, weak polarity items will be underspecified for all three polar features. Once the terms of the intended distinction (between strong and weak polarity items) is made precise, the analysis makes predictions about which types of polarity items can be found in natural languages. This is shown in Table 8.4 below.

TABLE 8.4.

TYPES OF POLARITY ITEMS		FEATURE (UNDER)SPECIFICATION	GENERALIZATION
STRONG	Negative	[+neg, 0 mod, 0 aff]	Strong polarity items have one,
	Modal	[0 neg, +mod, 0 aff]	and only one, specified feature
	Affirmative	[0 neg, 0 mod, +aff]	and no α-underspecified features
WEAK	Negative	[α neg, α mod, 0 aff]	Weak polarity items have at least
		[α neg, 0 mod, 0 aff]	one α-underspecified feature and
	Affirmative	[0 neg, α mod, α aff]	no specified feature
		[0 neg, 0 mod, α aff][23]	
	Bi-polar[22]	[α neg, α mod, α aff]	
		[α neg, 0 mod, α aff][24]	

The strong/weak distinction is not confined to the realm of negative polarity items, and it therefore might be relevant to check whether the direction of change identified for negative polarity items (see §8.3.2) extends to other kinds of polar entities. This will be the topic of the next section (§8.4.2). Afterwards another possible extension of the analysis will be sketched by looking at 'expletive negation' (§8.4.3).

8.4.2. *Positive indefinites in Romance*

Positive indefinites, like negative indefinites, were less restrictive in Old Romance than in some varieties of Modern Romance with respect to their licensing environment. Besides occurring in affirmative and in non-negative modal environments, as in Modern Romance, Old Romance positive indefinites were also allowed in negative sentences, receiving a 'negative meaning'. Sentences (39) and (40) from Old Spanish are relevant examples; see also (70) in the Appendix.

---

[22] The term 'bi-polar' is taken from van der Wouden (1994).

[23] In a language having an overt affirmative correlate of the overt negative marker, [0 neg, 0 mod, α aff] polarity items would obligatorily co-occur with it. Otherwise weak affirmative polarity items of this type are superficially indistinguishable from strong affirmative polarity items.

[24] If [α neg, 0 mod, α aff] bi-polar polarity items can be found in natural language, they will be licensed in negative and in non-negative assertive contexts, being excluded from non-negative modal contexts. Otherwise, a thoroughly worked out geometry of features will be needed in order to exclude the possibility of this type of polarity item in natural language.

(39) *OS*   *No* consientes   *algun* consejo ni   tienes   reposo
       not you-consent some advice   nor you-have rest
       'You don't take any advice, nor do you have any rest.'
       (Cf. Keniston 1937: 615)

(40) *OS*   No es mucho que sea yo de su cofradia   *no* sabendo
       not is much   that be I   of his brotherhood not knowing
       alguna cosa
       something
       'It's not significant that I belong to his brotherhood since I don't
       know anything.'
       (Cf. Keniston 1937: 616)

The above-mentioned trait of Old Romance positive indefinites was generally lost; in Modern Romance positive indefinites do not show the same capacity to appear in negative contexts. Examples (41) to (43) below, from Modern Portuguese, Modern French, and Modern Catalan, show that positive indefinites, in contrast to negative indefinites, are excluded from negative sentences.

(41) (*a*) *Port.*   A   Maria *não* comprou *nenhum* livro
            the Mary not bought   no   book
            'Mary didn't buy any book.'

    (*b*) *Port.*   *A   Maria não comprou *algum* livro
            the Mary not bought   some book
            'Mary didn't buy any book.'

(42) (*a*) *Fr.*   Marie n'   a   acheté *aucun* livre.
          Mary NE has bought no   book
          'Mary didn't buy any book.'

    (*b*) *Fr.*   *Marie n'   a   pas acheté *quelque* livre.
          Mary NE has NEG bought some   book
          'Mary didn't buy any book.'

(43) (*a*) *Cat.*   *No* vull   menjar *res*
           not I-want to-eat   nothing
           'I don't want to eat anything.'
           (Vallduví 1994: 289)

    (*b*) *Cat.*   **No* vull   menjar *alguna cosa*
           not I-want to-eat   something
           'I don't want to eat anything.'
           (Vallduví 1994: 289)

As for Spanish, Keniston (1937: 616) comments that as early as the sixteenth century 'Valdés considers that *No diga alguno* [not say someone—'nobody tell'] for *No diga ninguno* [not say no-one—'nobody tell'] is poor style'.

The fact that positive indefinites could occur in negative contexts in Old Romance, in contrast to Modern Romance, suggests that they evolved from polarity items α-underspecified for aff, neg, and mod features to polarity items α-underspecified for aff and mod features (cf. the data in §8.2), but o-underspecified for the neg-feature. That is, Old Romance positive indefinites were bi-polar polarity items which could match any kind of polar environment; by losing the α-underspecified value for the neg-feature, they evolved to being weak affirmative polarity items, therefore being excluded from negative contexts.

The parallel with the pattern of change observed with respect to negative indefinites is clear and the rationale seems to be the same. Positive indefinites (like negative indefinites) ceased to occur in a less salient licensing environment, an environment where competition between positive and negative indefinites left the former in a weaker position.

Affirmative polarity items did not go as far as negative polarity items in their polar narrowing. In general, they kept the ability to occur in two types of polar environments, whereas negative polarity items in the more innovative Romance languages were limited to a single polar environment. In terms of feature values, negative polarity items reduced their degree of underspecification, while affirmative polarity items simply reduced their degree of α-underspecification. In both cases, the effect is a loss of polar versatility which is, however, more radical with respect to negative polarity items.

It should be noted, however, that positive indefinites, like negative indefinites, can behave as strong polarity items, although this is not very common in Romance. A case in point is Sicilian (*Sic.*) *coccunu* 'someone, somebody', which displays the typical behaviour of a strong affirmative polarity item. As example (44) shows, *coccunu* is licensed in non-negative assertive contexts only, being excluded from both negative and modal environments.[25]

(44) (*a*) *Sic.*   Maria parrò ccu *coccunu*
            Maria spoke to   someone
            'Maria spoke to someone.'

     (*b*) *Sic.*   *Maria 'un parrò ccu *coccunu*
            Maria not spoke to   someone
            'Maria didn't speak to anybody.'

     vs.   Maria 'un parrò ccu *nuddu*
            Maria not spoke to   no-one
            'Maria didn't speak to anybody.'

     (*c*) *Sic.*   *Telefonò *coccunu*?
            called   someone
            'Did anybody call?'

---

[25] I am indebted to Delia Bentley for the Sicilian data.

> *vs.* Telefonò *nuddu?*
> called   no-one
> 'Did anybody call?'

(*d*) *Sic.* *Ddumannacci si veni *coccunu*
> ask-him   if come someone
> 'Ask him whether anyone is coming.'

> *vs.* Ddumannacci si veni *nuddu*
> ask-him   if come no-one
> 'Ask him whether anyone is coming.'

(*e*) *Sic.* *'Un criu   ca veni *coccunu*
> not I-think that come someone
> 'I don't think that anyone will come.'

> *vs.* 'Un criu   ca veni *nuddu*
> not I-think that come no-one
> 'I don't think that anyone will come.'

8.4.3. *'Expletive negation'*

Different authors have treated 'expletive negation' as a polarity item of the weak type (van der Wouden 1994, Espinal 1998). The reasoning behind this analysis is the fact that 'expletive negation' is licensed in the kind of non-negative modal contexts where weak negative polarity items and modal polarity items are licensed.

I would like to draw attention to another fact: the diachronic change that affected negative indefinites in Romance appears to correlate with a parallel change with respect to 'expletive negation'. Thus Portuguese, where the weak or modal character of negative indefinites was lost, does not generally license 'expletive negation'. Example (45) below shows the contrast between Old Portuguese and Modern Portuguese; examples (46) to (48) show the contrast between Portuguese and Italian, Portuguese and Spanish, and Portuguese and French, respectively.

(45) (*a*) *OP*   E   assi escapou o   comde Joham Fernandez de   *nom* seer
>   and so   escaped the count Joham Fernandez from not to-be
>   morto
>   killed
>   'And in that way the count J. F. escaped from being killed.'
>   (Cf. Ali 1931: 99)

(*b*) *Port.*   E   assim escapou o   conde Joham Fernandez de   (*não)
>   and so   escaped the count Joham Fernandez from (not)
>   ser   morto
>   to-be killed
>   'And in that way the count J. F. escaped from being killed.'

(46) (a) *It.*   L' ho   fermato, prima che (*non*) si   facesse
him I-have locked   before that (not) himself would-make
male
harm
'I locked him in before he would harm himself.'
(Manzotti and Rigamonti 1991: 292)

(b) *Port.*   Fechei-o,   antes que (*não) se   magoasse.
I-locked-him before that (not)   himself would-harm
'I locked him in before he would harm himself.'

(47) (a) *Sp.*   Ernesto prefiere ser   escéptico que (*no*) tragarse
Ernesto prefers to-be sceptical than (not) to-swallow
semejantes disparates
such   nonsense
'Ernesto prefers to be sceptical rather than swallowing such
nonsense.'
(Bosque 1980: 81)

(b) *Port.*   O Ernesto prefere ser   céptico do que (*não) engolir
the Ernesto prefers to-be sceptical than   (not) to-swallow
tais disparates.
such nonsense
'Ernesto prefers to be sceptical rather than swallowing such
nonsense.'

(48) (a) *Fr.*   Je crains qu' il *ne* vienne (≠ Je crains qu' il *ne* vienne *pas*)
I fear   that he NE come   I fear   that he NE come   NEG
'I fear he will come.'   'I fear he will not come.'
(Mauger 1968: 374)

(b) *Port.*   Temo que ele (*não) venha.
I-fear that he (not)   comes
'I fear he will come.'
(Ungrammatical with the intended meaning)

Ambiguity between modal polarity items and strong negative polarity items
was lost in Portuguese with words such as *nenhum* 'no, no one', *nada* 'nothing',
ninguém 'nobody'.[26] A correlative departure from ambiguity might have affected
the word *não* 'not'. Under this hypothesis, rather than being seen as an 'expletive negative' head, an entity whose existence in natural language would be
under Minimalist assumptions quite puzzling, so-called 'expletive negation'
might be seen as a modal head, i.e. the overt manifestation of a [+mod] Pol. Old

---

[26] This appears to have happened during the nineteenth century (see Martins 1996). Before the
change took place, Portuguese belonged in the same linguistic group as Galician, Spanish, Italian,
and French.

Portuguese *não* would therefore be ambiguous between a modal and a negative head, while in Modern Portuguese it tends to be just a negative head.[27]

The question remains of why the overt realization of the modal head is identical with the negative head.[28] I leave this subject open for future research.

8.5. CONCLUSION

Throughout this chapter I have looked at diachronic and geographical variation in Romance in order to provide a unitary account of the intricacies of the behaviour of polarity items (context sensitivity/interaction with negation) in different but formally, and historically, related grammars. The comparative approach which has been adopted has led to a clear view of the formal and historical relationship between those grammars, to a better understanding of the Old Romance state of affairs, and to a syntactically motivated definition of a typology of polarity items, which is based on a distinction well established in the semantics literature, the 'weak'/'strong' distinction.

The analysis which has been proposed makes crucial use of the 'phonology-borrowed' notion of underspecification, and is consistent with the observations in the semantics literature that 'the phenomenon of polarity is essentially of a purely lexical nature' (Zwarts 1993) and that 'there is no way in which a binary system may account for the rich variety of polarity items we find in natural language' (van der Wouden 1994: 29).

With respect to what drives historical change, we have seen that both negative and positive indefinites evolved towards reducing their degree of variable underspecification, thereby becoming more restrictive with respect to their licensing contexts. This is the direction we would expect for change given current assumptions on the relation between language acquisition and language change. If children rely on strong positive empirical evidence in order to make decisions while building up their grammars, they may well not identify a less salient polar environment as a licensing context for certain kinds of polarity items. Competition between negative and positive indefinites in non-negative modal contexts makes this kind of context a less salient licensing environment for negative polarity items than negative contexts. Negative contexts, on the other hand, being particularly salient as a licensing environment for negative polarity items, are the

---

[27] Examples of (exclamative) sentences where 'expletive negation' can still be found in Modern Portuguese are given in Martins (1996).

[28] Note however that the modal head is not homophonous with every negative head found in languages with 'expletive negation'. In Modern Greek the head *den* 'not' can only express true negation, 'expletive negation' being conveyed by the negative complementizer *mipos* 'that-not' (cf. van der Wouden 1994). Similar facts hold with respect to Classical Latin where *ne* '(that)-not' in opposition to *non* 'not' might express 'expletive negation'—moreover *ne* is also the overt realization of an interrogative suffix. On the other hand, in languages like French, where the true negator is not a head, there is no superficial identity between 'negation' and 'expletive negation' (cf. example (48a) above).

kind of context where positive indefinites (when competing with negative indefinites) are expected to be in a weaker position.[29]

Finally it should be noted that in the case under consideration, lexical ambiguity appears as an intermediate stage in the transition of polar words to restriction to a single polar context.

8.6. APPENDIX

8.6.1. *Old Romance (cf. §8.2.1)*

(49) (a) OP que *nehũu nõ* scapou
            that no-one not escaped
            'that no one escaped (death)'
            (*Crónica Geral de Espanha de 1344*. Cintra, ed. 1954: 107)

     (b) OP avya   grande vontade   de *nõ* leixar   *nehũus* do
            he-had great   determination of not to-leave no-one from-the
            bando de Pompeo
            group of Pompeo
            'He was determined not to leave alive anyone from Pompeo's group.'
            (*Crónica Geral de Espanha de 1344*. Cintra, ed. 1954: 111)

(50) (a) OC E Astor de Mares *neguna* vegada *nos*   moch de
            and Astor de Mares not-one time   not-himself moved from
            son caval
            his horse
            'And Astor de Mares didn't move from his horse at any time.'
            (Cf. Llorens 1929: 91 and 62)

     (b) OC *No* avia   *negun* refugi
            not there-was no   refuge
            'There wasn't any refuge.'
            (Cf. Llorens 1929: 89 and 61)

(51) (a) OI *Gente neuna non* v'   arrivava
            people not-one not there arrived
            'Nobody arrived.'
            (Cf. Meyer-Lübke 1900: 777)

     (b) OI *Non* li   fece motto *niente*
            not them did fun   nothing
            'They weren't amused by anything.'
            (Cf. Meyer-Lübke 1900: 780)[30]

---

[29] It is not impossible, however, that a bi-polar polarity item reduces its degree of variable underspecification in the direction of becoming a weak negative polarity item and eventually a strong negative polarity item. The data we have dealt with do not show this kind of change, but see the case of Italian *veruno* treated in Ramat (1998). Other polar words inherited from Latin followed the same path.

[30] See Molinelli (1988: 44–55) for other relevant examples, taken from sources representative of different varieties of 'Old Italian'.

(52)   OP   Viste-me   nunca andar em demanda com *ninguém* senão hũa   em
             you-saw-me never to-be in fight   with nobody   except once in
             Santarem?
             Santarém
             'Have you ever seen me fighting with anyone except for once in
             Santarém?'
             (Cf. Ali 1931: 201)

(53)   *Old Galicien-Leonese*
             que *ningun* omne que en suas heredades nin en seus omnes metir
             that no   man that in his properties nor in his men   puts
             mano . . . que peyte mil   mors. e   perda quanto   ouuer
             hand   that pays thousand mors. and loses as-much-as might-have
             'that any person who causes damage to his properties or his men . . .
             pay a thousand *moravedis* (units of money) and lose everything he
             might have'
             (*Foros de Castel Rodrigo.* Cintra 1959: 22)

(54)   OC   Si sarayns fugen o *nul hom* los troba ans   que ayen
             if Saracens escape or no man them find before that they-have
             pasat   Lobregat, e'ls reté
             crossed Lobregat them return
             'If there are Muslims who escape or if anyone find them before they
             have crossed Lobregat, they are to be returned (to their lords).'
             (Cf. Camus Bergareche 1988: 433)

(55)   OS   desean   que sus obras sean   más perfectas que *ningunas*
             they-wish that their works might-be more perfect   than no
             otras
             others
             'They wish that their works might be more perfect than any others.'
             (Cf. Keniston 1937: 611)

(56)   OI   Ogni volta que *niente* sentite
             every time that nothing you-feel
             'every time that you feel something (whatever it is)'
             (Cf. Meyer-Lübke 1900: 778)

(57)   OS   Antes que *nadie* se lo demandase yo lo avia ya   prometido
             before that nobody him it asked   I it had already promised
             'I promised that to him before anybody else could question him about
             it.'   (Cf. Keniston 1937: 611)

8.6.2. *Modern Romance: Romanian, north-eastern Italian dialects (Venetian) (cf.
§8.2.2.1)*

(58)   *Rom.* Întreabă-l dacă a   văzut pe *nimeni* / *cineva*
              ask-him if   has seen   no-one / someone
              'Ask him whether he saw anyone.'

(59)   *Rom.* Dacă ai   nevoie de *nimic / *ceva*,   spune-mi
                 if   you-have necessity of nothing / something, tell-me
                 'If you need anything, let me know.'

(60)   *Ven.* Dime   come che *nisun / *qualcheduni* pol esser cosí semo
                 tell-me how that no-one / someone   can be   so   stupid
                 'Tell me how anyone can be so stupid.'

(61)   *Ven.* No credo che vegna   *nisuni / *qualcheduni*
                 not I-think that will-come no-one / someone
                 'I don't think that anyone will come.'

8.6.3. *Modern Romance: Spanish, Galician, Italian, French (cf. §8.2.2.3)*

(62)   *Sp.*   Prefiero quedarme   aquí que ir   a *ningún* sitio
                 I-prefer to-stay-myself here than to-go to no   place
                 'I would rather stay here than go anywhere.'
                     (Cf. Bosque 1980: 81)

(63)   *It.*   Ha telefonato *nessuno*?
                 has called   nobody
                 'Did anyone call?'

(64)   *Fr.*   Pensez-vous que *personne* ait   *rien*   fait pour
                 think-you   that nobody   might-have nothing done to
                 m'aider?
                 me help
                 'Do you think that anyone might have done anything to help me?'
                     (Cf. Milner 1979: 81)

(65)   *Fr.*   Pierre est plus gentil qu' *aucun* de ces amis
                 Pierre is   more nice   than none of his friends
                 'Pierre is nicer than any of his friends.'
                     (Cf. Milner 1979: 81)

(66)   (*a*) *It.*   Hai   visto *niente*?
                       have-you seen nothing
                       'Did you see anything?'

        (*b*) *It.*   Hai   visto *qualcosa*?
                       have-you seen something
                       'Did you see anything?'
                           (Cf. Bernini and Ramat 1996: 119)

(67)   (*a*) *Fr.*   Avez-vous jamais rencontré *personne* de ce   genre?
                       have-you never met   nobody   of that type
                       'Have you ever met anyone like that?'
                           (Cf. Milner 1979: 81)

        (*b*) *Fr.*   Avez-vous jamais rencontré *quelqu'un* de ce   genre?
                       have-you never met   somebody of that type
                       'Have you ever met anyone like that?'

8.6.4. *Modern Romance: Portuguese (cf. §8.2.2.4)*

(68) (*a*) *Port.*   *Perguntava-se   se teria   telefonado *ninguém.*
    he-asked-himself if would-have called   nobody
    'He wondered if anybody had called.'

  (*b*) *Port.*   Perguntava-se   se teria   telefonado *alguém.*
    he-asked-himself if would-have called   somebody
    'He wondered if anybody had called.'

(69) (*a*) *Port.*   *Se precisares de *nada,*   diz-me.
    if you-need of nothing tell-me
    'If you need anything, let me know.'

  (*b*) *Port.*   Se precisares de *alguma coisa,* diz-me.
    if you-need of something   tell-me
    'If you need anything, let me know.'

8.6.5. *Positive indefinites in Romance: Old Portuguese (cf. §8.4.2)*

(70) *OP*   *nem* era *alguũ*   ousado   de lhe   tall cousa dizer
    nor was someone courageous of to-him such thing to-say
    'Nobody dared to tell that to him.'
    (Fernão Lopes, *Crónica de D. João I.* Freire, org. 1977: 6)

9

Relabelling

JOHN WHITMAN

9.1. INTRODUCTION

Minimalist approaches to diachronic syntax have focused primarily on phenomena that can be accounted for in terms of changes in feature strength, such as innovation or loss of verb movement. Roberts (1997) shows how the same basic approach extends to changes in phrasal constituent order (concretely, the shift from OV to VO order in English) within the antisymmetry framework of Kayne (1994), where head-final constituent order across languages is transformationally derived. A transformational account of word-order variation across languages as well as within languages makes it possible to account for a large portion of the phenomena that have traditionally attracted the attention of historical syntacticians in terms of a single mechanism: presence or absence of a feature forcing a particular movement operation.

Despite the impressive potential coverage of such a theory, there remains an important class of changes that are not obviously analysable in terms of gain or loss of a movement operation. This is the class of 'reanalyses' in Langacker's general sense: 'a change in the structure of an expression or class of expressions that does not involve any immediate or intrinsic modification of its surface manifestation' (1977: 59). An example widely cited in the grammaticalization literature is the reanalysis of serial verbs as prepositional phrases (Lord 1973, 1976, Li and Thompson 1973, Heine and Reh 1984), as in (1).

(1)

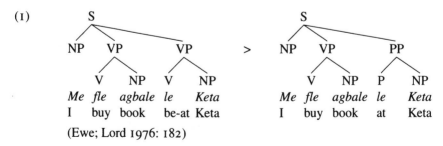

(Ewe; Lord 1976: 182)

In Lord's analysis of this development, the only change is in the category label of the serial verb 'be-at' and its projection. In a Principles and Parameters approach to syntactic change, reanalysis of this sort would involve a change in the d-structure representation of the pattern; in fact, in that approach, reanalysis in Langacker's sense might be analysed as change restricted to d-structure representations.[1]

Under a Minimalist approach to syntactic change this move is unavailable, as there is no general level of pre-transformational structure corresponding to an underlying representation in the traditional sense. The pressure is thus on in this framework to represent (1) in very much the way Lord presents it: as a change in the category of 'be-at' and its projection which induces no modification of surrounding structure. In this chapter I will attempt to develop an account of syntactic reanalysis based on the idea that the crucial element in the process is change in the categorial status of the head, what I will call 'relabelling', borrowing the term from Harris and Campbell (1995). Two factors seem to me at the outset to favour this approach to syntactic reanalysis.

The first is an empirical one. Grammaticalization theorists have long argued that grammatical reanalysis proceeds from lexical change, as in Heine and Reh's statement: ' reanalysis is the result of, or has been triggered by, certain processes like Desemanticization or Expansion. This assumption is based on the claim that grammaticalization starts with individual lexical items which, by changing their own syntactic and morphosyntactic status, are responsible for an overall transformation of the syntactic structures in which they occur' (1984: 96). The empirical basis for this claim is that examples like (1) proceed from individual lexical items: Kwa languages are analysed as gaining some prepositions from serial verbs, but other serial verbs remain. Let us consider the reanalysis in (1) in terms of a Minimalist conception of phrase structure. Under this conception, the head of the VP undergoing reanalysis is not the word-level category V, but the lexical item *lè* 'be-at':

(2)

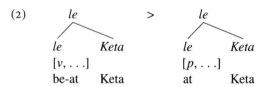

In (2) neither the head of the phrase (the lexical item *lè*) nor its label (projected from *lè*) changes its identity. Instead, what changes is the categorial feature of this lexical item: if Lord's description of the change is correct, the categorial feature changes from v to p. Certain consequences follow from this change: for example, the projection headed by *lè* can no longer check a feature of T.

---

[1] Lightfoot's (1979) treatment of 'radical reanalysis' appears to be very close to such an approach within an REST framework. In this approach, changes such as the reanalysis of modals from verbs to categories base-generated under Aux, and the same serial verb > preposition and serial verb > complementizer reanalyses discussed here are treated as changes affecting the rules of the base component.

Viewed this way, the term 'relabelling' is something of a misnomer. The identity of the head and the label derived from it are exactly what do not change in (2). I retain the term because it captures the notion of a change in category with no attendant change in structure. The important point here is that this treatment is completely consistent with the claim that reanalysis proceeds lexical item by lexical item.[2]

The second factor in favour of the conception of reanalysis as relabelling is that this move makes it possible to treat reanalysis and innovation or loss or transformational movement in similar ways: both proceed from a change in the feature of a head. Reanalysis is change in a categorial feature; gain or loss of overt movement occurs when features such as a *wh-* or case-feature undergo a change in strength.

The body of this chapter explores how far the conception of reanalysis as relabelling can be extended, beginning with relatively straightforward cases of reanalysis.

9.2. SIMPLE REANALYSIS AS RELABELLING

Both the example of verb > preposition reanalysis in (1) and verb > complementizer reanalysis in (3) are instances of what we might call 'simple relabelling': under standard accounts (see Lord 1976, Heine and Reh 1984 for verb > complementizer reanalyses) no change occurs in the affected projection except a change in the categorial identity of its head.[3]

(3)

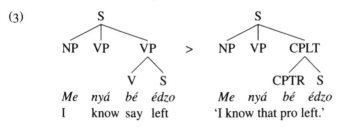

Me   nyá   bé   édzo   *Me   nyá   bé   édzo*

I   know   say   left   'I know that pro left.'

(Ewe; Lord 1976: 182)

Again, restating this change in Minimalist terms in (4), the categorial feature of *bé* 'say' changes from *v* to *c*:

---

[2] The claim that reanalysis proceeds in a 'lexically' determined fashion has been disputed (e.g. Lightfoot 1979: 100). Resolving the issue far exceeds the scope of this chapter, but I would point out that in the framework proposed here, while relabelling (change in categorial feature) is chiefly visible in its effects on individual lexical items, changes in feature strength associated with a functional category (resulting in gain or loss of an overt movement operation) is predicted to be visible in the behaviour of whole syntactic categories.

[3] We see in §9.5 that this is an oversimplification: a change in the internal structure of the projection follows from the changes V>P and V>C.

(4)

In terms of visible consequences, Lord reports that complementizer *bé* no longer takes tense-aspect marking or pronoun prefixes, properties of verbs in serial constructions but not complementizers (1976: 180), and that *bé* also appears in positions where we would expect a projection of C but not V to appear, such as purpose CPs (1976: 184).

Cases such as these are relatively uncontroversial examples of categorial change; Minimalism contributes only the idea that what changes is a categorial feature. The more ambitious proposal that I would like to explore in this chapter is that syntactic reanalysis always proceeds from relabelling, in the sense of change in a categorial feature without any change in surrounding syntactic structure.

(5)   *Relabelling*
        The first step of syntactic reanalysis is restricted to relabelling, where
        relabelling refers to a change in the categorial feature of a head. The
        result of relabelling must be well formed independently of any changes
        outside the minimal domain of the relabelled item.

For the definition of minimal domain, see Chomsky (1995: 178). In the cases relevant to this chapter, the minimal domain of a head consists of its complement and the specifier of the minimal–maximal projection that contains the head. (5) amounts to the hypothesis that syntactic reanalyses can be accounted for in terms of changes to a subset of the features of an individual head, without changes in larger units of structure.

'Simple' reanalyses like V>P and V>C in (1) and (3) (confining ourselves for the time being to Lord's analyses of these changes) satisfy (5), but other alleged instances of syntactic reanalysis do not. For example, Harris and Campbell (1995: 62) follow Ebert's (1978: 12) interpretation of Visser (1966: 967–8) in claiming that English *for*-infinitivals result from reanalysis of matrix *for*-NP as a complementizer followed by an infinitival subject (see also Stockwell 1976). On this view, the matrix PP [*for* NP] and infinitive complement in examples like (6) is the input to a reanalysis where *for* is reanalysed as infinitival complementizer and NP is reanalysed as subject of the infinitive (7):

(6)   [it is bet for me] [to sleen my self than ben defouled thus]
        (Chaucer; Harris and Campbell 1995: 62 citing Ebert 1978: 12)

(7)   [it is better] [for me to slay myself . . .]

Stated in terms of changes in the possible expansions of VP, this reanalysis is equivalent to replacing expansion (8*a*) with (8*b*):

(8) (*a*)   V [$_{PP}$ for NP] [$_{IP}$ PRO to VP] >

(*b*)   V [$_{CP}$ for [$_{IP}$ NP to VP]

Such a reanalysis would be a counter-example to (5). Relabelling *for* as a complementizer is unproblematic, in fact comparable to the serial V > C reanalysis discussed by Lord. The problem is that, given (5), there is no way to formulate a change which results in the object of a matrix PP being reanalysed as the subject of a subordinate clause. No change in the categorial features of *for* produces this result. While (8) is stated in terms of changes in phrase structure, (5) restricts the domain of reanalysis to changes in the features of heads.

In fact Lightfoot (1976: 22–5, 1978: 186–9) presents a very different account of the genesis of *for*-infinitivals. Lightfoot shows that the *for*-infinitival pattern without overt subject (*for to* VP) consistently appears in Middle English data one to two hundred years before corresponding patterns with overt subjects (*for* NP *to* VP). Lightfoot suggests that the previously emergent *to* VP infinitival pattern had NP-like properties and thus came to be selected by the preposition *for*.[4] The *for* NP *to* VP pattern emerges as the *to*-infinitival loses its nominal properties. Lightfoot's scenario is consistent with (5). Rephrased in Minimalist terms, *for* (like all transitive prepositions) bears a D-feature which must be checked by a nominal complement. When *to*-infinitivals appear as the complement of *for* they must bear a nominal feature that is able to check the D-feature of *for*. In the majority of Modern English varieties, where *to*-infinitivals lose this feature, *for* may take an infinitival complement only when it includes an NP subject able to check the D-feature of *for*. None of these changes require reference to the pattern in (8*a*).

In the sense in which 'syntactic reanalysis' has normally been used, that is, replacement of one syntactic pattern by another with identical post-syntactic form, the pattern in (8*a*) cannot have undergone a reanalysis resulting in the pattern in (8*b*), because there is no evidence that any variety of English has ever lost the pattern in (8*a*). A weaker notion of reanalysis might be invoked, where *for* first becomes analysable as a complementizer only in the context of (8*a*); but as Stockwell (1976: 33) acknowledges, this is directly contradicted by the data cited by Lightfoot showing that subjectless *for*-infinitives emerge first. I therefore see no reason to recognize (8*a*)>(8*b*) as an actual instance of reanalysis.[5]

---

[4] Warner (1982: 115–27) argues for a different view, where Middle English *for to* is a (complex) infinitive marker and *for* 'grammatically unrelated to the preposition'. However, Warner also confirms the finding of earlier researchers that *for (to)* infinitivals are far more likely to appear in adjunct position than elsewhere. If in fact the pattern could be shown to originate in adjunct position, the possibility of a reanalysis like (6)>(7) could be conclusively rejected.

[5] Stockwell (1976) interprets Visser (1966: 968) as endorsing the occurrence of a reanalysis of the form (8*a*)>(8*b*), but when Visser refers to '[t]his shift in the interdependence of the constituent parts of the sentence', he is simply referring to the indubitable fact that the pattern V *for* NP *to* VP becomes structurally ambiguous in English. The fact that he goes on to speculate that the advent of the complementizer *for* in the V *for* NP *to* VP context may have been influenced by use of *for* as

This example brings up the crucial issue of what exactly the protagonists of syntactic reanalysis are. Traditionally, reanalysis has been viewed as a type of grammar change, that is, change in the repertory of basic structural patterns made available by the grammar of a language, as in (8). This conception of diachronic change has of course been criticized, most famously by Andersen (1973, 1989), who argues that the concept of changes involving direct mappings between grammars at distinct diachronic stages is suspect, as speakers do not have direct access to the grammars of earlier stages of the language. The issue is further vexed in the case of syntactic change, due to the difficulty of determining the units of a 'diachronic correspondence' in Andersen's sense. This is precisely the problem in the case of the alleged reanalysis in (8). The protagonists of the 'diachronic correspondences' in (1) and (3) have been taken to be the structural patterns associated with particular lexical items: the structural pattern VP associated with a Ewe *lè* 'be-at' at one diachronic stage corresponds to the structural pattern PP at another stage. But it is not clear how the structural pattern (8*a*) in Middle English 'corresponds' to the subsequent pattern in (8*b*), as (8*a*) persists in the grammar, and (8*b*) has a different meaning (that is, a different thematic role structure). The idea that (8*a*) is reanalysed as (8*b*) seems to be based on the hypothesis that the surface pattern in (8*a*) plays a causal role in the *innovation* of (8*b*) (again using Andersen's term) by individual speakers. But it is not clear how this hypothesis could be proven, and as Lightfoot shows, it is not supported by the historical chronology.

Under the Minimalist conception of syntactic change that I have sketched above, the protagonists of syntactic change, including reanalysis, are heads (in the unmarked case, overt lexical items). Thus, following Lightfoot's scenario for the development of *for*-infinitivals, the protagonists of change are *for*, and *to*, the head of *to*-infinitivals. The changes involving these heads may be outlined as follows.

(9) (*a*)   *for* gains a subcatgegorization feature allowing it to select infinitival complements. At this stage, the head of *to*-infinitivals (presumably *to*) bears a nominal feature which can check the D-feature of *for*.

(*b*)   *to*-infinitivals lose their nominal feature. No change takes place in the features of *for*, but *for* now may occur with infinitival complements only when they contain a subject able to check its D-feature.

Note that in terms of (5), neither of the steps of (9) involve reanalysis, since *for* does not undergo a change in categorial feature. It is possible that at some stage subsequent to (9*a*), *for* in infinitivals undergoes a change in categorial feature from *p* to *c* (for example, when *for-to* infinitivals begin to appear in subject

complementizer in other contexts (such as adjunct infinitivals) suggests that Visser indeed does not consider the former context to be the original source of complementizer *for*.

position), but this is controversial, as some accounts of infinitival *for* analyse it as a preposition in Modern English (e.g. Emonds 1985).

9.3. RELABELLING IN SERIAL CONSTRUCTIONS

This section explores the consequences of (5) for reanalysis in serial verb constructions under a more articulated theory of the structure of these constructions. Collins (1993, 1997) develops such a theory based on the insight that the first verb (V_1) takes a projection of the second verb (V_2) as its complement (see also Campbell 1989, Larson 1991, among others), and that the argument 'shared' between the two verbs originates as the specifier of V_1, controlling *pro* in the specifier of V_2. This leads to the analysis in (10) for the Ewe example in (1) prior to reanalysis of V_2 as a preposition.

(10)

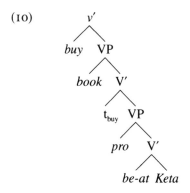

The surface order V_1 NP V_2 . . . results from movement of V_1 to the head of a higher verbal projection (here represented as the 'light verb' head of vP in Chomsky 1995).

The hypothesis in (5) makes the following prediction about syntactic reanalysis in serial verb constructions given an analysis like (10) (or any serial verb construction where the projection of V_2 is a complement of V_1).

(11)   In serial constructions of the form V_1 NP V_2 . . ., where V_1 is the main verb, V_2 may be reanalysed as the head of a PP, but V_1 may not.

As we saw in §9.2, reanalysis of V_2 as P is a 'simple' reanalysis, merely changing the categorial feature of the complement of V_1.[6] Reanalysis of V_1 as P, on the other hand, would result in (12b).

---

[6] The issue of structural changes internal to the reanalysed PP, such as elimination of the specifier position hosting *pro*, is taken up in §9.5.

(12) (a)   >   (b)

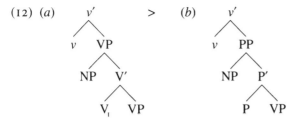

From a pre-theoretic standpoint, the development in (12) deprives the clause of a main verb; more technically, it eliminates a category capable of checking the V-feature of v (and subsequently T), and requires P to take a VP complement. (12b) is therefore ill-formed in several respects. Thus while reanalysis of V_2 as P (or as C) is countenanced under (5), similar reanalysis of V_1 is not.

A complete survey of the literature on verb > preposition reanalyses exceeds the scope of this chapter, but it is possible to make some preliminary predictions about where support or counter-exemplification of (11) is likely to be found.[7] The relative order of serial verbs is widely described as being constrained by an 'iconicity' condition (Y. Li 1993: 499), which stipulates that the linear order of V_1 and V_2 in a serial construction must reflect the temporal of the events they represent. Under the iconicity condition, verbs such as 'be-at' (as a candidate for reanalysis as a locative preposition) or 'give' (a candidate for reanalysis as a benefactive or dative preposition) occur in the position of V_2 and are thus unproblematic from the standpoint of (11).

The largest class of potential counter-examples to (11) is composed of serial verbs such as 'take' or 'hold' in the V_1 position, often introducing an instrumental argument. Despite claims to the contrary, the literature on serial V>instrumental P reanalyses appears not to provide clear examples of V_1 undergoing such a reanalysis. For example, Lord's (1973: 280–92) discussion of serial V > comitative P reanalyses includes a case in Yoruba (and possibly Ewe and Fon) where the reanalysed comitative P can introduce an instrumental argument. However the source for the reanalysis, a verb meaning 'be included among, be together with' occurs in V_2, not V_1 position. Lord contrasts the reanalysed comitative P with verbs in the same languages of the 'take' type in the V_1 position, which have not undergone reanalysis. Similarly, Durie's (1988) survey of instrumental prepositions in Oceanic (a family which abundantly attests reanalyses of V>P as well as 'intermediate' categories variously labelled 'verbids',

---

[7] Asymmetries in the consequences of V>P reanalyses for V_1 as opposed to V_2 have been discussed in previous literature. For example, Givon (1975: 87) points out that V>P reanalysis of V_1 should result in S–INSTRUMENT–V–O and S–ACCUSATIVE–O–V–X word orders. Hyman (1975) rejects Givon's claim that reanalysed serial verbs play a major role in word-order change in Niger-Congo.

'verbal prepositions', etc.) shows no case where instrumental P originates from V_1. Only one of the ten languages surveyed by Durie has an instrumental marker which also functions independently as a verb, but in this language, Puluwat, the marker in question is the verb 'give', an archtypical V_2:

(13)   wo pwe   ngan-iy-áy efór suupwa
         you HORTATIVE give-TR-1SG cigarette
         'Give me a cigarette.'

(14)   yi pwe   yatipa ngan-i   laayif
         I FUTURE slice   give-TR knife
         'I will slice (it) with a knife.'
              (Durie 1988: 7)

A case for $V_1 > P$ reanalysis is made by Lord (1982), who analyses a class of 'object markers' in Akan, Ga, and Idoma as resulting from reanalysis of a verb with the meaning 'take, hold' in the V_1 position of a serial construction. In the case of Akan, Lord cites nineteenth-century authors who show *de*, the morpheme in question, functioning as an independent verb; at the same time, *de* had the function of marking instrumental and comitative arguments, objects, and causatives. The first two of these functions are shown in (15–16).

(15)   O-de eñkrante tya duabasa
         he-DE sword   cut branch
         'He cut off a branch with a sword.'
              (Lord 1982: 281)

(16)   O-de mfoníni bi   kyèré nè bá
         he-DE picture certain show his child
         'He shows his child the picture.'
              (Lord 1982: 281)

In present-day Akan, *de* has ceased to function as an independent verb. It also does not inflect for tense and aspect. The question is whether *de* has become a preposition. Lord argues that it has, on the basis of the loss of inflection and independent verbal function, but other researchers have not accepted this view. Thus Campbell (1989) argues in detail that *de* is a verb.[8]

Lord observes that the object markers in the Benue-Kwa languages she studies are remarkably similar to the Chinese object marker *ba* in range of function and historical source. Since the historical provenience, categorial status, and syntactic position of *ba* have been intensively studied over the past twenty-five years,

---

[8] Like Lord, many grammaticalization theorists have taken inability to appear as an independent verb as criterial for prepositional status. Thus Givon (1984: 229) claims that Yoruba *fi* 'take, use' has undergone $V_1 >$ instrumental P reanalysis. But Bamgbose (1972: 42–3) specifically rejects this criterion, and argues that *fi* is a verb.

I turn to an examination of this item in the next section to investigate further the validity of (11).

9.4. THE DEVELOPMENT OF CHINESE *BA*

Chinese provides surely the best known case of an alleged $V_1 > P$ reanalysis. Mandarin *ba* functioning as a pre-verbal 'object marker' in contexts like (17) is generally considered to have arisen from the serial construction exemplified in (18), where *ba* has its original 'unbleached' meaning 'hold, grasp' (Wang 1958, Li and Thompson 1974, Peyraube 1985).[9]

(17)   Zhangsan ba Lisi pian le
        Zhangsan BA Lisi cheat PERF
        'Zhangsan cheated Lisi.'

(18)   Zui ba zhuyu   zixi   kan
        drunk take dogwood carefully look
        'Drunk, (I) take the dogwood and look at it carefully.'
        (Tu Fu, eighth century, cited by Wang 1958: 411)

The details of the change relating the modern object marking or 'disposal'[10] pattern in (17) and the serial pattern in (18) are not uncontroversial. A number of linguists, most recently Mei (1990) (see also Sun 1996) have argued that an earlier pattern involving the morpheme *yi*[11] 'use, with' provided a model for the object-marking function of the disposal construction in general. Regardless of these details, it is the case that *ba* has made the change from V_1 in serial constructions like (18) to an item which cannot appear as an independent verb and lacks such characteristics of main verbs as the ability to be followed by aspect markers. These are exactly the considerations that led Lord (1982) to analyse Akan *de* as a preposition.

A number of linguists have analysed present-day Mandarin *ba* as a preposition, including specialists on its historical development such as Peyraube (1985, 1996) and Sun (1996). This is also the view of Li (1990) in a Principles and Parameters

---

[9] *Ba* is one of a complex of original verbs including *jiang* 'take' and *chi* 'hold' that underwent parallel developments; specialists in Chinese historical syntax generally treat them together (Wang 1958: 410, Peyraube 1996: 168). While *ba* survives in the object-marking function in Modern Mandarin, *jiang* is its counterpart in Cantonese (Sun 1996: 60).

[10] As is well known, the ability of objects to appear pre-verbally with *ba* is restricted by their specificity and the aspectual status of the nuclear verb phrase. The traditional label 'disposal form' refers to the aspectual restrictions in particular. Lord (1982) notes the parallels between these restrictions and those found with the object-marker constructions in Benue-Kwa.

[11] *Yi* itself is generally analysed as a preposition (Chinese *jieci*: Wang 1958: 336). If the argument that *yi* provided an analogical model for *jiang* and *ba* in the disposal form can be shown to entail that the latter assumed the exact grammatical status of *yi*, then the categorial status and syntactic position of *yi* in earlier Chinese becomes crucial for the argument here. This issue must be left for future research.

framework. However, there are two alternative views of the categorial status of *ba*: as a verb (Hashimoto 1971, Ross 1991, Bender 2000), and as the head of a functional projection (Sybesma 1992, Zou 1993, Takahashi 1997, Paul 1999) which takes the projection of the verb to the right of *ba* as its complement. Bender effectively marshals the arguments for *ba* as a verb, and addresses the major counter-arguments against this view. These include the fact that *ba* cannot be followed by aspect markers, cannot be used as a one-word answer to a yes–no question, and has a restricted distribution in the A-not-A question form. Bender shows that each of these properties holds true of other verbs, such as *rang* 'let' in the case of the aspect marker restriction, and *renwei* 'think, consider' in the case of the other two restrictions. At the same time, Ross, Zou, and Bender summarize the many respects in which *ba* does not pattern with Ps in Chinese:

(19) (*a*)　*ba* and the following NP never dislocate as a constituent.

    (*b*)　*ba* and the following NP do not allow coordination with clear PPs
        (Zou 1993: 732 *contra* Li 1990)

    (*c*)　*ba* contributes to the addition of an external (subject) argument in
        the so-called 'causative' *ba* pattern

Property (19*a*) in particular contrasts with the case of $V_2 > P$ reanalysis involving *yu* 'give' (later a dative/benefactive and finally comitative preposition 'with') in Middle Chinese and Early Mandarin, studied by Peyraube (1986, 1996). Peyraube shows that after *yu* becomes predominant in the ditransitive serial construction in (20), it begins to appear pre-verbally with the indirect object, as in (21) (examples cited from Sun 1996: 22).

(20)　　Jii　chi　ci　bao　　yu　zhu xiongdi
　　　　then take this treasure give his　brother
　　　　'Then take this treasure to his brothers.'
　　　　　(*Dazhengzang shengjing*)

(21)　　Yu lao seng　guo　jing　shui-ping
　　　　for old monk pass clean water-bottle
　　　　'(Someone) rinsed the bottle clean for the old monk.'
　　　　　(*Zutangji*)

The ability to occupy more than one position in the clause is taken to be criterial for the PP status of *yu* and the following NP (Peyraube 1996: 182). This property is not shared by *ba* and the following NP, which are fixed in their immediate pre-verbal position:

(22) (*a*)　*Ba Lisi Zhangsan pian le
       BA Lisi Zhangsan cheat PERF

    (*b*)　*Zhangsan pian le　　ba Lisi
       Zhangsan cheat PERF BA Lisi
       'Zhangsan cheated Lisi.'

Property (19c) has received different accounts in different frameworks. For example, Sybesma (1992) argues that the causer role in causative *ba* sentences like (23) (from Sybesma 1992: 154–5) is contributed by the head of a projection he labels CAUSP; the head of this projection may be filled by raising the verb, as in (23b), or by inserting *ba*.

(23) (a) Zhei jian   shi   ba Zhangsan ku lei   le
        this CLASSIFIER matter BA Zhangsan cry tired ASPECT
        'This matter got Zhangsan tired from crying.'
    (b) Zhei jian   shi   ku lei   le   Zhangsan
        this CLASSIFIER matter cry tired ASPECT Zhangsan
        'This matter got Zhangsan tired from crying.'

On the other hand Ross (1991) and Bender (2000) argue that the causer role is contributed by *ba* itself. Whether the causer role in *ba* causatives is provided by a higher head whose position may be occupied by *ba* or whether *ba* itself assigns that role, neither scenario is compatible with an analysis of *ba* as a preposition. From a cross-linguistic standpoint, while adpositions are commonly associated with addition of adjunct roles within VP, they are not associated with addition of external roles as in a causative pattern. It is therefore difficult to see how the *ba* causative pattern in (19c) could be accounted for under an analysis of *ba* as preposition.

In this section I have reviewed recent analyses of the categorial status of Mandarin *ba*, by far the best-studied example of a putative $V_1 > P$ reanalysis. These studies provide strong arguments that *ba* is not in fact a preposition. The issue of whether *ba* heads a (lexical) verbal projection or a functional projection is immaterial to the question at hand, since either analysis is consistent with the hypothesis in (11). To see this, compare the earlier serial verb structure (24) with the analysis of *ba* as higher verb (25).

(24)   (=18)

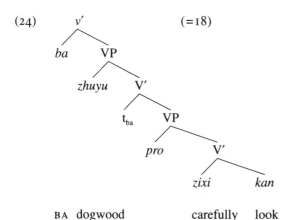

BA   dogwood   carefully   look

(25)   (=17)

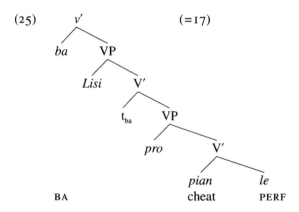

(25) involves no change at all in the categorial status or structural position of *ba*. As in the serial construction (24), the NP in the specifier of the VP headed by *ba* controls an empty category in the specifier of its complement.[12]

The structure in (25) is essentially unchanged on the analysis of *ba* as a functional head. All that differs in this analysis is that the matrix NP *Lisi* appears in the specifier of *ba* as the result of movement. As Takahashi (1997) points out, the surface word order of *ba* and the associated NP suggests that *ba* is still raised to a higher position such as *v* in (25). In terms of feature change, *ba* ceases to assign a thematic role to the associated NP, and gains a strong feature that forces movement to its specifier.

The background for this discussion has been the hypothesis (5) that reanalysis in serial constructions must begin by relabelling. This led to the prediction in (11) that while V_2 in serial constructions may undergo reanalysis, V_1 may not. We then examined the *ba* 'object marker' pattern in Chinese and saw that although *ba* in this pattern has undergone some change (in the identity of its complement, and perhaps its thematic role-assigning properties), *ba* has not been reanalysed as a preposition.

9.5. PRUNING

Although (5) requires that changes in the categorial features of a head be independent of any changes outside its minimal domain, it allows for the possibility that relabelling might be accompanied by changes within the minimal domain of the head. Even in the cases of 'simple' serial $V_2 > P$ reanalysis discussed in §9.3, it seems that such changes occur. Thus under Collins' analysis of serial

---

[12] It is possible that the complement of *ba* in (25) is a larger projection than VP, at least in patterns such as the *ba* causative in (23*a*). In such patterns, the controlled empty category shown in the specifier of this category in (25) cannot be restricted to internal arguments of V_2. Under the analysis in (25), this would be the only change between (25) and the serial pattern in (24).

constructions as in (10), V_2 assigns a thematic role to *pro* in its specifier; but
when V_2 is reanalysed as C as in (4), it no longer assigns this role. The same is
true of at least some cases of $V_2 > P$ reanalysis. For instance, the preposition *yu*
'with' (originally a serial V_2 'give') discussed in §9.4 occurs only in pre-verbal
position and has a comitative function in present-day Mandarin:

(26)   Zhe jian   shi   yu   ni   mei   guanxi
        this CLASSIFIER matter with you not-have connection
        'This mattter has nothing to do with you.'

Both of these facts indicate that its projection has ceased to contain a *pro*
controlled by the object.

    Let us assume that in these cases the only relation between the head (ori-
ginally V_2) and its specifier is that the former assigns the latter a thematic role,
and that this relationship is eliminated when the categorial change takes place.
As a result, no category is merged in the specifier of the reanalysed P. Due to
the prohibition on non-branching projections, the reanalysed projection of P is
'pruned'. This result is shown in (27), using Mandarin *yu* 'with' as an example.

(27)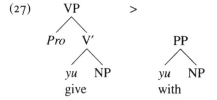

The term 'pruning' is taken from Ross (1967), where it refers to an operation
which removes projections that have been rendered non-branching as the result
of a transformational operation. Here the term refers not to a syntactic operation,
but the consequence of a change that makes a syntactic position cease to be
the target for merge or movement, resulting in a non-branching projection. In a
theory which disallows non-branching projections, the consequence of such a
change is elimination of the projection. Pruning is a relatively straightforward
structural change within the minimal domain of a relabelled head. In the following section I examine a more complex case.

9.6. SPECIFIER > HEAD REANALYSIS

The literature on syntactic reanalysis has included cases which involve greater
modification of structure than the 'simple' renalyses discussed above. In this
section I will focus on one such case, reanalysis of a subject pronoun as a copula. I will argue that a Minimalist treatment is in fact consistent with (5).

    In a number of languages, subject pronouns are reanalysed as copulas, as first
discussed from a comparative standpoint by Li and Thompson (1977). Modern
Mandarin *shi* 'be' has such a source, from an original function as a proximal

demonstrative 'this' (Wang 1958, Peyraube and Wiebusch 1995). (28), cited by Li and Thompson (1977: 421) from the *Lun yu* (500 BCE) shows the pattern without an overt medial copula typical of this period of Chinese.[13] (29) shows an example where *shi* clearly functions as a demonstrative (1977: 423).

(28)   Zi yu: ru ji ye
         Zi say: you tool PARTICLE
         'Confucius says: "You are a tool." '
             (*Lun yu*)

(29)   Zi yu *shi* ri   ku
         Zi at this day cry
         'Confucius cried on this day.'
             (*Lun yu*)

In this period it is also possible to find examples of *shi* as a resumptive pronominal subject with a nominal predicate, as in (30) from Peyraube and Wiebusch (1995: 393).

(30)   Fu   yu gui   *shi* ren zhi suo   yu   ye
         riches and honour this men 's NOMINALIZER desire PARTICLE
         'Riches and honour, this is what men desire.'   (*Lun yu*)

The pattern in (30) is held by the authors cited above to be the source construction for the reanalysis of *shi* as a copula.[14] In examples prior to 200 BCE it is often difficult to determine whether *shi* functions as a subject resumptive pronoun or copula (Peyraube and Wiebusch 1995: 396–7), but Peyraube and Wiebusch cite examples such as the following from the second century BCE where *shi* occurs twice, first as subject pronoun and next as copula, confirming that the latter function has been established (1995: 398):

(31)   Shi *shi* lie   gui
         this is   violent ghost
         'This is a violent ghost.'
             (*Shuihudi Qin mu zhujian*)

---

[13] The sentence-final particle *ye* in (28) is analysed by many scholars as a clause-final copula (e.g. Peyraube and Wiebusch 1995: 389–90). *Ye* is common in examples from the Late Archaic (500–100 BCE) containing *shi* where it is difficult to determine whether the latter is pronoun or copula. It seems likely that the decline of *ye* and the establishment of *shi* as medial copula are related phenomena, but clarifying this relationship requires a clear structural analysis of *ye*.

[14] Peyraube and Wiebusch discuss and reject alternative analyses, which attempt to relate copular *shi* to its earlier adjectival/adverbial function 'right/truly' (clearly related to to its demonstrative source, as with English 'thus'), or to its affirmative/focus function (likewise derivable from the demonstrative source). I am indebted to Erwin Chan for discussion of this debate.

As Li and Thompson (1977) and subsequent authors have shown, reanalysis of a subject resumptive pronoun as a copula is a widely attested phenomenon. The structural adjustment involved in such a reanalysis is not just a simple categorial change on the part of the pronoun. Not only must the pronoun change from pronoun to copula, it must change its structural status from specifier of the clausal projection (subject) to head of a verbal projection. Let us see how this change is consistent with (5), first by positing a structure for the subject–resumptive pronoun pattern in (30).

(32)   (=30)

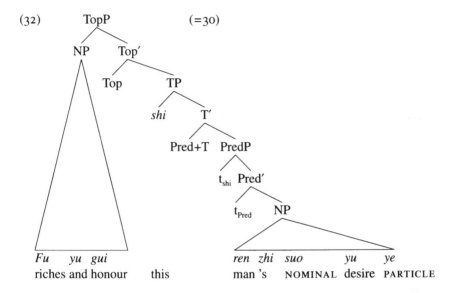

| Fu | yu gui | | this | ren zhi suo | yu | ye |
| riches and honour | | | | man 's NOMINAL | desire | PARTICLE |

I have followed conventional practice in assuming that a left-dislocated phrase binding a resumptive pronoun resides in the specifier of a higher projection, Topic Phrase in (32). The subject pronoun *shi* originates in the specifier of the projection where it is predicated of the NP *ren zhi suo yu* 'what man desires'. This projection is identified as PredP following Bowers (1993); its crucial properties are that it selects a predicate NP as complement and has a phonetically null head whose categorial feature may check the V-feature of T.[15] *Shi* raises to Spec,TP to check the strong D-feature of T and satisfy the Extended Projection Principle; the categorial feature of the empty copula checks the V-feature of T. *Shi* in this structure is both a maximal projection and a head. As it is a pronoun, I will assume its category is D.

Change of the categorial feature of *shi* from *d* to *v* is accompanied by the change in structural status shown in (33):

---

[15] I assume that Pred is a subtype of the category V.

(33)   TopP   (=31)

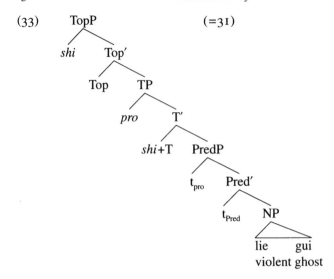

Let us consider how this change takes place. When the categorial feature of *shi* changes from *d* to *v*, *shi* becomes available to select the predicate NP and check the *v*-feature of T; it therefore can be merged with the predicate NP to form PredP. The category Pred assigns a thematic role to its specifier (Bowers 1993); an empty pronominal is available in Chinese to be merged in this position. The empty pronominal subject raises to check the D-feature of T, and *shi* raises to check its V-feature.

Thus the change from pronoun to copula forces a change in the identity of the head and specifier of PredP, but these changes are internal to the minimal domain of *shi*. (5) requires that relabelling of *shi* be independent of any changes outside its minimal domain. This predicts that change in status of the left-dislocated phrase in Spec,TopP to subject in Spec,TP occurs independently of the reanalysis of *shi* as copula; that is, this phrase may retain its left-dislocated status after reanalysis of *shi*, as in (33). Although this possibility is difficult to confirm in the case of earlier Chinese, it can be confirmed in the case of a parallel development in Saramaccan.

McWhorter (1997) discusses the same development of the Saramaccan copula *da* from an element corresponding to the English demonstrative *that*.

(34)   Mi da   i   tata
        I   COPULA your father
        'I am your father.'

Assuming a development parallel to what we have described for Chinese *shi* above, after reanalysis of *da* as a copula, structure outside the minimal domain of *da* is unchanged: subject position is occupied by a null pronoun, and the clause-initial NP retains its left-dislocated status, as in (35).

(35)   [$_{TopP}$ Mi [$_{TP}$ pro [$_{T'}$ da   i   tata]]]
         I   COPULA your father

McWhorter provides three pieces of data which suggest that a representation like (35) is correct. First, he shows that the third person subject pronoun form co-occurring with copular *da* must be the topic form *hɛn* rather than the non-topic form *a*. This is shown in the contrast between the non-copular sentence (36*a*) and the copular sentence (36*b*) with a third person pronominal subject.

(36) (*a*)   A tei   faka koti di gwamba
             he take knife cut the meat
             'He cut the meat with a knife.'
             (McWhorter 1997: 98)

    (*b*)   Hɛn/*A da   di Gaama
            he   COPULA the chief
            'He is the chief.'
            (McWhorter 1997: 98)

Second, McWhorter observes that the copula is normally obligatory in modern Saramaccan (37), but must be dropped in sentences with predicate fronting (38). The ungrammaticality of predicate fronting with *da* can be explained if subjects with *da* are always topicalized or left-dislocated. Predicate fronting over a topicalized or left-dislocated constituent results in a violation of Relativized Minimality, as in English (39).

(37)   Disi *(da)   mi tata
         this COPULA my father
         'This is my father.'
         (McWhorter 1997: 90)

(38)   Mi tata,   disi (*da)
         my father this COPULA
         'This is my father.'
         (McWhorter 1997: 90)

(39)   *Smart, my father he is.

Similarly, McWhorter observes that *da* must be dropped in *wh*-questions (40). Again this is explained because *wh*-movement over topicalized or left-dislocated subjects violates Relatived Minimality (41).

(40)   Un   buku di-de (*da/dɛ)
         which book that   COPULA
         'Which book is that?'
         (McWhorter 1997: 91)

(41)   *Which book, that is it?

The data cited by McWhorter indicate that the overt subject NP in *da* copular sentences remains in a topicalized or left-dislocated position even after reanalysis of *da* as copula, showing that resumptive pronoun > copula reanalysis need not be accompanied by immediate change in the status of the topicalized or left-dislocated NP to subject.

9.7. CONCLUSION

The objective of this chapter has been to develop an account of syntactic re-analysis formulated in terms of changes in the features of lexical items rather than correspondences between syntactic patterns or rules of historically distinct grammars. The relabelling hypothesis in (5) claims that reanalyses begin with a change in the categorial feature of a head, and that the structural consequences of this change (pruning resulting from a change in thematic role assignment, or change from specifier to head status) are limited to the minimal domain of that head.

The relabelling hypothesis says nothing about the 'causes' of syntactic re-analysis. From the standpoint of (5), 'book' might as easily undergo the categorial change N>copula as a resumptive pronoun. The hypothesis in effect sets an upper limit for possible types of reanalysis: it allows the range of reanalyses in serial verb and copular constructions that we have reviewed, while ruling out changes that affect structure over larger syntactic domains. The hypothesis presents what might be called a lexical conception of a type of change that has been thought to be quintessentially syntactic.

PART III

Mechanisms of Syntactic Change

2

Movement

10

The Value of Definite Determiners from Old Spanish to Modern Spanish

MONTSE BATLLORI and FRANCESC ROCA

10.1. INTRODUCTION

This chapter focuses on the analysis of determiners and offers a comparative approach by paying special attention to the syntactic and semantic properties of the definite article and the demonstrative in Modern Spanish and Old Spanish (see F. Roca 1997 and Batllori 1996, respectively). Our main goal is to show that in Old Spanish the behaviour of *el*, *la*, *los*, *las* can only be explained by referring to two subsystems of grammar. The more general one is the innovative grammar or subsystem in which these forms function as discourse anaphors (in the same way as *is*, *ea*, *id* did in Latin). This amounts to saying that the syntactic change from a demonstrative to a definite article had already started in Late Latin. On the other hand, Old Spanish retains an older subsystem, dubbed 'etymological' in this chapter, with forms that express deictic meaning (i.e. they function as demonstratives rather than as their Modern Spanish counterparts, which display the typical properties associated with the head D). This suggests that the grammatical change from Latin to Old Spanish and, consequently, from the etymological Old Spanish grammar to Modern Spanish involves the reanalysis of *ille*, *illa*, *illud* as functional heads that lack all the syntactic and semantic properties of demonstratives.

As will be seen, the structure put forward in F. Roca (1997) explains the main properties of nominal expressions in both Old Spanish and Modern Spanish and provides the means for a unitary account of determiners in both periods and also for their evolution from one stage to the other. This structure postulates the existence of two different levels of determination (labelled as DP and DemP) and can be outlined as follows:

This work has been sponsored by the following research projects: PB96-1199-C04-03 and PB95-0656 (DGICYT-MEC), 1997SGR00125 (Generalitat de Catalunya), PB96-0457-C03-01 and PB96-1199-C04-01 (DGICYT-MEC), 1997SGR00193 (Generalitat de Catalunya), PB-98-0884 (DGICYT-MEC), and 1999SGR00114 (Generalitat de Catalunya).

[$_{DP}$ D [$_{DemP}$ Dem [. . . [Poss] . . . [NP] . . .]]]

This analysis can account for the fact that Modern Spanish admits the coexistence of the definite article and the demonstrative (*el libro este* 'lit. the book this'), which seems to be ungrammatical in Old Spanish given the lack of empirical evidence. In order to explain this contrast, we claim that in one of these Old Spanish grammars the nature of *ille* descendants is close to demonstratives. This leads us to state that in the Old Spanish etymological grammar *el, la, los, las* as well as demonstratives are not the head D, but the head Dem, whereas in Modern Spanish and in the Old Spanish innovative grammar, which is the most general one, they correspond to the head D and demonstratives to the head Dem. Therefore, they go through an evolution that involves a change from being a head Dem to being a head D, which according to the analysis we put forward implies the loss of syntactic movement from Dem to D.

10.2. THE ANALYSIS OF DETERMINERS

10.2.1. *The definite article and the demonstratives in Modern Spanish*

In Modern Spanish, the definite article and the demonstratives clearly differ in both their syntactic behaviour and their semantic properties. These differences concern several syntactic constructions and aspects of grammar such as the linear order with respect to the noun, constructions with an empty N, generic readings in nominal expressions and adjectives introduced by the particle *tan* 'so', among others.[1] These properties will be reviewed below by comparing Old and Modern Spanish data, but first we should examine the facts related to the syntactic position of the definite article and the demonstratives, which is the most relevant contrast from a purely syntactic point of view and reflects the proper structure of the whole DP.

The definite article and the demonstrative both appear in a prenominal position, which is the unmarked position for any determiner in Spanish. However, they differ in the fact that in some cases the demonstrative can follow the noun or the noun plus an adjectival or prepositional complement, whereas the definite article cannot:

(1) (*a*)   el   libro
          the book
    (*b*)   *libro el
          book the
    (*c*)   *este libro el
          this book the

---

[1] See Leonetti (1996) and F. Roca (1997) for a detailed discussion of these differences from a semantic and a syntactic point of view respectively.

(2) (*a*) este libro
            this book
    (*b*) el libro este
            the book this
            'this book'
    (*c*) el libro viejo ese / el libro ese viejo
            the book old   that / the book that old
            'that old book'
    (*d*) el libro de latín aquel / el libro aquel de latín
            the book of Latin that / the book that of Latin
            'that book on Latin'

The examples (2*c–d*) show that the postnominal demonstrative can precede or follow the AP/PP modifiers rather freely, suggesting that the adjacency to the noun is not very strict. Although the construction with the postnominal demonstrative is subject to some restrictions, like the obligatory presence of the definite article preceding the noun, the contrast holds independently because the definite article cannot follow the noun under any circumstance, even if another definite determiner like the demonstrative precedes the whole expression, as the ungrammaticality of (1*c*) indicates.[2]

The coexistence of the definite article and the demonstrative constitutes a strong argument against the analysis of the two determiners as the same head. So, we consider that they must be treated as two different elements and we assume the analysis put forward by F. Roca (1997), according to which the definite article and the demonstrative are the heads of two different functional projections. Each functional projection constitutes a different level of determination within nominal expressions: the highest level is exclusive to the definite article and corresponds to the DP proposed by Abney (1987); the second level is a lower projection located in the complement position of the head D, headed by the demonstrative and labelled DemP.[3] The basic structure of a DP would be the following:

---

[2] There are, however, some nominal constructions where the demonstrative is postnominal and no definite article occurs:

(i) el aplazamiento de la reunión, *posibilidad esta* que no es deseada por nadie, . . .
    the postponing   of the meeting possibility this that not is desired by nobody

These nominal expressions have a very limited syntactic distribution: they can only appear as an appositive complement and they never act as arguments, the typical role of DPs, according to Longobardi (1994). Given that the nominal expression in (i) does not display all the properties of DPs, we can conclude that it is not a complete DP in the sense we will develop in this work. The element that allows a nominal expression to act as a true DP is the head D, which usually corresponds to the definite article. Thus, in the case where we have a definite article without any specific content (that is, an expletive article), its syntactic role will be to ensure that the whole expression is a DP.

[3] In fact, this projection would correspond to any determiner other than the definite article like indefinites, quantifiers, or demonstratives. Here we label it as DemP because we will deal only with demonstratives.

(3) $[_{DP} [_{D'} D [_{DemP} [_{Dem'} Dem . . . [NP]]]]]$

In (3) we abstract away from the different functional categories that are postulated between NP and DemP; here, the most relevant points are the facts that D takes the DemP as its complement and that the NP is generated in a lower position.[4] This analysis can account for all the nominal constructions which contain a demonstrative, either prenominal or postnominal. The derivation of a DP like *este libro* 'this book' would follow from two different movements: NP movement to the specifier position of DemP and raising of the head Dem up to the head D.[5] This can be seen in the following representation:

(4) $[_{DP} [_{D'} este_i [_{DemP} [_{NP} libro]_j [_{Dem'} t_i . . . t_j]]]]$

The derivation of the construction with the postnominal demonstrative (*el libro este* 'the book this') only differs in the fact that the movement of the demonstrative to the head D does not take place in the overt syntax and, then, the head D is occupied by the definite article (the movement of the NP to Spec,DemP applies in both cases):

(5) $[_{DP} [_{D'} el [_{DemP} [_{NP} libro]_j [_{Dem'} este . . . t_j]]]]$

One of the main points of this approach is that the relationship between the head D and the head Dem, that has been expressed in terms of head raising, appears as a kind of expletive replacement: the movement of Dem to D can take place before Spell Out (4) or after Spell Out (5). In the latter case, the demonstrative remains *in situ* in the overt syntax and the head D is occupied by an expletive. This clearly suggests that, whenever we have a demonstrative, the head D will have no content by itself. Such a prediction is borne out by the fact that all the semantic and syntactic properties of the DPs in which the definite article and the demonstrative co-occur depend exclusively on the demonstrative, never on the definite article. The only role of the head D in these configurations

---

[4] There are, within the generative framework, several analyses of demonstratives as a category different from the definite article. The one put forward in F. Roca (1997) and adopted here either differs completely or coincides with them only in some aspects. For instance, the treatments of Giusti (1995) and Brugè (1996) differ completely both in the status of the demonstrative, which they consider as specifier of a functional projection, and in the kind of movement the demonstrative undergoes (XP movement instead of head movement). Bernstein (1997) also considers the demonstrative to be a specifier, but she notes that it must raise to D as a head. Cornilescu (1992) also establishes two levels of determination with a DetP projection below the DP, but she concedes a double possibility for the demonstrative, that can be a head, when it acts as a determiner, or a specifier, when it is like a pronoun. We keep away from such a distinction and consider that it is always the head Dem of the DemP. See F. Roca (1997) for the problems that these approaches posit in the case of Spanish. The analysis and the derivation we assume have, at some extent, a connection with the ones postulated by Zamparelli (1996) from a semantic perspective.

[5] Both movements are motivated, in accordance with the Minimalist Programme, by attraction to check some features. The features involved are related to the informational content of the elements that precede the head Dem and to the [+/–def] value of the whole DP. F. Roca (1999) discusses the properties of these operations and their final motivation.

will be, according to Longobardi (1994), to ensure that the whole nominal expression can act as an argument. The validity of this prediction is exemplified by the behaviour of the construction with the definite article and the postnominal demonstrative (from now on the 'Art–N–Dem' construction) with respect to the generic interpretation of nominals and to adjectives introduced by *tan* 'so', which constitute two of the main syntactic and semantic differences between the two determiners.

In Spanish, some DPs can have a generic reading when they are introduced by the definite article, as in the example (6*a*). But the demonstrative does not allow for this reading (# indicates that the generic reading is not available):

(6) (*a*)　La ballena está en peligro de extinción
　　　　　the whale is   in danger of extinction
　　　　　'Whales are in danger of extinction.'

　　(*b*)　#Esta ballena está en peligro de extinción.
　　　　　this whale is   in danger of extinction.
　　　　　'This whale is in danger of extinction.'

The only possible reading for (6*b*) is the one referring to a specific whale or to a specific type of whale (the blue whale for instance), which is a possible reading with demonstratives (see Vergnaud and Zubizarreta (1992) on the type/token distinction). The interpretation of the 'Art–N–Dem' construction coincides completely with that of the prenominal demonstrative:

(7)　　　#La ballena esta está en peligro de extinción.
　　　　　the whale this is   in danger of extinction
　　　　　'This whale is in danger of extinction.'

Adjectives introduced by the particle *tan* 'so' show the opposite behaviour: they are impossible with the definite article, but grammatical with a demonstrative.

(8) (*a*)　*el libro tan viejo
　　　　　the book so old
　　(*b*)　ese libro tan viejo
　　　　　this book so old

Again, the construction in which the definite article and the demonstrative coexist follows the same pattern as the demonstrative and is grammatical with this particle:

(9)　　　el libro ese tan viejo
　　　　　the book this so old

If the presence of the determiner played a role in the syntactic and semantic properties of the 'Art–N–Dem' construction, we should expect the phrase in (9) to be ungrammatical (as (8*a*) is). The fact that the definite article does not induce ungrammaticality in (9) must be interpreted in the sense that it actually does not have any relevance in the syntactic and semantic properties of the construction. The element that determines these properties is, as in the preceding case of generic NPs, the demonstrative. This points to the conclusion that the definite article that appears in the 'Art–N–Dem' configurations has no real value and that it should be analysed as an expletive.[6]

From a purely theoretical point of view, the analysis sketched in (4)–(5) relies on the same grounds as the analysis of DPs put forward in Kayne (1994). The relation that holds between the determiner in D and the NP is the same as the one postulated in Kayne's analysis for possessives and internally headed relatives. In (10) we reproduce the structures for relative clauses and for possessives according to his view ((5) is repeated as (10d)):

(10) (a) $[_{DP}$ the $[_{CP}$ [two pictures of John's]$_i$ $[_{C'}$ that $[_{IP}$ you lent me t$_i$]]]]

    (b) $[_{DP}$ D $[_{C/PP}$ [two pictures]$_i$ $[_{C/P'}$ of $[_{IP}$ [John] ['s t$_i$]]]]]

    (c) $[_{DP}$ la $[_{C/PP}$ [voiture]$_i$ $[_{C/P'}$ de $[_{IP}$ [Jean] $[_I$ t$_i$]]]]]

    (d) $[_{DP}$ el $[_{DemP}$ $[_{NP}$ libro]$_j$ $[_{Dem'}$ este . . . t$_j$]]]

The NP always ends up in the specifier position of the functional projection immediately below DP. Thus, we consider that the relationship between D and NP goes along the same lines in Kayne's analysis and in the one we postulate. In addition, our analysis can account for all the occurrences of postnominal demonstratives in Spanish. We have already seen that the postnominal demonstrative can precede or follow the adjectives or the prepositional phrases that modify the noun:

(11) (a) el libro viejo ese
       the book old   that

    (b) el libro ese viejo
       the book that old
       'that old book'

(12) (a) la casa aquella con dos jardines
       the house that   with two gardens

    (b) la casa con dos jardines aquella
       the house with two gardens that
       'that house with two gardens'

These facts can be explained if we consider that the NP and its modifiers are two independent constituents (as in Kayne's approach) and that the constituent moved to Spec,DemP can be complex and include the AP/PP modifiers (as in

---

[6] F. Roca (1997) shows that this is the case with all the differences noted between the definite article and the demonstrative.

the relative structure (10*a*), for instance). Under this view, the fact that the PP or AP complement is left behind (and appears on the right) would be analogous in a Kaynian approach to the cases of extraposition within sentences (we could have, then, extraposition inside nominals).[7]

10.2.2. *The definite article and the demonstratives in Old Spanish*

As is well known, although literary Latin lacks determiners, it has a system of demonstratives which are basically used to express deixis *ad oculos* concerning speech acts and its participants. Besides the demonstratives *hic* 'this', *iste* 'this', and *ille* 'that', Latin has an anaphoric pronoun, mainly used as the antecedent of a relative clause (*is, ea, id—is homo qui . . ., is qui . . .*), an identity pronoun (*idem, eadem, idem* 'the same'), and an emphatic pronoun (*ipse, ipsa, ipsum* 'one and the same'). The loss of *is, hic*, and *ille* due to phonetic erosion through evolution brings about restructuring of the demonstrative system in Late Latin.

As for the value of Latin *ille*, Harris (1980: 141–56) states that *ille*, while retaining at least at first its demonstrative functions, was also used both as a 'personal' and an 'anaphoric' pronoun (these both also being [+definite], [–proximity]). Notice the comment concerning the fact that *ille* retains some of its demonstrative functions in Late Latin. As will be shown, Old Spanish *el, la, los, las* display characteristics which reflect their demonstrative origins: (*a*) they cannot coexist with demonstratives, (*b*) generic nominals do not admit these forms, (*c*) both *el, la, los, las* and the demonstratives are attested in empty noun constructions, and (*d*) they both appear in structures with an adjective introduced by *tan* 'so'. Therefore, the syntactic and semantic nature of these forms is clearly different from the equivalent Modern Spanish determiners. It could be said that Old Spanish *el, la, los, las* are part of a demonstrative system whose elements display a single and a reinforced variant in each case. These reinforced variants are the result of the prefixation of **accu* to single variants. **Accu* corresponds to the contraction of *ad* (a Latin preposition that became a prefix in Romance), *ecce* (a Latin adverbial particle used to reinforce deictic value, meaning 'here it is', or 'over here'), and *eum* (the accusative form of the anaphoric pronoun *is, ea, id*). In fact, the use of reinforced variants is documented in Plautus (e.g. *eccillum video* 'I see that over there' and *eccistam video* 'I see this over here'), and thus the origin can be attributed to a development of colloquial Latin. Notice that Plautus frequently uses *eccum* (< *ecce eum*) instead of *ecce*.

The demonstrative system documented in the *Poema de Mío Cid* (twelfth century) displays the following pattern: *este logar* 'this place' (< *iste*), **essa** *santidad* 'this holiness' (< *ipsa*) and **la** *mi mugier* 'that my wife' (< *illa*) in contrast to

---

[7] This approach is better than the analyses that treat the demonstrative as a specifier, which are led to state that the postnominal demonstrative must follow adjectives but precede PPs. See Brugè (1996) or Giusti (1995), who assume the existence of the functional architecture above NP put forward by Cinque (1994).

aqueste escano 'this bench here' (< **accu iste*), *aquessa corrida* 'this dash here' (< **accu ipsa*) and *aquelas villas* 'those villages there' (< **accu illas*).

The change from *ille* to the definite article seems to have taken a long time during which two possible competing internalized grammars or linguistic subsystems coexist as proposed by Kroch (1989*b*). In one of these grammars, which could be called etymological, *el* maintains its deictic value, generic nominal constructions display null articles and the *el+su+*noun constructions are generated in the same way as *este+su+*noun structures. In the other grammar, which can be defined as the innovation, *el* has already lost its deictic value, generic nominal constructions are introduced by *el* and the co-occurrence of *el* with the prenominal possessive is ungrammatical. The latter grammar involves grammaticalization and parametric variations as discussed in Roberts (1993*b*).

As for Old Spanish, Batllori (1996) analyses the distribution of *ille* descendants and points out that both [+referential] and [−referential] nominals admit the absence of determiners, as in (13).

(13) (*a*) E   quando alçava Moyses sos manos, vencia Israel. *Manos de*
            and when   raised Moses his hands, won   Israel. Hands of
            Moysen eran pesadas . . .
            Moses   were heavy . . . (*Fazienda*: 73)

     (*b*) Dixo el angel: 'descalçaras   *pies*, que el logar en que
            Said the angel: you-will-undress feet, that the place in which
            estas,   [santo] es' . . . (*Fazienda*: 98) / Quando lo   uio doña
            you-are [holy] is   when   him saw lady
            Ximena a *pies* se le   echaua (*Cid*, v. 1594)
            Ximena to feet her of-him threw

     (*c*) E   crebantaredes todas *cibdades encastelladas* (*Fazienda*: 131) /
            And broke   all   cities   fortified
            De   diestro a Lilon las torres, que *moros*   las   han / *Moros*
            From right   to Lilon the towers, that Arabians them have   Arabians
            le   reçiben / Que non   lo sepan *moros*   nin *christianos*
            him meet   that neither it know Arabians nor Christians
                (*Cid*, v. 398, 712, 145)

In (13*a*) the bare noun *manos* 'hands' functions as a subject, in (13*b*) *pies* 'feet' acts as an object (a direct object, in the first sentence, and an adverbial object, in the second one) and in both cases the bare noun is [+referential], while in (13*c*) the bare nouns are generic and therefore [−referential].

Thus, Old Spanish has two different subsystems of grammar for *ille* descendants. In the innovative grammar they have already been reanalysed as discourse anaphors and examples such as the ones in (13) would not be generated, whereas in the etymological one these examples would be commonplace and *el*, *la*, *los*, *las* behave as demonstratives.

When *el, la, los, las* pair with demonstratives in expressing deictic value, the [+referential] interpretation can be achieved by the use of the null article, as a reflex of the literary Latin system of determination. The absence of the definite article can also be related to the [−referential] feature subject to lexical head government, at LF, which enables it to be interpretable at this level.

The Old Spanish etymological grammar has no overt D heads and both the demonstratives and the definite articles are generated under the head Dem. The definite article progressively loses its deictic features and develops an anaphoric feature to be checked under the D head; this brings about the extension of its use with nominals which do not show deictic values (generic nouns, nouns with referential uniqueness, and abstract and mass nouns). As shown in (14), in the innovative grammar the definite article functions as a discourse anaphor (i.e. a real D head):

(14) (*a*)   En vn otero Redondo (*Cid*, v. 554)
             in a round hillock (indefinite meaning)

      (*b*)   Bien puebla   *el otero* (*Cid*, v. 557)
             well (he) settles the hillock

      (*c*)   Derredor *del otero*, bien çerca del   agua (*Cid*, v. 560)
             around   the hillock, pretty close to-the water

The coexistence of two competing grammatical subsystems allows an explanation of the variation between the presence and absence of definite articles that do not convey any difference in meaning, as can be seen in the examples below:

(15) (*a*)   los moros   nos   van *del campo* (*Cid*, v. 755)
             the Arabians not-them go   from-the field

      (*b*)   los moros   non ficaran   en *campo* (*Cid*, v. 2354)
             the Arabians not will-stay in field

      (*c*)   a *los pies* le   cayo (*Cid*, v. 2025)
             to the feet to-him fell

      (*d*)   a *pies* se le   echava (*Cid*, v. 1594)
             to feet her to-him threw

      (*e*)   dizes   *verdat* (*Cid*, v. 3386)
             (you) say truth

      (*f*)   quem   digades   *la verdat* (*Cid*, v. 2139)
             that-to-me (you) say the truth

In the language of the *Poema de Mío Cid*, which is taken as the starting point for the chronology of the extension of the definite article, human generic nouns follow two patterns. In the pattern used more frequently, nouns are introduced by the definite article *el, la, los, las*, as shown in (16):

(16) (*a*)   enbia   sus cartas pora Leon e   a Sancti Yaguo, / *Alos*
            (he) sends his letter to   Leon and to Santiago   / to-the
            portogaleses & a galizianos / E   *alos*   *de Carrion* &
            Portuguese   and to Galician / And to-those of Carrion and
            avarones castellanos (*Cid*, vv. 2977–9)
            to-men   Castilian

      (*b*)   que sea *el pueblo* de moros   & *dela yente* christiana
            that be the village of Arabians and of-the people Christian
                (*Cid*, v. 901)

      (*c*)   Grande duelo auien *las yentes christianas*   (*Cid*, v. 29)
            Great grief had the people Christian

In the pattern used less frequently, which corresponds to the etymological
grammar, they are always nouns used without determiners or demonstratives, as
in (17).

(17) (*a*)   Con el Rey van *leoneses & mesnadas galizianas*
            with the king go Leoneses and armies   Galician
                (*Cid*, v. 1982)

      (*b*)   E   non la tolliesse dent   *Christiano* (*Cid*, v. 1788)
            and not her took out from-there Christian

      (*c*)   De noche lo   lieuen, que non lo vean *christianos*   (*Cid*, v. 93)
            at night him bring that not him see Christians

      (*d*)   *Moros*   le   Reçiben (*Cid*, v. 712)
            Arabians him receive

Likewise, the examples in (18) display a generic construction, which is in this
case a reflex of Latin *omnia res*. They are the only examples that can be found
in the *Poema de Mío Cid* corresponding to generic structures that lack *el*, *la*, *los*,
las and are introduced by the universal quantifier *todo*. They must also be regarded as constructions produced by the etymological grammar.

(18) (*a*)   Et guarnir uos de   *todas armas*   commo uos dixieredes aqui
            and supply you with all   weapons as   you said   here
            (*Cid*, v. 1872)

      (*b*)   Tanta   buena espada *contoda guarnizon* (*Cid*, v. 3244)
            so-many good swords with-all complements

      (*c*)   Bauieca el so cauallo; De *todas guarnizones* muy bien es
            Bauieca the his horse; of all   complements very well is
            adobado (*Cid*, v. 1715)
            provided

      (*d*)   Vanssele acogiendo   yentes de *todas partes* (*Cid*, v. 403)
            go-to-him taking.refuge people of all   parts

According to Company (1991*a*, *b*), mass and abstract nouns do not display definite articles systematically until the fifteenth century. In the twelfth century, however, both types of nouns can occur either with *el* or without it (see the examples below). Despite the fact that Company comments on the sporadic presence of the definite article with mass and abstract nouns before the fifteenth century, she does not offer an explanation for the variation documented in the previous centuries. Under our analysis, the explanation lies in the existence of two different structures generated by two subsystems of grammar as if the speaker had two registers, which alternate in use, a colloquial one (the innovative grammar) and a formal one (the etymological grammar). This situation gives rise to two possible interpretations of the data. It could be the case that (19) displayed bare nouns corresponding to the etymological grammar and (20) showed definite articles corresponding to the innovative grammar whose meaning would be that of the discourse anaphor. Nevertheless, it could also be the case that (20) expressed the etymological grammar and thus that these forms were demonstratives, which would respect the chronology proposed by Company.

(19) (*a*)   *Grand alegreya* va   en tre   essos christianos (*Cid*, v. 0797)
            great   happiness goes between these Christians

  (*b*)   Non ayades *pauor* por que me   veades lidiar (*Cid*, v. 1653)
          not have   fright because to-me see   fight

  (*c*)   Non dizes *verdad* amigo   ni ha señor (*Cid*, v. 3386)
          not say   truth   to-friend nor to sir

(20) (*a*)   Grant fue *el alegria*   que fue por   el palaçio (*Cid*, v. 1770)
            great was the happiness that was around the palace

  (*b*)   perdiendo   van   *el pauor* (*Cid*, v. 1670)
          through-losing (they) go the fright

  (*c*)   dezir uos   he   *la verdad* (*Cid*, v. 0947)
          say   to-you have the truth

In fact, the following examples suggest that the ones in (20) are nouns preceded by a demonstrative, since in (21) the elements that introduce the mass noun in (*a*) and the abstract noun in (*b*) are demonstratives.

(21) (*a*)   Beuemos so vino &   comemos *el so pan* (*Cid*, v. 1104)
            drink   his wine and eat   the his bread

  (*b*)   Que non sopiesse ninguno *esta su poridad* (*Cid*, v. 680)
          that not knows   anybody this his secrecy

As for nouns expressing uniqueness of reference, they also display variation with respect to the presence or absence of the determiner, as can be seen in the following examples:

(22) (*a*)　Antes sere　　　con uusco que *el sol* quiera Rayar (*Cid*, v. 231)
　　　　　before (I) will-be with you　than the sun wants to-shine

　　(*b*)　*El yuierno* es exido, que *el marſo* quiere entrar (*Cid*, v. 1619)
　　　　　the winter is gone, that the March wants to-enter

　　(*c*)　iuntaras　　　comigo fata dentro en *la mar* (*Cid*, v. 2416)
　　　　　(you) will-join with-me until inside in the sea

(23) (*a*)　El vno es en *parayso*, ca　el otro non entro (*Cid*, v. 350)
　　　　　the one is in paradise, since the other not enter

　　(*b*)　*Dios* que esta en *ſielo*　dem　　dent buen galardon (*Cid*, v. 2126)
　　　　　God who is　in heaven give-me then good prize

　　(*c*)　Entraron sobre *mar*, en las barcas son . . . (*Cid*, v. 1627)
　　　　　entered on　sea, in the boats (there) are

　　(*d*)　si plogiere a *Criador* (*Cid*, v. 1665)
　　　　　if pleased to Creator

To sum up, once the definite article is identified with the default realization of the [referential] feature, its movement from Dem to D is no longer postulated by language learners and the definite article is generated under D. As for possessives, at the beginning they are generated in a lower position, but they soon compete with the definite article for the expression of the [+referential] feature and start raising to the D head. This leads to the ungrammaticality of the 'Art–Poss–N' construction. Notice, on the one hand, that Mexican Spanish has completed this process of substitution and in this variety the possessive is generally used instead of the definite article as a discourse anaphor. On the other hand, the demonstratives, which only raise to the D head when neither the definite article nor a prenominal possessive intervene, are the only elements that can coexist with the definite article (as the default realization of the expletive features) and prenominal possessives nowadays.

We can say then that the evolution from a demonstrative (a head Dem) to a determiner (the head D) had already started in Late Latin. Old Spanish displayed two different subsystems of grammar whose realizations relied on code-switching in the same way as a bilingual speaker changes from one language to the other or a monolingual one switches from a colloquial register to a formal one. The etymological grammar seems to have existed until the seventeenth century at least (see Girón Alconchel (1998) for a study of the reinforced variants of demonstratives).

There are clear differences in the syntactic use and the semantic value of determiners between the Old Spanish etymological grammar and Modern Spanish, which have already been examined in Batllori and Roca (1998). These differences show that in this Old Spanish system the definite article behaves like Modern Spanish demonstratives and that, consequently, it has to be analysed as the head Dem rather than as the head D. The syntax of Old Spanish possessives differs also from that of Modern Spanish. The reason for this contrast is due to the argument status of the possessive in Old Spanish, which enables it to introduce a noun modified by a restrictive relative clause and to coexist with an article when prenominal. The following example illustrates both properties:

(24)   todos *los mjs vasallos que aqui son fi[n]ados* serian   por su
           all   the my disciples that here are killed   would-be by his
           señor este dia vengados
           master this day revenged
                 (*Poema de Fernán González*, fol. 32r)

The syntactic contexts that indicate that demonstratives and articles behave exactly in the same way in the Old Spanish etymological subsystem but not in Modern Spanish mainly concern the coexistence of both determiners, which is not possible in the former but grammatical in the latter. The fact that this construction is not ruled out in the older system shows that the demonstrative and the definite article should be analysed as the same element. The behaviour with respect to the generic reading of nominals, which is not allowed in NPs headed by the definite article or the demonstrative in the Old Spanish etymological grammar, suggests that they are both deictic. Nominal structures with an empty nominal head and also clauses introduced by *tan* 'so' are grammatical in Old Spanish with both the definite article and the demonstrative. This is additional evidence for the deictic value of the definite article which reinforces its treatment as a Dem head.

10.3. CONCLUSION

In this chapter we have argued that the evolution of definite determiners from Latin and Old Spanish to Modern Spanish can be viewed as loss of derivational steps involving movement. In Modern Spanish the only element that is a true determiner (D head) is the definite article, whereas demonstratives are 'Dem-class' elements. In contrast, earlier stages of the language had an etymological subsystem of grammar in which there were no lexical elements specified as D heads, and the descendant of Latin *ille*, as well as the rest of demonstratives, were Dem heads.

We have also argued that this difference can be captured by the following structure of nominal projections:

(25)   [$_{DP}$ D [$_{DemP}$ Dem [. . . [Poss] . . . [NP] . . .]]]

The structure in (25) is valid for both Modern Spanish and Old Spanish nominals. The main syntactic differences we can observe between the two periods are due to the fact that the definite article is the head Dem in the Old Spanish etymological grammar and that it has changed to the head D in Modern Spanish and in the Old/Middle Spanish innovative grammar. As for demonstratives, they occupy the lower head Dem both in Modern Spanish and Old Spanish:

(26)   Old Spanish: [$_{DP}$ D [$_{DemP}$ el/este/ese/aquel [NP . . .]]]
         Modern Spanish: [$_{DP}$ el [$_{DemP}$ este/ese/aquel [NP . . .]]]

The evidence for this analysis consists of constructions with postnominal determiners, generic phrases, empty nouns, *tan* clauses and possessives, but further support can be found by taking into account other syntactic contexts that distinguish the definite article from demonstratives. Among them we can mention proper nouns, where no difference between determiners is noticed in Old Spanish, contrary to Modern Spanish, the deictic value present in Old Spanish *el*, *la*, *los*, *las* but not in their Modern Spanish counterparts, and the ability of the definite article to introduce a sentential subject, which is not attested in Old Spanish.

Our approach also gives an account of the fact that constructions with a definite article and a demonstrative are grammatical in Modern Spanish, but not in Old Spanish, and for the syntax of possessives in Spanish (coexistence with a definite article, a defining relative clause, etc.). In Old Spanish possessives do not behave as true determiners because they do not raise to the DP domain. This can be due to the fact that Old Spanish has not completely developed a head D, that is, a head with all the syntactic and semantic properties of the highest level of determination. In contrast, in Modern Spanish we have such a functional head, and both the raising of possessives and the postnominal demonstrative are possible.

APPENDIX

Admyte (*Archivo Digital de Manuscritos y Textos Españoles*). Madrid: Micronet, S.A.
    [Examples from: *Poema de Fernan González*]
Calila. Thirteenth century. *Calila e Dimna*, ed. J. M. Cacho Blecua and M. J. Lacarra. Madrid: Castalia, 1987.
Celestina. Last decade of the fifteenth to beginning of the sixteenth century. Fernando de Rojas. *La Celestina*, ed. D. S. Severin. Madrid: Cátedra, 1989.
Cid. Twelfth century. *Poema de Mio Cid. Facsímil de la edición paleográfica*, ed. R. Menéndez Pidal. Madrid: Dirección General de Archivos y Bibliotecas, 1961.
CORDE (*Corpus diacrónico del Español*). Madrid: Real Academia Española. [Examples from: *Libro de Buen Amor, Consolatoria de Castilla, Guzmán de Alfarache, Segunda Carta de Hernán Cortés, El sacrificio de la Misa, Tractado de Amores*]
Fazienda. Thirteenth century. Almerich, Arcidiano de Antiochia. *La Fazienda de Ultra Mar. Biblia Romanceada et Itinéraire Biblique en prose castillane du XIIe siècle*, ed. M. Lazar. Salamanca: Acta Salmanticensia, XVIII, Núm. 2, 1965.
González Ollé, F. *Lengua y literatura españolas medievales*. Madrid: Arco Libros, 1993.
    [Examples from: *Fueros Navarros, Auto de los Reyes Magos*]
Lucanor. Fourteenth century. Don Juan Manuel. *El Conde Lucanor*. Madrid: Castalia.
Zifar. Fourteenth century. *El libro del Cauallero Zifar* (*El libro del Cauallero de Dios*), ed. Ch. Ph. Wagner. University of Michigan, Ann Arbor: Kraus Reprint, 1929.

11

From OV to VO in Swedish

LARS-OLOF DELSING

11.1. INTRODUCTION

In this chapter, I present new data on the change from OV to VO in Old Swedish and Early Modern Swedish. Like several other languages (see e.g. Pintzuk 1991 on English and Hróarsdóttir 1999*b* on Icelandic), Swedish goes through a stage where there is variation in the surface word order of the verb and its object(s). My investigation shows that during the fourteenth, fifteenth, and sixteenth centuries both OV and VO word orders are possible. The Swedish data indicate that the choice between OV and VO is not arbitrary, but to a large extent dependent on the form of the object.

I use the Minimalist framework (as outlined in Chomsky 1993 and 1995). I will, however, use the old label I (for INFL) in cases when I do not want to choose between the labels AgrS and T. I refer to two object positions, the right-hand complement of the VP and the Specifier of AgrOP. The latter of these I identify as a position below sentence negation. I assume (with Kayne 1994) that clause structure is universally head initial, and thus that the underlying object position is to the right of the verb. Object verb order is then derived by movement of the object to Spec,AgrOP.

I discuss optionality of movement in general, and I will make precise an empirical generalization about the position of objects in Swedish. In short, objects with an empty D-position are found in preverbal position, whereas objects with a structurally filled D-position are found postverbally. I will also give an account of the three main stages Swedish goes through: the initial OV-grammar, an intermediate grammar that has variation depending on the form of the object, and the modern pure VO-grammar.

I thank the audience of the Diachronic Generative Syntax Workshop 5 for useful comments. I am very grateful to the editors of this volume for many comments and suggestions on this chapter. I also thank Ute Bohnacker, Elisabeth Engdahl, Cecilia Falk, Gunlög Josefsson, Christer Platzack, and Henrik Rosenkvist for comments on previous versions of this chapter. All errors are mine. Most of the investigation has been conducted within the project *Det nordiska artikelsystemet* ('The Nordic Article System'), funded by the Swedish research council for humanities and social sciences, HSFR.

The chapter is organized as follows. The investigation is presented in §11.2, where I show that for three centuries, Swedish has variation between OV and VO. I also show that only certain object types show this variation, whereas other types consistently occur postverbally. In §11.3, I discuss the specific structures of the two types of objects established in the investigation. I argue that objects that are consistently postverbal have a filled D-position, whereas this is not so for other objects. In §11.4, I discuss optionality of movement in general, and I outline an analysis in terms of licensing conditions for objects. In §11.5, the diachronic development of verb–object order is presented in brief. In §11.6 conclusions are presented.

11.2. THE INVESTIGATION

In this section, I present the results of an investigation of the order of non-finite verb and its object(s) in Swedish during the period 1270–1600. For reasons of space, not all details of the investigation can be presented here. A more detailed presentation of the data can be found in Delsing (1999).

11.2.1. *Sources*

I have investigated sixteen Old Swedish (1225–1525) and Early Modern Swedish (1526–1732) texts. The Swedish originals were written during the period 1270–1600. The texts are sometimes referred to on their own, but they are often grouped into five periods, according to the date of composition of the Swedish original. The number of words is an approximation. Full titles of the individual texts and some information about them can be found in Appendix A.

1270–1300	ÖgL and UL	49,000 words
1300–1375	Leg and Mos	179,900 words
1375–1450	Jär, Greg, Birg, and MPI	182,300 words
1451–1530	Val, Did, Regl, Link, and Troja	183,400 words
1530–1600	Petri, Swart, and Brahe	186,200 words

All these texts are computerized, and I have searched them for all non-finite forms of verbs.

11.2.2. *Principles of data collection and classification*

I have chosen to use a large corpus (at least in comparison to other corpus studies of Old Swedish) that allows removal of all cases that might be ambiguous or uncertain. In my investigation, I have also been careful to exclude structures that have not been affected by the general shift from OV to VO.

Old Swedish is (like Modern Swedish) a rigid V2 language. Furthermore, Old Swedish had raising of V to I past the sentence adverbial in embedded clauses. Like Modern Icelandic, Old Swedish had Stylistic Fronting, i.e. movement of objects or other constituents to a position in front of the finite verb in subjectless subordinate clauses. Old Swedish also has topicalization of objects in main clauses. In these cases, the object is clearly in neither of the two relevant positions, Spec,AgrOP or the complement of VP, and I will therefore disregard these cases. Objects will only be considered in relation to non-finite verbs.

The finer details of the principles of data collection are given in Appendix B. In general, all clauses with a finite auxiliary followed by a non-finite main verb are relevant. Out of these structures, I have excerpted all cases with an object of an active, personal construction (i.e. a construction with a full argument as subject). If verbs/verb phrases are coordinated, only the object of the first non-finite verb is excerpted.

Turning to the objects, it is necessary to exclude some of them, because they have a fixed position already in the earliest texts. In particular, we see that clausal objects (subordinate or infinitival clauses) are always postverbal. We also observe that objects containing a negative element are invariably preverbal and will therefore not be investigated here. Even in Modern Swedish, negative objects are still placed in front of non-finite verbs. Other objects are obligatorily placed after the verb. Consider the Modern Swedish examples in (1)–(2).

(1)	Jag har ingenting sett	*Jag har sett ingenting
	I have nothing seen	I have seen nothing
(2)	*Jag har honom/mannen sett	Jag har sett honom/mannen
	I have him/man-the seen	I have seen him/man-the

In other words negative objects have not been part of the general change from OV to VO, and they are therefore not included in the investigation.[1]

All nominal objects are analysed as DPs (except for those used with light verbs, which are analysed here as NPs; see §§11.2.3 and 11.3). Crucial to the analysis is whether the head of the DP is empty or filled; DP objects are therefore categorized according to their heads. Personal pronouns and proper names are treated as separate categories, and the remaining objects are classified as follows:

(3)   *Classification of objects*

indefinite article	en hæst	a horse
definite suffixed article	hæstin	horse-the
demonstrative pronoun	then/thenni hæst	this horse
determinative pronoun	then hæst som . . .	the horse that . . .
possessive pronoun	min/hans hæst	my/his horse

---

[1] A common alternative to (1) is a structure with sentence negation and a postverbal object variable, as in (i).

(i) Jag har inte sett någonting
   I   have not seen anything

genitival attribute	ens mans hæst	a man's horse
cardinal numeral	thre hæstar	three horses
indefinite pronoun	alle/nokre hæstar	all/some horses
bare noun (no determiner)	hæst/hæstar	horse/horses

The prenominal definite article (which is used only when the DP contains an adjective: *then svarti hæstin* 'the black horse-the') is identical in form to the demonstrative pronoun and is therefore included in the same category. Determinative pronouns (which are always followed by a relative clause) are morphologically distinct from demonstratives and articles. The term 'indefinite pronouns' is a bit misleading. This class contains all DPs introduced by an indefinite pronoun (i.e. a quantifier), or an element that triggers a comparative clause/phrase introduced by *som* or *än* ('as' or 'than').[2] Notice that DPs without a lexical noun, such as *then gamle* 'the old (one)', *nokra* 'some', are grouped according to their determiner, together with DPs containing a lexical noun. Coordinated objects are treated as a separate group irrespective of their determiners.

If two determiners are present in the same DP, the highest (leftmost) determiner is given precedence, i.e. *thetta mit hus* 'this my house', is seen as a DP with a demonstrative. An exception is made for indefinite pronouns, which are found both before and after definite determiners. Definite determiners are always given precedence over indefinite pronouns, i.e. *alle mine män* 'all my men', is seen as a DP with a possessive pronoun.

11.2.3. *The position of objects*

DP objects not containing negative elements are placed both before and after the non-finite verb in all my texts. The OV-frequency is however very high in the oldest texts (around 80%). In these texts we may find specific explanations for postverbal objects. Most are either heavy or part of a small clause (see further §11.5 below).

Already at the beginning of the fourteenth century, the OV-frequency drops drastically, and by the end of that century the OV-frequency is only some 10%. The OV-frequency raises again in the fifteenth century, and slowly decreases to around 5% by the end of the sixteenth century. This development of OV order has been partly known since Wenning (1930).

The result raises several questions, for instance: Is the drop in the fourteenth century a parameter shift? How can the variation be explained? The answers to these questions can be given, I think, if we consider the form of the object. The

---

[2] For instance this group includes noun phrases with *sami*: *samu böker* (*som*), '(the) same books (as)', comparative/superlative adjectives: *äldre böker* (*än*), 'older books (than)', or adjectival phrases containing degree adverbs: *lika gamla böker* (*som*), 'as old books (as)', etc. These phrases with graded adjectives should make up a group of their own, but since they show the same behaviour as indefinite pronouns, the two categories are grouped together here (see further Delsing 1999).

primary results are presented in Table 11.1. (Where the total is less than 25, percentages are placed in brackets.)

TABLE 11.1. *Objects of different types in three text groups*

Object	Laws (1270–1300)			MosLeg (1300–1350)			Others (1375–1600)		
	OV	VO	%OV	OV	VO	%OV	OV	VO	%OV
Bare noun	277	41	87%	66	237	22%	33	543	6%
Indefinite article	0	0	—	3	11	(21%)	1	161	1%
Numeral	27	12	69%	6	17	(26%)	0	54	0%
Indefinite pronoun	37	11	77%	56	79	41%	138	247	36%
Definite article	22	34	39%	13	75	15%	6	454	1%
Demonstrative	9	3	(75%)	12	27	31%	48	152	24%
Determinative	0	7	(0%)	2	26	7%	3	82	4%
Possessive pronoun	48	25	66%	22	215	9%	51	642	7%
Genitive	17	13	57%	8	103	7%	3	190	2%
Proper name	0	0	—	2	35	5%	1	227	0%
Personal pronoun	151	48	76%	211	271	44%	561	1,493	27%
Coordinated noun phrases	6	28	18%	5	116	4%	6	267	2%
TOTAL	594	222	**73%**	406	1212	**25%**	851	4512	**16%**

Apart from the general decrease in OV-frequency over time, Table 11.1 shows that only five categories exhibit a high rate of OV after 1375: personal pronouns, DPs with attributive pronouns (demonstrative, possessive, and indefinite) and bare nouns. Two categories show low rates of OV already in the earliest period (1270–1300), namely the two inherently heavy object types: coordinated objects and DPs with a determinative pronoun and a relative clause. I will assume that these two categories are primarily VO for reasons of heaviness, and whatever the nature of this heaviness rule, they are not really affected by the main shift from OV to VO. If we consider the other object categories, we can divide them into two groups as illustrated in Table 11.2 below. Notice that although the frequency of OV for bare nouns and NPs with possessive pronouns is lower than for the

TABLE 11.2. *Position of different object types in texts after 1375*

OV very scarcely attested		OV well attested	
Proper name	0%	Personal pronoun	27%
Indefinite article	1%	Bare noun	6%
Definite article	1%	Demonstrative pronoun	24%
Genitival attribute	2%	Possessive pronoun	7%
Cardinal numeral	0%	Indefinite pronoun	36%

other three categories, it still seems high enough for these two categories to be included in this group; see also the discussion on bare nouns below.

The lowest OV-frequency among the categories to the right in Table 11.2 is found with bare nouns. Most of these bare nouns are however of a special type. Consider the examples in (4).

(4) *Bare noun objects*   *Compare the verbs*
   (*a*)   thy   vilde   iak ey mik *loff*   vita (Birg)   lofua 'praise'
           therefore wanted I   not me praise give

   (*b*)   för än han haffde *hämdh* giort (Link)   hämna 'revenge'
           before he had   revenge made

   (*c*)   som   eder skulo *hynder* göra (Troja)   hindra 'hinder'
           which you should obstacle make

The examples in (4) contain a light verb and a semantically heavy bare noun, often a noun which has the root in common with a verb. The examples in (4) can be paraphrased with a single verb. I will call these constructions 'light verb constructions'.[3] As a working definition, I have picked out a group of verb–object combinations as light verb constructions, in order to be able to quantify them. I have selected a group of common lexical verbs which often occur together with a bare noun of the type described above. The selected verbs are listed in (5) and the selected nouns are listed in (6).

(5)   *hava* (have), *fanga/fa* (catch/get), *taka* (take), *giva* (give), *veta* (know), *vinna* (win), *tappa* (lose), *göra* (make/do), *bära* (bear).

(6)   *behof, nödh, tharf* (need); *hedher, lof, pris, ära* (praise, honour); *skadha, men* (damage, hurt); *hämdh* (revenge); *hinder* (obstacle); *hiälp* (help); *radh* (advice), *bot* (cure); *under* (wonder); *avund* (envy); *vitne* (testimony); *göm* (care); *rön* (experience), *skuld* (guilt), *plikt* (duty); *vissa* (knowledge); *akt* (intention); *siger* (victory); *makt, vald* (power).

The nouns in (6) have been picked out by independent criteria, namely that they have a verbal counterpart, and that they occur with an argument *thes*. This word is originally the genitive singular of the neuter third person pronoun, but is rather a prepositional clitic in the texts, i.e. an element that replaces a whole prepositional phrase. This word *thes* is normally moved away from the noun, which is not possible for other genitival attributes (see further Delsing 1998*a*). Consider (7), where *thes* is best analysed as a prepositional clitic moved away from the noun.

---

[3] The light verb constructions are sometimes called support verb constructions, as in Delsing (1998*a*) and van Durme and Schøsler (1998).

(7) (a) thäs hafuin ij ära (Iv)
　　　　THES have you honour
　　　　'You have honour (because) of that.'

　(b) tess gaff han ey myken akt (RK2)
　　　　THES gave he not much attention
　　　　'He did not give much attention to that.'

　(c) thes faan j rön (ST)
　　　　THES get you experience
　　　　'You will get experience of that.'

If we divide bare objects in the texts into light verb constructions and other constructions according to the selected verbs and nouns in (5) and (6), we find that the two groups behave quite differently. This is illustrated in Table 11.3.

TABLE 11.3. *Object placement for bare nouns*

	Light verb VPs			Other VPs		
	OV	VO	%OV	OV	VO	%OV
1270–1300	5	0	(100%)	272	41	87%
1301–1375	8	24	25%	58	213	21%
1376–1450	5	14	(26%)	3	172	2%
1451–1525	16	19	46%	6	125	5%
1526–1600	1	22	(4%)	2	187	1%

As can be seen from Table 11.3, light verb constructions show a high OV-frequency also after 1375, whereas other predicates have a very low frequency after 1375. Moreover, many of the OV examples categorized as 'Other VPs' could in fact be analysed as light verb constructions, although they are not listed in (5) and (6). It seems as if light verb constructions are fully possible in preverbal position, whereas this is very rare for other bare objects. Thus we can revise the earlier grouping of different object types.

(8)　　*Type I* (almost only VO)　　*Type II* (OV or VO)

　　　　Proper name　　　　　　　Personal pronoun
　　　　Definite article　　　　　Demonstrative pronoun
　　　　Genitival attribute　　　　Possessive pronoun
　　　　Ordinary bare noun　　　　Bare noun with light verb
　　　　Indefinite article　　　　　Indefinite pronoun
　　　　Cardinal numeral

Let us look first at the diachronic development of the two object types, shown in Table 11.4. It is clear from Table 11.4 that in the first two texts, Type I and Type II objects behave similarly. But starting with Leg, the behaviour of the two types diverges. Objects of Type I cease to occur in preverbal position by the end

TABLE 11.4. *Percentage of preverbal objects according to object type*

Text	Date	Type I		Type II	
		OV	%OV	OV	%OV
ÖgL	c.1280	191 / 267	72%	147 / 206	71%
UL	1297	147 / 171	86%	103 / 131	79%
Leg	1276–1307	20 / 66	30%	69 / 110	63%
Mos	c.1330	70 / 478	15%	240 / 815	29%
Jär	c.1385	4 / 86	5%	52 / 164	32%
Greg	late 14th c.	2 / 41	5%	25 / 94	27%
Birg	late 14th c.	1 / 213	0%	66 / 515	13%
MPI	c.1400	0 / 73	0%	16 / 110	15%
Val	c.1450	0 / 34	0%	58 / 146	40%
Did	c.1450	5 / 123	4%	122 / 455	27%
Regl	1450–1500	1 / 80	1%	40 / 106	38%
Link	late 15th c.	0 / 98	0%	134 / 203	66%
Troja	1529	4 / 85	5%	98 / 312	31%
Petri	c.1530	3 / 486	1%	107 / 735	15%
Swart	1560	2 / 183	1%	85 / 380	22%
Brahe	c.1580	0 / 94	0%	17 / 189	9%

of the fourteenth century, whereas the frequency of preverbal objects of Type II actually increases in the fifteenth century.[4,5]

11.3. OBJECT TYPES

In the previous section we found that from around 1300 on, objects are divided into two types, one that is invariably postverbal, and one that can be found on either side of the verb. The division of objects into these two types of noun phrases is surprising. The two types cannot be characterized by familiar features such as [±clitic/weak] or [±definite].

I propose that the significant difference between objects of Type I and objects of Type II concerns the highest functional head in the noun phrase, here taken to be D. I propose that the various sorts of object DPs in Type I have a filled D-position in common, and that object DPs of Type II may have an empty D-position.

[4] The two slight deviances in Table 11.4, where Type I objects have OV order after 1375 include some bare objects in Did, mostly of the type that can be seen as light verb constructions, and some cases of definite nouns (with a suffixed article) in Troja. I have no good explanation for the latter.

[5] The two types of objects that have been established in this investigation are not known from earlier investigations of Old Scandinavian. Hróarsdottir's (1999b) investigation of Old Icelandic gives examples of Type I objects in front of the verb. However, I cannot tell from her examples whether such cases are found during the whole period of variation in Icelandic (from the fourteenth to the nineteenth century). Further research is needed to determine whether Icelandic has a similar division of objects to Swedish.

The history of Icelandic is different from that of Old Swedish. Swedish was much more exposed to Low German influence (and thus to foreign OV-structures). Swedish also developed an indefinite article during the fourteenth century, whereas Icelandic never did.

Concerning the objects of Type I, it is quite obvious that the D-position is filled by the ordinary prenominal indefinite article. This is also arguably so for the suffixed definite article. It has been claimed several times in the literature that a noun with the definite suffixed article in Scandinavian is raised to D (see e.g. Delsing 1988, 1993, Taraldsen 1990, Holmberg and Sandström 1996).

I will also assume (following Delsing 1993) that proper names and bare nouns have covert articles in Swedish. The assumption is based on the existence of overt articles in such noun phrases in several languages. The article with proper names is well known from e.g. Portuguese, Greek, and Austronesian languages. The article with uncountables and 'bare' plurals is well known from French. In Northern Swedish dialects both types of articles are found, the proprial article is prenominal, whereas the article used with uncountables and bare plurals is suffixed. The two types are illustrated in (9) and (10); see further Delsing (1993: chapter 2).

(9)　　n　Erik å　a　Lisa ska jift sä　　　　　(Northern Swedish)
　　　　ART Erik and ART Lisa will marry

(10)　　Hä　finns vattn-e　däri　hinken　　　　　(Northen Swedish)
　　　　There is　　water-ART there-in bucket-the

The next group within Type I involves noun phrases with genitival attributes. Those are often argued to have genitival -s in the D-position. This option is discussed for English by Abney (1987). Swedish genitival -s behaves exactly like its English counterpart, and it is assumed to be situated in D (see Delsing 1991, 1993, 1998b, Holmberg and Sandström 1996, Josefsson and Platzack 1998). From the first half of the fifteenth century we can find indications that genitival -s is situated in D; for instance some group genitivals are found. The D-position however seems to have a strong Spec-feature already by 1300, when genitival attributes become obligatorily prenominal (as shown in Delsing 1991).[6]

The last group within Type I involves noun phrases with cardinal numerals. These are often assumed to be generated in a lower functional phrase (Num or Q). A special NumP has also been suggested (first by Ritter 1988). Noun phrases like *de tre husen* 'the three houses' indicate that numerals (at least in definite noun phrases) are generated below D. Thus, numerals are the only category of Type I that does not seem to be directly linked to the D-position. This is not in accordance with my general assumption, and I will leave it as an exception.[7]

If we now turn to Type II, we see that it includes bare nouns of light verbs, personal pronouns, and noun phrases with attributive pronouns. I claim that these objects may leave the D-position empty; thus it is necessary for me to show that attributive pronouns are merged in a lower functional projection than D, and that

---

[6] In order to have the same terminology for clauses and noun phrases I prefer the terms head-feature and spec-feature to the V-features and NP-features of Chomsky (1995).

[7] A possible way to maintain the generalization would be to stipulate obligatory movement of numerals to D in indefinite noun phrases.

nouns in light verb constructions and personal pronouns can be lower than D.

First, the objects of light verb constructions can be argued to differ from other bare nouns precisely with respect to the D-position. One argument in favour of such an analysis is that bare nouns in light verb constructions are clearly harder to pronominalize (as pointed out by e.g. van Durme and Schøsler 1998). This would indicate that they are NPs rather than DPs, which has been argued for, e.g. by Laka (1993) for Basque, and by myself for Swedish. In Delsing (1998*a*), I argue that the complement in light verb constructions lacks a D-position, i.e. they are NPs and not really arguments of the verb, but constitute a part of the predicate. The argument is primarily based on facts from languages which practically always have overt articles on arguments, such as French and Northern Swedish. These languages lack articles in light verb constructions, as in French: *il a (*du) besoin de . . . [he has* ARTICLE *need of . . .].*

Second, attributive pronouns are often assumed to be base generated in functional projections below the D-position. In Delsing (1993) and (1998*a*), I argue extensively for the view that possessive pronouns should be generated in an intermediate functional projection between D and N, as is shown in (11). The argument is based on facts from Scandinavian, which shows that possessive pronouns and full DP genitivals are very different; they co-occur, and they have different surface distributions. Moreover, possessive pronouns seem to be pure heads, whereas the genitival phrases are DPs. Possessive pronouns co-occur with definite articles in several languages, e.g. Italian. Thus, I argue that possessive pronouns are heads which are found below D (and obligatorily raised to D in Modern Germanic).[8]

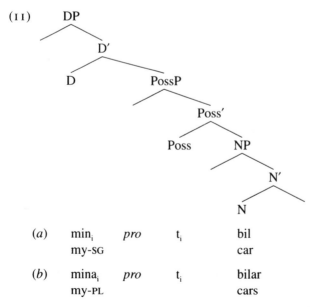

(11)   DP

               D′

     D   PossP

                    Poss′

               Poss   NP

                         N′

                     N

(*a*)	min_i	*pro*	t_i	bil
	my-SG			car
(*b*)	mina_i	*pro*	t_i	bilar
	my-PL			cars

---

[8] The possessive pronoun is seen as an agreement cluster, agreeing with both the small pro possessor in Spec,Poss and with the head noun.

Demonstrative and indefinite pronouns are sometimes seen as elements belonging to lower functional categories too (see e.g. Delsing 1993 and Vangsnes 1996).

Third, personal pronouns can be argued to be found in either the D- or the N-position. In (12) we find the personal pronoun in the D-position, whereas it is arguably in the N-position in vocative noun phrases in Modern Swedish, as shown in (13).

(12)   vi (fattiga) bönder
        we (poor) peasants

(13)   snälla du!
        dear you

Thus, we find that for all the cases of categories in Type II, it has been argued that the attributive pronoun or the head noun or personal pronoun is generated in a position lower than D, either in a lower functional position or in N.

To conclude, Type I objects are invariably postverbal and they have a filled D-position. Type II objects are found on either side of the verb and they can leave the D-position empty. The strongest and most interesting version of my proposal would be that Type II objects always have a filled D-position when postverbal, and that they always have an empty D-position when they are preverbal. If one can show this we can dispense with optionality all together in this matter. However, this remains to be shown. I do not at the moment have the necessary diagnostics to determine whether a constituent is situated in D or in a lower position.[9]

11.4. SYNTACTIC VARIATION AND OBJECT LICENSING

In this section, I consider the phenomenon of syntactic optionality more generally, and I present one way of implementing the empirical generalization discussed above. In short, I suggest that movement of the object to Spec,AgrOP is as costly as head movement within the DP, and that the two movements have the same effect with regard to object licensing. It will be shown that this analysis correctly describes the position of objects in Swedish from the fourteenth to the sixteenth century. Future research is necessary to determine whether a similar analysis can be used to describe an extended period of variation between OV and VO in other languages.

The fact that several languages have optional OV for a long period has presented a problem for diachronic linguistics in the 1980s and 1990s. Within the

---

[9] There are cases where it is more plausible to assume a filled D-position, i.e. in cases like (12). These are, however, very few. The examples that I have found are postverbal, as predicted by my proposal.

(i) iak *haver svikit*   **tik iomfru** (Did)
     I   have betrayed   you virgin

more traditional variant of the Principles and Parameters framework (as presented e.g. in Lightfoot 1991), syntactic change was predicted to be rather
abrupt. One will have to allow for some variation during a shorter period, due
to stylistic variation, geographical and social diffusion of change, etc. One
would, however, not expect languages to have two variants with opposite parameter values for many centuries as is observed for Swedish in this study, and in
other studies on English, Icelandic, and Yiddish (see e.g. Pintzuk 1991 and 1997,
Hróarsdottir in this volume, and Santorini 1992 respectively).

One way to solve the problem of extended variation is to assume that there is
a double base in word order, i.e. that both OV and VO can be the underlying
orders for one and the same language. This line of reasoning has been put forward by Anthony Kroch and his associates for English (see e.g. Kroch 1994,
Pintzuk 1991 and 1997) and by Rögnvaldsson (1996) for Icelandic. A double
base is seldom proposed for modern languages. The linguist is almost always
able to make precise the reason for the variation in her/his own language, a language where (s)he has access also to negative data. I believe that much of the
variation found in languages of the past can, at closer scrutiny, be shown to be
an epiphenomenon.

If one believes in a uniform phrase structure for all languages, one has to
account for variation in other ways. In a Minimalist framework there are two
such ways. The first solution is that the observed variation is just an epiphenomenon, i.e. the two variants have different LFs or different numerations and are
thus not comparable, in the sense of Chomsky (1995: 225 ff.). The other possibility is to state that the two variants are comparable, but that there are two equally
costly derivations, as has recently been proposed for the OV–VO-variation of
Middle English, by van der Wurff (1997).

Looking at the syntactic variation of Swedish during the fourteenth, fifteenth,
and sixteenth centuries, we might suspect that the OV–VO-variation is due to
different LF representations, such as scope differences. Such differences can be
found in Yiddish, where for instance bare nouns are found on both sides of the
verb, but with scope differences (see Diesing 1997: 393). It is not implausible
that such factors play a role in Swedish too, but to detect them in older languages is very hard.

In this study, the variation has been shown to be connected to another part of
syntax, namely the form of the object. In this section I outline an analysis in
which OV order is derived from VO structure, where the two derivations have
the same numeration. Thus, I think that the variation can be accounted for within
an antisymmetric Minimalist framework.

Combining the observations of the empirical investigation presented in §11.2
and the assumptions of the structure of the DP, presented in §11.3, we can see
that noun phrases with a filled D-position belong to Type I, i.e. objects that
almost always follow the verb. I assume that Swedish has licensing requirements
to the effect that the D-position of the object must be filled, or the object must

be licensed by movement to Spec,AgrOP.[10] I propose the following requirement on object licensing in Swedish.

(14) *Object Licensing Requirement* (OLR; to be revised)
  (*a*)   Fill the D-position (by merge in D or movement to D), or
  (*b*)   Move the argument (to Spec,AgrOP).

In other words the object may be licensed either internally, by (14*a*), or externally, by (14*b*). The OLR makes use of external and internal licensing as alternatives. This idea is similar to the theory proposed in Bittner and Hale (1996). They claim that licensing of direct cases (accusative and ergative) can be reduced to the ECP: arguments with an empty highest functional projection (which they take to be K, for Kase) must be licensed externally, i.e. by the ECP. Compare also Weerman (1997).

Type I objects, i.e. noun phrases with overt or covert articles in the D-position, are internally licensed automatically, and (under standard economy assumptions) they must not move. Hence, we predict that they be placed postverbally. Type II objects are not licensed automatically, but they may be licensed in two different ways. The head noun or an attributive pronoun generated in a lower functional projection may move (by head movement) to D, thus licensing the D-position internally (the *a*-clause). Alternatively, the D-position is left empty, and the whole phrase is instead moved to Spec,AgrOP in order to be licensed externally (the *b*-clause).

Merging an article in the D-position will give a numeration that is different from a construction with no article. The two derivations are thus not comparable, and should not compete. The movement alternative of the *a*-clause and the movement of the *b*-clause do however involve the same numerations.[11] I assume that the OLR can be fulfilled at equal cost by these derivations. This means that head movement to D is equally costly as movement of DP to Spec,AgrOP.

11.5. THE DIACHRONIC DEVELOPMENT

I will now take a closer look at the different stages in the development. I will identify the three following stages.

---

[10] Here and in the following, I talk about AgrOP. The data are a bit more complicated, though. Normally, personal pronouns are almost always found in a position to the left of the negation, whereas non-pronominal objects are found to the right of it. I take higher (pronominal) position to be OV order with subsequent object shift. Object shift is always impossible when the verb intervenes between the object-shift position and the ordinary object position (Holmberg 1986). Thus the object can only be shifted from the preverbal position.

[11] It might be argued that the two numerations are not the same, since they include functional heads with different features: D with a strong feature versus AgrO with a strong feature. I will assume either that features are added as items are taken from the numeration, and therefore are not part of the numeration, or else that numerations differ only if there are differences in non-instantiated features.

V-grammar (until around 1300)
Variation grammar (until around 1600)
VO grammar (from around 1600)

The first stage, the OV stage, is an underlying OV-grammar with particular exceptions, due to other independent properties of that grammar. The best representative of this grammar (in my investigation) is the Provincial Law of Uppland (UL).[12] UL has 302 DP/NP objects of the type specified in this investigation; 64 (21%) are found after the verb. Taking a closer look at these VO-structures of UL, we find that 25 of them are of the 'heavy type'; these are coordinations, DPs with clausal attributes or elements which are found after postverbal adverbials.

Out of the remaining 39 examples, we find that a substantial number of instances constitute subjects of small clauses. 22 examples are of this type, indirect objects and objects with objective predicatives, objects in ECM constructions, and objects with different prepositional phrases.

(15) (*a*)   tha skulu fædhærnis frændær [. . .] skiptæ *hwarium sin lot*
              then should father's relations   partition each   their part
              (UL, Äb 11)

     (*b*)   thær skal han giöræ *sik*   orthiuffwæ (UL, Mb 48)
              there shall he make himself innocent (prove his innocence)

     (*c*)   ther aghu swæriæ *witni*   a han (UL, Mb 37)
              they have to-swear witness on him

I think that it is fair to say that subjects of small clauses are over-represented among the VO objects. For the remaining seventeen objects, we find that some belong to a relatively recent paragraph and that others cluster in short passages of the text. I assume that these examples can be seen as recent additions to the law, reflecting a later stage of the language. If this is correct we have three kinds of VO-configurations in UL.

(16)   heavy constituents
         recently added paragraphs
         subjects of small clauses

About the first type I will have nothing interesting to say. Phonologically/ syntactically heavy constituents prefer the right-hand periphery of the clause in many languages, and they will have to be given a separate explanation in any case. The second type can be seen as representing the new grammar. The third type of examples must, however, be derived by the old OV-grammar.

---

[12] The Provincial Law of Östergötland is a bit older, but the manuscript is later, and this law is well known for its modern language, for instance with regard to the definite article (Larm 1936: 79, Ståhle 1988: 123–4).

A possible way to account for the VO examples involving small clauses would be to rephrase the Object Licensing Requirement (OLR) above to the effect that objects might be licensed not only in Spec,AgrOP but also in other spec-positions, for instance in the specifier position of a small clause. In such a case we would have to assume that the small clause head, such as a particle, preposition, or adjective would enter a head chain with the main verb.[13] Still abstracting away from the heavy DP cases we would get (17).

(17) *Object Licensing Requirement* (OLR, revised)
    (*a*)   Fill the D-position (by merge in D or movement to D), or
    (*b*)   License the argument in a position which is in a Spec-head relation with the verbal chain (by merge or move)

The *a*-clause above would account for the fact that noun phrases with a filled D-position are postverbal. The *b*-clause above would account for those Type II objects that have to move to Spec,AgrOP. What I have not shown is that the D-position is filled in the Type II objects that are placed postverbally. This investigation still remains to be done.[14]

As can be seen from Table 11.1, there is an increase of OV-structures in the fifteenth century. I do not think that this should be taken as a change of grammar but rather of language use. This increase is simultaneous with a heavy influence of Low German on the Swedish language. The influence results in a stream of loan words and it is extensive enough to involve the borrowing of prefixes and suffixes. A further indication that the phenomenon is one of performance and not of competence is the relatively large difference between the individual texts.

Lastly, I will speculate about the loss of OV in Swedish. The OV-percentage has dropped to some 6% in the latest text in my investigation (Brahe from the 1580s). I have not made a thorough investigation of OV order in the seventeenth century, so what I say must be preliminary.

I have investigated two texts from the mid-seventeenth century. I have followed the same principles of excerption as in the main investigation, but I have only studied infinitival verbs, not participles.[15] One of the texts (Gyllenhielm from 1640) shows quite a high OV frequency: 24% (compared to 9% with infinitives in the three chronicles from the sixteenth century, Petri, Swart, and Brahe).

---

[13] The close relation between the small clause head and the verb is probably based on selection. This relation is often signalled by incorporation in Old as well as Modern Swedish, where we find complex verbs like *utskicka*, *dödförklara*, 'out-send', 'dead-declare'.

[14] The OLR as stated in (17) should probably be capable of extension to other arguments as well, in particular subjects. However, the *b*-clause will license all external arguments, since they are merged in Spec,VP, and thus in a Spec-head relation with the verbal chain. Thus, the external argument is licensed as an argument; the placement at Spell Out is determined by other principles of the grammar such as the EPP.

[15] In the main investigation, the OV-frequency is generally slightly higher with participles than with infinitives.

Furthermore the difference between Type I and Type II is not as clear as in the older texts, and we also find several cases of co-ordinations preverbally. Type I objects and coordinations have a common OV frequency of 9% in Gyll, compared to 0.7% in the sixteenth-century chronicles. Thus it seems that Gyllenhielm does not use the same licensing conditions for objects as earlier generations did.

The other text (Horn from 1657) hardly has any OV examples at all. Only 5 out of 394 objects are preverbal (1.3%). Thus it seems as if Horn has a pure VO-grammar (with a few relics of OV order, however).

The two investigated texts are very different, and both are different from the earlier texts. A great variance in this respect can also be found in other investigations.[16] As far as I can see, the most plausible interpretation of these data is that Swedish has a pure VO-grammar by the middle of the seventeenth century. This is reflected in Horn, and the OV examples in Gyll do not seem to follow the same rules as in earlier texts. My best guess is that this is due to a literary style with no basis in the spoken language.

If it is correct that OV order is lost in the first half of the seventeenth century, it would be interesting to try to link it to other changes in the grammar from this period. Syntactic changes from this period are studied e.g. by Platzack (1983) and Falk (1993*b*). The most noticeable change is the loss of V-to-I raising. Two other changes, the introduction of expletive subjects and the loss of Stylistic Fronting are taken to be connected with V-raising. I now propose that the loss of OV is also connected to the loss of V-raising.

The Object Licensing Requirement (OLR) proposed here requires that the object either be in a Spec-head relation to the verb chain or that it have a filled D-position. Loss of OV can then either be due to a more consistent use of head movement to D or to the loss of a Spec-head relation in AgrOP. In the first case there is no obvious link to V-raising. In the other case, however, there is.

If the AgrO is weak, which I hypothesize, the only way to fill this position is by attraction from a higher head. When V-to-I-movement is lost, the verb will not go through AgrO. This eradicates the local relation between Spec,AgrOP and the lexical verb chain. Movement of the object is thus no longer an alternative for licensing the object.[17] This will force obligatory head movement to D within the noun phrase, since all noun phrases will now have to satisfy the OLR by the *a*-clause.

---

[16] Platzack (1987) has investigated eighteen texts from the period 1625–1750; one of his variables is OV word order, albeit his principles of data collection are different from the ones I have used. In the twelve texts written before 1725, we find a great deal of variation in OV-frequencies, from 1% up to 42%, with no development over time.

[17] Alternatively the loss of V-raising could be said to make object movement impossible, because Spec,AgrOP and Spec,VP would no longer be equidistant, and movement across the subject in Spec,VP would be blocked. Such an analysis is proposed by van der Wurff (1997). It is however hard to apply this to Swedish, since Swedish still has movement of negative objects (as illustrated in (1) above). Equidistance must apply to all objects and it cannot be used to rule out movement of only some objects.

If the development sketched above is correct, we would expect to find changes within the noun phrase in seventeenth-century Swedish. It is a fact that there have been changes since the sixteenth century. For instance possessive pronouns could co-occur with indefinite pronouns in the sixteenth century, indicating that possessive pronouns were not inherently definite, and presumably not always moved to D. These changes are not sufficiently investigated to say when they took place and if they were contemporaneous with the loss of OV and V-to-I.

11.6. CONCLUSIONS

In this chapter I have presented an extensive investigation of the order of non-finite verbs and objects in Swedish; the time span of the period is from 1270 to 1600. The investigation shows that in the earliest texts, OV is predominant, and VO instances involve heavy constituents, subjects of small clauses or recently added passages. We find a drastic drop in OV frequency around 1300, and during the fourteenth, fifteenth, and sixteenth centuries both OV and VO are allowed, but there is a significant rise in OV frequencies in the fifteenth century. Furthermore I have provided data that indicates the loss of OV by the middle of the seventeenth century in the spoken language.

During the period when Swedish allows both OV and VO, two different sorts of objects can be identified. Type I objects include noun phrases with proper names as heads, bare nouns, noun phrases with indefinite or definite suffixed articles, and noun phrases with genitival attributes or cardinal numerals. These objects are (almost) never found in preverbal position. Type II objects include personal pronouns, bare nouns in light verb constructions, and noun phrases with attributive pronouns (demonstrative, possessive, indefinite). These objects are found both preverbally and postverbally. Type I objects are argued to have a filled D-position, whereas Type II objects may leave the D-position empty.

The result of the investigation and the interpretation of the different structures of Type I and Type II objects have led me to propose the Object Licensing Requirement, which states that objects are licensed either by filling the D-position within the object DP, or by a Spec-head relation with the head chain of the verb. In the former case the object remains in the complement of VP. In the latter case the requirement is fulfilled in small clauses, but leads to movement to AgrOP in most cases. I have shown that the two different derivations can be viewed as equally costly.

The development of verb–object order in Swedish can thus be described in three steps. First Swedish has an OV grammar where almost all DP objects are moved to Spec,AgrOP. The only ones that are left to the right are subjects of small clauses and some heavy objects.

Then comes a 300-year period (1300–1600, approximately) of variation, where we find both OV and VO. Most importantly the OV/VO variation can be shown to follow certain rules. Objects of Type I are preverbal, whereas objects of type II may be either preverbal or postverbal.

Lastly, I have also speculated on the possible connection between the loss of OV and the loss of V-to-I-movement in Swedish.

APPENDICES

Appendix A. Sources

Birg   *Birgittas uppenbarelser*. The Revelations of Saint Birgitta, books 1–3. Translation from Latin. Original from the end of the fourteenth century, MS from the beginning of the fifteenth century (106,600 words). SFSS 9: 1, ed. G. E. Klemming.

Brahe *Per Brahes krönika*. Historical chronicle. Original from 1580s, contemporary MS (26,300 words). *Per Brahe d.ä: s fortsättning av Peder Swarts krönika I och II*, ed. Ahnfeldt, Lund 1896–7.

Did   *Didrik af Bern*. Chivalrous tale. Hand A (more than half the text). Translation from Old Norse. Original from 1450s, MS from the end of the fifteenth century (53,200 words). SFSS 10: 1–205, Ed. Hyltén-Cavallius.

Greg   *Gregorius av Armenien*. The legend of Gregory of Armenia. Original from the end of the fourteenth century, MS A from c.1420, MS D (used for lacunas in A) from c.1450. (19,000 words). SFSS 15, ed. G. E. Klemming.

Gyll   Carl Carlsson Gyllenhielm, *Egenhändige anteckningar rörande tiden 1597–1601*. Personal notations. Historiska handlingar 20. Stockholm 1905. Original MS from around 1640.

Horn   Agneta Horn, *Beskrivning över min vandringstid*. Authobiography, ed. G. Holm *Nordiska texter och undersökningar* 20. Uppsala 1959. Original MS from 1657.

Iv   Ivan Lejonriddaren. SFSS 50, ed. E. Noreen. Original from 1303, MS from 1400–25.

Jär   *Järteckensboken*. Book of Miracles, translation from Latin. MS from 1385, original probably a few years earlier (28,800 words). SFSS 22: 2–128, ed. G. E. Klemming.

Leg   *Fornsvenska legendariet*. The Old Swedish Legendary, parts from Codex Bureanus, excluding poetry and a short passage added later. Original from 1276–1307, MS from around 1350 (35,100 words). SFSS 7: 1, ed. G. Stephens.

Link   *Linköpingslegendariet*. Fifteen legends, translated from Latin/German by Nils Ragvaldi. Original from the end of the fifteenth century, MS from 1526 (49,300 words). SFSS 7: 1–3. Ed. G. Stephens. In the edited text the fifteen legends are found in volume: 7: 1: 331–6; 7: 2: 660–75; 7: 3: 64–9, 154–96, 262–320, 386–480.

Mos   *Pentateuchparafrasen*. Paraphrase of the Pentateuch. Original around 1330, MS (MB I B) from 1502 (144,800 words). SFSS 60, ed. O. Thorell.

MP I *Den äldsta postillan*. The oldest Swedish homily (half the text). Original around 1400, MS from the beginning of the fifteenth century (27,900 words). SFSS 23: 1, ed. G. E. Klemming.

ÖgL   *Östgötalagen*. Provincial Law of Östergötland: Kristnubalk (1–26), Edsöre (26–46), Egna salur (131–52) and Bygdabalk (185–232). Original from 1280s, MS from around 1350 (24,800 words). SSGL 2, ed. C. J. Schlyter.

Petri   *En Swensk Cröneka af Olavus Petri.* Historical chronicle. Original from 1530s, MS from 1540s (108,000 words). *Samlade Skrifter af Olavus Petri*, Vol. 4, ed. J. Sahlgren, Uppsala 1917.

Regl   *Constitutiones, St Augustini Regel, Lucidarium.* Original and MS from the second half of the fifteenth century (21,500 words). SFSS 9: 5: 3–106, ed. G. E. Klemming.

RK2   Rimkrönikon 2, Karlskrönikan. SFSS 17:2, ed. G. E. Klemming. Original from around 1450, MS from around 1452.

ST   Siælinna Thrøst. SFSS 79, ed. S. Henning. Original from around 1425, MS from around 1440.

Swart   *Peder Swarts krönika.* Historical chronicle. Original MS from 1560 (51,900 words). *Konung Gustaf I:s krönika*, ed. N. Eden, Stockholm 1912.

Troja   *Historia Trojana.* Half the text (1–173). Translation from Latin. Original MS from 1529 (44,200 words). SFSS 29, ed. R. Geete.

UL   *Upplandslagen.* Provincial Law of Uppland: Stadfästelsebrev (3–6), Företal (6–8), Konungsbalk (87–101), Ärvdabalk (Äb) (103–29), Manhelgisbalk (Mb) (129–78), and Jordabalk (179–202). Original from 1297, MS a few years later (24,200 words), SSGL 3, ed. C. J. Schlyter.

Val   *Namnlös och Valentin.* Chivalrous tale. Original from *c.*1450, MS a few years later (15,200 words). SFSS 52, ed. Wolff.

SSGL = Samling af Sveriges Gamla Lagar [Collection of Sweden's Old Laws]

SFSS = Svenska Fornskrifts-sällskapets skrifter [Publications by the Swedish Ancient Texts Society]

Appendix B. Principles of Data Collection

Apart from the general guidelines for data collection presented in §11.2, the following details should be noted.

In control infinitivals in Old Swedish, V-raising seems to be rare but still possible, as indicated by the example in (i).

(i) enghin ær loffwat *at lyuga ey* før siælfsins æller annars liff (Mos 211)
     nobody is allowed *to lie not* for his-own or someone-else's life

In an example like (i), we can conclude that the verb is not in its base position because of the position of negation, and in such cases the relative order of verb and object cannot tell us anything about the base position of the object. Therefore, objects in control infinitivals are excluded from the investigation.

In Old Swedish (as in Modern Swedish) the infinitival marker *at* may be deleted with many verbs. Thus, we have to differentiate between main verbs selecting control infinitivals (with or without the infinitival marker *at*) and auxiliaries taking a VP-complement. The long time span of the investigation makes it impossible to find a good formula for identifying auxiliaries. I have however taken advantage of the fact that infinitival clauses never occur in preverbal position, either in OV-structures or in Stylistic Fronting cases. Thus, a verb that is found with a non-finite verb in front of it cannot be seen as an ordinary verb selecting an infinitival clause, but must be seen as an auxiliary. Using this as the main criterion, I classify the verbs in (ii) as auxiliaries. The two verbs in (iii) regularly take a past participle; these verbs are also counted as auxiliaries.

(ii) *kunna* (can), *lär* (is-said-to), *magha* (may), *mona* (might), *måste* (must), *plägha* (usually-do), *skula* (shall), *vilia* (will), *ägha* (own)

(iii) *hava* (have), *gita*, (may/can)

Clauses with non-finite auxiliaries are left aside, since it is not clear whether a non-finite auxiliary selects an AgrOP, a VP, or something else, i.e. whether there is always a preverbal object position in these cases.

Furthermore, passive or impersonal verbs are not excerpted. In Modern Icelandic it is possible to show that these verbs take oblique subjects (see e.g. Sigurðsson 1989), but in Old Scandinavian, it is much harder to know whether the experiencers are subjects or objects. Both opinions have been argued for. Rögnvaldsson (1991) and Barðdal (1997) argue for the existence of oblique subjects in Old Icelandic, pointing out the fact that these arguments have a frequency distribution different from other objects. Falk (1997), on the other hand, argues that frequency is not enough; the odd behaviour of experiencer arguments with impersonal verbs can be attributed either to their subjecthood or to the fact that they are the highest argument. Because of the lack of positive evidence for the subject status of these elements in Old Swedish, Falk doubts the existence of oblique subjects in Old Swedish. Since the subject or object status of the arguments in these constructions is debatable, they are omitted from the investigation.

In verb coordinations, second conjuncts are also excluded from the investigation, since it is very hard to know what is coordinated (AgrOPs, vPs, VPs etc.), i.e. it is not clear that a second conjunct always has a preverbal object position.

It would be of interest to get a clear picture of other categories than objects. For instance we would like to know about complements in existential constructions, but in preverbal position these are impossible to distinguish from ordinary subjects. Thus they are excluded. PP complements and predicative noun phrases would also be of interest for a study like this, but they are hard or impossible to distinguish from adverbial PPs and complements in existential clauses, respectively, so they are not excerpted.

Lastly, from around 1400 to 1700, written Swedish shows influences of German embedded word order, i.e. the finite verb is clause final. In such cases the object always precedes the non-finite verb. This phenomenon is often considered to be just a literary convention. I will have nothing new to say about this type of clause, and I exclude it from the investigation, since it is unclear whether it is a part of the mental grammar (see Falk 1993b: 158 and references cited there). Sometimes the verb-final order in embedded clauses is taken to be connected with the OV-order diachronically. For instance, Platzack (1983) shows that both disappear from the written language at roughly the same time.

12

The Evolution of *Do*-Support in English Imperatives

CHUNG-HYE HAN

12.1. INTRODUCTION

This chapter presents an analysis of the syntactic evolution of English imperatives from Late Middle English to the Early Modern period, specifically of the increasing frequency of *do*-support in negative imperatives. I show that the development of *do*-forms in negative imperatives cannot be explained with a clause structure that has only one INFL projection and one NegP, as assumed in Roberts (1985) and Kroch (1989*b*). I therefore propose a more articulated clause structure, which I argue is already necessary to explain the syntax of Middle English infinitivals. In particular, I argue that the syntax of negative infinitivals in Middle English can be accounted for if we posit two possible syntactic positions for negation and an intermediate functional projection, which I assume to be an Aspect Phrase (AspP), between the two negation projections. The more articulated clause structure proposed here enables us to distinguish two types of verb movement: movement over the lower negation and movement over the higher negation. I show that the patterns of the development of *do*-support in imperatives as well as the patterns of the development of *do*-support in questions and negative declaratives can be explained if the loss of verb movement occurs in two steps in the history of English: the loss of the higher movement precedes the loss of the lower movement.

For data relating to the development of *do*-forms in various linguistic contexts, I use the online version of Ellegård's (1953) collection of clauses maintained by Anthony Kroch. The source for the data relating to Middle English infinitivals is the Penn–Helsinki Parsed Corpus of Middle English (PPCME) (Kroch and Taylor 1994*b*).

I am extremely indebted to Anthony Kroch for encouraging me to pursue this topic and for many helpful discussions along the way. I also thank Beatrice Santorini, Ann Taylor, Alexander Williams, the audience at DIGS 5 and the anonymous reviewers for helpful comments.

12.2. DATA AND ISSUES

12.2.1. *Development of imperatives in English: a short survey*

In Old English (*c.*850–*c.*1150), imperatives pattern with questions: the verb precedes the subject, even when the subject is pronominal, in both types of sentences. This is shown in (1) and (2).

(1)   Beo þu on ofeste
        be   you in haste
        'Be quick.'
            (*Beowulf* 386)

(2)   Hwi sciole we oþres   mannes niman?
        why should we another man's   take
        'Why should we take those of another man?'
            (Ælfric, *Lives of Saints* 24.188)

As in Pintzuk (1991) and Kroch and Taylor (1997), I assume that weak pronouns in Old English occur at the CP–IP boundary, so that the fact that the verb precedes the pronominal subject implies that the verb is located in C°.

In Middle English (*c.*1150–*c.*1500), the imperative verb also precedes the subject, as shown in (3).

(3) (*a*)   Naske ȝe of cunseil
             not-ask you of counsel
                (*Ancrene Riwle* II.58.569)

     (*b*)   Helpe þou me
             help   you me
                (*The Earliest Prose Psalter* 150.2290)

     (*c*)   Goo ȝe . . . ynto þe payne of helle
             go   you . . . into the pain of hell
                (*Mirk* 4.80)

In the case of negative imperatives with the negative adverbial *not*, the subject precedes *not*, and the verb precedes the subject. This is illustrated in (4).

(4) (*a*)   Ne hide þou noȝt fram me þyn comaundement
             NE hide you not from me your commandment
                (*The Earliest Prose Psalter* 146.2169)

     (*b*)   Depart þou nouȝt fro   me
             depart you not   from me
                (*The Earliest Prose Psalter* 24.594)

     (*c*)   medyl ȝe not wyth hym
             meddle you not with him
                (*Margery Kempe* I, 56.218)

The word order in Middle English imperatives also shows that the imperative verb occupies C⁰.

In Early Modern English (*c.*1500–*c.*1700), imperatives show the same word order as in Middle English. But imperatives with *do*-support are also attested. In imperatives with an overt subject and with *do*-support, auxiliary *do* precedes the subject, as shown in (5). In imperatives with an overt subject but without *do*-support, the verb precedes the subject, as shown in (6).[1]

(5) (a) Rather, O God! do thou have mercy on us (323 355–8–34)

    (b) but I will be your good lord, do you not doubt (361 O:4–2–39)

    (c) Do you and your fellows attend them in (361 M:5–1–106)

(6) (a) And feare ye nott them which kyll the body (310 mt10–28)

    (b) Forbid ye hym not (310 lk9–50)

    (c) doubte thou not all thinges rightly orderd be (356 90–25)

The fact that auxiliary *do* or the main verb precedes the subject suggests that *do* or the verb occupies C⁰.

In Present-day English, negative imperatives require *do*-support. In negative imperatives with an overt subject, auxiliary verb *do* and negation *n't* must precede the subject, as in (7).[2]

(7) (a) Don't you worry!

    (b) Don't anybody move!

An affirmative imperative does not allow *do*-support unless it is an emphatic imperative. In an affirmative imperative with an overt subject, the subject must precede the verb, as in (8).

(8) (a) You come here!

    (b) Nobody move!

In emphatic affirmative imperatives with auxiliary *do* and an overt subject, *do* must precede the subject. This is shown in (9).

(9) (a) Do somebody open the window!

    (b) Do at least some of you show up for the party!

---

[1] Early Modern English examples in this chapter are taken from the sources in Ellegård (1953). They are identified using Ellegård's system, with his source number preceding his reference. The full references of the sources are given in the Appendix to this chapter.

[2] The imperative subject appears to be able to precede *do*, as in (i). But the imperatives in (i) are degraded unless there is an intonational break between *you* and the rest of the sentence. This strongly suggests that the apparent subjects in sentences such as in (i) are not sentential subjects, but vocatives, which are considered to be outside the clause structure and do not have a structural relation with any element in the clause.

(i) (a) You don't drink the water

    (b) You do not leave the room

In Present-day English imperatives, the data suggest that while auxiliary *do* is located in C°, the lexical verb is located lower in the clause.

12.2.2. Do-*support*

In Present-day English, auxiliary *do* is required in *yes–no* questions, non-subject *wh*-questions, negative declaratives (i.e. those containing *not*), and of course negative imperatives.

(10) (*a*)   Did you finish?
     (*b*)   What did you finish?
     (*c*)   I did not finish.
     (*d*)   Don't finish!

Ellegård provides a quantitative study of the development of *do*-forms in various constructions using a collection of sentences extracted from texts ranging in time from Late Middle English to the eighteenth century. Figure 12.1 is from Ellegård (1953: 162). It plots the relative frequency of *do*-forms in affirmative and negative declaratives, affirmative and negative questions, and negative imperatives, based on a sample of more than 10,000 tokens. After the middle of the sixteenth

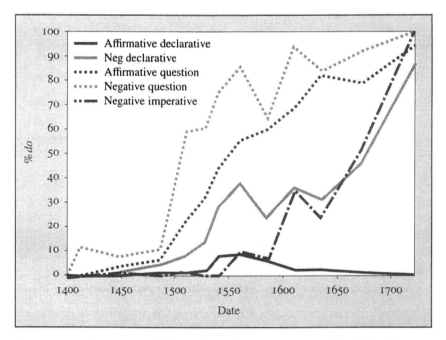

FIGURE 12.1. Percentage of *do*-forms in various sentence types (from Ellegård 1953: 162)

century, the frequency of *do* in affirmative declaratives declines steadily until, by 1700, the use of *do* in this environment is prohibited. The frequency of *do* in negative declaratives and both affirmative and negative questions rises continuously and sometime after the eighteenth century *do* is obligatory in these environments.

According to a common analysis of Middle English clause structure, questions have V–I–C movement and declaratives have V–I movement. Supporting evidence for this analysis comes from word-order facts: in questions the verb precedes the subject, as in (11), and in declaratives the verb precedes *not*, as in (12), and adverbs, as in (13)

(11) *Questions*

(*a*) *Bileuest thou* this thing?
(*The New Testament*, Wycliffe XI, 20.1033)

(*b*) And lo, what *seith Seneca* in this matere?
(Chaucer, *Melibee* 290.C2.237)

(12) *verb* + not

(*a*) I *herde nott* from you syns
(*Paston Letters* 450.602)

(*b*) but he *spack not* one worde
(Caxton, *History of Reynard the Fox* 52.278)

(13) *verb* + *adverb*

(*a*) and [he] *suffryd euer*   grete penaunce for Goddis sake in weryng
and [he] suffered always great penance   for God's sake in wearing
of the heyre
of the hair (*Life of St Edmund* 165.61)

(*b*) Here men *vndurstonden ofte*   by þis ny3t þe ny3t of synne
here men understood   often by this night the night of sin
(*Wycliffite Sermons* I, 477.605)

According to Roberts (1985) and Kroch (1989*b*), English lost V–I movement for lexical verbs in the middle of the sixteenth century. When V–I movement was lost, only *be*, auxiliary *have*, and modal verbs, such as *can*, *may*, *must*, etc. could appear in I°. Based on the behaviour of indicative sentences, Roberts (1985) argues that the rise of *do*-forms is a reflex of the loss of V–I movement. As V–I movement was lost, INFL-lowering replaced it (or verb movement to I° at LF, as in Chomsky 1991, 1993) and so the verb remains *in situ*. In questions, the requirement that the material in I° overtly move to C° persists; thus, auxiliary *do* is inserted in I° as a last resort device and then moves to C°. Examples of questions with *do*-support are given in (14).

(14) *Questions*
    (*a*)   and wherfore doth the earth sustaine me? (304 25–24)
    (*b*)   Dyd ye wryte this with your owne hande? (308 96–25)
    (*c*)   doeste thou enuy to him the monarchye of the thing mortal?
        (326 109–30)

In negative declaratives, negation blocks INFL-lowering (or verb movement to I^o at LF), stranding the material in I^o. Again, auxiliary *do* is inserted in I^o to support the stranded material as a last resort device. Examples of negative declaratives with *do*-support are given in (15).

(15) *Negative declaratives*
    (*a*)   They dyde not set theyr mynde on golde or rychesse (305 35–23)
    (*b*)   Christ dyd not praye for Iames and Iohan & for the other (305 319–11)
    (*c*)   but the shepe did not heare them (310 jn10–8)

Kroch (1989*b*) provides empirical support for the proposal that the rise of *do*-forms is a reflex of the loss of V–I movement by showing that the rate of the rise of *do*-forms in various contexts, such as questions, negative declaratives, and affirmative declaratives, is the same up to the middle of the sixteenth century (why this is evidence is discussed in §12.5.2).

Comparing the development of *do*-forms in negative declaratives and negative imperatives gives rise to an interesting puzzle. The development of *do*-forms in the two contexts does not show the same pattern. As can be seen in Figure 12.1, up to the end of the sixteenth century the relative frequency of *do* in negative imperatives was as low as that in affirmative declaratives. Then after 1600, there was a big change in the development of negative imperatives. The relative frequency of *do* in negative imperatives jumped to the much higher rate found in negative declaratives, and subsequently the two negative environments evolved identically. If *do*-support is triggered when negation intervenes between V^o and I^o, it is mysterious why the development of *do*-forms in negative imperatives patterns with negative declaratives only after 1600.

Comparing the development of *do*-forms in questions and imperatives gives rise to another puzzle. In Middle English, subject–verb inversion is attested in both questions and imperatives, indicating verb movement to C^o for both types of sentences, as was shown in (3) and (11). If *do*-support is triggered in questions as a reflex of the loss of V–I movement, as proposed in Roberts (1985) and Kroch (1989*b*), then we expect to see imperatives pattern with questions with respect to the development of the corresponding *do*-forms. However, as can be seen in Figure 12.1, the rate of use of *do*-forms in negative imperatives is much lower than the rate of use of *do*-forms in questions at all periods prior to the completion of the change. It is only after 1700 that the rate of use of *do*-forms in negative imperatives catches up with the rate in questions. As for affirmative imperatives with *do*-forms, the relative frequency is extremely low. The relative frequency of *do* in affirmative imperatives never exceeds 1% according to Ellegård (1953), who therefore does not plot them in Figure 12.1. Here are some examples of negative imperatives and affirmative imperatives with *do*-support:

(16) *Negative imperatives*

    (*a*)   Sir, do not marvel if I do bless your coming hither (344 21–17)

    (*b*)   Alas syr kinge Pepyn doo not moue your selfe in Ire (304 46–13)

    (*c*)   doe not wrong the gentleman, and thy selfe too (360 I: 435)

(17) *Affirmative imperatives*

    (*a*)   Rather, O God! do thou have mercy on us (323 355–8–34)

    (*b*)   Do you let it alone (350 7–24)

    (*c*)   Do you and your fellows attend them in (361 M: 5–1–106)

In Present-day English, although *do*-support is required in negative imperatives, it is not allowed in (non-emphatic) affirmative imperatives. If both questions and imperatives had verb movement to C°, then it is mysterious why there should be this asymmetry in the rate of development of *do*-forms in questions and negative imperatives. Moreover, if both questions and imperatives had verb movement to C°, it is even more mysterious why *do* in affirmative imperatives is not categorical, whereas it is in questions.

12.2.3. *Issues*

I summarize below the issues raised by the data considered so far:

• Why does the development of *do*-forms in negative imperatives statistically pattern with negative declaratives only after 1600?
• Why do affirmative imperatives not pattern with questions in the development of *do*-forms? That is, why do affirmative imperatives not require *do*-support in Present-day English?
• Why does the development of *do*-forms in negative imperatives statistically pattern with negative declaratives and not with negative questions after 1600?

12.3. INFINITIVALS IN MIDDLE ENGLISH

Before addressing the issues raised in §12.2, I discuss a new set of data from Middle English negative infinitivals. We will see that the word order attested in negative infinitivals in Middle English provides evidence for the inventory of functional projections and their relative positioning in English clause structure. We will then see that the questions raised in §12.2 can be given an elegant account if the clause structure proposed here is adopted.

12.3.1. *Infinitive verb and negation*

For negative infinitivals, Middle English allowed both '*not–to*–verb' order (as in (18)) and '*to*–verb–*not*' order (as in (19)), as attested in the PPCME.

(18) *not–to*–verb

   (*a*) þat sche wuld   vwche-save *nowth to labowre* aȝens ȝw jn þis
       that she would promise   not   to labour against you in this
       matere tyl ȝe kom hom
       matter until you come home
          (*Paston Letters* 221.310)

   (*b*) that they that ben sike of hir body ben worthy to ben hated but
       that they that are sick of their body are worthy to be hated but
       rather worthy of pite wel more worthy *nat to ben* hated
       rather worthy of pity even more worthy not to be hated
          (Chaucer, *Boethius* 449.C2.379)

(19) *to*–verb–*not*

   (*a*) *to sorow noght* for hys syn as he sulde do
       to sorrow not   for his sin as he should do
          (Rolle, *Form of Living* 99.260)

   (*b*) And herfore monye men vson   wel *to come not* in bedde
       and therefore many   men are-accustomed well to come not in bed
       wiþ schetis, but be hulude aboue þe bed
       with sheets but be covered above the bed
          (*Wycliffite Sermons* I, 479.641)

Table 12.1 provides the number of infinitivals with '*to*–verb–*not*' and '*not–to*–verb*' order ranging from Early to Late Middle English. I did not find any tokens from the corpus in the first two periods. But importantly the counts show that in the third and fourth periods, 50% of negative infinitivals have '*to*–verb–*not*' order.

TABLE 12.1 '*not–to–verb*' *and* '*to–verb–not*'
order in negative infinitivals

	not–to–verb	*to–verb–not*
1150–1250	0	0
1250–1350	0	0
1350–1420	10	4
1420–1500	4	10

For the counts in Table 12.1, I excluded purpose infinitival clauses in the form of '*not–to*–verb'. This is because the *not* in '*not–to*–verb' may be negating the entire purpose clause and so may not be a sentential negation of the infinitival clause.

    According to Frisch (1997), *not* in Middle English is either a VP-adjoined adverbial, or a sentential negation. Let us assume that the infinitive marker *to* originates and stays in a fixed position, namely I°, and that *not* originates and stays in a fixed position lower than I° as a head of NegP, as in (20).

(20)   [$_{IP}$ [$_I$ to] [$_{NegP}$ not [$_{VP}$ . . . verb . . .]]]

Given the phrase structure in (20), the word order '*to*–verb–*not*' can be derived only if the verb moves across *not* and right-adjoins to I°. But this is an unattractive solution in that we are forced to admit right-adjunction in syntax. Moreover, the phrase structure in (20) cannot derive the word order '*not*–*to*–verb'. Alternatively, if *to* is in I°, and *not* originates and stays in a fixed position higher than I°, as in (21), then the word order '*not*–*to*–verb' can be derived. But there is no way to derive the word order '*to*–verb–*not*' with this phrase structure.

(21)   [$_{NegP}$ not [$_{IP}$ [$_I$ to] [$_{VP}$ . . . verb . . .]]]

12.3.2. *Two possible positions for negation*

If there are two possible structural positions for negation in the clause structure of English (see Zanuttini 1991, 1997), then both the '*to*–verb–*not*' and the '*not*–*to*–verb' order in Middle English can be accommodated. Motivations for positing two structural positions for negation exist in Present-day English as well. In this section, I discuss what they are and determine where the two negations are located in the phrase structure of a sentence.

In *to*-infinitivals, *not* can either precede or follow *to*, as shown in (22). If *to* is structurally fixed, then the variable word order calls for two possible locations for negation.

(22) (*a*)   I promise not to be late
      (*b*)   I promise to not be late

Furthermore, in declaratives with a modal verb, negation *not* can occur either before or after an adverb, or in both positions, as shown in (23).

(23) (*a*)   John would not often eat meat dishes
      (*b*)   John would often not eat meat dishes
      (*c*)   John wouldn't often not eat meat dishes

Following Cinque (1999), let us assume that adverbs occur in fixed positions. Since *often* occupies the same position in the sentences in (23), the fact that negation *not* can be located above or below the adverb suggests again that there are two possible locations for negation.

The higher negation requires *do*-support for lexical verbs (as in (24)), and it licenses negative polarity items (NPIs) (as in (25)).

(24) (*a*)   *John not often eats meat dishes
      (*b*)   John does not often eat meat dishes

(25)   John would not often eat any meat dishes

The lower negation also requires *do*-support for lexical verbs (as in (26)), and it also licenses NPIs (as in (27)).[3]

---

[3] Unlike in negative sentences in which *do* is adjacent to *not*, in negative sentences in which *do* is separated from *not* by an adverb, *do* is emphatic, as in (26*b*). I do not have an explanation for this fact.

(26) (*a*)   *John often not eats his vegetables
      (*b*)   John does often not eat his vegetables

(27)   John would often not eat any vegetables

In addition, both the higher negation and the lower negation have similar scope properties. For instance, both the sentences in (28) are ambiguous in that the negation can take either wide scope or narrow scope with respect to the universal quantifier of the subject NP. The ambiguous readings are paraphrased in (29).

(28) (*a*)   All of the players will not certainly drop the ball
      (*b*)   All of the players will certainly not drop the ball

(29) (*a*)   For all x, x is a player, x will not drop the ball ($\forall$ > not)
      (*b*)   It is not the case that for all x, x is a player, x will drop the ball
              (not > $\forall$)

Given that the syntactic behaviour of the lower negation is similar to that of higher negation, I conclude that the lower negation heads its own NegP projection, just like the higher negation.

There are, however, some differences between the syntax of the lower negation and the higher negation. For instance, the higher negation determines the polarity of the tag question but the lower negation does not, as shown in (30).

(30) (*a*)   John wouldn't often eat any vegetables, would he?
      (*b*)   John would often not eat any vegetables, wouldn't he?

One may argue that the reason for this contrast is that the higher negation is a sentential negation and the lower negation is a constituent negation. The account proposed in this chapter does not hinge on this matter. The crucial point here is that both the high and low negations are syntactic heads each of which projects NegP and requires *do*-support for lexical verbs. And the contrast attested in (30) can simply be attributed to the structural difference between the two negations: that is, one negation is higher in the structure than the other.

So where are the higher negation and the lower negation located in the phrase structure of a sentence? The variable word order of negative infinitivals in Middle English suggests an answer. The word order '*not–to*–verb' indicates that the higher negation is located immediately above *to*, and the word order '*to*–verb–*not*' suggests that the lower negation is located somewhere below *to*. Let us assume that TP is the highest functional projection for tensed clauses and that in infinitivals TP does not project at all (following Baltin 1993). Such a phrase structure for infinitivals reflects the fact that the infinitive does not have tense morphology.[4] Let us further assume that *to* is in a functional head that hosts

---

[4] For a different approach in which infinitivals are tensed, see Chomsky (1981), Stowell (1982), Pollock (1989), Zanuttini (1991).

mood features, namely M°. Then, the higher negation is immediately above MP, deriving the word order '*not–to*–verb'.

Supporting evidence for the assumption that infinitivals do not project TP and that infinitive *to* cannot occupy T° is provided by Baltin (1993), who points out that negation can never precede finite auxiliaries, as shown in (31).

(31) (*a*) *John not will leave
      (*b*)   John will not leave

If finite auxiliaries occupy T°, the highest functional head for tensed clauses, and negation occurs lower than T°, as I have assumed, then finite auxiliaries cannot follow negation as shown in (31*a*). Furthermore, if *to* also occurred in T°, then *to* should not be able to follow negation. But the fact is that *to* can either precede or follow negation. Thus, *to* cannot be in T°, and it therefore occupies a functional head lower than T°.[5] Infinitive *to* contributes the modality of irrealis (cf. Stowell 1982 and Portner 1992). Therefore the appropriate functional head for infintive *to* is M°. The clause structure in which the tense projection is higher than the (irrealis) mood projection is consistent with Cinque's (1999) proposal for the universal hierarchy of functional projections.

As for the lower negation, I propose that it occupies a position intermediate between MP and VP. The skeletal phrase structure assumed here for English is given in (32).[6]

(32)

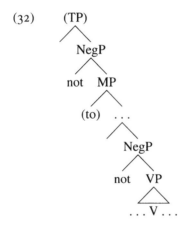

---

[5] The clause structure assumed here for English is similar to Baltin (1993). The main difference is that in Baltin (1993), AgrOP projects immediately below TP and *to* is placed in AgrO°, whereas I do not assume the existence of AgrP. Instead, I assume that MP projects below TP and *to* is placed in M°.

[6] Zanuttini (1991) also argues that English has two positions for negation. The analysis proposed here differs from Zanuttini (1991) in that she assumes that the presence of the higher negation is parasitic on the presence of a tense phrase, whereas I make no such assumption. As a consequence, unlike the analysis proposed here, Zanuttini is forced to assume that infinitivals project TP.

12.3.3. *Infinitive verb movement*

I propose that the '*to*–verb–*not*' order in Middle English is derived by the movement of the verb over the lower negation to an intermediate position between M°
and the lower Neg°, which I assume to be a head of aspect (Asp°) that encodes
(im)perfectivity. If infinitives move over the lower NegP, then we expect to find
cases in which the infinitive verb precedes *not* and *not* in turn precedes a participle or a direct object. Such cases can be found in the PPCME, as illustrated
in (33) and (34).

(33) *to*–verb–*not*–participle
   (*a*)   and said mayster parson, I praye you *to be not displeasyd*
          and said master parson I pray you to be not displeased
               (Caxton, *Prologues and Epilogues* 88.176)

   (*b*)   Ha! What it es mykell to be worþi lovyng and *be noght loved*!
          ha what it is much to be worth loving and be not   loved
               (Rolle, *Form of Living* 88.52)

(34) *to*–verb–*not*–direct object
   (*a*)   *to conforme noght his will* to Gods will, *to gyf noght entent* till hes
          to conform not   his will to God's will, to give not   heed to his
          prayers   (Rolle, *Form of Living* 99.263)
          prayers

   (*b*)   and *to spille not oure tyme*, be it short be it long at Goddis
          and to waste not our time, be it short be it long at God's
          ordynaunce   (Purvey, *Prologue to the Bible* I, 56.73)
          ordinance

A widely accepted diagnostic for verb movement is adverb placement with respect to the verb. In Middle English finite clauses, adverbs such as *often* and
ever usually follow the tensed verb, as in (13) (repeated below as (35)). If these
adverbs are VP-adjoined, then the fact that the tensed verbs precede the adverbs
suggests that the verb moves over the adverb.

(35) (*a*)   and [he] *suffryd euer*   grete penaunce for Goddis sake in
          and [he] suffered always great penance   for God's sake in
          weryng of the heyre
          wearing of the hair
               (*Life of St Edmund* 165.61)

   (*b*)   Here men *vndurstonden ofte* by þis ny3t þe ny3t of synne
          here men understood   often by this night the night of sin
               (*Wycliffite Sermons* I, 477.605)

In Middle English infinitival clauses, adverbs can also follow the infinitive, as
shown in (36). This suggests that in Middle English infinitive verbs can also
undergo movement.

(36) (*a*) Monye men han a maner *to ete ofte* for   to drynke
            many   men have a manner to eat often in-order to drink
            (*Wycliffite Sermons* I, 478.631)

     (*b*) þe oþur was þat God wold ȝeue hur þat grace, to hur þat was þe
            the other was that God would give her that grace, to her that was the
            modur of God *to do euer*   plesaund seruyse to God
            mother of God to do always pleasing service to God
            (*Sermons from the MS Royal* 256.260)

There is some evidence from adverb placement that the head which hosts verbal aspect is located low in the clause structure. Cinque (1999) argues that different classes of adverbs each occur in a fixed position in the specifier of a different functional projections and that these functional projections are hierarchically structured. Based on this premise, he derives a universal hierarchy of functional projections. In particular, he observes that in English (just as in other languages), aspectual adverbs such as *completely* must follow other classes of adverbs, as shown in (37) and (38).

(37) (*a*) He rarely completely eats his vegetables
     (*b*) *He completely rarely eats his vegetables

(38) (*a*) He hasn't yet completely ruined it
     (*b*) *He hasn't completely yet ruined it

Based on this fact he concludes that the aspect projection in English is located quite low in the clause structure, lower than tense projection and mood projection.

In summary, I have shown that Middle English phrase structure for clauses allows two possible positions for negation based on the data from negative infinitivals. I have also argued that in Middle English, infinitive verbs move over the lower negation to an intermediate position between M^o and the lower Neg^o. Moreover, I have argued that infinitivals do not project TP and that *to* is in M^o, which is located lower than the higher Neg^o. The phrase structure for infinitivals that I adopt is given in (39). If the proposed analysis is correct, then Middle English infinitivals are like their Present-day French counterparts in that the infinitive verb can move to an intermediate functional head (see Pollock 1989 for an account of French infinitivals). The difference is that infinitive verb movement is optional in French but it is feature-driven obligatory movement in Middle English. The phrase structure for tensed clauses in Middle English is similar to that for infinitivals, except that in tensed clauses, TP projects as the highest functional projection and the verb moves all the way up to T^o, as shown in (40).

(39) $[_{NegP} [_{Neg} \text{ not }] [_{MP} [_{M} \text{ to }] [_{AspP} [_{Asp} V_i] [_{NegP} [_{Neg} \text{ not }]$
          $[_{VP} \ldots t_i \ldots]]]]]$

(40) $[_{TP} [_T V_i] [_{NegP} [_{Neg}$ not $] [_{MP} [_M t_i] [_{AspP} [_{Asp} t_i] [_{NegP} [_{Neg}$ not $]$
         $[_{VP} \cdots t_i \cdots]]]]]]$

12.4. THE DEVELOPMENT OF *DO*-SUPPORT IN IMPERATIVES

12.4.1. Do-*support in Present-day English*

At this point, I need to clarify the mechanism I am assuming for *do*-support in Present-day English given the clause structure in (40). The facts are: (*a*) *do*-support is required in questions (except for subject *wh*-questions), and negative declaratives for lexical verbs, but prohibited for *be* and auxiliary verbs, and (*b*) *do*-support is prohibited for affirmative declaratives. The explanations for these facts in the literature are largely based on the widely accepted assumptions that auxiliary verbs and *be* undergo overt movement to INFL (which is equivalent to T^o in the clause structure in (40)), that lexical verbs undergo movement at LF in Present-day English, and that negation is a head that blocks this LF verb movement (cf. Chomsky 1991, Roberts 1993*a*).

In questions, tense features in T^o must move to C^o in the overt syntax. *Be* or auxiliary verbs in questions overtly move to T^o and then they further move to C^o, carrying along tense features, thereby satisfying the requirement that tense features overtly move to C^o. On the other hand, lexical verbs are stuck *in situ* in the overt syntax, and so they cannot carry the tense features to C^o in the overt syntax. As a last resort, *do* is inserted in Asp^o and moves through M^o and T^o to C^o carrying along tense.

In negative declaratives, negation blocks LF verb movement, and so for lexical verbs *do* is inserted in Asp^o as a last resort and it moves through M^o to T^o checking verbal features. But negation does not block overt verb movement, and so *be* and auxiliary verbs do not require *do*-support (hence prohibiting it for reasons of economy). Affirmative declaratives do not require *do*-support for lexical verbs (as well as *be* and auxiliary verbs) since there is nothing that blocks LF verb movement. The question that arises is why negation blocks LF verb movement but not overt verb movement. Here, I just refer the readers to Chomsky (1991) and Roberts (1993*a*) for two possible accounts. For the purposes of this chapter it does not matter which particular account is adopted.

12.4.2. *Verb movement in imperatives*

Imperative verbs lack tense in their morphological make-up, just as infinitive verbs do. I take this to mean that TP does not project at all in imperatives, as represented in (41).[7]

(41) $[_{CP} [_C] [_{MP} [_M] [_{AspP} [_{Asp}] [_{VP} \cdots [V] \cdots]]]]$

---

[7] Zanuttini (1991) argues for Romance that imperatives do not project a tense phrase.

Supporting evidence for this comes from the fact that modal verbs such as *must, can, might, should*, etc. cannot occur in imperatives. If modal verbs are merged in T° and if imperatives do not project tense phrase, then we expect modal verbs to be barred from imperatives.

In Old English and Middle English, the word order in imperatives suggests that the imperative verb is in C°. If we adopt the phrase structure in (41) for imperatives, then the imperative verb moves to Asp°, M°, and then to C°. Under this analysis, imperatives are similar to infinitivals in that the verb moves to Asp°, but they differ in that the verb moves further to C°.[8]

12.4.3. Do-*support in imperatives*

12.4.3.1. *Negative Imperatives*

As noted earlier, the standard view in the literature is that the development of *do*-support is a reflex of the loss of V–I movement for lexical verbs in the history of English. Under the more articulated clause structure proposed here, we are able to divide up V–I movement into M–T movement, Asp–M movement and V–Asp movement.

Recall that *do*-forms in negative imperatives are almost non-existent before the end of the sixteenth century, but gain ground rapidly after 1600. I propose that this is a reflex of the loss of V–Asp movement, which begins at the end of the sixteenth century. As V–Asp movement disappears, overt verb movement to C° is replaced with LF verb movement to C°. But when Asp° and V° are separated by negation *do*-support is required as a last resort device since LF verb movement is blocked by the intervening negation.[9] *Do* is inserted in Asp°, and then it moves to C°, deriving *do*–(subject)–*not*–verb order, as represented in (42). Some examples of negative imperatives with *do*-support are given in (43).

(42) $[_{CP} [_{C} do_i] [_{MP} [_{M} t_i] [_{AspP} [_{Asp} t_i] [_{NegP} [_{Neg} not] [_{VP} \ldots verb \ldots]]]]]$

---

[8] A reviewer noted that the presence of AspP is strange in imperatives, since some have denied that perfect imperatives exist. However, perfect imperatives are indeed possible, as shown in Davies (1986).

(i) (*a*)   Do at least have tried it before you begin to criticize   (Davies 1986, ch.1, 88)
    (*b*)   Don't have eaten everything before the guests arrive   (Davies 1986, ch.1, 89)

Moreover, progressive imperatives and perfective imperatives are possible as well, as in (ii).

(ii) (*a*)   Be waiting for me in front of the gate
     (*b*)   Eat up the cake!

Given these facts, positing an AspP for imperatives is not without some motivation.

[9] An alternative approach to why *do*-support is required in negative sentences is given in Bobaljik (1995). According to Bobaljik, *do*-support is triggered by a PF adjacency requirement between the morphology in INFL and the verb. Given this approach, I can say that *do*-support is required in negative imperatives because negation blocks PF adjacency between the morphology in the functional heads and the verb.

(43) (*a*)   Do not send me any letters (363 W:212a–33)
     (*b*)   but I will be your good lord, do you not doubt (361 O:4–2–39)
     (*c*)   Do not bite your thumbs, sir (364 N:281a–7)

The loss of V–Asp movement requires *do*-support in negative imperatives with higher negation as well: as V–Asp movement is lost, further verb movement to M^0 and to C^0 is prohibited, and overt verb movement to C^0 is replaced by LF verb movement to C^0. When negation intervenes between M^0 and C^0, LF verb movement to C^0 is blocked, and so *do*-support is required. In the spirit of Baltin (1993), the high negation has a clitic-like nature in that it must adjoin onto an adjacent verbal element. Thus, in negative imperatives with *do*-support and high negation, auxiliary *do* and the negation move to C as a unit, deriving the '*do–not–*(subject)*–verb*' order as illustrated in (44).

(44) (*a*)   Good brother, do not you envy my fortunate achievement
             (361 W: 3–1–86)
     (*b*)   Don't read this, you little rogue, with your little eyes (379 61–20)
     (*c*)   But don't lose your money (379 13–16)

12.4.3.2. *Affirmative imperatives*

Following Roberts (1985) and Kroch (1989*b*), I assume that as English lost verb movement for lexical verbs, questions, which require overt verb movement to C^0, resorted to *do*-support. Under the articulated clause structure assumed here, *do* is inserted in Asp^0 and then moves through M^0 and T^0 to C^0. This is represented in (45).

(45) $[_{CP}\ [_C\ do_i\ ]\ [_{TP}\ subject\ [_T\ t_i\ ]\ [_{MP}\ [_M\ t_i\ ]\ [_{AspP}\ [_{Asp}\ t_i\ ]\ [_{VP}\ \ldots\ verb\ \ldots\ ]]]]]$

Since imperatives also show overt verb movement to C^0, we expect the development of *do*-forms in affirmative imperatives to pattern with questions. However, the relative frequency of *do*-forms of affirmative imperatives has never exceeded 1%. In Present-day English, *do*-forms are restricted to emphatic affirmative imperatives, as illustrated in (46).

(46) (*a*)   Do come early
     (*b*)   Do enjoy the movie

The proposed phrase structure for imperatives differs from that of questions: imperatives do not project TP, whereas questions do. I argue that this is exactly why the development of *do*-forms in affirmative imperatives does not pattern with that of questions. In questions, as overt verb movement is lost, the tense feature in T^0 is stranded. But even after the loss of overt verb movement, the requirement that features in T^0 overtly move to C^0 persists. As a last-resort device for movement to C^0, the stranded tense feature is supported by *do*, which then overtly moves to C^0. But imperatives contain no functional head with tense features. This means that once overt verb movement to C^0 is replaced by LF movement, the requirement that features in T° move to C° cannot apply to imperatives, and so imperatives do not develop *do*-forms.

12.5. SEQUENTIAL LOSS OF VERB MOVEMENT

If we assume the articulated clause structure proposed here, we can imagine two different ways in which the loss of verb movement can proceed: (*a*) the loss of V–Asp movement, and M–T movement begin simultaneously; (*b*) the loss of M–T movement historically precedes the loss of V–Asp movement. In the rest of §12.5, I will show that possibility (*b*) makes the correct predictions for the overall statistical patterns shown in Figure 12.1: the loss of M–T movement begins at the beginning of the fifteenth century, and the loss of V–Asp movement begins at the end of the sixteenth century. At this point, I know of no evidence that indicates when exactly the loss of Asp–M movement begins. For the purposes of this chapter, I will simply assume that Asp–M movement is string vacuous and is lost in conjunction with the loss of M–T movement. The validity of the argument presented here does not hinge on when the loss of Asp–M movement takes place.

In a series of works on syntactic change, Kroch develops a model of change that accounts for the gradual replacement of one form by another form (Kroch 1989*a*, *b*, 1994; see also Pintzuk 1991, Santorini 1992, Taylor 1994). According to Kroch, the gradual change in the relative frequencies of two forms is a reflex of the competition between two grammars, rather than a series of grammatical reanalyses. In particular, Kroch argues that the statistical pattern in the development of *do*-forms reflects the competition between the old grammar that has V–I movement for lexical verbs and the new one that has lost it. In time, the grammar without V–I movement wins, at the expense of the grammar that has V–I movement.

Extending Kroch's grammar competition model to the proposed analysis here, I make a conjecture as to how the loss of M–T and V–Asp movements proceeds. I hypothesize that at the beginning of the fifteenth century, the competition between the grammar with M–T movement and the one without such M–T movement begins. Before the grammar with M–T movement completely loses out, the competition between the grammar with V–Asp movement and the one without such V–Asp movement begins at the end of the sixteenth century. The grammar without V–Asp movement is constrained not to have M–T movement (as well as Asp–M movement), since the loss of lower verb movement prevents the verb from moving higher up. Thus, at this point, competition between three grammars is taking place: one grammar with both M–T and also V–Asp movement, a second grammar with V–Asp movement but no M–T movement, and a third grammar with neither V–Asp nor M–T movement. In what follows, I will discuss some evidence for the hypothesis that the loss of M–T movement precedes the loss of V–Asp movement in the history of English.

12.5.1. Do-*support in negative imperatives and negative declaratives*

As shown in Figure 12.1, by 1575, the relative frequency of *do*-forms in negative declaratives is almost 40 per cent, whereas the frequency of *do*-forms in negative imperatives is remarkably low. But at the end of the sixteenth century, the frequency of *do*-forms in negative imperatives suddenly rises, and around 1600, the development of *do*-forms in negative imperatives is roughly the same as in negative declaratives.

Given the articulated clause structure proposed here, in declaratives in Middle English, the verb moves all the way up to T^o, as represented in (40). Negative declaratives formed with higher negation require *do*-support when M–T movement is lost. Moreover, all negative declaratives, whether formed with higher or lower negation, require *do*-support when V–Asp movement is lost. If the loss of M–T movement begins at the beginning of the fifteenth century, we expect to find *do*-support in negative declaratives well before 1575. And this is indeed what we see in Figure 12.1.

On the other hand, in the proposed phrase structure for imperatives, TP does not project at all. Thus, in imperatives in Middle English, the verb moves to Asp^o and to M^o and then directly to C^o, as represented in (47).

(47) $[_{CP} [_C V_i] [_{NegP} [_{Neg} \text{ not }] [_{MP} [_M t_i] [_{AspP} [_{Asp} t_i] [_{NegP} [_{Neg} \text{ not }]$
        $[_{VP} \ldots t_i \ldots]]]]]]$

The absence of T^o in imperatives means that the loss of M–T movement has no consequences for the development of *do*-forms in negative imperatives. But the loss of V–Asp movement does. If the loss of V–Asp movement begins at the end of the sixteenth century, we do not expect to find much *do*-support in negative imperatives before 1600. As shown in Figure 12.1, our expectation is supported.

Another difference between negative declaratives and negative imperatives has to do with the development of *do*-forms with *be* and auxiliary *have*. While negative imperatives require *do*-support with these verbs, negative declaratives prohibit it. Ellegård's data contain two negative imperatives with *be* in the seventeenth century, and both of them have *do*-support, as shown in (48).

(48) *Negative imperatives*
    (*a*)   Well then, don't be so tedious, Mr. Presto (379 107–5)
    (*b*)   I mean decently, don't be rogues (379 174–17)

The standard view of why negative declaratives with an auxiliary verb prohibit *do*-support is that auxiliary verbs undergo overt movement. The question then is why auxiliary verbs in imperatives do not undergo overt movement, hence requiring *do*-support when negated. The answer lies in the presence or the absence of the tense projection. That is, auxiliary verbs can undergo overt movement only when the clause is tensed. Following Chomsky (1995), let us think of movement as attraction. Then tense features in T^o attract auxiliary verbs, allowing them to move up to T^o. If there is no tense projection, then there is no tense feature to attract auxiliary verbs. I have assumed that imperatives are not tensed and so do not project a tense phrase. This means that auxiliary verbs cannot be attracted by tense features, and so they must remain *in situ*.

12.5.2. Do-*support in questions and negative declaratives*

Figure 12.1 shows that *do*-support was much more favoured in questions than in negative declaratives. By 1575, while the frequency of *do*-forms is 40 per cent in negative declaratives, it is almost 60 per cent in affirmative questions and almost 90 per cent in negative questions. The difference in the frequency of *do*-forms in questions and negative declaratives can be explained if the loss of M–T movement precedes the loss of V–Asp movement.

In questions, the loss of M–T movement leads to *do*-support, and *do* moves to C°. On the other hand, in negative declaratives, the loss of M–T movement does not necessarily correlate with the development of *do*-support because negative declaratives have two possible analyses. That is, a negative declarative can be formed with negation either in the higher NegP (as in (49)) or the lower NegP position (as in (50)). During the period in which M–T movement is being lost and before the period in which the loss of V–Asp movement begins, if (49) is chosen, then *do*-support is required, and if (50) is chosen, then *do*-support is not required. This explains why the frequency of *do*-forms in negative declaratives is much lower than in questions before 1600. When V–Asp movement is lost after 1600, both analyses in (49) and (50) require *do*-support and so the frequency of *do*-forms in negative declaratives rises rapidly.

(49) $[_{TP} [_T] [_{NegP} [_{Neg}] [_{MP} [_M] [_{AspP} [_{Asp}] [_{VP} \ldots \text{verb} \ldots]]]]]]$

(50) $[_{TP} [_T] [_{MP} [_M] [_{AspP} [_{Asp}] [_{NegP} [_{Neg}] [_{VP} \ldots \text{verb} \ldots]]]]]]$

Kroch (1989*a*, *b*) has argued that the rise of *do*-forms is a reflex of an abstract grammatical change, the loss of V–I movement, by showing a correlation between the rise of *do*-forms in the various linguistic contexts up to 1575. The rates of the change in *do*-support were shown to be constant across these contexts using logistic regression. However, his calculation for the rate in negative declaratives is based on a set of sentences that includes both high and low negation, since he was assuming a clause structure with one NegP. According to the analysis proposed here, only high negation is relevant for the rise of *do*-forms in negative declaratives before 1575. What this means is that in order to get an accurate measure, sentences formed with low negation should not be counted in the calculation of the rate of rise of *do*-forms in negative declaratives. This distinction has implications for the constant rate effect of change in *do*-support discussed in Kroch.[10]

---

[10] The implications of high versus low negation towards the constant rate effect of the development of *do*-support is a topic of my current research.

The proposed analysis also explains why the development of *do*-forms in negative imperatives patterns with that of negative declaratives and not with that of negative questions after 1600. In negative questions, *do*-support takes place because of the requirement of overt tense-feature movement to C^0, and due to the presence of negation which blocks LF verb movement. When V–Asp movement is lost, the requirement for overt tense-feature movement to C^0 does not apply in imperatives since imperatives are not tensed. The only source for *do*-support in negative imperatives is therefore the presence of negation, which blocks LF verb movement. We have seen that *do*-support in negative declaratives is also due to the presence of negation. Hence, it is not surprising that negative imperatives pattern like negative declaratives with respect to the development of *do*-forms after 1600.

Some questions remain: (*a*) Why is the frequency of *do*-forms in negative questions always higher than in affirmative questions prior to the completion of the loss of verb movements? (*b*) Why does the frequency of *do*-forms drop suddenly in negative questions and in negative declaratives during 1560–90? (*c*) Why do infinitivals and subjunctives in Present-day English not have *do*-support? For a possible answer to the third question, see Han (2000).

12.6. CONCLUSION

I have argued that the syntax of Middle English infinitivals can be explained if we allow two possible positions for negation and an intermediate functional projection, which I assume to be an aspect phrase (AspP), between the mood phrase (MP) and the verb phrase (VP). I was able to account for the patterns of *do*-support in various sentence types based on the articulated clause structure that I have proposed for Middle English. In particular, I have proposed that the development of *do*-support in negative imperatives is a reflex of the loss of V–Asp movement. That is, as V–Asp movement was lost, the verb in imperatives moves to C^0 at LF. In negative imperatives, *do*-support is required as a last resort device because negation blocks LF verb movement. I have also argued that the differences and similarities attested in the statistical patterns of the development of *do*-forms between imperatives and questions, between imperatives and declaratives, and between questions and declaratives can be explained if the loss of M–T movement precedes the loss of V–Asp movement in the history of English.

APPENDIX

This appendix lists the abbreviations and their full names for the texts from Late Middle English and Early Modern English that are cited in this chapter. I refer to the texts by the abbreviations specified in Ellegård (1953).

[302] William Atkynson. *De Imitatione Christi*. 1502. Ed. J. K. Ingram. London: Early English Text Society, ES 63, 1893.

[304] *Valentine and Orson.* 1505. Ed. A. Dickson. London: Early English Text Society, OS 204, 1936.

[305] John Fisher. *The English Works.* 1509–21. Ed. J. E. B. Mayor. London: Early English Text Society, ES 27, 1876.

[308] Robert Whittinton. *The Vulgaria.* 1519. Ed. B. White. London: Early English Text Society, OS 187, 1931.

[310] William Tindale. *The Four Gospels.* 1525. Ed. J. Bosworth. The Gothic and Anglo-Saxon Gospels. London, 1865.

[323] Hugh Latimer. *Letters.* c.1525–55. Ed. G. E. Corrie. *Remains of Bishop Latimer.* Parker Society 10, 1845.

[326] John Palsgrave. *The Comedy of Acolastus.* 1540. Ed. P. L. Carver. London: Early English Text Society, OS 202, 1935.

[344] *Palace of Pleasure.* 1566. Ed. Haworth. *An Elizabethan Story Book.* London, 1928.

[350] Richard Mulcaster. *Elementarie.* 1582. Ed. E. T. Campagnac. Tudor and Stuart Library. London, 1925.

[356] Queen Elizabeth. *Boethius.* 1593. Ed. C. Pemberton. London: Early English Text Society, OS 113, 1899.

[360] Ben Jonson's *Plays.* 1598–1609. Ed. W. Bang. *Ben Jonsons Dramen*, in *Materialien zur Kunde des Älteren Englischen Dramas*, VII: 1–2. 1905–8.

[361] George Chapman. *Plays.* 1606–12. Ed. T. M. Parrot. London, 1914.

[363] John Webster and Thomas Dekker. *Westward Ho; Northward Ho.* 1607. Ed. Alex Dyce. *The Works of John Webster.* London, 1857.

[364] Thomas Dekker. *Seven Deadly Sins of London.* 1606. Ed. E. Arber. English Scholars' Library 7, 1879.

[379] Jonathan Swift. *Journal to Stella.* 1710. Ed. Harold Williams. Oxford, 1948.

13

Interacting Movements in the History of Icelandic

ÞORBJÖRG HRÓARSDÓTTIR

13.1. INTRODUCTION

A central question in the comparison of OV- and VO-languages is whether the difference results from having more object movements in OV-languages, or more verb movements in VO-languages. In this chapter, I will argue that although the uniform VO-base hypothesis with overt versus covert leftward movement of objects yields positive results in the synchronic analysis of the Old(er) Icelandic VP, it cannot easily handle the diachronic aspect. Instead, I will agree with the original proposal of Haider (1992) that there are good reasons to assume that the verb moves more in VO-languages. Haider thinks of this verb movement as head movement. However, this could also be a VP-movement, provided that the complements have first moved out of this VP. This is the path that Johnson (1996), Hinterhölzl (1997), and Kayne (1998) take. More exactly, they suggest that VO-order might in some cases result from shifting a remnant VP containing the verb across complements extracted from the VP.

Generalizing this idea, I will propose that the crucial difference between OV and VO languages is simply that OV-languages lack the VP-preposing Modern English and other VO languages have. The picture is slightly more complicated for mixed OV/VO languages such as Old English, Old Icelandic, Afrikaans, and Dutch. However, I will show that it is possible to construct a theory with a universal base which derives all the attested OV and VO word-order patterns, by means of three main transformations: (*a*) obligatory and universal leftward movement of the direct object out of the VP (to [Spec,AgrOP] in the functional domain), together with (*b*) optional extraction of the embedded VP from the matrix VP in Old(er) Icelandic, followed by (*c*) obligatory preposing of the remnant VP, containing at least the finite auxiliary verb, in all VO-languages, including all stages of Icelandic.

It will be argued that the preposing of the remnant VP will always mask the object movement, deriving VO word order only, as long as the option of extracting the embedded VP from the matrix VP has not been chosen.

13.2. LOSS OF OV WORD ORDER

Although it is a well-known fact that Modern Icelandic has pure SVO word order, several other orders of the VP-internal arguments were possible at earlier stages in the history of Icelandic, including both pure and mixed OV word-order patterns, in addition to VO word order (cf. Sigurðsson 1988; Rögnvaldsson 1994/1995, 1996; Indriðason 1987; Hróarsdóttir 1996, 1998, 1999*a*, 1999*b*, to appear). The attested OV word-order patterns were lost at the beginning of the nineteenth century, despite the fact that Icelandic has had rich subject–verb agreement morphology and case morphology throughout its history. It is generally assumed that both Old and Modern Icelandic have obligatory overt movement of the finite verb to Infl, in both main and subordinate clauses, since the difference with regard to the position of the finite verb in main and subordinate clauses in Icelandic is insignificant, unlike most of the other Germanic verb-second languages, such as the Mainland Scandinavian languages, and German and Dutch.

The frequency of the different word-order patterns was studied in various texts dating from the fourteenth to the nineteenth century, in addition to personal letters dating from the nineteenth century. A list of the sixteen texts used for this study is given in Appendix A, together with bibliographical information. These texts are literary works, all in reliable editions based directly on the original composition. Approximately 25–30 pages (resulting in 500–1000 lines) were extracted from each text, where possible, until a corpus of approximately 5,000 sentences containing at least one non-finite verb had been reached, exhibiting either OV or VO word order. Letters by seventy-five individuals were studied, approximately three letters from each writer (150 lines), and they were divided into seven groups, with approximately ten writers in each. Only letters when the year of the author's birth is known were used. The first group has letters from speakers born 1730–50 and the last group has letters from speakers born 1850–70. In all the texts and letters, 4,875 clauses were extracted, of which 3,497 were counted as VO and 1,378 clauses as OV, where OV-order is taken to include not only clauses where a nominal object precedes the main verb, but also clauses where other complements of the main verb precede it (PPs, adverbials, adjectives, and other non-finite verbs). In (1) are shown some simple sentences with OV word order to exemplify the classification into the various types of the complements. Example (1*a*) shows a sentence containing a preverbal complement that is a nominal object, (1*b*) shows an example of a preverbal prepositional phrase, (1*c*) is an example of a preverbal adverb, (1*d*) shows a preverbal adjective, example (1*e*) shows a preverbal particle, and finally, examples (1*f–g*) show sentences where the non-finite main verb occurs to the left of the non-finite auxiliary. All of the complements included in the main study here are ungrammatical in a preverbal position in Modern Icelandic, except for negative and quantified complements.

(1) (a)   so Þorsteinn skyldi *lífinu*   tapa
             so Þorsteinn should life-the lose
             'so that Þorsteinn should die'

(b)   að þú mættir *hjá mér* vera nokkra daga
             that you could with me stay few   days
             'that you could stay with me for a few days'

(c)   því   var riddarinn *hingað* sendur
             therefore was knight-the here   sent
             'Therefore, the knight was sent here.'

(d)   at þið munit nu   *satt* segja
             that you will   now true say
             'that you will now tell the truth'

(e)   áður   sól var *niður* runnin
             before sun was down slid
             'before the sun had gone down'

(f)   at vitinn   hefir *brendr* verit
             that lighthouse-the has burned been
             'that the lighthouse has been burned'

(g)   Þú munt *frétt* hafa, að . . .
             You will heard have, that . . .
             'You will have heard, that . . .'

All sentences that show signs of OV-order were counted as OV (either 'pure' or 'mixed' order). A few examples of this classification are in (2) to (4). (2) illustrates pure OV-order, and (3) and (4) show examples of the possible mixed orders.

(2) Pure OV word order

(a)   að hann hafi *hana* drepið
             that he   had her   killed
             'that he had killed her'

(b)   að þú . . . hafir *það bréf* fengið
             that you . . . have that letter received
             'that you have received that letter'

(c)   að eg skal *þér það* allvel launa
             that I   shall you it   well reward
             'that I shall reward you well for it'

(d)   að eg mundi *hann sigrað* geta
             that I   would him   defeat could
             'that I would be able to defeat him'

(3) Mixed word order: one non-finite verb plus two objects

    (*a*)   hafer þu *þinu lidi*   jatat   *þeim*
           have you your assistance promised them
           'if you have promised them your assistance'

    (*b*)   þa uilldi hann nu   giarna *hialp* weita *leoninum*
           then wanted he   now readily help give lion-the
           'Then, he readily wanted to help the lion.'

    (*c*)   Hafdi þa   huorgi *sari*   komit *a annann*
           had   then neither wound got   on other
           'Neither had been able to wound the other.'

(4) Mixed word order: two non-finite verbs plus one object

    (*a*)   að hann skyldi aldrei *mega*   *sól sjá*
           that he   should never be-allowed sun to-see
           'that he should never be allowed to see the sun'

    (*b*)   þeir quaðuz eigi *þat mundu gera*
           they said   not it   would do
           'They claimed they would not do it.'

    (*c*)   at hann mun *raða vilja ferðum sínum*
           that he   will decide want journeys his
           'that he will want to decide his own journeys'

The main results for the frequency of OV-order are shown in Tables 13.1 and 13.2. Table 13.1 shows the rate of the frequency of OV-order in each of the texts, and letters from each age group studied, and Table 13.2 contains similar information for each century. There is no distinction made between main and embedded clauses here. The last seven rows in Table 13.1 are letters.

OV-orders occurred most frequently in texts dating from the fourteenth to seventeenth centuries (from an average of 58.2% to 50.0%) and decreased to an average of 37.0% in texts from the eighteenth century. OV word order then gradually disappeared in texts and letters dating from the nineteenth century. These results are in accordance with earlier studies on OV-order in Old(er) Icelandic (cf. Rögnvaldsson 1994/1995, 1996; Indriðason 1987). The OV-orders therefore showed a remarkable stability for at least five or six centuries. The first important decline seems to occur in the language of writers in the eighteenth century, until OV word order almost disappears in the nineteenth-century texts. This rapid disappearance of OV-orders is especially interesting since the frequency seems to have been quite stable in the preceding centuries.

Finally, all the complements, pre- and postverbal, were divided into four main groups according to their type (DPs, PPs, non-finite verbs, or another type, including adverbials, adjectives, verbal particles, and single prepositions). See Hróarsdóttir (1999*b*) for a more thorough study of each of these four types and their subclassification. The frequency of each type of these complements, in both

TABLE 13.1. *Number of clauses with OV- and VO-orders (in each text)*

Texts		All clauses			
		OV	VO	Total	% OV
early 14th century	Finn	78	46	124	62.9%
mid 14th century	Guðm	43	54	97	44.3%
late 14th century	Árn	41	32	73	56.2%
late 14th century	Dín	68	33	101	67.3%
early 15th century	Sig	81	47	128	63.3%
late 15th century	Vikt	59	65	124	47.6%
early 16th century	Afs	29	24	53	54.7%
late 16th century	Morð	100	79	179	55.9%
late 17th century	Skál	43	103	146	29.5%
late 17th century	Árm	182	108	290	62.8%
*c.*1700	Munn	73	87	160	45.6%
early 18th century	J.Ey	15	15	30	50.0%
early 18th century	Bisk	25	50	75	33.3%
late 18th century	Próf	48	85	133	36.1%
early 19th century	Álf	138	123	261	52.9%
early 19th century	Esp	18	116	134	13.4%
1. age group	1730–1750	88	250	338	26.0%
2. age group	1750–1770	47	203	250	18.8%
3. age group	1770–1790	65	345	410	15.9%
4. age group	1790–1810	45	342	387	11.6%
5. age group	1810–1830	36	425	461	7.8%
6. age group	1830–1850	27	418	445	6.1%
7. age group	1850–1870	29	447	476	6.1%
		1,378	3,497	4,875	

pre- and postverbal positions, is given in Table 13.3. The frequencies for texts from each century have been assembled here.

As indicated in Table 13.3, there is no significant general difference between the frequency of preverbal NPs and preverbal PPs; both types also seem to have

TABLE 13.2. *Number of clauses with OV- and VO-orders (in each century)*

Texts	All clauses			
	OV	VO	Total	% OV
14th century	230	165	395	58.2%
15th century	140	112	252	55.6%
16th century	129	103	232	55.6%
17th century	298	298	596	50.0%
18th century	88	150	238	37.0%
19th century	493	2,669	3,162	15.6%
	1,378	3,497	4,875	

TABLE 13.3. *Type of pre- and postverbal complements (in each century)*

	Nominal objects			PPs		
	$DO\text{-}V_{main}$	$V_{main}\text{-}DO$	% preverbal	$PP\text{-}V_{main}$	$V_{main}\text{-}PP$	% preverbal
14th c.	98	120	45.0%	47	42	52.8%
15th c.	67	77	46.5%	36	46	43.9%
16th c.	64	64	50.0%	29	36	44.6%
17th c.	148	209	41.5%	70	112	38.5%
18th c.	31	105	22.8%	28	60	31.8%
19th c.	202	1,544	11.6%	147	998	12.8%
	610	2,119	22.4%	357	1,294	21.6%
	Non-finite verbs			XPs		
	$V_{main}\text{-}V_{aux}$	$V_{aux}\text{-}V_{main}$	% preverbal	$XP\text{-}V_{main}$	$V_{main}\text{-}XP$	% preverbal
14th c.	25	7	78.1%	103	25	80.5%
15th c.	7	8	46.7%	61	14	81.3%
16th c.	16	11	59.3%	45	16	73.8%
17th c.	17	22	43.6%	142	55	72.1%
18th c.	6	13	31.6%	40	24	62.5%
19th c.	36	273	11.7%	191	728	20.8%
	107	334	24.3%	582	862	40.3%

declined at a very similar rate. Let us now turn to the cases where the preverbal complement is a non-finite verb. This variable seems to have occurred with a similar average frequency in texts and letters from the fifteenth to the nineteenth century as nominal objects and PPs. The average frequency for this type of complements in the fourteenth century is higher than for both nominal objects and PPs. The last group, called XPs in Table 13.3, is not immediately comparable to the other three groups since it contains various types of complements, or small clause predicates, as already mentioned: adverbials, adjectives, verbal particles, and single prepositions. Only adverbials and adjectives that are complements of the main verb were counted as small clause predicates here, that is, predicates that are subcategorized by the verb, leaving the discussion of both PP adjuncts and other adjuncts aside for now. See Hróarsdóttir (1999*b*) for a further discussion of these types.

13.3. THE IMPLICATIONAL RELATIONSHIP OF RESTRUCTURING AND UNIVERSAL BASE VO ORDER

13.3.1. *Introduction*

In this section, I will focus on the fact that several different features of OV-order all disappeared from Icelandic at the same time, arguing that this is not accounted for in earlier proposed analyses of the derivation of OV/VO word order. Ultimately, I will propose that VO-order is derived by remnant VP-preposing.

In addition to deriving all attested VO and OV word-order patterns, the proposal can give a unification (by implicational relationship) between the three word-order patterns shown in (5).

(5) (a) V_{fin} . . . Object–V_{aux}–V_{main}
    (b) V_{fin} . . . V_{aux}–Object–V_{main}
    (c) V_{fin} . . . V_{main}–V_{aux}

These three word-order patterns are typical examples of restructuring in the West Germanic languages; (5*a*) is the typical pattern of restructuring (long DP-movement) in Dutch, (5*b*) is a case of verb-projection raising typical for West Flemish, Swiss German, and South Tyrolean, and (5*c*) is the standard pattern of verb-raising in Standard German. Furthermore, these word-order patterns all disappeared simultaneously in the history of Icelandic (see Hróarsdóttir 1999*b*).

13.3.2. *VO by object-movement*

Let us begin by assuming a uniform VO-base hypothesis, with overt versus covert leftward object movements. According to Kayne (1994), all languages have S–H–C order. Chomsky (1995: chapter 4) adopts a similar position. Zwart (1993, 1997), Koster (1995), and Lattewitz (1996) have extended these insights by showing that this approach yields positive results in the analysis of Dutch and German, and Roberts (1997) and van der Wurff (1997) also argue that Old and Middle English can plausibly be analysed as head-initial. Kayne's system can also account nicely for the word order variation in the Old(er) Icelandic VP; assuming that the object could move either 'short' (within the VP) or 'long' (out of the VP), and that the main verb could move individually and adjoin to the non-finite auxiliary. (6) illustrates possible argument movements for some common word-order patterns in Old(er) Icelandic.

(6) (a) V_{fin} . . . $[_{VP} [V_{aux}–V_{main}–object]]$ (no movement)
    (b) V_{fin} . . . $[_{VP} [V_{main}–V_{aux}–object]]$ (V-raising)
    (c) V_{fin} . . . $[object–[_{VP} [V_{aux}–V_{main}]]]$ (object moves long)
    (d) V_{fin} . . . $[object–[_{VP} [V_{main}–V_{aux}]]]$ (V-raising + object moves long)
    (e) V_{fin} . . . $[_{VP} [V_{aux}–object–V_{main}]]$ (object moves short)

On this hypothesis, Old(er) Icelandic had two optional movements which resemble obligatory movements postulated for German/Dutch by Zwart (1993). First, the main verb can optionally adjoin to the left of a (non-finite) auxiliary, as in (6*b*). Second, the object may optionally move to a specifier position to the left of the verbs, as in (6*c–d*) (with and without V-raising). In addition, Old(er) Icelandic had one more option *not* observed in Standard German, namely short object movement, as in (6*e*), where the landing site of the object precedes the main verb but not the auxiliary (that is, movement of the object internal to the VP).

   More exactly, OV word order would involve raising of the object to [Spec,AgrOP] for Case-checking reasons, both inside and out of the VP. The object movement would be triggered by the strong N-feature of AgrOP, in agreement with the assumption that overt movement is triggered by the necessity to eliminate the strong features in the Spec-head configuration in the functional domain (Chomsky 1993).

Therefore, I conclude that Kayne's (1994) system can account for the word order in the Old(er) Icelandic VP, and the argument movements necessary to derive the existing patterns, but at the price of optionality since the feature triggering the complement movement would be of variable strength. If we follow Kayne's (1994) antisymmetry proposal, according to which all languages have S–H–C order, and combine it with Chomsky's (1993) hypothesis that objects always have their case checked in [Spec,AgrOP], we have to assume that Old(er) Icelandic had a choice between overt and covert object movement to [Spec,AgrOP], whereas Modern Icelandic only has this movement in covert syntax. The optionality of the complement movements in Old(er) Icelandic seems to violate Chomsky's (1993) principle of Procrastinate, which says that covert movements are preferred to movements before Spell Out. If movement can be procrastinated, we expect it always to be. Hence, the optionality in complement movement might concern the strength of features of functional heads that trigger the movement. One possible way to get around the economy problems is then simply to assume that while AgrOP and PredP have weak N-features in Modern Icelandic (postponing the movements of DPs, PPs, and small clause predicates until LF), they have had optionally (weak and) strong features in Old(er) Icelandic, forming both VO- and OV-orders.

Although I have shown that it is possible to derive all the attested word-order patterns by assuming SVO word order base with overt versus covert object movements in the history of Icelandic, this hypothesis does not easily handle the diachronic aspect. With regard to the word order within (and out of) the VP, Old Icelandic differs from Modern Icelandic in three major aspects, as shown in (5), repeated in (7).

(7) (a) V_{fin} . . . Object–V_{aux}–V_{main}
    (b) V_{fin} . . . V_{aux}–Object–V_{main}
    (c) V_{fin} . . . V_{main}–V_{aux}

All these three word-order patterns are ungrammatical in Modern Icelandic (abstracting away from negative and quantified phrase constructions). The striking fact is that all these three leftward movement processes seem to have disappeared from the language at the same time in the history of Icelandic. Furthermore, the possibility of placing nominal objects, on the one hand, and PPs and small clause predicates, on the other hand, to the left of the main verb also seems to have disappeared from the language at the same time.

Given a uniform VO-base for all stages in the history of Icelandic, together with leftward movements of the complements, the difference noted between Old and Modern Icelandic, the language change in question, must be explained by use of feature strength, as already mentioned: strong versus weak N-features in both AgrOP and PredP. However, this proposal would leave some important questions unanswered. First, if the decline of the OV word order was subject to the disappearance of the strong features in question, it would be necessary to assume that the N-features in AgrOP and PredP both became obligatorily weak at exactly the same time in the history of Icelandic. This is not easily accounted for within this framework. There is nothing in the theory that predicts or explains this fact.

Second, the hypothesis does not connect the decline of the three operations shown in (7). It is possible, though, to connect the first two operations, the long and the short object movement, if the short object movement was a necessary step in the derivation of the long object movement. Thus, when the short object movement disappeared, so did the long object movement. However, the third leftward movement, the movement of the non-finite main verb to the left of the non-finite auxiliary verb, would always be independent of the object movements (this is, for instance, supported by the difference between German and Dutch). Hence, there is nothing in the theory that leads us to expect this process to have disappeared from the language at the same time as the other two leftward movement processes.

Third, there is the question of morphology. More exactly, the question of why the relevant features triggering the overt leftward movements in question have been weakened (or lost their possibility of being strong) in the history of Icelandic. According to my proposal, the old language contained optional leftward movements of the complements in overt syntax, while these are ungrammatical in overt syntax in the modern language. Hence, the parameter change in question has to do with the loss of the relevant strong N-features, leading to the impossibility of movements due to UG-internal economy condition (the Procrastinate Principle). This leads to the question of why the relevant strong N-features disappeared from the language, and why they disappeared at the same time.

It is a well-known fact that languages with rich case morphology have freer word order than languages without rich case-morphology, which tend to have a more rigid word order. Roberts (1997), for instance, has recently linked the cause of word order changes in the history of English to inflection—more precisely, the loss of morphological case marking. This implies that some morphological changes might have occurred in the late Icelandic period, causing the decline of OV word order. However, this does not have any empirical support since the agreement system and case in Modern Icelandic are as rich as they were in Old Icelandic. In fact, Icelandic has the richest overt inflectional system of any modern Germanic language.

13.3.3. *Remnant VP-preposing*

13.3.3.1. *Introduction*

Due to the shortcomings of the uniform VO-base hypothesis, as proposed earlier, with regard to the diachronic aspect, it might be desirable to revise the proposal in the direction of a theory of interacting movements. Because there has not been any overt weakening of the status of the morphological system in the history of Icelandic, I will propose that the morphological features relevant for the triggering of leftward object movements in Old(er) Icelandic were indeed not weakened. Instead, the objects still have to move to the left of the main verb (say, to [Spec,AgrOP]) in overt syntax in Modern Icelandic.

My proposal has properties in common with Kayne's (1998) analysis of negative/focus constructions. In this chapter, I want to generalize Kayne's proposal. In his paper, Kayne does not propose that every single instance of VO in English involves VP-preposing. In particular, he does not propose there that ordinary non-quantified, non-negative, non-focused objects involve a derivation with VP-preposing. More precisely, Kayne (1998) claims that there are no covert movements, so that it is necessary to postulate overt movements of (quantified, negative or focused) arguments to the left of the VP, followed by a remnant VP-fronting to the left of the already extracted arguments, deriving VO word order again. One of the aims of Kayne's paper is to account for negative phrase constructions, the difference between English and the Scandinavian languages. The Scandinavian negative phrase construction has some similarity with the English construction 'I have seen nobody', which Kayne argues involves a step parallel to the Icelandic preposing, with the difference that in English there is a further operation (lacking in Icelandic) that 'undoes' the change in word order affected by the first preposing step. In other words, negative as well as quantified and focused arguments must exit the VP. However, he claims that the second step in the derivation, the VP-preposing, only takes place in English and not in Icelandic nor the Mainland Scandinavian languages.[1]

Generalizing this idea, I propose that the crucial difference between VO-languages (like English) and OV-languages (like Dutch) is that the OV-languages lack the last step in the derivation, that is, the VP-preposing. In VO-languages, on the other hand, the overt movement of the objects is masked by the subsequent movement of the VP. Thus, the landing site of the objects in OV-languages is not obscured by VP-preposing the way it is in VO-languages (see also Hinterhölzl 1997 and Johnson 1996). In sum, the proposal makes it possible to eliminate covert movement altogether and replace it with a combination of overt movements.

The picture is a bit more complicated for mixed OV/VO languages, such as Old(er) Icelandic, especially since it follows from the generalized remnant VP-preposing analysis that Icelandic must have been a VO-language throughout its history. However, I will show that it is possible to derive all the attested OV word-order patterns in Old(er) Icelandic with the tools of this framework, by means of three main derivations: (*a*) obligatory movement of the direct object

---

[1] This can be made consistent with our proposal by assuming that Icelandic and the Mainland Scandinavian languages have VP-preposing, as well as English, but not to a position higher than the fronted negative/quantified phrase.

out of the VP (to [Spec,AgrOP] in the functional domain) at all stages in the history of Icelandic, together with (*b*) optional extraction of the embedded VP from the matrix VP in the old language, followed by (*c*) obligatory preposing of the remnant VP, containing at least the finite auxiliary verb in VO-languages, including all stages of (attested) Icelandic.

The main advantage with this proposal is that, in addition to deriving the attested word-order patterns, we can account for the decline of the various leftward movement processes. More exactly, this proposal has an answer to the diachronic question, addressed earlier: why all the various OV word-order patterns disappeared from the language at the same time in the history of Icelandic.

13.3.3.2. *Outline*

The diachronic problem, as mentioned, is that we do not want three unrelated changes. Hence, it is necessary to unify (*a*), (*b*), and (*c*) in example (7), repeated below.

(7) (*a*) V_{fin} . . . Object–V_{aux}–V_{main}
     (*b*) V_{fin} . . . V_{aux}–Object–V_{main}
     (*c*) V_{fin} . . . V_{main}–V_{aux}

On the earlier proposed DP/PP-movement approach (the uniform VO-base hypothesis), no unification (by implicational relationship) is possible. That is, there is no reason to expect the loss of the verb cluster [V_{main}–V_{aux}] to have caused the loss of leftward movement of objects, nor vice versa. Therefore, I will attempt unification by reversing the implicational relationship, that is, I will show that the loss of the three word-order patterns in (7) holds on two plausible assumptions.

The first assumption is that (Germanic) VO derives from OV by raising the verb across the object overtly extracted from VP, and that Old Icelandic in fact was a VO-language. More precisely, Old(er) Icelandic has the preposing of the finite VP (typical for VO-languages), but it also has the VP-out-of-VP phenomenon, characteristic of OV-languages such as German, and the [V_{main}–V_{aux}] pattern (unlike Dutch which does not have this VP-out-of-VP option).

So far, I have remained vague as to exactly how the finite verb comes to end up preceding its complements. As suggested in recent work by Kayne (1998), Hinterhölzl (1997), H. Koopman and Szabolcsi (1997), I will now assume that the verb can only be raised as a part of a (remnant) VP raising to [Spec,FP] above the positions of the complements extracted from it. On this view, the intermediate structure [Object [V_{fin} [V_{main} t_{Object}]]] would still only yield the VO-order [V_{fin}–V_{main}–Object] (as a result of raising the matrix VP). In order to get [V_{fin}–Object–V_{main}], we must have a further step leading to [Object [V_{main} t_{Object}] [V_{fin} t_{VP}]], that is, the embedded VP must extract from the matrix VP. This extraction is arguably also what leads to the [V_{main}–V_{aux}] word order in general.

Therefore, if the [V_{main}–V_{aux}] option is lost, the Modern Icelandic strict VO-order is an automatic consequence, since both [V_{main}–V_{aux}] and [Object–V_{main}] are derived by the same process. Hence, only one parametric change is needed to account for the change from Old to Modern Icelandic.

13.3.3.3. *Implementation*

I assume that the sentence in Old and Modern Icelandic (in fact, in all Germanic VO-languages) is constructed as shown in (8), that is, uniformly VO where each verb has its own VP-projection and PredP-projection.[2]

(8) (*a*)   *Initial order*:

FP [$_{\text{AgrOP}}$ [$_{\text{PredPfin}}$ [$_{\text{VPfin}}$ **V$_{\text{fin}}$** [$_{\text{PredPaux}}$ [$_{\text{VPaux}}$ **V$_{\text{aux}}$** [$_{\text{PredPmain}}$
[$_{\text{VPmain}}$ **V$_{\text{main}}$ object**]]]]]]]

(*b*)   *Initial order*:

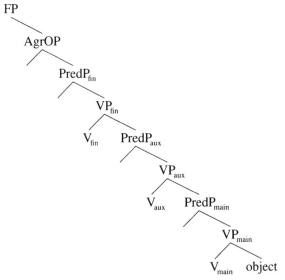

Moreover, in Old and Modern Icelandic (both VO-languages), each extended verb-projection contains FP which attracts VP to its Spec, across intervening complements. This happens whether the verb is finite or not, an auxiliary verb or a main verb. Thus, 'short' object movement always leads to VO-order, and the object must have moved 'long' in order to derive OV-order in Old(er) Icelandic. In order to obtain successive cyclic application of VP-extraction resulting in intermediate structures of the form [[V$_{\text{main}}$ V$_{\text{aux}}$] [V$_{\text{fin}}$ . . .]], I take VP-extraction to be PredP-extraction, that is, VP-extraction is to be implemented as movement to [Spec,PredP], where PredP is immediately above the VP. Assuming that only the VP, not the PredP, raises to [Spec,FP] (across the complements), the final step of the derivation always puts the finite verb in front of its complements.

Finally, the movements must obey the following constraints. First, VP for each

---

[2] In what follows, I will only show a somewhat simplified version of this, leaving out AgrOP and FP as well as all empty heads (AgrO, Pred, etc.).

verb (finite or non-finite, modal or auxiliary or main verb) is attracted to the
specifier of its own FP across intervening material. However, if PredP-extraction
has first occurred, VP cannot move to the specifier of its own FP. Second, the
object must move to some [Spec,AgrOP] position. It moves as far as it can,
depending upon the status of the projections that dominate it (coherent vs. incoherent). If all the FPs are coherent, the object moves to [Spec,AgrOP$_{fin}$],
otherwise it lands in [Spec,AgrOP] of the lowest incoherent projection.

The three main transformations are shown in the following tree-structures,
both for Old(er) and Modern Icelandic, where the crucial difference is that the
VP-out-of-VP option (where PredP$_{main}$ moves to [Spec,PredP$_{fin}$]) has been lost in
the modern language.

(9)   *Old(er) Icelandic*

   (*a*)   First step: PredP$_{main}$ moves to [Spec,PredP$_{fin}$]

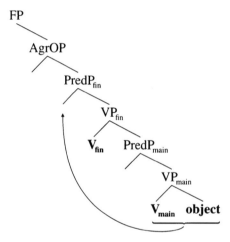

   (*b*)   Second step: DP moves to [Spec,AgrOP]

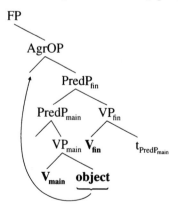

(c)   Third step: VP$_{fin}$ (remnant finite VP) moves to [Spec,FP]

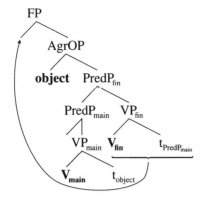

This derives the OV word order [V$_{fin}$–object–V$_{main}$].

(10)   *Modern Icelandic*

(a)   First step: DP moves to [Spec,AgrOP]

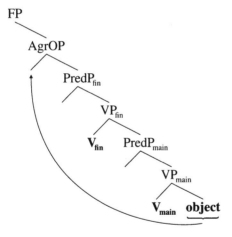

(*b*)   Second step: VP$_{fin}$ (remnant finite VP) moves to [Spec,FP]

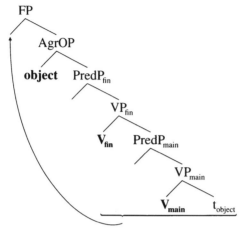

This derives the VO word order [V$_{fin}$–V$_{main}$–object].

Let us now compare these derivations to the earlier proposed argument movements, where (11) to (19) illustrate the possible derivations for some common word-order patterns in Old(er) Icelandic, given the tools of our proposal. The derivations shown in (11) and (12) would be the analysis of a (Modern Icelandic) VO sentence. There are actually two options to derive pure VO word order, depending on whether the complement is coherent/transparent or incoherent.[3] In (11), the object moves long, and if nothing else can be extracted, the finite VP preposes, containing not only the finite verb, but also the non-finite ones; thus, they end up to the left of the moved object. In (12), the object has moved short, and since this is a VO-language, the verb (the main verb) must move in front of it, deriving VO word order again.

(11)   [*V$_{fin}$–V$_{aux}$–V$_{main}$–object*]

(*a*)   Initial order:

[$_{PredPfin}$ [$_{VPfin}$ **V$_{fin}$** [$_{PredPaux}$ [$_{VPaux}$ **V$_{aux}$** [$_{PredPmain}$ [$_{VPmain}$ **V$_{main}$ object**]]]]]]

(*b*)   Object moves long (coherent complement):

object [$_{PredPfin}$ [$_{VPfin}$ **V$_{fin}$** [$_{PredPaux}$ [$_{VPaux}$ **V$_{aux}$** [$_{PredPmain}$ [$_{VPmain}$ **V$_{main}$**
t$_{object}$]]]]]]

(*c*)   VP$_{fin}$ moves to [Spec,FP]:

[$_{VPfin}$ **V$_{fin}$** [$_{PredPaux}$ [$_{VPaux}$ **V$_{aux}$** [$_{PredPmain}$ [$_{VPmain}$ **V$_{main}$** t$_{object}$]]]]] **object**
[$_{PredPfin}$ t$_{VPfin}$]

---

[3] I use the label 'IC' for 'Incoherent Complement' in the following examples. Hinterhölzl (1997), among others, assumes that there are two types of full sentential infinitival complements: incoherent/ opaque CPs and coherent/transparent CPs. While the coherent infinitives are *transparent* for several types of extraction processes/restructuring effects, the incoherent infinitives block long-distance scrambling/restructuring. See further discussion in Hróarsdóttir (1999*b*).

(12) $[V_{fin}-V_{aux}-V_{main}-object]$

  (a) Initial order:

    $[_{PredPfin} [_{VPfin}$ **V**$_{fin}$ $[_{PredPaux} [_{VPaux}$ **V**$_{aux}$ $[_{PredPmain} [_{VPmain}$ **V**$_{main}$ **object**$]]]]]]$

  (b) Object moves short (incoherent complement):

    $[_{PredPfin} [_{VPfin}$ **V**$_{fin}$ $[_{PredPaux} [_{VPaux}$ **V**$_{aux}$ **[object]** $[_{PredPmain} [_{VPmain}$ **V**$_{main}$
    $t_{object}]]]]]]$

  (c) VP$_{main}$ moves to [Spec,FP]:

    $[_{PredPfin} [_{VPfin}$ **V**$_{fin}$ $[_{PredPaux} [_{VPaux}$ **V**$_{aux}$ $[_{IC} [_{VPmain}$ **V**$_{main}$ $t_{object}]]$ **[object]**
    $[_{PredPmain}$ $t_{VPmain}]]]]]$

Example (13) shows the derivation of a simple OV word order, derived by the
possibility of extracting VPs out of VPs (moving PredPs into Spec of PredPs by
cyclic application).

(13) $[V_{fin}-object-V_{main}]$

  (a) Initial order:

    $[_{PredPfin} [_{VPfin}$ **V**$_{fin}$ $[_{PredPmain} [_{VPmain}$ **V**$_{main}$ **object**$]]]]$

  (b) PredP$_{main}$ moves to [Spec,PredP$_{fin}$] (the German option):

    $[_{PredPfin} [_{PredPmain} [_{VPmain}$ **V**$_{main}$ **object**$]]$ $[_{VPfin}$ **V**$_{fin}$ $[t_{PredPmain}]]]$

  (c) Object moves long:

    object $[_{PredPfin} [_{PredPmain} [_{VPmain}$ **V**$_{main}$ $t_{object}]]$ $[_{VPfin}$ **V**$_{fin}$ $[t_{PredPmain}]]]$

  (d) VP$_{fin}$ moves to [Spec,FP]:

    $[_{VPfin}$ **V**$_{fin}$ $[t_{PredPmain}]]$ **object** $[_{PredPfin} [_{PredPmain} [_{VPmain}$ **V**$_{main}$ $t_{object}]]$ $[t_{VPfin}]]$

Example (14) illustrates the derivation of the $[V_{main}-V_{aux}]$ order, previously called
V-raising. This order now simply reflects the VP-out-of-VP option. Alternatively,
it is possible to derive this order in a more complex way, as shown in (15),
depending on the relative position of the object in this respect.

(14) $[V_{fin}-V_{main}-V_{aux}]$

  (a) Initial order:

    $[_{PredPfin} [_{VPfin}$ **V**$_{fin}$ $[_{PredPaux} [_{VPaux}$ **V**$_{aux}$ $[_{PredPmain} [_{VPmain}$ **V**$_{main}]]]]]]$

  (b) PredP$_{main}$ moves to [Spec,PredP$_{aux}$] (the German option):

    $[_{PredPfin} [_{VPfin}$ **V**$_{fin}$ $[_{PredPaux} [_{PredPmain} [_{VPmain}$ **V**$_{main}]]]$ $[_{VPaux}$ **V**$_{aux}]]$ $[t_{PredPmain}]]$

  (c) VP$_{fin}$ moves to [Spec,FP]:

    $[_{VPfin}$ **V**$_{fin}$ $[_{PredPaux} [_{PredPmain} [_{VPmain}$ **V**$_{main}]]]$ $[_{VPaux}$ **V**$_{aux}]$ $[t_{PredPmain}]]$ $[_{PredPfin}$
    $t_{VPfin}]$

(15) $[V_{fin}-V_{main}-V_{aux}]$

  (a) Initial order:

    $[_{PredPfin} [_{VPfin}$ **V**$_{fin}$ $[_{PredPaux} [_{VPaux}$ **V**$_{aux}$ $[_{PredPmain} [_{VPmain}$ **V**$_{main}]]]]]]$

  (b) PredP$_{main}$ moves to [Spec,PredP$_{aux}$] (the German option):

    $[_{PredPfin} [_{VPfin}$ **V**$_{fin}$ $[_{PredPaux} [_{PredPmain} [_{VPmain}$ **V**$_{main}]]]$ $[_{VPaux}$ **V**$_{aux}]]$ $[t_{PredPmain}]]$

(c) PredP$_{aux}$ moves to [Spec,PredP$_{fin}$] (the German option):

$[_{PredPfin} [_{PredPaux} [_{PredPmain} [_{VPmain} \mathbf{V_{main}}]] [_{VPaux} \mathbf{V_{aux}}] [t_{PredPmain}]] [_{VPfin} \mathbf{V_{fin}}$ $t_{PredPaux}]]$

(d) VP$_{fin}$ moves to [Spec,FP]:

$[_{VPfin} \mathbf{V_{fin}} t_{PredPaux}] [_{PredPfin} [_{PredPaux} [_{PredPmain} [_{VPmain} \mathbf{V_{main}}]] [_{VPaux} \mathbf{V_{aux}}$ $[t_{PredPmain}]]] [t_{VPfin}]]$

In (16) to (19), there are examples showing that by combining these three derivations—VPs out of VPs, object movement, and finite VP-preposing—it is possible to derive all the various OV (pure and mixed) word-order patterns. These are the only three main derivational possibilities (two of them are obligatory), and the option is simply whether or not we choose to take VPs out of VPs and how often. This analysis also has one big advantage that many other analyses of OV/VO word order must stipulate: it does not permit the derivation of $[V_{main}$–O–$V_{aux}]$ word order, nor $[V_{main}$–O–$V_{fin}]$ for languages like Old English, where movement of VP$_{fin}$ to [Spec,FP$_{fin}$] is not obligatory.

(16) $[V_{fin}$–V_{main}–V_{aux}–*object*]

(a) Initial order:

$[_{PredPfin} [_{VPfin} \mathbf{V_{fin}} [_{PredPaux} [_{VPaux} \mathbf{V_{aux}} [_{PredPmain} [_{VPmain} \mathbf{V_{main}} \mathbf{object}]]]]]]$

(b) PredP$_{main}$ moves to [Spec,PredP$_{aux}$] (the German option):

$[_{PredPfin} [_{VPfin} \mathbf{V_{fin}} [_{PredPaux} [_{PredPmain} [_{VPmain} \mathbf{V_{main}} \mathbf{object}]] [_{VPaux} \mathbf{V_{aux}}$ $[t_{PredPmain}]]]]]$

(c) Object moves long:

$\mathbf{object} [_{PredPfin} [_{VPfin} \mathbf{V_{fin}} [_{PredPaux} [_{PredPmain} [_{VPmain} \mathbf{V_{main}} t_{object}]] [_{VPaux} \mathbf{V_{aux}}$ $[t_{PredPmain}]]]]]$

(d) VP$_{fin}$ moves to [Spec,FP]:

$[_{VPfin} \mathbf{V_{fin}} [_{PredPaux} [_{PredPmain} [_{VPmain} \mathbf{V_{main}} t_{object}]] [_{VPaux} \mathbf{V_{aux}} [t_{PredPmain}]]]]$ $\mathbf{object} [_{PredPfin} t_{VPfin}]$

(17) $[V_{fin}$–*object*–V_{aux}–$V_{main}]$

(a) Initial order:

$[_{PredPfin} [_{VPfin} \mathbf{V_{fin}} [_{PredPaux} [_{VPaux} \mathbf{V_{aux}} [_{PredPmain} [_{VPmain} \mathbf{V_{main}} \mathbf{object}]]]]]]$

(b) PredP$_{aux}$ moves to [Spec,PredP$_{fin}$]

$[_{PredPfin} [_{PredPaux} [_{VPaux} \mathbf{V_{aux}} [_{PredPmain} [_{VPmain} \mathbf{V_{main}} \mathbf{object}]]]] [_{VPfin} \mathbf{V_{fin}} t_{PredPaux}]]$

(c) Object moves long:

$\mathbf{object} [_{PredPfin} [_{PredPaux} [_{VPaux} \mathbf{V_{aux}} [_{PredPmain} [_{VPmain} \mathbf{V_{main}} t_{object}]]]] [_{VPfin}$ $\mathbf{V_{fin}} t_{PredPaux}]]$

(d) VP$_{fin}$ moves to [Spec,FP]:

$[_{VPfin} \mathbf{V_{fin}} t_{PredPaux}] \mathbf{object} [_{PredPfin} [_{PredPaux} [_{VPaux} \mathbf{V_{aux}} [_{PredPmain} [_{VPmain}$ $\mathbf{V_{main}} t_{object}]]]] [t_{VPfin}]]$

(18) $[V_{fin}-V_{aux}-object-V_{main}]$

    (*a*)   Initial order:

        $[_{\text{PredPfin}}\,[_{\text{VPfin}}\,\mathbf{V_{fin}}\,[_{\text{PredPaux}}\,[_{\text{VPaux}}\,\mathbf{V_{aux}}\,[_{\text{PredPmain}}\,[_{\text{VPmain}}\,\mathbf{V_{main}}\,\mathbf{object}]]]]]]$

    (*b*)   PredP$_{\text{main}}$ moves to [Spec,PredP$_{\text{aux}}$]

        $[_{\text{PredPfin}}\,[_{\text{VPfin}}\,\mathbf{V_{fin}}\,[_{\text{PredPaux}}\,[_{\text{PredPmain}}\,[_{\text{VPmain}}\,\mathbf{V_{main}}\,\mathbf{object}]]\,[_{\text{VPaux}}\,\mathbf{V_{aux}}$
        $t_{\text{PredPmain}}]]]]$

    (*c*)   Object moves short (incoherent complement):

        $[_{\text{PredPfin}}\,[_{\text{VPfin}}\,\mathbf{V_{fin}}]\,\mathbf{object}\,[_{\text{PredPaux}}\,[_{\text{PredPmain}}\,[_{\text{VPmain}}\,\mathbf{V_{main}}\,t_{\text{object}}]]\,[_{\text{VPaux}}\,\mathbf{V_{aux}}$
        $t_{\text{PredPmain}}]]]$

    (*d*)   VP$_{\text{aux}}$ moves to [Spec,FP]:

        $[_{\text{PredPfin}}\,[_{\text{VPfin}}\,\mathbf{V_{fin}}]]\,[_{\text{IC}}\,[_{\text{VPaux}}\,\mathbf{V_{aux}}\,t_{\text{PredPmain}}]]\,\mathbf{object}\,[_{\text{PredPaux}}\,[_{\text{PredPmain}}$
        $[_{\text{VPmain}}\,\mathbf{V_{main}}\,t_{\text{object}}]]\,[t_{\text{VPaux}}]]$

(19) $[V_{fin}-object-V_{main}-V_{aux}]$

    (*a*)   Initial order:

        $[_{\text{PredPfin}}\,[_{\text{VPfin}}\,\mathbf{V_{fin}}\,[_{\text{PredPaux}}\,[_{\text{VPaux}}\,\mathbf{V_{aux}}\,[_{\text{PredPmain}}\,[_{\text{VPmain}}\,\mathbf{V_{main}}\,\mathbf{object}]]]]]]$

    (*b*)   PredP$_{\text{main}}$ moves to [Spec,PredP$_{\text{aux}}$]:

        $[_{\text{PredPfin}}\,[_{\text{VPfin}}\,\mathbf{V_{fin}}\,[_{\text{PredPaux}}\,[_{\text{PredPmain}}\,[_{\text{VPmain}}\,\mathbf{V_{main}}\,\mathbf{object}]]\,[_{\text{VPaux}}\,\mathbf{V_{aux}}$
        $t_{\text{PredPmain}}]]]]$

    (*c*)   PredP$_{\text{aux}}$ moves to [Spec,PredP$_{\text{fin}}$]:

        $[_{\text{PredPfin}}\,[_{\text{PredPaux}}\,[_{\text{PredPmain}}\,[_{\text{VPmain}}\,\mathbf{V_{main}}\,\mathbf{object}]]\,[_{\text{VPaux}}\,\mathbf{V_{aux}}\,t_{\text{PredPmain}}]]\,[_{\text{VPfin}}$
        $\mathbf{V_{fin}}\,t_{\text{PredPaux}}]]$

    (*d*)   Object moves long:

        $\mathbf{object}\,[_{\text{PredPfin}}\,[_{\text{PredPaux}}\,[_{\text{PredPmain}}\,[_{\text{VPmain}}\,\mathbf{V_{main}}\,t_{\text{object}}]]\,[_{\text{VPaux}}\,\mathbf{V_{aux}}\,t_{\text{PredPmain}}]]$
        $[_{\text{VPfin}}\,\mathbf{V_{fin}}\,t_{\text{PredPaux}}]]$

    (*e*)   VP$_{\text{fin}}$ moves to [Spec,FP]:

        $[_{\text{VPfin}}\,\mathbf{V_{fin}}\,t_{\text{PredPaux}}]\,\mathbf{object}\,[_{\text{PredPfin}}\,[_{\text{PredPaux}}\,[_{\text{PredPmain}}\,[_{\text{VPmain}}\,\mathbf{V_{main}}\,t_{\text{object}}]]$
        $[_{\text{VPaux}}\,\mathbf{V_{aux}}\,t_{\text{PredPmain}}]]\,[t_{\text{VPfin}}]]$

Given the remnant VP-hypothesis, all the OV word-order patterns shown above would disappear as soon as the possibility of the extraction of VPs out of VPs (PredPs into Spec of PredPs) was lost. In other words, the remnant finite VP will always necessarily contain all the non-finite verbs in addition to the finite verb (in the appropriate order), and the preposing of this remnant VP will always mask the object movement, deriving VO word order only.

Finally, word-order patterns with PP complements could in principle be regarded as ambiguous: either the PP moves into the lowest [Spec,PredP] position, and then moves along with the main verb when PredP$_{\text{main}}$ moves to [Spec, PredP$_{\text{fin}}$], or, the PP moves long in a similar way to long DP-movement. There are reasons to choose the latter derivation here for PPs, but the former for verbal particles, instead of a derivation where both the particle and the PP undergo 'long' movement (see Hróarsdóttir 1999b). The existence of word-order patterns with a verbal particle would be consistent with the proposal of allowing only verbal particles, VPs, and PredPs in [Spec,PredP] and having a separate F_{XP} position above PredP for PPs. In sum, it seems that the term 'PredP' in the Koster/Zwart sense is simply a cover term for a projection licensing non-DP arguments, whereas the notion 'PredP' in the outline of our basic analysis is more specific. It refers to a projection whose Spec-position may host a VP (and a particle). Hence, based on the existence of $[PP-V_{aux}-V_{main}]$ and the absence of $[particle-V_{aux}-V_{main}]$ in Old(er) Icelandic, I claim that particles can either move 'short' (local) or stay *in situ*. PPs (and other full phrase predicates), on the other hand, can move long. So far I have remained vague as to where exactly the PP moves. I will conclude by claiming that PPs move to a special PP-position (call it [Spec,AgrPP]), rather than moving to the highest [Spec,PredP]. Hence, it becomes necessary to depart from the formulation of 'PredP' in the sense of Koster/Zwart and rather think of 'PredP' in the sense of Hinterhölzl.

13.3.4. *Summary*

In sum, the remnant VP-preposing hypothesis can account for all the various attested pure and mixed word-order patterns in Old(er) Icelandic, in addition to providing the diachronic account by explaining the language change in question in terms of a single parameter change, leading to the superficial loss of all the other attested OV word-order patterns. In the end, the relative base order of the verb and the object plays no role in the analysis, in particular since the object always moves. This gives the comparative Germanic correlation set out in Table 13.4.

TABLE 13.4. *Comparative Germanic Correlation (CGC)*

	VP-preposing	VP-out-of-VP
Icelandic, English, The Mainland Scandinavian languages	yes	no
Old(er) Icelandic	yes	optional
German	no	yes
Dutch	no	no

An additional step in the derivation raises the finite verb to the verb-second position. This movement applies (in main clauses) in the Germanic verb-second languages, and both in subordinate and main clauses in Icelandic. As discussed in the following section, I assume this verb movement to the verb-second position to be a head movement, rather than VP-raising.

The Comparative Germanic Correlation in Table 13.4 raises the following three problems. First, in languages where both VP_{fin} movement to $[Spec,FP_{fin}]$ and PredP movement to [Spec,PredP] are optional (like Old English), in clauses with three verbs (finite, aux, and main), it is possible to derive $[V_{aux}-V_{main}-V_{fin}]$ word order by moving $PredP_{aux}$ to $[Spec,PredP_{fin}]$. However, this order is not attested in any West Germanic language unless V_{fin} is an auxiliary (cf. Zwart 1996). This, in some ways, is the [V_{main}–O–V_{aux}] problem in another guise, since it is a head-initial VP embedded in a head-final VP. The generalization that must be captured is that if the highest VP is head-final in surface word order, then all of the embedded VPs must be head-final as well. Second, the picture is more complicated for the history of English: OV word order is found (at a low frequency) throughout Middle English, but in the Penn–Helsinki Parsed Corpus of Middle English, there is only one instance of [V_{fin}–V_{main}–V_{aux}] order out of 1,048 clauses with three verbs of the relevant type (Susan Pintzuk, p.c.). Third, this analysis does not handle all the possibilities for the order of verbs within verb clusters in languages like Dutch, where so-called verb raising is optional and other orders are possible (see Zwart 1996 for a full discussion).

13.4. VERB MOVEMENT, VP-MOVEMENT, AND V2

The question whether the VO word order of Icelandic results from more verb movement or more VP-movement than in related OV-languages is related to the behaviour of verbal particles in the Germanic VO- and OV-languages. There are two interesting facts to note in this respect as discussed in Taraldsen (to appear). First, the ordering with respect to the verb is [particle–verb] in the OV-languages, while it is [verb–particle] in the VO-languages. Second, while the particle can precede the DP object in (most) VO-languages, it invariably follows all complements in the Germanic OV-languages. This is illustrated for Icelandic in (20) and Dutch in (21).

(20) (*a*)   Hann hendir kettinum út
         he   throws cat-the   out

     (*b*)   Hann hendir út   kettinum
         he   throws out cat-the

(21) (*a*)   Hij schakelt het licht uit
         he turns   the light off

     (*b*)   *Hij schakelt uit het licht
         he turns   off the light

     (*c*)   omdat   hij het licht uitschakelt
         because he the light off-turns

     (*d*)   *omdat   hij uit het licht schakelt
         because he off the light turns

As Hinterhölzl (1997) and Taraldsen (to appear) both mention, certain occurrences of verbal particles in the Germanic languages cannot be derived by incorporation in terms of head movement, but must involve some XP-movement instead. This is actually one of the main motivations for Hinterhölzl's analysis of verb-raising in terms of an XP-movement of a VP or some bigger projection.

In Dutch, a verbal particle can either precede the verb cluster (created by verb-raising), or it can become part of the verb cluster, as illustrated in (22) (examples from Hinterhölzl 1997: 9).

(22) (*a*)　dat Jan Marie op wil　　bellen
　　　　　　that Jan Marie up wants call

　　　(*b*)　dat Jan Marie wil　　op bellen
　　　　　　that Jan Marie wants up call
　　　　　　'that Jan wants to call up Marie'

In Old(er) Icelandic, only the latter possibility is possible for preverbal particles (resulting from short particle movement in Old(er) Icelandic). 'If we assume that verb-particles in Dutch are not licensed via incorporation but by XP-movement to either [Spec,PredP] or [Spec,F1P], then the cases in which a to-infinitive has been raised with its particle that are so problematic for the standard theory [. . .] fall in place nicely [. . .]' (Hinterhölzl 1997: 16). This is illustrated in (23) below.

(23)　　　dat Jan [Marie]$_{TP}$ probeerde [$_{CP}$ [$_{F1P}$ [$_{PP}$ op] te [$_{VP}$ bellen t$_{PP}$]] t$_{TP}$]
　　　　　that Jan Marie　tried　　　　　　　　　up to　　　call
　　　　　'that Jan tried to call up Marie'

Assuming a uniform and universal S–H–C order of constituents (in the spirit of Kayne 1994), it not only becomes necessary for the direct object to follow the verb in base word order (regardless of whether it is a surface OV- or VO-language), it also becomes necessary for the verbal particle to occur in a postverbal position. I assume the particle to constitute a small clause together with the DP object; hence the base word order for both the OV- and the VO-languages must be along the lines shown in (24).

(24) [$_{VP}$ verb [$_{SC}$ DP [particle]]]

　　　(*a*)　henda kettinum út　　　　　　　　　　　　　　　　*(Icelandic)*
　　　　　　throw cat-the　out

　　　(*b*)　slå lyset　　av　　　　　　　　　　　　　　　　　*(Norwegian)*
　　　　　　turn light-the off

　　　(*c*)　schakel het licht uit　　　　　　　　　　　　　　　*(Dutch)*
　　　　　　turn　　the light off

According to my remnant VP-preposing hypothesis, the first step in the derivation must raise the direct object obligatorily out of the VP into [Spec,AgrOP] in all the languages, as illustrated for Icelandic and Dutch in (25).

(25) [$_{AgrOP}$ DP [$_{VP}$ verb [$_{SC}$ t$_{DP}$ [particle]]]]

　　　(*a*)　kettinum hendir út　　　　　　　　　　　　　　　*(Icelandic)*
　　　　　　cat-the　　throws out

(b)   het licht schakelt uit   (*Dutch*)
       the light turns   off

The second step in the derivation distinguishes the two languages, and OV- and VO-languages in general, where the remnant VP raises to [Spec,FP] above the extracted direct object. As a result, the verb is situated to the left of its complements (even in embedded non-verb-second clauses). As noted earlier, the particle can at this point be situated inside the VP, as a result of it raising together with the verb within the remnant VP, acquiring its position to the left of the object. As no such movement applies in OV-languages, according to our hypothesis, the particle cannot raise across the object in OV-languages. This is illustrated in (26).

(26)   [$_{FP}$ [$_{VP}$ verb [$_{SC}$ t$_{DP}$ [particle]]] [$_{AgrOP}$ DP t$_{VP}$]]
        hendir út   kettinum   (*Icelandic; remnant VP-preposing*)
        throws out cat-the

The third step in the derivation, then, raises the finite verb to the verb-second position. This movement applies in both Icelandic (both main and subordinate clauses) and in main clauses in Dutch (since Dutch is a verb-second language in main clauses), but not in English. I wish to claim that the verb movement to the verb-second position is a head movement, rather than VP-raising. This is illustrated for main clauses in (27). If the verb movement to the verb-second position is a head movement, it follows directly that only the finite verb, and not the particle, can raise higher than the negation.

(27)   verb [$_{FP}$ [$_{VP}$ t$_{verb}$ [$_{SC}$ t$_{DP}$ [particle]]] [$_{AgrOP}$ DP t$_{VP}$]]

       (a)   schakelt het licht uit
              turns   the light off

       (b)   hendir (ekki) út   kettinum
              throws (not) out cat-the

This correctly excludes the particle from preceding the DP object in Dutch and other OV-languages, since they lack the remnant VP-preposing.

As already mentioned, on our remnant VP-preposing hypothesis, a particle can be raised across a DP object as part of the remnant VP. This is exemplified for Modern Icelandic in (28) and (29) below. In (28), the particle does not exit the VP, but moves along with VP$_{fin}$ when it moves to [Spec,FP], while in (29), the particle exits the VP and thus stays behind when the finite VP moves. This particle raising needs to precede the other postulated movements, as indicated in (29).

(28) (a)   Jón   hefur hent   út kettinum
            John has   thrown out cat-the

     (b)   Initial order:
            [$_{PredPfin}$ [$_{VPfin}$ **V$_{fin}$** [$_{PredPmain}$ [$_{VPmain}$ **V$_{main}$** **DP particle**]]]]

    (c)   DP moves long:

        DP [$_{PredPfin}$ [$_{VPfin}$ **V$_{fin}$** [$_{PredPmain}$ [$_{VPmain}$ **V$_{main}$** t$_{DP}$ **particle**]]]]

    (d)   VP$_{fin}$ moves to [Spec,FP]:

        [$_{VPfin}$ **V$_{fin}$** [$_{PredPmain}$ [$_{VPmain}$ **V$_{main}$** t$_{DP}$ **particle**]]] **DP** [t$_{PredPfin}$]

(29) (a)   Jón hefur hent   kettinum út
        John has   thrown cat-the   out

    (b)   Initial order:

        [$_{PredPfin}$ [$_{VPfin}$ **V$_{fin}$** [$_{PredPmain}$ [$_{VPmain}$ **V$_{main}$** **DP particle**]]]]

    (c)   Particle moves to [Spec,PredP$_{main}$]:

        [$_{PredPfin}$ [$_{VPfin}$ **V$_{fin}$** [$_{PredPmain}$ **particle** [$_{VPmain}$ **V$_{main}$** **DP** t$_{particle}$]]]]

    (d)   DP moves short (incoherent complement):

        [$_{PredPfin}$ [$_{VPfin}$ **V$_{fin}$**] **DP** [$_{PredPmain}$ **particle** [$_{VPmain}$ **V$_{main}$** t$_{DP}$ t$_{particle}$]]]

    (e)   VP$_{main}$ moves to [Spec,FP]:

        [$_{PredPfin}$ [$_{VPfin}$ **V$_{fin}$**]] [$_{IC}$ [$_{VPmain}$ **V$_{main}$** t$_{DP}$ t$_{particle}$]] **DP** [$_{PredPmain}$ **particle**]
        [t$_{VPmain}$]

In most OV-languages, then, the particle movement must be obligatory, while in Icelandic and Norwegian, it is optional. This explains why particles in the Germanic OV-languages must follow all complements of the verb. Since PredP is situated below AgrOP, the hypothesis correctly predicts the ungrammaticality of the pattern [particle–DP–verb] in the Germanic OV-languages.

13.5. CONCLUSIONS

In this chapter, two ways to account for the loss of OV word-order patterns in the history of Icelandic were discussed, both in line with a uniform VO-base hypothesis. I discussed the possibility of loss of overt leftward movements of objects, leading to covert movements only in Modern Icelandic. On this view, the parameter change in question would have to do with the loss of the relevant strong features in the functional domain: the N-features of both AgrOP and PredP. Hence, the word-order change, the decline of OV word order, would be described as a reflection of a parameter change, eliminating the relevant strong N-features in [Spec,AgrOP] and [Spec,PredP], within the VP, leading to the unavailability of overt movement of objects (DPs, PPs, and small clause predicates) to the left of the main verb, which in turn has led to the unavailability of scrambling (movement of objects to [Spec,AgrOP] and [Spec,PredP] outside the VP). It was argued that although this approach might yield positive results in the analysis of the Old(er) Icelandic VP, it does not easily handle the diachronic aspect.

    Therefore, I put forward a theory of remnant VP-preposing, which has properties in common with Kayne's (1998) analysis of negative/focus constructions. In short, I assumed three main transformations: (*a*) obligatory leftward movement of the direct object out of the VP (to [Spec,AgrOP] in the functional domain) at all stages in the history of Icelandic, in addition to (*b*) optional extraction of the embedded VP from the matrix VP in Old(er) Icelandic, followed by (*c*) obligatory preposing of the remnant VP, containing the finite auxiliary verb, in Old(er) and Modern Icelandic.

The only major drawback I can see with this proposal is that it needs to explain why the third leftward movement process, the extraction of VPs out of VPs, was lost—a question I do not have an answer to.[4] However, any other analysis seems to have to face this same problem, and at least I have pinpointed the diachronic aspect (the language change in question) to only one parameter change; the loss of a single movement, which is preferable to having to explain three unrelated but simultaneous changes. Of course, this proposal also has to assume a certain optionality with respect to the derivation of OV word-order patterns in Old(er) Icelandic, especially with regard to long versus short object movement, but this optionality problem seems to be a side effect that every possible framework also has to face to some extent.

In sum, we are able to account for all the various attested word-order patterns in Old(er) Icelandic, in addition to providing the diachronic account by explaining the language change in question in terms of a single parameter change. After the loss of the possibility of extracting the embedded VP from the matrix VP, the remnant finite VP will always necessarily contain all the non-finite verbs in addition to the finite verb (in the appropriate order), and the preposing of this remnant VP will always mask the object movement, deriving VO word order only. Hence, I have claimed that the Old(er) Icelandic VP resembled the Modern Icelandic VP much more than it appears to do at first sight, and that the analysis of Icelandic word order is much closer to that of the West Germanic OV-languages than previously believed.

APPENDICES

Appendix A: Primary texts

Ármanns rímur eftir Jón Guðmundsson lærða (1637) og Ármanns þáttur eftir Jón Þorláksson, pp. 91–121. Ed. Jón Helgason. Íslenzk rit síðari alda, vol. I. Copenhagen: Hið íslenzka bókmenntafélag, 1948. [Söguþáttur af Ármanni og Þorsteini gála (Árm). A short narrative story. Date of composition: late seventeenth century. Approximately 900 lines studied (the whole text).]

Árna saga biskups. Ed. Þorleifur Hauksson. Reykjavík: Stofnun Árna Magnússonar in Iceland, 1972. [Árna saga biskups (Árn). Story of bishops. Date of composition: 1375–1400. Approximately 500 lines studied.]

---

[4] Maybe there is no explanation in structural linguistic terms, but only in sociolinguistic terms: a certain type of word order became unfashionable (Anders Holmberg, p.c.).

Biskupasögur Jóns prófasts Haldórssonar í Hítardal. Með viðbæti. Skálholtsbiskupar 1540–1801. Reykjavík: Sögufélagið, 1903–10. [Biskupasögur Jóns prófasts Haldórssonar (Bisk). Story of bishops. Date of composition: 1720–30. Approximately 500 lines studied.]

Dínus saga drambláta. Ed. Jónas Kristjánsson. Riddarasögur I. Reykjavík: Háskóli Íslands, 1960. [Dínus saga drambláta (Dín). Chivalric romance. Date of composition: 1375–1400. Approximately 500 lines studied.]

Ferðasaga úr Borgarfirði vestur að Ísafjarðardjúpi sumarið 1709, ásamt lýsingu á Vatnsfjarðarstað og kirkju. Eptir Jón Eyjólfsson í Ási í Melasveit. Blanda II. Fróðleikur gamall og nýr, pp. 225–39. Reykjavík: Sögufélagið, 1921–3. [Ferðasaga úr Borgarfirði (J. Ey). Travelogue; a story from a journey. Date of composition: 1709. Approximately 335 lines studied (the whole text).]

Finnboga saga ramma. Ed. Hugo Gering. Halle: Verlag der Buchhandlung des Waisenhauses, 1879. [Finnboga saga ramma (Finn). Heroic epic. Date of composition: 1330–70. Approximately 500 lines studied.]

Íslands Árbækur í söguformi. Af Jóni Espólín fyrrum Sýslumanni í Skagafjarðar Sýslu. Copenhagen: Hið íslenzka bókmenntafélag, 1843. [Jón Espólín (Esp). Annual stories, in epical form. Date of composition: first half of the nineteenth century. Approximately 650 lines studied.]

Íslenzkar þjóðsögur og ævintýri. Nýtt safn, vol. VI, pp. 1–39. Collected by Jón Árnason. Ed. Árni Böðvarsson and Bjarni Vilhjálmsson. Reykjavík: Bókaútgáfan Þjóðsaga, 1961. [Álfarit Ólafs í Purkey (Álf). Folk tale, fairy tale. Date of composition: 1820–30. Approximately 650 lines studied.]

Morðbréfabæklingar Guðbrands biskups Þorlákssonar, 1592, 1595 og 1608, með fylgiskjölum. Reykjavík: Sögufélagið, 1902–6. [Afsökunarbréf Jóns Sigmundssonar (Afs). Document/formal letter. Date of composition: 1502–6. Approximately 375 lines studied (the whole text). Transcript made by Bishop Guðbrandur Þorláksson, 1592.]

Morðbréfabæklingar Guðbrands biskups Þorlákssonar, 1592, 1595 og 1608, með fylgiskjölum. Reykjavík: Sögufélagið, 1902–6. [Morðbréfa-bæklingar Guðbrands biskups (Morð). Document. Date of composition: 1592. Approximately 700 lines studied.]

Munnmælasögur 17. aldar. Ed. Bjarni Einarsson. Íslenzk rit síðari alda, vol. VI. Reykjavík: Hið íslenzka fræðafélag í Kaupmannahöfn, 1955. [Munnmælasögur 17. aldar (Munn). Folk tales, in oral tradition. Date of composition: 1686–7. Approximately 700 lines studied.]

Saga Guðmundar Arasonar, Hóla-biskups, eptir Arngrím ábóta. *Biskupa sögur,* vol. II, pp. 1–220. Copenhagen: Hið íslenzka bókmenntafélag, 1878. [Saga Guðmundar Arasonar, Hóla-biskups (Guðm). Story of bishops. Date of composition: 1350–65. Approximately 650 lines studied.]

Sigurðar saga þǫgla. Ed. M. J. Driscoll. Reykjavík: Stofnun Árna Magnússonar in Iceland, 1992. [Sigurðar saga þǫgla (Sig). Icelandic romance. Date of composition: early fifteenth century. Approximately 1000 lines studied.]

Sögu-þáttur um Skálholts biskupa fyrir og um siðaskiptin. *Biskupa sögur,* vol. II, pp. 235–65. Copenhagen: Hið íslenzka bókmenntafélag, 1878. [Sögu-þáttur um Skálholts biskupa (Skál). Story of bishops. Date of composition: late seventeenth century. Approximately 800 lines studied.]

Viktors saga og Blávus. Ed. Jónas Kristjánsson. Riddarasögur II. Reykjavík: Handrita-stofnun Íslands, 1964. [Viktors saga og Blávus (Vikt). Chivalric romance. Date of composition: *c*.1470. Approximately 500 lines studied.]

Æfisaga Jóns prófasts Steingrímssonar eptir sjálfan hann. Reykjavík: Sögufélagið, 1913–16. [Æfisaga Jóns prófasts Steingrímssonar (Próf). Biography. Date of composition: 1785–91. Approximately 800 lines studied.]

Appendix B: Bibliographical information for the nineteenth-century letters

Biskupinn í Görðum. Sendibréf 1810–1853. Ed. Finnur Sigmundsson. Íslenzk sendibréf II. Reykjavík: Bókfellsútgáfan, 1959.

Bjarni Thorarensen, Bréf, vol. I. Ed. by Jón Helgason. Safn Fræðafélagsins um Ísland og Íslendinga XIII. Copenhagen: Hið Íslenzka Fræðafélag í Kaupmannahöfn, 1943.

Doktor Valtýr segir frá. Úr bréfum Valtýs Guðmundssonar til móður sinnar og stjúpa 1878–1927. Ed. Finnur Sigmundsson. Íslenzk sendibréf V. Reykjavík: Bókfellsútgáfan, 1964.

Frásögur um fornaldarleifar 1817–1823, vol. I. Ed. Sveinbjörn Rafnsson. Reykjavík: Stofnun Árna Magnússonar, 1983.

Frásögur um fornaldarleifar 1817–1823, vol. II. Ed. Sveinbjörn Rafnsson. Reykjavík: Stofnun Árna Magnússonar, 1983.

Geir biskup góði í Vínarbréfum 1790–1823. Ed. Finnur Sigmundsson. Íslenzk sendibréf VII. Reykjavík: Bókfellsútgáfan, 1966.

Gömul Reykjavíkurbréf 1835–1899. Ed. Finnur Sigmundsson. Íslenzk sendibréf VI. Reykjavík: Bókfellsútgáfan, 1965.

Hafnarstúdentar skrifa heim. Sendibréf 1825–1836 og 1878–1891. Ed. Finnur Sig-mundsson. Íslenzk sendibréf IV. Reykjavík: Bókfellsútgáfan, 1963.

Konur skrifa bréf. Sendibréf 1797–1907. Ed. Finnur Sigmundsson. Íslenzk sendibréf III. Reykjavík: Bókfellsútgáfan, 1961.

Magnús Stephensen, Brjef. Ed. Hið Íslenska Fræðafjelag í Kaupmannahöfn. Safn Fræðafjelagsins um Ísland og Íslendinga IV. Copenhagen, 1924.

Sendibréf frá íslenzkum konum 1784–1900. Ed. Finnur Sigmundsson. Reykjavík: Helgafell, 1952.

Skrifarinn á Stapa. Sendibréf 1806–1877. Ed. Finnur Sigmundsson. Íslenzk sendibréf I. Reykjavík: Bókfellsútgáfan, 1957.

Þeir segja margt í sendibréfum. Ed. Finnur Sigmundsson. Reykjavík: Bókaútgáfan Þjóðsaga, 1970.

14

Verb Movement in Slavonic Conditionals

DAVID WILLIS

14.1. INTRODUCTION

A striking feature of the historical development of the morphosyntax of a number of Slavonic languages is the reanalysis of what were once inflected conditional auxiliaries as uninflected conditional-mood markers. Such a development has taken place in East Slavonic (Russian, Ukrainian, and Belorussian), Slovak, Lower Sorbian, Slovene, Macedonian, and to some extent also in Serbian.[1] The details of the development vary among the different languages. In Slovak, for instance, the conditional marker co-occurs with the perfect tense, and a form of agreement has been reintroduced; in others it co-occurs with the former past participle alone. The purpose of this chapter is to examine some of the asymmetries between the conditional auxiliary and other auxiliaries in two historical varieties of Slavonic in the hope of moving towards an account of why the loss of an inflected conditional auxiliary should be a feature of Slavonic. The chapter begins (§14.2) by examining the conditional in Old Church Slavonic, a language whose morphosyntactic rules for the conditional may resemble those of the Slavonic parent language. The conditional auxiliary in Old Church Slavonic is traditionally termed a semi-enclitic. This section examines how this term can be integrated into a formal linguistic framework (Principles and Parameters or Minimalism). It is claimed that the conditional auxiliary undergoes movement from T° to C°. The existence of this movement can be deduced from the behaviour of the conditional with respect to negation and pronominal clitics. The second variety under consideration (§14.3) is Old Russian. It is argued that, as compared to Old Church Slavonic, the clitic and non-clitic forms of the auxiliary have been redistributed in Old Russian. For one form, second and third person singular *by*, movement was obligatory. This created the conditions for a change, discussed in §§14.3.4–6, whereby C° became a basic rather than derived position

---

[1] For details of these developments, see Stanislav (1967–73: III.451–2) and Pauliny (1981: 191–2) for Slovak; Stone (1993: 638) for Lower Sorbian, and more generally also Panzer (1967: 24–32).

for the conditional auxiliary. This change is a case of grammaticalization of movement, a process whereby an item acquires the characteristics of the position to which it habitually moves. The implications of such a process for historical linguistics more generally are discussed in §14.4.

14.2. OLD CHURCH SLAVONIC

14.2.1. *The language and its texts*

Old Church Slavonic is the language of a canon of religious texts associated with the missionary activity of SS Cyril and Methodius in Moravia between 863 and 869 and of their followers in the South Slavonic lands in the following two centuries. The texts themselves are written in a South Slavonic dialect, based on the Bulgarian-Macedonian dialect then spoken to the north of the Greek city of Salonika, and the canonical texts date in their current form from the ninth and tenth centuries.

Most of the texts are translated from Greek. For some aspects of historical syntax, this may be a serious problem, and on the whole we should be careful about inferring Old Church Slavonic word-order patterns from the available texts. However, the Old Church Slavonic periphrastic conditional had no direct equivalent in Greek, and the patterns found in the texts are therefore more likely to be representative of contemporary Slavonic usage.

The discussion of Old Church Slavonic is based on exhaustive extraction of conditionals from the Old Church Slavonic Gospels, supplemented by data on other constructions primarily from these texts, but also by available data from other Old Church Slavonic texts, in particular the *Codex Suprasliensis*. Gospel examples are cited from the *Codex Marianus* unless indicated otherwise.

14.2.2. *The conditional in Old Church Slavonic*

The conditional in Old Church Slavonic, as is the general pattern in other conservative Slavonic varieties, is formed using the conditional of the verb *byti* 'to be' plus the active past participle ('*l*-participle').[2] An example is given in (1), and the relevant Old Church Slavonic and (for comparison) Old Russian paradigms are set out in Table 14.1 (see Vaillant 1948: 298). Notice that the second and third person singular forms are identical in all cases, and are the only forms with a zero inflectional ending. The two Old Church Slavonic paradigms coexist, and may reflect dialect differences.[3]

---

[2] Slavonic languages have both an active past participle, used alongside an auxiliary to form periphrastic tenses and aspects in the active voice (perfect, pluperfect, etc.), and a passive past participle, used adjectivally or in constructions resembling passives in other languages.

[3] The *bimĭ* paradigm is historically a conditional, whereas the *byxŭ* paradigm is an earlier aorist form redeployed as a conditional. Synchronically, both are used only as conditionals.

(1)   Ašte *bi*   *věděla* darŭ b[o]žii . . . ty *bi*
        if   would-2SG know-PP gift God's   you would-2SG
        prosila u   nego i *dalŭ* ti *bi*   vodǫ živǫ.
        ask-PP with him and give-PP you would-3SG water living
        'If you knew God's gift . . . you would ask him and he would give
        you the water of life.'
            (John 4: 10)

TABLE 14.1. *The paradigm of the conditional auxiliary in
Old Church Slavonic and Old Russian*

	Old Church Slavonic		Old Russian
first person singular	bimĭ	byxŭ	byx"
second person singular	bi	by	by
third person singular	bi	by	by
first person plural	bimŭ	byxomŭ	byxom"
second person plural	biste	byste	byste
third person plural	bǫ, bišę	byšę	byša
first person dual	—	byxově	byxovi
second person dual	—	bysta	bysta
third person dual	—	bysta, byste	bysta

The conditional is one of a number of periphrastic verbal forms in the language.
Periphrastic forms using the active past participle express also the perfect,
pluperfect, and future perfect. Old Church Slavonic also has an elaborate clitic
system, with which the auxiliaries interact. The behaviour of the auxiliaries is,
however, not entirely consistent with that of typical clitics in the language, and
this is reflected in the fact that auxiliary forms of *byti* have traditionally often
been termed 'semi-enclitics' (Vaillant 1948: 360, 1977: 263–4; Večerka 1989:
42). The 'semi-enclitic' behaviour of the auxiliary will be investigated by examining its interaction with clitics and negation.

14.2.3. *Predicate movement*

First, however, a basic analysis of a movement phenomenon is required in order
to deal with other aspects of the syntax of conditionals. In addition to allowing
the auxiliary–participle order of the first two conditional clauses in (1), Old
Church Slavonic allows the participle to precede the auxiliary as in (2) (and also
in the third conditional clause in (1)). This pattern is permitted in all periphrastic
verbal constructions.

(2)   . . . i *poslušala bi*   vasŭ
            and obey-PP   would-3SG you-ACC
        '. . . and it would (have) obey(ed) you.'   (Luke 17: 6)

    This is part of a wider phenomenon whereby a variety of complements may
precede the auxiliary or even a main verb that selects them. For instance, passive

(adjectival) past participles may appear to the left of the verb *byti* 'to be', as in (3); adjectives may precede their copula, as in (4); and secondary predicate noun phrases may precede their verb, as in (5). It is desirable to develop a unitary account of these phenomena, which henceforth I shall term collectively 'predicate movement', using the term 'predicate' to cover the variety of participial, adjectival, and nominal elements that participate in the construction.

(3) Vamŭ   že   i   vlasi glavy   vĭsi ištŭteni sǫtŭ
     you-DAT PRT also hairs head-GEN all count-PP are
     'Every hair of your head is counted.'
         (Matt. 10: 30)

(4) Brakŭ   ubo gotovŭ estŭ
     wedding PRT ready is
     'For the wedding is ready.'
         (Matt. 22: 8)

(5) Xramŭ moi xramŭ molitvě   narečetŭ sę
     temple my temple prayer-DAT call-3SG REFL
     'My temple is called a temple of prayer.'
         (Matt. 21: 13)

In some of these cases the moved predicate is clearly phrasal, as can be seen from the example in (5) (also Matt. 3: 11, 3: 15, 6: 26, 10: 31, 13: 32, 14: 33, etc.). Therefore, in order to maintain a unitary account of all these phenomena, it is necessary to assume phrasal movement to be involved, rather than head movement.

As for the landing site of this movement, clitic placement may offer some clues. The participle or other element in this construction must precede a pronominal clitic, but precedes the sentential clitics *bo* 'therefore', and *že* 'contrast marker' only if these clitics would otherwise end up in the disallowed clause-initial position (see Večerka 1989: 58 on the special case of the interaction of sentential clitics and the conditional). That is, there is absolute parallelism between a pronominal clitic, like *mi* in (6), and a sentential clitic, like *že* in (7), when nothing precedes that participle or similar element. This is shown in (6) and (7).

(6) Dana   mi   estŭ vĭsěka vlastĭ na neb[e]se i na zemi
     given-PP me-DAT is every power over heaven and over earth
     'Every power over heaven and earth is given to me.'
         (Matt. 28: 18)

(7) Rečeno že bystŭ
     say-PP PRT was
     'But it was said.'   (Matt. 5: 31)

When some element precedes, a sentential clitic may precede the participle, as with *že* in (8), whereas a pronominal clitic still follows the participle. Thus we have the sentence in (9*a*), rather than (9*b*) or (9*c*), either of which would parallel (8).

(8)   G[lago]ljǫ vamŭ   ěko nikotory že   pror[o]kŭ prijętenŭ estŭ vŭ
        say-ISG   you-DAT that no   PRT prophet   accept-PP is   in
        otečŭstvii svoemŭ
        homeland his
        'I say to you that no prophet is accepted in his homeland.'
            (Luke 4: 24)

(9)   A otŭ načęla   sŭzŭdaniju,
            and from beginning creation-DAT

    (a) mǫža i ženǫ sŭtvorilŭ ě   estŭ b[og]ŭ
         man and woman create-PP them is   God

    (b) *mǫža i ženǫ ě   sŭtvorilŭ estŭ bogŭ
         man and woman them create-PP is   God

    (c) *mǫža ě   i ženǫ sŭtvorilŭ estŭ bogŭ
         man them and woman create-PP is   God
         'And from the beginning of creation, God created them man and
         woman.'   (Mark 10: 6)

This fact suggests that moved predicate phrases move across the site of pronominal clitics, but ordinarily, that is, in the absence of overriding prosodic requirements, they do not move across sentential clitics. To put this another way, the
relative ordering of predicate phrases and sentential clitics is sensitive to prosodic
rules of clitic placement in this instance, whereas the relative ordering of the
predicate phrase and pronominal clitics is not. Predicate phrases therefore move
to a position between sentential clitics and pronominal clitics. They may undergo
a further movement process in order to save a (sentential) clitic stranded in initial position (for instance prosodic inversion, in the sense of Halpern 1995 and
King 1996). The relative ordering of positions required is therefore that given in
(10a). A suggested implementation of this ordering is given in (10b).

(10) (a)   sentential   landing site   pronominal   origin of
           clitics   for predicate   clitics   predicate
                          movement   phrases

(b)

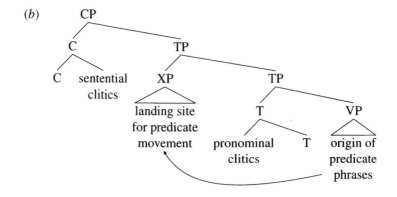

Assuming that sentential clitics right-adjoin to C° and pronominal clitics left-adjoin to a lower functional head, such as T°, then predicate movement can be identified as movement to a position between these two. Since it is movement of a phrase it must be to a phrasal position rather than a head position. Given this, it is natural to assume that the movement is akin to topicalization, and involves movement to adjoin to the phrasal projection TP.

Given the claim that this movement is movement of a phrase, we must further assume that if a participle alone moves leaving behind a direct object, as is the case with the participle *dalŭ* 'given' and the direct object *vodǫ živǫ* 'water of life' in the third clause of (1), it is the entire verb phrase (VP) that moves, with the direct object either raising out of the verb phrase into either an object agreement projection (AgrOP) or a light verb projection (vP) or scrambling to an adjoined position.[4]

14.2.4. *Negation*

Old Church Slavonic shows an asymmetry in the position of negation between the conditional and another periphrastic verbal form, the perfect. In the perfect, formed from the present tense of *byti* 'to be' and the (active) past participle, the negative marker *ne* must appear in initial position within the verb group, irrespective of whether the participle precedes the auxiliary, as in (11), or vice versa, as in (12). For full details of Old Church Slavonic negation, see Večerka (1989: 33–7, 1995).

(11)   . . . i   *ne   uvĕdĕlŭ   jesi*   byvŭšaago   vĭ nemĭ
          and NEG ascertain-PP be-2SG what-happened in it
       '. . . and you have not ascertained what happened in it.'
       (*Su.* 475.10–11)

(12)   *Nĕstŭ   umrŭla* nŭ *sŭpitŭ*
          NEG-be-3SG die-PP but sleeps
       'She has not died, but is sleeping.'
       (Luke 8: 52)

Predicate movement does not move an element across negation, as (11) shows. Assuming that the position of negation is constant, this suggests that predicate movement moves an element to a position following negation. Orders where the negative marker intervenes between auxiliary and past participle (in either order) are not attested, except for minor cases involving the verb *dokonĭčati* 'to finish'

---

[4] The most widely advocated analyses involve either movement of the past participle alone to I° (T°), or some head position immediately dominating the verb phrase (Bošković's 1995 'participle movement'), or movement of the past participle to C°, or some relatively high clausal position ('long head movement', Lema and Rivero 1989, Rivero 1991, 1993, 1994). Both analyses involve head movement only. However, the current position is justified by the need to maintain a parallel between leftward movement of past participles and leftward movement of other predicate constituents, a parallel not possible within these analyses.

(Večerka 1989: 34). Večerka (1989: 34) finds the pattern where the auxiliary immediately follows the negative, as in (12), to be four times as frequent as the one where the lexical verb immediately follows the negative, as in (11).

It might be expected that a parallel distribution would hold for the conditional, but this turns out not to be the case. As with the periphrastic perfect, the negative marker in the conditional may precede both auxiliary and lexical verb, provided that the auxiliary precedes the lexical verb (Sławski 1946: 23–4). That is, there is a parallel for (12). This is illustrated in (13).

(13)   . . . ašte bi   sǐde bylŭ, *ne   bi*   bratrŭ moi *umrŭlŭ*
             if   would-2SG here be-PP NEG would-3SG brother my die-PP
             'If you had been here, my brother would not have died.'
             (John 11: 21)

Surprisingly, however, the negative may also intervene between the auxiliary and lexical verb, although this order is attested less frequently than the dominant negation–auxiliary–verb order:

(14)   Dobrěa bi   bylo emu   ašte sę *bi*   *ne*
             better   would-3SG be-PP him-DAT if   REFL would-3SG NEG
             rodilŭ   č[lově]kŭ tŭ
             be-born-PP man   that
             'It would be better for him, if that man had never been born.'
             (Matt. 26: 24)

Another order (negation–verb–auxiliary) is attested rarely, only twice in the Gospels (Večerka 1989: 35). Both cases are in main clauses (also Luke 12: 39):

(15)   Ašte ne bi   otŭ b[og]a bylŭ sŭ,   *ne moglŭ*
             if   NEG would-3SG from God   be-PP this-one NEG be-able-PP
             bi   tvoriti ničesože.
             would-3SG do   anything
             'If he were not from God, he would not be able to do anything.'
             (John 9: 33)

I have attempted to give statistical data summarizing the various orders in Table 14.2. The data for the perfect are inferred from Večerka's (1989: 34) description of word order with the perfect in all the canonical Old Church Slavonic texts.[5] Exact data could not be derived from that source, and the figures in the perfect column of Table 14.2 are therefore approximations only, based on

---

[5] The canonical Old Church Slavonic texts are the *Codex Zographensis, Codex Assemanianus, Savvina Kniga, Psaltericum Sinaiticum, Euchologium Sinaiticum, Clozianus, Codex Suprasliensis,* and *Kiev Leaves.*

Večerka's comments about word order in the perfect in the canonical Old Church Slavonic texts.[6] The two instances of the order auxiliary–negation–participle involve *ne dokončati* 'to fail to finish', which is probably a single lexicalized unit and can therefore be excluded. Data for the conditional are given for the Gospels in the *Codex Marianus* and for the assorted religious texts in the first thirty-nine chapters of the *Codex Suprasliensis*.[7] Throughout, instances of constituent negation and negation of the synthetic conditional of *byti* 'to be' are excluded.

TABLE 14.2. *Word order in negative verbal forms in Old Church Slavonic*

Type of periphrasis	Perfect	Conditional	
		Marianus	*Suprasliensis*
Word-order pattern			
negation–auxiliary–participle	>70	16	24
auxiliary–negation–participle	2	1	14
negation–participle–auxiliary	*c.*18	2	0
participle–negation–auxiliary	0	0	0

The difference between the perfect and the conditional can be attributed to the structure of embedded clauses. Conditionals appear more frequently in embedded clauses than in main clauses, whereas perfect forms show the reverse distribution. In the *Codex Suprasliensis*, of the thirty-eight relevant instances of conditionals, sixteen are in main clauses, and in all of them negation precedes the auxiliary. Similarly, in the *Codex Marianus*, negation always precedes the auxiliary in main clause conditionals. In the twenty-two embedded conditionals in the *Codex Suprasliensis* both patterns are found, with auxiliary-first order predominating.

These patterns can be accounted for by proposing that the complementizers used with conditionals in embedded clauses may 'attract' the conditional auxiliary to a position earlier than it would otherwise have occupied. This accounts for the fact that examples of the order auxiliary–negation–participle do not appear in main clauses, where, in the absence of a complementizer, such attraction does not take place. With overt complementizers the possibility of this movement is variable. Those with which the conditional most frequently occurs favour this attraction. Večerka (1989: 35) notes that the sequence complementizer *a* 'if' +conditional auxiliary (with no intervening material) is more or less fixed in Old Church Slavonic. The absence of this complementizer in conditional clauses in the *Codex Marianus* is partly responsible for the low frequency of auxiliary–

---

[6] Večerka states that there are over seventy instances of the order negation–auxiliary–participle in the perfect in the canonical Old Church Slavonic texts, and that this pattern outnumbers the order negation–participle–auxiliary by about four to one.

[7] Data for the *Codex Suprasliensis* were extracted using the electronic version of the text in the Corpus Cyrillo-Methodianum Helsingiense of the University of Helsinki.

negation patterns in that text. The complementizer *a* differs from such other 'conditional' complementizers as *da* 'in order that' in requiring rather than merely permitting the verb in its clause to be conditional. Although *da* readily appears with a conditional verb, it appears substantially more frequently with verbs in the indicative (Bräuer 1957). This is perhaps why attraction of the conditional auxiliary over negation is optional with *da*. This optionality can be illustrated by the differing redactions of Luke 4: 42, given according to the *Codex Marianus* in (16a) and *Codex Zographensis* in (16b).

(16) (a) . . . drŭžaaxǫ i,   da *ne bi*   *otŭšelŭ* otŭ nixŭ

(b) . . . drŭžaaxǫ i,   da *bi ne*   *ošĭlŭ* otŭ nixŭ
          held-3PL him that NEG-would-3SG-NEG leave-PP from them
     '. . . and they held him, so that he would not leave them.'
     (Luke 4: 42)

A third complementizer *ašte* 'if' also readily (although again, only optionally) appears with the conditional, and, like *da*, optionally attracts the conditional auxiliary to a position preceding negation and other intervening material (see the variation in the Gospel redactions discussed in Večerka 1989: 35–6).[8] This movement takes place in (17a) (=(14)) (cf. *Su.* 165.14, 442.17), but not in (17b) (cf. Matt. 24: 22, Mark 13: 20, 14: 21, John 9: 33, 15: 22, 15: 24).

(17) (a) . . . ašte sę   *bi*   *ne   rodilŭ*   č[lově]kŭ tŭ
          if   REFL would-3S NEG be-born-PP man   that
     '. . . if that man had not been born.'
     (Matt. 26: 24)

(b) Ašte *ne   bimĭ*   *prišelŭ* i   gl[agol]alŭ imŭ . . .
     if   NEG would-1SG come-PP and speak-PP   them-DAT
     'If I had not come and spoken to them . . .'
     (John 15: 22)

It is worth emphasizing that the crucial difference between *a*, on the one hand, and *da* and *ašte* on the other, is the fact that while the former occurs exclusively with conditional verbs, the latter both allow (in fact, favour) indicatives. When an indicative verb is used, it does not need to occupy a position adjacent to *da*. In (18), the indicative verb *bǫdete* is not adjacent to the complementizer *da*.[9]

---

[8] Unlike *da*, the norm seems to be for *ašte* not to attract the auxiliary: the pattern in (17b) is clearly the majority one.

[9] See also the examples listed in Bräuer (1957: 56, 60, 76–7), and discussion of such examples in MacRobert (1980: 63, 87) and Večerka (1989: 54–6).

(18) Vĭnemlĕte   milostynę vašeję ne   tvoriti prĕdŭ
      be-careful-IMP-2PL alms   your NEG do-INF in-front-of
      čl[o]v[ĕ]ky da vidimi bǫdete   imi
      people   that seen   be-FUT-2PL by-them
      'Be careful not to give alms in front of other people so that you
      should be seen by them.'
          (Matt. 6: 1)

Why should conditional movement be optional with *da* and *ašte* but compulsory with *a*? It seems natural to link this to the fact that *a* 'if' requires a
conditional clause, whereas the other complementizers do not.[10]

It can be concluded that leftward movement of the conditional is compulsory
with *a*, but merely optional with *da* and *ašte*. As for main clauses, leftward
movement of the conditional, in so far as it is possible to judge, is ruled out:
auxiliary–negation–verb order does not seem to occur in main clauses.

Since the conditional auxiliary precedes negation, it must occupy a head-
position higher than negation. I shall assume a split IP, with the order of projections AgrP–NegP–TP, for reasons to do with the variation between Old Church
Slavonic and Old Russian. Old Church Slavonic auxiliaries normally occupy T°.
In conditional movement, the conditional auxiliary moves first to Agr°, then
moves further, right-adjoining to C°. Such movement is obligatory if the mood
phrase is selected by the complementizer *a*, optional if selected by *da* or *ašte*,
and impossible if the conditional is in a main clause.

(19)

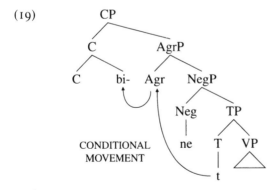

Notice that once movement from T° to C° has taken place, predicate movement of the participle to adjoin to TP will have no effect on the surface order,
since the auxiliary is no longer within TP. Irrespective of whether predicate

---

[10] Perhaps the sequence *a* + conditional auxiliary is stored as such in the lexicon and inserted
directly into C°. Agreement features would then raise covertly to C° in order to check for appropriate
subject–verb agreement.

movement takes place, the surface order will be auxiliary–negation–participle, representing either $[_{CP}$ auxiliary$_i$ $[_{NegP}$ negation $[_{TP}$ participle$_j$ t$_i$ $[_{VP}$ t$_j]]]]$ (if the participle has moved) or simply $[_{CP}$ auxiliary$_i$ $[_{NegP}$ negation $[_{TP}$ t$_i$ $[_{VP}$ participle$]]]]$ (if it has not).

This predicts that negation–verb–auxiliary order, derived through predicate movement in the absence of conditional movement, should be permitted, albeit infrequently, wherever it is possible to forgo conditional movement. It was shown in (15) that this is true in main clauses. Furthermore it would be expected, as one option, after *da* and *ašte*, although not after *a*, where conditional movement is obligatory. Although this order is not found with an active past participle, the sentences in (20) illustrate the equivalent configuration with a passive past participle *prědanŭ* 'handed over' in (20) (see also, with a predicative adjective, Luke 16: 12).

(20) . . . da *ne prědanŭ bimĭ* ljuděomŭ
         that NEG handed-over would-1 SG Jews-DAT
    '. . . that I might not be handed over to the Jews.'
    (John 18: 36)

14.2.5. *Pronominal clitics*

Another asymmetry is found in the positioning of pronominal clitics in the perfect and conditional (Večerka 1989: 59–63). The frequency of the various word order possibilities is given in Table 14.3, derived from data given in Večerka (1989: 63) for the canonical Old Church Slavonic texts.

Fundamentally, it is necessary to account for the fact that orders where the auxiliary precedes the pronoun are infrequent with the perfect (only six examples out of 157),[11] whereas this order is almost as frequent as the inverse order with

TABLE 14.3. *Word order with pronominal clitics in Old Church Slavonic periphrastic verbal forms*

Type of periphrasis	Perfect		Conditional	
	no.	%	no.	%
word-order pattern				
pronoun–auxiliary–participle	28	18	34	33
participle–pronoun–auxiliary	115	73	28	27
auxiliary–participle–pronoun	3	2	21	21
auxiliary–pronoun–participle	3	2	18	18
pronoun–participle–auxiliary	8	5	0	0
participle–auxiliary–pronoun	0	0	1	1

Source: Večerka (1989: 60)

---

[11] The availability of the order auxiliary–participle–pronoun may be due to an independent development favouring the position immediately following the lexical verb for the reflexive clitic *sę*, which is present in all three examples of this pattern.

the conditional. Examples are provided below. Cases where the pronoun precedes the auxiliary in the perfect are given in (21). Conditional examples are given in (22) and (23). In (22), the pronoun precedes the auxiliary as in the perfect. The auxiliary–pronoun orders characteristic of the conditional are illustrated in (23).

(21) (*a*) Vŭskǫjǫ *mę*   esi   ostavilŭ?
            why   me-ACC be-2SG leave-PP
            'Why have you left me?'
                (Matt. 27: 46)

       (*b*) . . . ěko *vŭzljubilŭ mę*   esi . . .
              for   love-PP   me-ACC be-2SG
            '. . . for you have loved me . . .'
                (John 17: 24)

(22) (*a*) Ašte *mę*   biste   znali . . .
            if   me-ACC would-2PL know-PP
            'If you knew me . . .'
                (John 14: 7)

       (*b*) . . . i *dalŭ   ti   bi*   vodǫ živǫ
              and give-PP you-DAT would-3SG water living
            '. . . and he would give you the water of life.'
                (John 4: 10)

(23) (*a*) . . . da *byxŭ*   pokajalŭ sę   kŭ bogu
              that would-1SG repent-PP REFL to God
            '. . . in order that I might repent before God.'   (*Su.* 167.2)

       (*b*) . . . da *bǫ*   i   prědali   vladyčŭstvu i   oblasti
              that would-3P him hand-over-PP possession and authority
              voevody
              governor
            '. . . in order that they would hand him over to the possession and authority of the governor.'
                (Luke 20: 20)

This distribution is consistent with previous assumptions, namely that the conditional auxiliary optionally right-adjoins to C°, whereas the perfect auxiliary generally does not. Continuing previous assumptions, I assume that pronominal clitics occupy a position left-adjoined to T°. Predicate movement remains adjunction to TP.

The orders in (21) are achieved without movement of the perfect auxiliary. The auxiliary occupies T°, and the pronominal clitic *mę* left-adjoins to T°. In (21*b*) the participle *izbavilŭ* undergoes predicate movement to adjoin to TP, appearing to the left of both clitic and auxiliary. The parallel conditional orders in (22*a*) and (22*b*) are produced in the same way: in these cases, conditional movement, which is optional or excluded in these contexts, has not occurred.

(24)

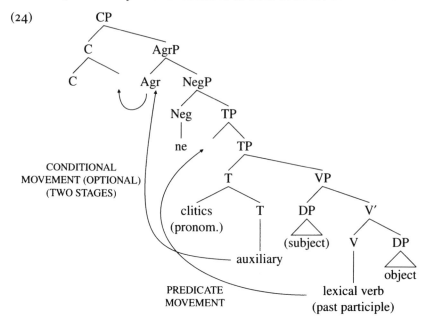

To produce the orders in (23), characteristic of the conditional, conditional movement must be invoked. In (23a), the conditional moves to C°, and there is also predicate movement of the lexical verb. The result is that both the conditional auxiliary and the lexical verb move to a position that precedes that of the pronominal clitic. In (23b), only conditional movement takes place, with the result that the auxiliary, but not the lexical verb, ends up in a position preceding the clitic. The overall schema is shown in (24).

This analysis links ordering of the conditional auxiliary with respect to negation to the ordering of the auxiliary with respect to pronominal clitics, and predicts the same distributional possibilities in both cases. The distributional possibilities in both cases are the same with the different complementizers. Thus, with the complementizers *da* and *ašte*, the conditional auxiliary is not obliged to precede pronominal clitics, although it may. This optionality is shown by the pair of examples with *da* in (25). In (25a) the order is complementizer–clitic–auxiliary (*da i bǫ*) (cf. Mark 12: 13, John 11: 53; *Su.* 275.6), freely alternating with, in the same environment, the order complementizer–auxiliary–clitic (*da bǫ i*) in (25b) (cf. Matt. 6: 16, Mark 7: 24, 9: 22, Luke 4: 29, 18: 15, 20: 20).

(25) (a) Otŭ togo že dĭne sŭvěštašę   da *i*   *bǫ*   ubili
      from that PRT day conspired-3PL that him-ACC would-3P kill-PP
      'From that very day they began to conspire to kill him.'
        (John 11: 53)

(b) . . . i   věsę   i   do vrŭxu gory   . . . da bǫ
        and took-3P him-ACC to top   mountain   that would-3PL
    i   nizŭbrinǫli
    him-ACC cast-down-PP
    '. . . and they took him to the top of the mountain in order to cast
    him down.'
        (Luke 4: 29)

Finally, there is variation between two syntactic patterns involving the
sentential clitic *bo* 'therefore'. This variation is illustrated in (26) and (27). In
(26), the sentential clitic *bo* follows the auxiliary in the context of the
complementizer *a*, whereas with *ašte* in (27) (see also *Su.* 241.27), the auxiliary
follows *bo*.

(26)   . . . a *by*   bo ne *molilŭ* *sę*   ne by   vŭstavilŭ
             if would-3SG PRT NEG pray-PP REFL NEG would-3SG rise-PP
         mrŭtvaago
         dead-GEN
         '. . . for if he had not prayed, he would not have risen from the dead.'
             (*Su.* 303.12–13)

(27)   Ašte bo *byxŭ*   ne *vědělŭ* ježe glagolǫtŭ . . .
         if   PRT would-1SG NEG know-PP that say-3PL
         'If I did not know that it is said . . .'
             (*Su.* 165.14–15)

This seems to suggest that conditional movement results in a closer relationship
between the complementizer and the auxiliary in the case of *a*. This can be
accounted for if it is claimed that conditional movement proceeds all the way to
C° only in the case of *a*, whereas it stops at an intermediate position, namely
Agr°, following *bo*, in the case of *ašte*.

14.2.6. *Integrating clitics and negation*

Pronominal clitics and negation rarely co-occur in the attested Old Church
Slavonic texts. The following comments are based on the eight examples found
in the *Codex Marianus* and *Codex Suprasliensis*, and must therefore be treated
with caution. When clitics and negation co-occur, two patterns are attested. In
one pattern the clitic appears early in the clause and the auxiliary and negation
follow, as in (28).

(28)   Dobrěa bi   bylo emu   ašte *sę*   *bi*
         better would-3SG be-PP him-DAT if REFL would-3PL
         ne *rodilŭ*   č[lově]kŭ tŭ
         NEG be-born-PP man   that
         'It would be better for him, if he had not been born.'
             (Matt. 26: 24)

This pattern is not consistent with (24). In order to account for it, we need to assume variation in the position of the pronominal clitics, suggesting for instance that in (28), the clitics occupy a higher position than T°, perhaps right-adjoining to C°. The participle remains in V°. It is well known that the modern South Slavonic languages differ from each other with respect to the rules for placement of pronominal clitics. In Serbo-Croat, clitics occupy a high clausal position which has been analysed as right-adjunction to C° (Progovac 1996). In Bulgarian (Hauge 1976, King 1996: 274–8, Tomić 1996: 814–32), pronominal clitics primarily occupy a fixed position relative to the verb, namely an immediately preverbal position. That is, Bulgarian pronominal clitics occupy a position within the verbal projection, whereas earlier stages of South Slavonic reserved a position within a higher projection. In the light of this, variation within Old Church Slavonic is not unexpected.

In any case, this is the only example of this order in the Gospel translations. In the other cases where negation and pronominal clitics co-occur in the Gospel translations and the *Codex Suprasliensis*, the norm seems to be for the pronominal clitic (always reflexive) to follow the lexical verb as in the two examples in (29) (also Mark 14: 21; *Su.* 442.30, 303.12, 401.20, 428.15, but the clitic intervenes between auxiliary and lexical verb in *Su.* 433.1):

(29)   . . . ašte *ne bišę prěkratili sę* dŭne ti,   *ne   bi*
       if   NEG would-3PL cease-PP REFL days these NEG would-3SG
       ubo   *sŭp[a]sl sę*   vĭsěka plŭtĭ
       therefore save-PP REFL any   flesh
       'If these days were not to cease, then no flesh would be saved.'
       (Matt. 24: 22)

Indeed, the passage of Mark paralleling (28) above (Mark 14: 21) manifests an order with the reflexive clitic *sę* following the participle, and the Matthew text in (29) in the Ostromir Gospels also shows the same order.

Again this suggests that the position of the reflexive clitic is subject to variation and change. It seems that, in (29), the pronominal clitic is contained within the verb phrase. Under the most straightforward analysis, the clitic is right-adjoined to the verb, and the verb remains in V°: [12]

(30)   [CP ašte [NegP ne [TP bišę [VP [V° [V° prěkratili] sę]] . . .]]]
       if   NEG   would-3P   cease-PP   REFL

14.2.7. *Conclusions about Old Church Slavonic*

Investigation of the Old Church Slavonic conditional leads us to the conclusion that the conditioning factor for conditional movement is the nature of the element in C°: conditional movement is obligatory with *a*, optional with *da* and *ašte*, and

---

[12] An alternative would be to move the lexical verb to a position outside the verb phrase (by predicate movement), and left-adjunction of the clitic to T°.

excluded in unembedded contexts. This means that in Old Church Slavonic it is possible to identify instances both where the auxiliary moves to C° and where it fails to move. The availability of both options makes clear the derived nature of the positioning of the auxiliary in C°, and favours faithful acquisition of the system.

14.3. OLD RUSSIAN

This section examines the properties of conditional movement in another variety of Slavonic, Old Russian, and concludes that the conditioning factors for conditional movement are different from those in Old Church Slavonic. As before, negation and clitic placement are used as diagnostics.

14.3.1. *Sources*

The analysis of Old Russian is based on exhaustive extraction of the conditionals in the Laurentian redaction of the Primary Chronicle (*Povest' Vremennyx Let*) (*PSRL* I) (1377), the chancery documents in *Gramoty Velikogo Novgoroda i Pskova* (*GVNP*) (twelfth to fifteenth centuries), the First Novgorod Chronicle (*NPL*) (second half of the thirteenth century to the mid-fourteenth century), and the birchbark documents edited by Zaliznjak in *Drevnenovgorodskij dialekt* (*DND*) (eleventh to fifteenth centuries). Although the earliest manuscript of the Primary Chronicle dates from 1377, the text was composed much earlier. Linguistically it represents a conservative variety of Old Russian with Church Slavonic influence, and will be used here to exemplify the most conservative stage of Old Russian. It also has the advantage that, unlike in the other texts, the conditional is used in it fairly frequently. The other texts seem to reflect contemporary practice more faithfully, but the paucity of examples from these texts (thirty-four tokens in *DND*, eighteen in *GVNP*, and thirteen in *NPL*) makes it impossible to be certain of the details of some of the developments.

14.3.2. *Negation*

In the majority of cases, the Old Russian conditional auxiliary precedes negation. This is the case in embedded clauses headed by all complementizers, and in this context auxiliary–negation order appears to be obligatory. Examples are found with the complementizers *a* 'in order that' (*DND* B69, B100), *ašče* 'if' (*PSRL* II.241.19), and *da* 'in order that' (*NPL* 73.34–5, *PSRL* I.30.24, 265.23):

(31)   . . . v"zdviže   kramolu meži   rus'skymi knjazi, da
               raised-3SG strife   between Russian   princes in-order-that
          byša   čelověci *ne* *žili*   mirno
          would-3PL people   NEG live-PP peacefully
          'He sowed strife among the Russian princes, in order that people
          should not live in peace.'
          (*NPL* 73.34–5)

However, in main clauses, the auxiliary generally follows negation, regardless of the person–number features of the auxiliary (*PSRL* I.10.2, 86.4, 108.27, 117.18, 178.22). Examples are given in (32). Other orders are discussed below.

(32) (*a*) Ašče bo by   perevoznik″ Kij, to *ne* *by*
         if   PRT would-3SG ferryman   Kij then NEG would-3SG
         xodil″ Carjugorodu
         go-3SG Constantinople-DAT
         'For if Kij had been a ferryman, then he would not have gone to
         Constantinople.'
         (*PSRL* I.10.2)

   (*b*) Ašče li bysta   vědala, to *ne* *bysta*   *prišla*
         if   Q would-3D know-PP then NEG would-3D come-PP
         na město se
         to place this
         'If they had known, then they would not have come to this place.'
         (*PSRL* I.178.22)

This can be dealt with within a framework structurally identical to that proposed for Old Church Slavonic above, since differences between Old Church Slavonic and Old Russian relate not to the processes themselves, but to the environments in which these processes are triggered. The conditional may undergo movement to C°, bypassing negation. Whereas in Old Church Slavonic this movement is obligatory only with the complementizer *a*, in Old Russian it appears to be obligatory, as far as negation is concerned, with all the relevant complementizers. The environment for conditional movement is therefore larger in Old Russian than in Old Church Slavonic.

14.3.3. *Clitics*

As before, a second source of evidence on this point is the relative ordering of auxiliaries and clitics. In main clauses, which in general seemed to exclude conditional movement in Old Church Slavonic, conditional movement is available in Old Russian but is conditioned by the person–number features of the auxiliary itself. Specifically, the second and third person singular form of the auxiliary, *by*, regularly precedes pronominal clitics (also *PSRL* I.110.20, 136.4, 136.13, 242.18):[13]

(33)   . . . [iz] oc′ju *by*   *sja*   *vyt′r′go*
             from eyes would-2SG REFL escape-PP
          '. . . you would have escaped from [other people's] eyes.'
             (*DND* A7, 1080s–1100s)

---

[13] An exception is perhaps *PSRL* I.263.1 in the Laurentian redaction (although not in other redactions of the same passage).

In the other forms the conditional auxiliary follows pronominal clitics (also *PSRL* I.254.7):

(34) Radi *sja   byxom"   jali*   po dan'
      happy REFL would-1PL agree-PP to tribute
      'We would happily agree to tribute.'
      (*PSRL* I.58.22)

This asymmetry holds irrespective of whether the participle has been fronted or not. The minimal pair *proslavil" by í* in (35) (also *PSRL* I.263.1), as against *požerli ny byša* in (36) demonstrates the same asymmetry with a fronted participle.

(35) Da ašče byxom   iměli   potščan'e i   mol'by prinosili bogu
      for if   would-1PL have-PP diligence and prayers bring-PP God-DAT
      za n', . . . *proslavil" by*   *í*
      for him   glorify-PP would-3SG him
      'For if we had been diligent and prayed to God for him, then He would have glorified him . . .'
      (*PSRL* I.131.11)

(36) Vnegda stati   čelověkom", ubo živy *požerli   ny byša*
      when   rise-up-INF people-DAT then alive devour-PP us would-3PL
      'When people rose up, they would devour us alive.'
      (*PSRL* I.242.18)

In embedded clauses, there is no such asymmetry: all forms of the auxiliary precede the clitics in clauses headed by the complementizers *a* and *da* 'in order that'. Relevant cases are given in (37). A case with a third person singular auxiliary is shown in (37a); a non-third-person auxiliary (first person dual) is given in (37b).[14]

(37) (a) Poslisja   k bratu . . .   da *by*   *ti*   *pomogl"*
         send-IMPER to brother-DAT that would-3SG you-DAT help-PP
         'Send to you brother . . . that he should help you.'
         (*PSRL* I.219.1)

     (b) Da *byxovi   sja   snjala*
         that would-1D REFL go-away-PP
         'We should go away.'
         (*PSRL* II.265.4)

---

[14] Textual variants suggest that productive use of the rule was lost during the fourteenth century. Consider the contrast in the form of (34) in the Laurentian redaction (1377) and the Hypatian redaction (early fifteenth century) of the Primary Chronicle. The Laurentian version appears in (34). By contrast, in the Hypatian redaction (*PSRL* II.47.8) the order of auxiliary and clitic is reversed (*byxom" sja jali*).

These facts can be accounted for by claiming that *by* undergoes obligatory conditional movement, whereas for other forms conditional movement is triggered by
the presence of an overt complementizer in C°.

However, there appears to be a contradiction here since the system proposed
to handle negation and that proposed to handle clitics are mutually exclusive.
Specifically, in main clauses, the form *by* must not undergo conditional movement in order for the correct order with auxiliary following negation to be maintained. On the other hand, in the context of pronominal clitics, *by* must undergo
conditional movement, in order to occupy a position preceding the clitic.

An account can be constructed if Old Russian conditional movement is
assumed to be a staged process. That is, *by* would always undergo 'short' conditional movement, even in main clauses, thereby skipping the clitic position,
but not negation. A mood projection (MP) has been proposed for Slavonic
elsewhere,[15] and may reasonably be adopted here between NegP and TP as the
host for the auxiliary when it undergoes short movement. Other forms of the
auxiliary do not undergo 'short' conditional movement unless they are required
by the presence of a relevant complementizer in C° to move all the way to C°.
The relevant configuration, covering the cases in (33) versus (32*a*), is represented in (38).

(38)

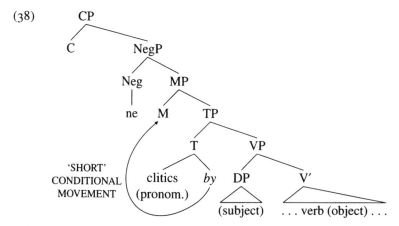

Any account must also be compatible with the Old Russian perfect. Here,
typical orders are negation–verb–auxiliary in (39), and auxiliary–negation–verb
in (40).

(39)   . . . *ne   myslil"   esm"*   do Pl'skovič' gruba   ničegože
              NEG think-PP be-ISG to Pskovians bad-GEN anything-GEN
          'I have not devised any evil against the Pskovians.'
          (*NPL* 66.6)

---

[15] For a mood projection in Macedonian, see Tomić (1996: 823–9), and for Balkan languages
generally Rivero (1994).

(40) . . . i zla do vas" *esm'* *ne* *myslil"* nikotorago že . . .
        and evil-GEN to you be-1SG NEG think-PP none PRT
  '. . . I have not devised any evil towards you . . .'
  (*NPL* 66.20)

Note the ungrammaticality of this second order in Old Church Slavonic (see Table 14.2) and the corresponding ungrammaticality of the Old Church Slavonic order negation–auxiliary–verb in Old Russian. In order to accommodate this, we must elaborate the account somewhat. The order in (40) is taken to be basic, with (39) representing an instance of predicate movement. Therefore, the perfect auxiliary underlyingly occupies a position above negation. The structure in (41) is assigned to the verbal form in (40): as before IP is split into AgrP and TP, with AgrP occupying a position above negation, and TP occupying a position below negation. The perfect auxiliary then occupies Agr° (presumably having moved there from T°), whereas the conditional auxiliary and the Old Church Slavonic auxiliaries occupy T° (perhaps moving covertly to check features in Agr°). Negation remains in Neg° and the verb in V°.

(41)

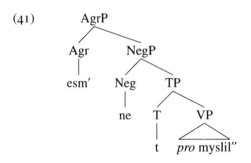

(42)

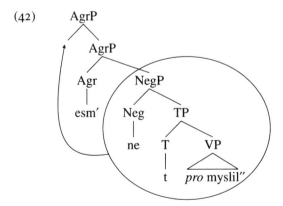

The verbal periphrasis in (39), represented in (42), is derived by movement of the verb to Neg°, followed by predicate movement of the whole negation-verb complex (NegP) to adjoin to AgrP.

14.3.4. *The historical development in later Russian*

In Old Church Slavonic each form of the auxiliary undergoes conditional movement to an equal extent. Effectively all forms of the auxiliary are 'semi-enclitic'.
In Old Russian, although the entire paradigm may reasonably be described as
semi-enclitic, since conditional movement occurs only in some cases, each form
is not equally clitic-like. The form *by* always undergoes movement of some kind.
In this section, I examine a related series of changes in the conditional system
of Old Russian, suggesting that they all represent a fundamental change in the
status of *by* from an inflectional element that moves to C^0 to a sentential clitic
base-adjoined to C^0. In terms of the general theory of language change, this
change is an example of loss of movement: a common derived structure is
reanalysed as underlying.

14.3.5. *Syntactic ambiguity*

Some sentences in which the conditional marker is in C^0 are syntactically ambiguous in the sense that they are in principle amenable both to an analysis where
the positioning of the conditional in C^0 is derived and one where it is underlying.
This is the case in the second and third person singular. Consider the third person singular conditional clause in (43). If *by* is present underlyingly in C^0, then
this sentence apparently contains no auxiliary and no finite verb. Under normal
circumstances, this would allow the movement analysis to be rejected during
language acquisition because it would require there to be main clauses lacking
a finite verb.

(43)   Ašče *by*   kto   dobro drugu   *činil″* . . .
          if   be-COND-3SG someone good another-DAT do-PP
          'If someone had done a good deed for someone else . . .'
             (*NPL* 82.4–5)

However, in Old Russian the third person singular perfect auxiliary is normally
null:

(44)   . . . knjaz′ velikyi poslal″ k vamo svoego syna . . .
          prince grand   send-PP to you self's son-ACC
          '. . . the Grand Prince sent you his son . . .'   (*GVNP* 35.4, 1302)

This opens up the possibility of an analysis of (43) where *by* is underlyingly in
C^0, and the auxiliary is null. Such an analysis is less easily available for the
second person singular *by*, since the second person singular perfect auxiliary (*esi*)
is mostly overt.

The 'correct' derived nature of the positioning of *by* could nevertheless still
be acquired by comparison with cases where the conditional is clearly in its
lower underlying position. Clearly, there are logically two ways of acquiring the
syntactic properties of the auxiliary. Either the syntactic properties of the whole
paradigm can be acquired as a single fact, or each member of the paradigm can

be learned individually. In Old Church Slavonic, it does not matter which approach the learner takes. Each member of the conditional paradigm appears both in the derived and underlying position. The appearance of each form in the underlying position will alert learners to the existence of this position. In Old Russian, however, it is important for accurate replication of the grammar that learners consider the paradigm as a whole. This is because the form *by* appears only in the derived position. If learners acquire *by* separately, there will be no evidence that it is underlyingly an auxiliary. On the other hand, if learners treat the whole conditional paradigm as a single unit, the evidence of other forms, which appear both in the derived and underlying position, will be sufficient for the learner to acquire conditional movement correctly.

The fact that *by* is the only monosyllabic member of the paradigm, and the fact that it contains no recognizable verbal (person–number) ending would have mitigated against it being treated as a part of a larger paradigm. Some learners will have begun by acquiring its syntactic properties separate from those of the other members of the paradigm. Such learners will acquire *by* as a mood marker (rather than auxiliary) base-generated within CP.

I hypothesize that *by* was reanalysed as underlyingly in C° at the latest early in the fourteenth century. The reanalysis applied both to third person singular *by* and to second person singular *by*. This left the auxiliary heads (Agr° and T°) filled by null auxiliaries.

In the second person singular, the auxiliary was usually overt, and therefore the option of filling the auxiliary 'slot' with an overt auxiliary in the second person singular becomes available immediately. The perfect auxiliary, the present tense of the verb *byti* 'to be', appears in the conditional alongside the conditional marker in the texts examined from the mid-fourteenth century. An example is given in (45).[16] All examples except one of perfect auxiliaries in the conditional in the texts examined are in the second person, whether singular or plural.

(45)   Dobyša čelom" nov"gorod'ci . . . arxiepiskopu . . . čto*by*
         asked-3PL   Novgorodians   archbishop-DAT   that+COND
         '*esi*   gospodine *exal"* narjadil" kostry   vo Orěxově.'
         be-2SG sir   go-PP set-up-PP defences in O.-PREP
         'The Novgorodians . . . asked the archbishop . . . that "you, Sir,
         should go and set up defences in Orexov".'
         (*NPL* 100.14–16)

Although this has sometimes been analysed as a hypercorrection (Nikiforov 1952: 139), its sheer frequency in texts of various stylistic levels suggests that it is a naturally occurring innovation. Notice also that the same innovation has

---

[16] See also other fourteenth- and fifteenth-century examples, with second person singular, *DND* G24, G40, G49 (four examples), G55, G63, G76, D9, D15; *GVNP* 53.12, 53.18; *NPL* 100.16, 100.19; and with second person plural *DND* G37, D13; *GVNP* 50.5, 50.6 (two examples), 96.10; *PSRL* I.197.9.

occurred in Slovak, where it is clearly a productive phenomenon (Stanislav 1967–73: III.451–2, Panzer 1967: 30–2, Pauliny 1981: 191–2).

The new configuration is illustrated in (46).

(46)

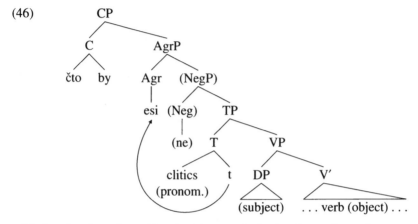

Notice that there is nothing in this reanalysis that forces loss of agreement. Both third person singular *by* and second person singular *by* may retain their agreement features even when they are base generated in C°. They (or perhaps the entire complex in C°, that is, *čtoby* in (46)) will select for an AgrP and TP headed by an auxiliary with the relevant person–number features. Effectively, at this stage, the conditional paradigm will be as in (47) (illustrated using the verb *činiti* 'to make, do'), with an agreeing conditional auxiliary in the plural and in the first person singular, but an uninflected particle accompanied by a perfect auxiliary carrying agreement in the other persons of the singular.

(47)   byx″ činil″   byxom″ činili
          by esi činil″   byste činili
          by ø činil″   byša činili

Gaps in the evidence of the Old Russian texts examined prevent us from establishing the existence of the stage hypothesized in (47) with any certainty. The following example, in which the synthetic form of the first person singular (*byx″ . . . postavile* 'I would build') is maintained alongside the innovative analytic form of the second person singular (*by esi . . . dale* 'you would give'), is perhaps suggestive that such a stage did indeed exist:

(48)   čto *by*   *esi*   g[ospodi]ne *dale*   měsce mně   na dorě
          that COND be-2SG sir   give-PP plot   to-me on cleared-land
          i   jaz″ *byx″*   g[ospodi]ne sobě   izbu *postavile* . . .
          and I   cond-1SG sir   self-DAT hut   build-PP
          'Sir, if you would give me a plot on the cleared land, then I would build myself a hut . . .'
              (*DND* G40, 1360s–80s)

The next stage is the elimination of agreement. *By* is still restricted to its original person–number combinations. It is reasonable to suppose that subject–complementizer agreement is difficult to acquire, given that complementizers do not normally carry agreement features. Some learners may fail to acquire the fact that *by* is restricted to two person–number combinations, and instead leave it unmarked for person and number. This will lead to a period of competition, since for four of the person–number combinations, both conditional auxiliary and conditional marker are now available in the plural and in the first person singular.

(49)   byx″ činil″ OR by esm′ činil″   byxom″ činili OR by esmi činili
       by esi činil″   byste činili   OR by este činili
       by ø činil″   byša činili   OR by ø činili

It is reasonable to suppose that, in such a competition, the analytic conditional marker will win out. Even at the start of the competition stage, *by* would be far more frequent in usage than any of the other forms, since it is the only option in the most frequent form, the third person singular.

Finally, with complete loss of the perfect auxiliary in both the perfect and conditional, agreement disappears throughout the paradigm. This last stage is attested only in the fifteenth century in the texts examined (*GVNP* 69.14, 339.14). For earlier cases, see Sobolevskij (1962: 244), from which the following example, dating from 1339, is taken:

(50)   Ašče *by*   slěpi   *byli* . . .
      if   COND blind-PL be-PP
      'If you (plur.) were blind . . .'
         (*Moscow (Sijskij) Gospels* 20v, John 9: 41)

14.3.6. *Positional restrictions*

Halpern (1995: 14) highlights the difference between second-word (2W) clitics and second-phrase (2D) clitics. The former appear in second position regardless of phrase boundaries, whereas the latter are sensitive to phrase boundaries and do not interrupt phrases. Within prosodic inversion analyses, second-constituent clitics appear in second position because some phrase moves over them, whereas second-word clitics, if they find themselves in a prohibited clause-initial position, undergo prosodic (phonological rather than syntactic) inversion with the phonological word that follows them. In conservative Old Russian the conditional auxiliary does not interrupt phrases. This follows from the analysis adopted above, since even when it acts as a clitic, the conditional auxiliary moves leftwards to particular syntactic positions, and never undergoes prosodic inversion. Modern Russian and later Old Russian *by* may appear within phrases (*GVNP* 50.8, 50.9; *PRP* 28.16, 28.17). A fifteenth-century example is given in (51).

(51)   A   gostju   *by*   našemu po vašei zemli put' *by*   *byl"*
    and merchants-DAT COND our   in your land road COND be-PP
    čist", a   ot   lixix" *by*   ljuděi   na puti pakosti
    clear and from evil   COND people-GEN on road trouble-GEN
    im"   *ne*   *bylo*
    them-DAT NEG be-PP
    'And the roads should be free to our merchants in your land, and there
    should be no trouble for them from evil people along the way.'
        (*GVNP* 50.8–9)

When *by* becomes an invariant conditional marker originating within C°, it remains a clitic, and is still subject to a restriction that it may not appear in clause-initial position. Before the change, in main clauses *by* moved to M° and no further, and could therefore satisfy this requirement so long as some constituent underwent predicate movement or topicalization. However, after the change, the position of *by* is fixed in C°, and there may be cases where it finds itself in the disallowed initial position, and hence subject to prosodic inversion with the following non-phrasal phonological word. This accounts for the innovation of the clause type in (51).

14.4. IMPLICATIONS FOR THEORIES OF SYNTACTIC CHANGE

I have outlined an account of change in Russian which involves a category change (from T° to C°). If it is accepted that C° represents a 'more grammatical' category on a continuum from most grammatical (functional) to least grammatical (lexical) categories, then this shift represents an instance of grammaticalization.

Movement of an element from an underlying position to a derived position can be removed from the grammar either by eliminating the movement itself or by treating the derived position as basic. The Russian case instantiates the second option, and is interesting from a theoretical perspective in that most well-studied instances of the elimination of movement, such as the loss of verb-second in French or the loss of verb-raising in English (see Roberts 1993*a*), instantiate the first option.

Grammaticalization of movement of this kind is attested elsewhere. One further example is the grammaticalization of the Welsh main clause affirmative complementizer *mi*. This was formerly a preverbal first-person-singular subject pronoun occupying [Spec,CP]. Since Welsh was (and is) a verb-initial language, this was a derived position. Movement was eliminated by reanalysing the pronoun as a complementizer, appearing underlyingly in C°. In Welsh this reanalysis can be recognized in two ways: the appearance of a new (postverbal) subject pronoun in clauses with *mi*, and, later, the spread of *mi* to clauses of all person–number combinations (for details see Willis 1998). Clearly the Welsh change shares a number of features of the Russian change. In particular, both undergo two stages: the reanalysis of an element as underlyingly in its derived position (C°), and the loss of agreement associated with its earlier underlying position. It remains to be seen whether these features allow the identification of 'grammaticalization of movement' as a type of syntactic change.

The Russian change also confirms the role of ambiguity in reanalysis, first highlighted in Timberlake's (1977) study of syntactic reanalysis. We can identify sentences of the type in (43), repeated here as (52), as the drivers of change.

(52)   Ašče *by*   kto   dobro drugu   *činil"* . . .
          if   be-COND-3SG someone good another-DAT do-PP
          'If someone had done a good deed for someone else . . .'
              (*NPL* 82.4–5)

Sentences of this sort were open to an ambiguous analysis by learners, either with *by* in C° and the participle accompanied by a null auxiliary, or with *by* as the auxiliary itself. It is doubtful whether the change could have proceeded without this preexisting ambiguity.

14.5. CONCLUSIONS

The two varieties of Slavonic analysed in this chapter share many common features in periphrastic verbal forms. However, they differ in the way in which the 'semi-enclitic' nature of the conditional auxiliary is realized. In Old Church Slavonic, all forms of the auxiliary underwent movement under certain conditions. This created the conditions for stability: no form of the auxiliary could be reanalysed as categorically distinct from the others. In Russian, however, the privileged status of the form *by* is evident even in the conservative language: only *by* underwent movement in all environments. I have argued that this created the conditions for change: the reanalysis of the Russian conditional auxiliary as a conditional marker can be viewed as grammaticalization of this movement to such an extent that the moved position is reanalysed as underlying.

APPENDIX: TEXTS CITED

Drevnenovgorodskij dialekt (*DND*), ed. A. A. Zaliznjak. Moscow: Jazyki Russkoj Kul'tury, 1995.

Gramoty Velikogo Novgoroda i Pskova (*GVNP*), ed. S. N. Valk. Moscow: Izdatel'stvo Akademii Nauk SSSR, 1949.

Novgorodskaja Pervaja Letopis' po Sinodal'nomu spisku (*NPL*) [*First Novgorod Chronicle*], ed. J. Dietze. Leipzig: Edition Leipzig, 1971.

Polnoe sobranie russkix letopisej (*PSRL*). Vol. I. *Lavrent'evskaja letopis' i Suzdal'skaja letopis' po Akademičeskomu spisku* [*Laurentian Chronicle*], II. *Ipat'evskaja letopis'* [*Hypatian Chronicle*]. Moscow: Izdatel'stvo Vostočnoj Literatury, 1962.

Putešestvija russkix poslov XVI–XVII vv. (*PRP*), ed. D. S. Lixačev. Moscow: Izdatel'stvo Akademii Nauk SSSR, 1954.

Quattuor Evangeliorum Codex Glagoliticus olim Zographensis nunc Petropolitanus [*Codex Zographensis*], ed. V. Jagić. Berlin: Weidmann, 1879.

Quattuor Evangeliorum Versionis Palaeoslovenicae Codex Marianus Glagoliticus [*Codex Marianus*], ed. I. V. Jagić. Graz [Berlin]: Akademische Druck- und Verlagsanstalt [Weidmann], 1960 [1883].

Suprasălski ili Retkov sbornik, ed. J. Zaimov and M. Kapaldo. Sofia: Izdatelstvo na Bălgarskata Akademija na Naukite, 1982.

Suprasl'skaja rukopis' (*Su.*) [*Codex Suprasliensis*], ed. S. Sever'janov. St Petersburg: Izdanie Otdelenija Russkogo Jazyka i Slovesnosti Imperatorskoj Akademii Nauk, 1904.

Old English and Middle English Sources

Where examples have been taken from the Brooklyn–Geneva–Amsterdam–Helsinki Parsed Corpus (Pintzuk, Haeberli, van Kemenade, Koopman, and Beths 2000) and either edition of the Penn–Helsinki Parsed Corpus of Middle English (Kroch and Taylor 1994*b*, 2000), the referencing conventions of those corpora have been followed. Listed below are the original publication details of texts from these corpora which have been used in examples, and other sources referred to in this volume.

Ælfric, *Catholic Homilies*
The Sermones Catholici or Homilies of Ælfric, ed. B. Thorpe. 2 vols. London, 1844, 1846.

Ælfric, *Homilies*, Pope
Homilies of Ælfric: A Supplementary Collection, ed. J. C. Pope. London: Early English Text Society, os 259, 260, 1967–8.

Ælfric, *Letters* (AELet3)
Ælfric's First and Second Letters to Wulfstan. In B. Fehr (ed.), *Die Hirtenbriefe Ælfrics in altenglischer und lateinischer Fassung*. Bibliothek der angelsächsischen Prosa IX. 1914: 68–144, 146–220. Hamburg: Verlag von Henri Grand.

Ælfric, *Letter to Wulfsige*. Ibid. 1–34.

Ælfric, *Lives of Saints* (ÆLS), ed. W. W. Skeat 1966 (1881–1900). London: Early English Text Society, os 76, 82, 94, and 114.

Ancrene Riwle (CMANCRIW)
Part I in *Ancrene Riwle Introduction and Part I*, ed. R. W. Ackerman and R. Dahood. Binghampton, NY: Medieval and Renaissance Texts and Studies 31, 1984.
Part II in *The English Text of the Ancrene Riwle*, ed. E. J. Dobson. London: Early English Text Society, os 267, 1972.

Apollonius of Tyre (ApT, APOLLO)
The Old English 'Apollonius of Tyre', ed. P. Goolden. Oxford: Oxford University Press, 1958.

Bede
Bede, *Ecclesiastical History*, in *The Old English Version of Bede's 'Ecclesiastical History of the English People'*, ed. T. Miller. London: Early English Text Society, os 95, 96, 1959 (1890–1).

Beowulf and the Fight at Finnsburg, ed. F. Klaeber. 3rd edn. Boston: Heath, 1950.

Boethius
King Alfred's Old English Version of Boethius 'De Consolatione Philosophiae', ed. W. J. Sedgefield. Oxford: The Clarendon Press, 1899.

Caxton, *Prologues and Epilogues*
The Prologues and Epilogues of William Caxton, ed. W. J. B. Crotch. London: Early English Text Society, os 176, 1956 (1928).

Caxton, William. *The History of Reynard the Fox Translated from the Dutch Original by William Caxton*, ed. N. F. Blake. London: Early English Text Society, os 263, 1970. (CMREYNAR)

Chaucer, Geoffrey, *The Riverside Chaucer*, ed. L. D. Benson. 3rd edn. Boston: Houghton Mifflin Company, 1987. (CMBOETH, CMCTPARS, CMCTMELI, CMASTRO)

ChronA, CHROA2
The Anglo-Saxon Chronicle, MS A, in *Two of the Saxon Chronicles Parallel*, ed. C. Plummer. Oxford: The Clarendon Press, Oxford, 1965 (1892).

Cura Pastoralis
King Alfred's West-Saxon Version of Gregory's Pastoral Care, ed. H. Sweet. London: Early English Text Society, os 45, 50, 1871.

The Earliest Complete English Prose Psalter, ed. K. D. Buelbring. London: Early English Text Society, os 97, 1891. (CMEARLPS)

GDC
Gregory the Great, *Dialogues*, MS C in *Bischofs Waerferth von Worcester Uebersetzung der Dialoge Gregors des Grossen*, ed. H. Hecht. Bibliothek der Angelsächsischen Prosa V. Leipzig: Georg H. Wigands Verlag, 1900.

GDH, GREGD3
Gregory the Great, *Dialogues*, MS H. Ibid.

Hali Meiðhad (CMHALI)
In *The Katherine Group. Edited from MS Bodley 34*, ed. S. T. R. O. d'Ardenne. Bibliotheque de la Faculté de Philosophie et Lettres de l'Université de Liège, CCXV. Paris: Société d'Edition 'Les Belles Lettres', 1977.

Holy Rood Tree
History of the Holy Rood-Tree, ed. A. S. Napier. London: Early English Text Society, os 103, 1894.

Kentish Sermons
In *Early Middle English Verse and Prose*, ed. J. Bennett and G. Smithers. 2nd edn. Oxford: Clarendon Press, 1968.

Lambeth Homilies (CMLAMB1, CMLAMBX1)
In *Old English Homilies and Homiletic Treatises . . . of the Twelfth and Thirteenth Centuries. First Series*, ed. R. Morris. London: Early English Text Society, os 29, 34, 1969 (1868).

Laws, Laws Ine, LAW2
Laws of Alfred, Æthelred, Cnut, Ine, William I, Late Laws. In *Die Gesetze der Angelsachsen*, ed. F. Liebermann. Halle: Max Niemeyer, 1903. Alfred's Introduction to Laws. Ibid. 26–46.

Life of St Edmund (CMEDMUND)
In *Middle English Religious Prose*, ed. N. F. Blake. York Medieval Texts. London: Edward Arnold, 1972.

Mandeville (CMMANDEV)
Mandeville's Travels, Translated from the French of Jean d'Outremeuse, vol. I, ed. P. Hamelius. London: Early English Text Society, OS 153, 154, 1919–23.

Margery Kempe (CMKEMPE)
The Book of Margery Kempe, vol. I, ed. S. B. Meech and H. E. Allen. London: Early English Text Society, OS 212, 1940.

Mirk (CMMIRK)
Mirk's Festial: A Collection of Homilies, by Johannes Mirkus (John Mirk), part I, ed. T. Erbe. London: Early English Text Society, ES 96. London, 1905.

Mirror of St Edmund (Thornton) (CMEDTHOR)
In *Religious Pieces in Prose and Verse from R. Thornton's MS*, ed. George G. Perry. London: Early English Text Society, OS 26. London, 1867, revised 1913.

Mirror of St Edmund (Vernon) (CMEDVERN)
In *Yorkshire Writers: Richard Rolle of Hampole and his Followers*, ed. C. Horstman. London, 1895.

Mowntayne
The Autobiography of Thomas Mowntayne, ed. J. Nichols. London: Camden Society 77, 1859.

The New Testament in English according to the version by John Wycliffe about A. D. 1380 and revised by John Purvey about A. D. 1388, ed. J. Forshall and F. Madden. Oxford: Clarendon Press, 1879. (CMNTEST)

Orosius
King Alfred's Orosius, part I, ed. H. Sweet. London: Early English Text Society, OS 79, 1959 (1883).

Paston Letters and Papers of the Fifteenth Century, part I, ed. N. Davis. Oxford: Clarendon Press, 1971.

Poema Morale
In the same volume as *Lambeth Homilies*.

Purvey, John, *Prologue to the Bible*, in *The Holy Bible, containing the Old and New Testaments, with the Apocryphal Books, in the Earliest English Versions Made from the Latin Vulgate by John Wycliffe and his Followers*, vol. I, ed. J. Forshall and F. Madden. Oxford: University Press, 1850. (CMOTEST, CMPURVEY)

Rolle, *The Form of Living* (CMROLLEP)
In *English Writings of Richard Rolle, Hermit of Hampole*, ed. Hope Emily Allen. Oxford, 1931.

St Benet (CMBENRUL)
The Northern Prose Version of the Rule of St. Benet, in *The Benedictine Rule. Three Middle-English Versions of the Rule of St. Benet and Two Contemporary Rituals for the Ordination of Nuns*, ed. E. A. Kock. London: Early English Text Society, os 120, 1902.

St Juliana (CMJULIA)
Liflade ant te Passiun of Seinte Iuliene, ed. S.R.T.O. d'Ardenne. London: Early English Text Society, os 248, 1961.

St Katherine (CMKATHE)
In the same volume as *Hali Meiðhad*.

St Margarete (CMMARGA)
In the same volume as *Hali Meiðhad*.

Sawles Warde (CMSAWLES)
In the same volume as *Hali Meiðhad*.

Sermons from the MS Royal (CMROYAL)
Middle English Sermons, edited from British Museum MS. Royal 18 B. XXIII, ed. W. O. Ross. London: Early English Text Society, os 209, 1940.

Trinity Homilies (CMTRINIT)
In *Old English Homilies of the Twelfth Century. Second Series*, ed. R. Morris. London: Early English Text Society, os 53, 1873.

Vices and Virtues (CMVICES1)
Vices and Virtues, part I, ed. F. Holthausen. London: Early English Text Society, os 89, 1888.

Wulfstan, *Homilies* (WHom, WULF3)
The Homilies of Wulfstan, ed. B. Bethurum. Oxford: Clarendon Press, 1957.

Wycliffite Sermons (CMWYCSER)
English Wycliffite Sermons, ed. A. Hudson. Oxford: Clarendon Press, 1983.

References

ABNEY, P. S. 1987. The English Noun Phrase in its Sentential Aspect. Ph.D. dissertation. MIT.

ABRAHAM, W. 1997. The interdependence of case, aspect, referentiality in the history of German: The case of the verbal genitive. In van Kemenade and Vincent (eds.), 29–61.

ACKEMA, PETER, and AD NEELEMAN. 1998. Optimal questions. *Natural Language and Linguistic Theory* 16.443–90.

—— —— 2000. Absolute ungrammaticality. In Dekkers, van der Leeuw, and van de Weijer (eds.), 297–301.

ACQUAVIVA, PETER. 1993. The Logical Form of Negation: A Study of Operator-Variable Structures in Syntax. Ph.D. dissertation. Scuola Normale Superior, Pisa. Published under the same title. New York: Garland, 1997.

ADAMS, J. N. 1994. Wackernagel's Law and the position of unstressed personal pronouns in Classical Latin. *Transactions of the Philological Society* 92.103–78.

ADAMS, MARIANNE. 1987*a*. From Old French to the theory of pro-drop. *Natural Language and Linguistic Theory* 5.1–32.

—— 1987*b*. Old French, Null Subjects, and Verb Second Phenomena. Ph.D. dissertation. University of California, Los Angeles.

AISSEN, JUDITH. 1998. Markedness and Subject Choice in Optimality Theory. MS. University of California at Santa Cruz.

ALEXIADOU, A. 1997. *Adverb Placement: A Case Study in Antisymmetric Syntax.* Amsterdam and Philadelphia: John Benjamins.

ALI, M. SAID. 1931. *Gramática histórica da língua portugueza.* S. Paulo: Melhoramentos. 1964 (7th edn).

ALLEN, CYNTHIA. 1995. *Case-Marking and Reanalysis: Grammatical Relations from Old to Early Modern English.* Oxford: Clarendon Press.

ÁLVAREZ, R., X. L. REGUEIRA, and H. MONTEAGUDO. 1986. *Gramática galega.* Vigo: Galaxia.

ANDERSEN, H. 1973. Abductive and deductive change. *Language* 48.765–94.

—— 1989. Understanding linguistic innovations. In Breivik and Jahr (eds.), 5–28.

ANDERSON, JOHN. 1997. *A Notional Theory of Syntactic Categories.* Cambridge: Cambridge University Press.

ARCHANGELI, DIANA. 1997. Optimality Theory: An introduction to linguistics in the 1990s. In Archangeli and Langendoen (eds.), 1–32.

—— and D. TERENCE LANGENDOEN (eds.). 1997. *Optimality Theory: An Overview.* Oxford: Blackwell.

—— and DOUGLAS PULLEYBLANK. 1994. *Grounded Phonology.* Cambridge, Mass.: MIT Press.

ARONOFF, MARK. 1994. *Morphology by Itself.* Cambridge, MA: MIT Press.

ARTSTEIN, RON. 1998. Hierarchies. MS. Rutgers University.

BADIA MARGARIT, A. M. 1962. *Gramática catalana*. Madrid: Gredos. 1980.

BAILEY, C.-J. 1973. *Variation and Linguistic Theory*. Washington, DC: Center for Applied Linguistics.

BAKER, MARK. 1995. *The Polysynthesis Parameter*. Oxford and New York: Oxford University Press.

BAKOVIC, ERIC. 1997. Complementizers, faithfulness and optionality. The Rutgers Optimality Archive at http://ruccs.rutgers.edu/roa.html

BALDWIN, J. M. 1896. A new factor in evolution. *American Naturalist* 30.441–51.

BALTIN, MARK R. 1993. Negation and clause structure. Paper presented at North Eastern Linguistics Society 23rd Annual Meeting. MS. New York University.

BAMGBOSE, A. 1972. What is a verb in Yoruba? In A. Bamgbose (ed.), *The Yoruba Verb Phrase*, 17–60. Ibadan: Ibadan University Press.

BARBOSA, PILAR et al. (eds.). 1998. *Is the Best Good Enough? Proceedings from the Workshop on Optimality in Syntax, MIT, May 19–21, 1995*. Cambridge, MA: MIT Press.

BARÐAL, J. 1997. Oblique subjects in Old Scandinavian. In *Working Papers in Scandinavian Syntax* 60. Dept. of Scandinavian Languages, Lund.

BATALI, J. 1998. Computational simulations of the emergence of grammar. In Hurford, Studdert-Kennedy, and Knight (eds.), 405–26.

BATLLORI, M. 1996. Aspectos tipológicos y cambio sintáctico en la evolución del latín clásico al español medieval y preclásico. Doctoral Dissertation. Universidad Autónoma de Barcelona.

—— and F. ROCA. 1998. Old Spanish versus Modern Spanish: The case of the definite article. MS. Universitat de Girona.

BATTYE, ADRIAN, and IAN ROBERTS (eds.). 1995. *Clause Structure and Language Change*. Oxford and New York: Oxford University Press.

BECKMAN, J. N., S. URBANCZYK, and L. WALSH (eds.). 1995. *Papers in Optimality Theory*. University of Massachusetts Occasional Papers 18. Amherst, MA: GSLA.

BENDER, E. 2000. The syntax of Mandarin *ba*: Reconsidering the verbal analysis. To appear in *Journal of East Asian Linguistics*.

BENINCÀ, PAOLA. 1994. *La variazione sintattica. Studi di dialettologia romanza*. Bologna: Il Mulino.

BERGEN, L. VAN. 1998. The indefinite pronoun *man*: 'nominal' or 'pronominal'? Paper presented at the 10th International Conference on English Historical Linguistics, University of Manchester.

BERNINI, G. and P. RAMAT. 1996. *Negative Sentences in the Languages of Europe: A Typological Approach*. Berlin and New York: Mouton de Gruyter.

BERNSTEIN, J. B. 1997. Demonstratives and reinforcers in Romance and Germanic languages. *Lingua* 102.87–113.

BERWICK, R. 1998. Language evolution and the minimalist program: the origins of syntax. In Hurford, Studdert-Kennedy, and Knight (eds.), 320–40.

BETHS, F. 1999. The history of *dare* and the status of unidirectionality. *Linguistics* 37.1069–110.

BICKERTON, D. 1981. *Roots of Language*. Ann Arbor: Karoma.

—— 1984. The language bioprogram hypothesis. *The Behavioral and Brain Sciences* 7.173–222.

—— 1988. Creole languages and the bioprogram. In F. Newmeyer (ed.), *Linguistics: The Cambridge Survey* II.267–84. Cambridge: Cambridge University Press.

—— 1998. Catastrophic evolution: The case for a single step from protolanguage to full human language. In Hurford, Studdert-Kennedy, and Knight (eds.), 341–58.

BIRNER, BETTY, and GREGORY WARD. 1993. *There*-sentences and inversion as distinct constructions: A functional account. *Proceedings of Berkeley Linguistics Society* 19.27–39.

BITTNER, M., and K. HALE. 1996. The structural determination of Case and Agreement. *Linguistic Inquiry* 27.1–68.

BOBALJIK, JONATHAN DAVID. 1995. Morphosyntax: The Syntax of Verbal Inflection. Dissertation. MIT.

—— and D. JONAS. 1996. Subject positions and the roles of TP. *Linguistic Inquiry* 27.195–236.

—— and H. THRÁINSSON. 1998. Two heads aren't always better than one. *Syntax* 1.37–71.

BÖRJARS, KERSTI, and CAROL CHAPMAN. 1998. Agreement and pro-drop in some dialects of English. *Linguistics* 36.71–98.

—— JOHN PAYNE, and ERIKA CHISARIK. 1999. On the justification for functional categories in LFG. In Butt and King (eds.).

—— NIGEL VINCENT, and CAROL CHAPMAN. 1997. Paradigms, periphrases and pronominal inflection: A feature-based account. *Yearbook of Morphology 1996*. 155–80.

BOŠKOVIĆ, ŽELJKO. 1995. Participle movement and second position cliticization in Serbo-Croatian. *Lingua* 96.245–66.

—— 1996. Selection and categorial status of infinitival complements. *Natural Language and Linguistic Theory* 14.269–304.

BOSQUE, I. 1980. *Sobre la negación*. Madrid: Cátedra.

—— 1996a. La polaridad modal. *Actas del Cuarto Congreso de Hispanistas de Asia*. Seúl: Asociación Asiática de Hispanistas.

—— 1996b. Sobre la gramática de los contextos modales. Paper presented at XI Congreso de ALFAL, Las Palmas.

BOWERS, J. 1993. The syntax of predication. *Linguistic Inquiry* 24.591–656.

BRÄUER, HERBERT. 1957. *Untersuchungen zum Konjunktiv im Altkirchenslavischen und im Altrussischen*. Slavistische Veröffentlichungen 11. Wiesbaden: Osteuropa-Institut an der Freien Universität Berlin.

BREIVIK, LEIV EGIL. 1989. On the causes of syntactic change in English. In Breivik and Jahr (eds.), 29–70.

—— and ERIK JAHR (eds.). 1989. *Language Change: Contributions to the Study of its Causes*. Berlin: Mouton de Gruyter.

BRESNAN, JOAN. 1982. Control and complementation. *Linguistic Inquiry* 13.343–434. Reprinted in Joan Bresnan (ed.), *The Mental Representation of Grammatical Relations*, 282–390. Cambridge, MA: MIT Press.

—— 1994. Locative inversion and the architecture of Universal Grammar. *Language* 70.72–131.

—— 1997. Optimal syntax. In Dekkers, van der Leeuw, and van de Weijer (eds.), 334–85.

—— 1998a. Explaining morphosyntactic competition. In Mark Baltin and Chris Collins (eds.), *Handbook of Contemporary Syntactic Theory*. Oxford: Blackwell.

—— 1998b. The emergence of the unmarked pronoun. To appear in G. Legendre, J. Grimshaw, and S. Vikner (eds.), *Optimality Theoretic Syntax*. Cambridge, MA: MIT Press.

BRESNAN, JOAN. 1998c. Pidgin genesis in Optimality Theory. In Butt and King (eds.).

BRISCOE, E. J. 1997. Co-evolution of language and of the language acquisition device. *Proceedings of the 35th Meeting of Assoc. for Computational Linguistics*, 418–27. Palo Alto, CA: Morgan Kaufmann.

—— 1998. Language as a complex adaptive system: Co-evolution of language and of the language acquisition device. In P. Coppen, H. van Halteren, and L. Teunissen (eds.), *8th Meeting of Computational Linguistics in the Netherlands*, 3–40. Amsterdam: Rodopi.

—— 1999. The acquisition of grammar in an evolving population of language agents. Electronic Transactions in Artificial Intelligence. Special issue: *Machine Intelligence* 16, ed. S. Muggleton. http://www.etaij.org/

—— 2000a, to appear. Grammatical Acquisition and Linguistic Selection. In Briscoe (ed.).

—— 2000b, to appear. Grammatical acquisition: Inductive bias and co-evolution of language and the language acquisition device. *Language* 76.

—— (ed.). 2000c, to appear. *Language Acquisition and Linguistic Evolution: Formal and Computational Approaches*. Cambridge: Cambridge University Press.

—— and A. A. COPESTAKE. 1999. Lexical rules in constraint-based grammar. *Computational Linguistics* 25:4.

BRUGÈ, L. 1996. Demonstrative movement in Spanish: A comparative approach. *University of Venice Working Papers in Linguistics* 6:1.

BUTLER, MILTON. 1980. *Grammatically Motivated Subjects in Early English*. Texas Linguistic Forum 16.

BUTT, MIRIAM, and TRACY HOLLOWAY KING (eds.). 1998. The Proceedings of the LFG '98 Conference. CSLI Proceedings On-Line. http://www-csli.stanford.edu/publications. Stanford, CA: CSLI.

—— —— (eds.). 1999. The Proceedings of the LFG '99 Conference. CSLI Proceedings On-Line. http://www-csli.stanford.edu/publications. Stanford, CA: CSLI.

BYBEE, JOAN *et al.* 1994. *The Evolution of Grammar*. Chicago and London: Chicago University Press.

CAMPBELL, R. 1989. The Grammatical Structure of Verbal Predicates. Ph.D. dissertation. UCLA.

CAMUS BERGARECHE, B. 1988. Aspectos históricos de la negación románica. Ph.D. dissertation. Universidad Complutense de Madrid.

CANALE, W. M. 1978. Word Order Change in Old English: Base Reanalysis in Generative Grammar. Ph.D. dissertation. University of Toronto.

CARDINALETTI, ANNA, and MICHAEL STARKE. 1994. Pronouns: A View from Germanic. MS. University of Venice.

—— and IAN ROBERTS. 1991. Clause Structure and X-Second. MS. University of Venice and University of Geneva.

CHOMSKY, NOAM. 1965. *Aspects of the Theory of Syntax*. Cambridge, MA: MIT Press.

—— 1981. *Lectures on Government and Binding*. Dordrecht: Foris.

—— 1986a. *Barriers*. Cambridge, MA: MIT Press.

—— 1986b. *Knowledge of Language*. New York: Praeger.

—— 1991. Some notes on economy of derivation and representation. In Robert Freidin (ed.), *Principles and Parameters in Comparative Grammar*. Cambridge, MA: MIT Press.

—— 1993. A minimalist program for linguistic theory. In K. Hale and S. J. Keyser (eds.), *The View from Building 20: Essays in Linguistics in Honor of Sylvain Bromberger*, 1–52. Cambridge, MA and London: MIT Press.

—— 1995. *The Minimalist Program*. Cambridge, MA and London: MIT Press.

—— 1998. *Minimalist Inquiries: The Framework*. MIT Occasional Papers in Linguistics 15.

—— and HOWARD LASNIK. 1993. The theory of principles and parameters. In J. Jacobs *et al.* (eds.), *Syntax: An International Handbook of Contemporary Research*, 506–69. Berlin: Mouton de Gruyter. Reprinted as Chapter 1 of Chomsky (1995).

CHRISTENSEN, K. K. 1986. Norwegian *ingen*: A case of post-syntactic lexicalization. In Ö. Dahl and A. Holmberg (eds.), *Scandinavian Syntax*, 21–35. Stockholm: University of Stockholm.

—— 1987. Modern Norwegian *ingen* and the ghost of an Old Norse particle. In R. D. S. Allen and M. P. Barnes (eds.), *Proceedings of the Seventh Biennial Conference of Teachers of Scandinavian Studies in Great Britain and Northern Ireland*, 1–17. London: University College London.

CINQUE, GUGLIELMO. 1990. *Types of A-Dependencies*. Cambridge, MA: MIT Press.

—— 1994. On the evidence for partial N-movement in the Romance DP. In G. Cinque, J. Koster, J. Y. Pollock, L. Rizzi, and R. Zanuttini (eds.), *Paths towards Universal Grammar: Studies in Honor of Richard S. Kayne*, 85–110. Washington, DC: Georgetown University Press.

—— 1999. *Adverbs and Functional Heads: A Cross-Linguistic Perspective*. Oxford Studies in Comparative Syntax. New York and Oxford: Oxford University Press.

CINTRA, L. F. LINDLEY (ed.). 1954. *Crónica Geral de Espanha de 1344 (Edição crítica do texto português)*. Lisboa: Imprensa Nacional—Casa da Moeda.

—— 1959. *A Linguagem dos Foros de Castelo Rodrigo*. Lisbon: Publicações do Centro de Estudos Filológicos.

CLARK, R. 1992. The selection of syntactic knowledge. *Language Acquisition* 2.83–149.

—— and I. ROBERTS. 1993. A Computational model of language learnability and language change. *Linguistic Inquiry* 24.299–345.

CLARK, R. A. J. 1996. Internal and External Factors Affecting Language Change: A Computational Model. M. Sc. Dissertation. University of Edinburgh.

COELHO DA MOTA, MARIA. 1997. Les traits *nombre* et *personne/nombre* en portugais— l'oral dans ses variétés. In Mireille Bilgar *et al.* (eds.), *Analyse linguistique et approches de l'oral. Recueil d'études offert en hommage à Claire Blanche-Benveniste*, 339–45. Louvain and Paris: Peeters.

COLE, PETER. 1987. Null objects in universal grammar. *Linguistic Inquiry* 18.597–612.

COLLINS, C. 1993. *Topics in Ewe Syntax*. Ph.D. dissertation. MIT.

—— 1997. Argument sharing in serial verb constructions. *Linguistic Inquiry* 27.391–444.

COMPANY, C. 1991*a*. *La frase sustantiva en el español medieval. Cuatro cambios sintácticos*. México: UNAM.

—— 1991*b*. La extensión del artículo en el español medieval. *Romance Philology* 44.4: 402–24.

CORNILESCU, A. 1992. Remarks on the determiner system of Rumanian: the demonstratives *al* and *cel*. *Probus* 4.189–260.

COSMIDES, L., and TOOBY, J. 1996. Are humans good intuitive statisticians after all? Rethinking some conclusions from the literature on judgement under uncertainty. *Cognition* 58.1–73.

CRESTI, ARIANNA. 1994. La flessione personale dell'infinito nel repertorio italiano. *Rivista italiana di dialettologia* 18.31–50.

CRISMA, P. 1999. Sintassi formale e lingue medievali: l'articolo in inglese antico. MS. Università di Padova.

CROFT, WILLIAM. 1990. *Typology and Universals.* Cambridge: Cambridge University Press.

—— 1995. Autonomy and functionalist linguistics. *Language* 71.490–531.

CULICOVER, PETER, and WENDY WILKINS. 1986. Control, PRO, and the Projection Principle. *Language* 62.120–53.

CUNEO, MARCO. 1997. L'uso dell'infinito nei dialetti liguri: infinito con soggetto espresso e infinito flesso nel dialetto di Cicagna (GE). *Rivista italiana di dialettologia* 21.99–132.

CZIKO, G. 1995. *Without Miracles: Universal Selection Theory and the Second Darwinian Revolution.* Cambridge, MA: MIT Press.

DALRYMPLE, MARY, *et al.* (eds.). 1995. *Formal Issues in Lexical-Functional Grammar.* Stanford, CA: CSLI Publications.

DAVIES, EIRLYS. 1986. *The English Imperative.* London, Sydney, Dover: Croom Helm.

DAWKINS, R. 1983. Universal Darwinism. In D. S. Bendall (ed.), *Evolution: From Molecules to Men*, 403–25. Cambridge: Cambridge University Press.

—— 1989. *The Selfish Gene.* Oxford: Oxford University Press. 2nd edn.

DE ROECK, A., R. JOHNSON, M. KING, M. ROSNER, and G. SAMPSON. 1982. A myth about center-embedding. *Lingua* 58.327–40.

DEACON, T. 1997. *The Symbolic Species: Co-evolution of Language and Brain.* Cambridge, MA: MIT Press.

DÉCHAINE, R.-M., and M. TREMBLAY. 1998. On category features. In C. Thiersch and G. Müller (eds.), *Glow Newsletter* 40.26–7.

DEGRAFF, MICHEL. (ed.). 1999. *Language Creation and Language Change: Creolization, Diachrony and Development.* Cambridge, MA. MIT Press.

DEKKERS, JOOST, FRANK VAN DER LEEUW, and JEROEN VAN DE WEIJER (eds.). 2000. *Optimality Theory: Phonology, Syntax, and Acquisition.* Oxford: Oxford University Press.

DELSING, L.-O. 1988. The Scandinavian Noun Phrase. In *Working Papers in Scandinavian Syntax* 42.57–79. Dept. of Scandinavian Languages, Lund.

—— 1991. Om genitivens utveckling i fornsvenskan [On the development of the genitive in Old Swedish]. In S.-G. Malmgren and B. Ralph (eds.), *Studier i svensk språkhistoria* 2.12–30. Nordistica Gothonburgensia 14. Göteborg.

—— 1993. *The Internal Structure of Noun Phrases in the Scandinavian Languages: A Comparative Study.* Dept. of Scandinavian Languages, Lund.

—— 1998a. Support verbs and the Argument rule. In van Durme and Schøsler (eds.), 63–88.

—— 1998b. Possession in Germanic. In A. Alexiadou and C. Wilder (eds.), *Possessors, Predicates and Movement in the Determiner Phrase*, 87–108. Linguistik Aktuell/Linguistics Today, Amsterdam and Philadelphia: John Benjamins.

—— 1999. Från OV-ordföljd till VO-ordföljd—en språkförändring med förhinder [From OV word order to VO word order]. *Arkiv för nordisk filologi* 114.151–232.

DENNETT, D. 1995. *Darwin's Dangerous Idea: Evolution and the Meanings of Life.* New York: Simon and Schuster.

DIESING, MOLLY. 1988. Word order and the subject position in Yiddish. *Proceedings of NELS* 18.124–40.

—— 1997. Yiddish VP Order and the Typology of Object Movement in Germanic. *Natural Language and Linguistic Theory* 15.369–427.

DIKKEN, MARCEL DEN, and ALMA NÆSS. 1993. Case dependencies: The case of predicate inversion. *The Linguistic Review* 10.303–36.

DOBSON, E. J. 1972. *The English Text of the Ancrene Riwle edited from B. M. Cotton MS. Cleopatra C VI.* London: Oxford University Press.

—— 1976. *The Origins of Ancrene Wisse.* Oxford: Clarendon Press.

DOWTY, D., P. WALL, and S. PETERS. 1981. *An Introduction to Montague Semantics.* Dordrecht: Reidel.

DRESHER, E. B. 1999. Charting the learning path: Cues to parameter setting. *Linguistic Inquiry* 30.27–67.

DURIE, M. 1988. Verb serialization and 'verbal prepositions' in Oceanic languages. *Oceanic Linguistics* 27:1–2.1–23.

DURME, KAREN VAN, and LENE SCHØSLER. 1998. Valency and Verb Typology. In van Durme and Schøsler (eds.), 1–7.

—— —— (eds.) 1998. *Studies in Valency IV: Valency and Verb Typology.* Odense: Odense University Press.

EBERT, R. P. 1978. *Historische Syntax des Deutschen.* Stuttgart: Sammlung Metzler.

EINENKEL, E. 1912. Die englische Verbalnegation. *Anglia* 35.187–248.

ELLEGÅRD, ALVAR. 1953. *The Auxiliary Do: The Establishment and Regulation of its Use in English.* Gothenburg Studies in English 2. Stockholm: Almqvist and Wiksell.

EMONDS, J. 1985. *A Unified Theory of Syntactic Categories.* Dordrecht: Foris.

ESPINAL, M. T. 1998. Expletive negation, negative concord and feature checking. MS. Universitat Autònoma de Barcelona.

FALK, CECILIA. 1993a. Non-Referential Subjects and Agreement in the History of Swedish. Ph.D. dissertation. University of Lund.

—— 1993b. Impersonal Subjects in the History of Swedish. Dept. of Scandinavian Languages, Lund.

—— 1997. *Fornsvenska upplevarverb* [Old Swedish experiencer verbs]. Lundastudier i nordisk språkvetenskap A 49. Lund: Lund University Press.

FARRELL, PATRICK. 1990. Null objects in Brazilian Portuguese. *Natural Language and Linguistic Theory* 8.325–46.

FERRARESI, GISELLA. 1991. Die Stellung des gotischen Verbs im Licht eines Vergleichs mit dem Althochdeutschen. Tesi di Laurea. University of Venice.

FISCHER, O., A. VAN KEMENADE, W. KOOPMAN, and W. VAN DER WURFF. 2000. *The Syntax of Early English.* Cambridge: Cambridge University Press.

FODOR, J. D. 1981. Does performance shape competence? *Phil. Trans. Royal Society of London.* B295. 285–95.

—— 1998. Unambiguous triggers. *Linguistic Inquiry* 29.1–36.

FOULET, L. 1930. *Petite syntaxe de l'ancien français.* Paris: Librairie Ancienne Honoré Champion.

FRANK, R. and S. KAPUR. 1996. On the use of triggers in parameter setting. *Linguistic Inquiry* 27.623–60.

FREIRE, A. BRAANCAMP (org). [1915] 1977. *Fernão Lopes, Cronica del Rei Dom Joham I de boa memoria e dos Reis de Portugal o decimo* I. Lisbon: Imprensa Nacional—Casa da Moeda.

FRISCH, STEFAN. 1997. The change in negation in Middle English: A NEGP licensing account. *Lingua* 101.21–64.

GERDTS, DONNA. 1993. Mapping Halkomelem grammatical relations. *Linguistics* 31.591-621.

GIANNAKIDOU, A. 1994. The semantic licensing of negative polarity items and the Modern Greek subjunctive. In A. de Boer, H. de Hoop, and H. de Swart (eds.), *Language and Cognition* 4.55–68. Groningen. Yearbook 1994 of the research group for Theoretical and Experimental Linguistics of the University of Groningen.

—— 1997. *The Landscape of Polarity Items*. Groningen Dissertations in Linguistics 18.

GIBSON, E. 1998. Linguistic complexity: Locality of syntactic dependencies. *Cognition* 68.1–76.

—— and K. WEXLER. 1994. Triggers. *Linguistic Inquiry* 25.407–54.

GIRÓN ALCONCHEL, J. L. 1998. Sobre el reajuste morfológico de los demostrativos en el español clásico. In C. García Turza *et al.* (eds.), *Actas del IV Congreso Internacional de Historia de la Lengua Española*. Logroño and Bilbao: Publicaciones de la Universidad de la Rioja-Editorial Didot.

GIUSTI, G. 1995. The categorial status of determiners. MS. Università di Venezia.

GIVÓN, T. 1975. Serial verbs and syntactic change: Niger-Congo. In C. Li (ed.), *Word Order and Word Order Change*, 113–48. Austin, TX: University of Texas Press.

—— 1984. *Syntax: A Functional Typological Introduction*. Amsterdam and Philadelphia: John Benjamins.

GOLD, E. M. 1967. Language identification in the limit. *Information and Control* 10.447–74.

GOLDSMITH, J. A. (ed.). 1995. *The Handbook of Phonological Theory*. Cambridge, MA and Oxford: Blackwell.

GONDAR, FRANCISCO. 1978. *O infinitivo conxugado en galego*. University of Santiago de Compostela, Anejo 13, Verba, Anuario Gallego de Filología.

GRIMSHAW, JANE. 1997. Projection, heads and optimality. *Linguistic Inquiry* 28.373–422.

—— 1998. Constraints on constraints. Paper delivered at the symposium 'Is Syntax Different?', CSLI, Stanford University, 12–13 December 1998.

HAEBERLI, E. 1991. *The Neg Criterion and Negative Concord*. Mémoire de Licence. Université de Genève.

—— 1996. Clitics in West Flemish. In Halpern and Zwicky (eds.), 135–64.

—— 1998. Some aspects of the distribution of non-pronominal subjects in Old and Middle English. Paper presented at the 10th International Conference of English Historical Linguistics, University of Manchester.

—— 1999. *Features, Categories and the Syntax of A-positions: Synchronic and Diachronic Variation in the Germanic Languages*. Ph.D. dissertation. Université de Genève.

—— 1999. On the Word Order 'XP–Subject' in the Germanic Languages. *The Journal of Comparative Germanic Linguistics* 3.1–36.

HAEGEMAN, L. 1995. *The Syntax of Negation*. Cambridge: Cambridge University Press.

HAIDER, HUBERT. 1992. Branching and discharge. *Arbeitspapiere des Sonderforschungs-bereichs 340* 23. University of Stuttgart.

HAIMAN, JOHN. 1985. *Natural Syntax*. Cambridge: Cambridge University Press.

HALE, M. 1998. Diachronic syntax. *Syntax* 1.1–18.

HALL, J. 1920. *Selections from Early Middle English 1130–1250*. Oxford: Clarendon Press.

HALPERN, AARON L. 1995. *On the Placement and Morphology of Clitics*. Stanford, CA: CSLI Publications.

—— and ARNOLD M. ZWICKY (eds.). 1996. *Approaching Second: Second Position Clitics and Related Phenomena*. Stanford, CA: CSLI Publications.

HAN, CHUNG-HYE. 2000. *The Structure and Interpretation of Imperatives: Mood and Force in Universal Grammar*. Series in Outstanding Dissertations in Linguistics. New York, London: Garland Publishing, Inc.

HARLEY, HEIDI. 1995. Subjects, Events, and Licensing. Ph.D. dissertation. MIT.

HARRIS, A. and L. CAMPBELL. 1995. *Historical Syntax in Cross-Linguistic Perspective*. New York: Cambridge University Press.

HARRIS, M. 1978. *The Evolution of French Syntax: A Comparative Approach*. Harlow: Longman.

—— 1980. The marking of definiteness in Romance. In J. Fisiak (ed.), *Historical Morphology*, 141–56. Berlin: Mouton de Gruyter.

HASHIMOTO, A. 1971. Mandarin syntactic structures. *Unicorn* 8.1–149.

HAUGE, KJETIL RÅ. 1976. *The Word Order of Predicate Clitics in Bulgarian*. Meddelelser 10. Oslo: Universitetet i Oslo, Slavisk-Baltisk Institutt.

HAWKINS, J. A. 1994. *A Performance Theory of Order and Constituency*. Cambridge: Cambridge University Press.

HEINE, BERND, ULRIKE CLAUDI, and FRIEDERIKE HÜNNEMEYER. 1991. *Grammaticalization. A Conceptual Framework*. Chicago and London: The University of Chicago Press.

—— and M. REH. 1984. *Grammaticalization and Reanalysis in African Languages*. Hamburg: Helmut Buske.

HELLAN, L., and C. PLATZACK. 1995. Pronouns in Scandinavian languages: An overview. *Working Papers in Scandinavian Syntax* 56.47–69. Dept. of Scandinavian Languages, Lund.

HERBURGER, E. 1998. Spanish n-words: Ambivalent behavior or ambivalent nature? In U. Sauerland and O. Percus (eds.), *The Interpretive Tract*, 87–102. MIT Working Papers in Linguistics 25.

HEYCOCK, CAROLINE, and YOUNG-SUK LEE. 1989. Subjects and predication in Korean and Japanese. In Hajime Hoji (ed.), *Japanese/Korean Linguistics* II.239–54. Stanford, CA: CSLI.

HILL, B. 1977. The twelfth century Conduct of Life, formerly the Poema Morale or a Moral Ode. *Leeds Studies in English* 9.97–144.

HINTERHÖLZL, ROLAND. 1997. A XP-movement account of restructuring. MS. University of Southern California.

HJELMSLEV, LOUIS. 1954. La stratification du langage. *Word* 10.163–88. Reprinted in Louis Hjelmslev, *Essais linguistiques*, 36–68. Copenhagen: Nordisk Sprog- og Kulturforlag, 1970.

HOEKSTRA, TEUN, and RENÉ MULDER. 1990. Unergatives as copular verbs: Locational and existential predication. *The Linguistic Review* 7.1–79.

HOGG, RICHARD M. (ed.). 1992. *The Cambridge History of English* I, *The Beginnings to 1066*. Cambridge: Cambridge University Press.

HOLMBERG, A. 1986. Word Order and Syntactic Features in the Scandinavian Languages and English. Doctoral dissertation. University of Stockholm.

—— 1993. Two subject positions in IP in Mainland Scandinavian. *Working Papers in Scandinavian Syntax* 52.29–41. Dept. of Scandinavian Languages, Lund.

—— and G. SANDSTÖM. 1996. Scandinavian possessive constructions from a Northern Swedish viewpoint. In J. R. Black and V. Motapanyane (eds.), *Microparametric Syntax and Dialect Variation*. Current Issues in Linguistic Theory 139. Amsterdam and Philadelphia: John Benjamins.

HOPPER, PAUL, and ELIZABETH TRAUGOTT. 1993. *Grammaticalization*. Cambridge: Cambridge University Press.

HORNSTEIN, NORBERT. 1999. Movement and control. *Linguistic Inquiry* 30.69–96.

HRÓARSDÓTTIR, ÞORBJÖRG. 1996. The decline of OV word order in the Icelandic VP: A diachronic study. *Working Papers in Scandinavian Syntax* 57.92–141. Dept. of Scandinavian Languages, Lund.

—— 1998. *Setningafræðilegar breytingar á 19. öld; þróun þriggja málbreytinga*. Málfræðirannsóknir 10. Reykjavík: Málvísindastofnun Háskóla Íslands.

—— 1999a. VP-preposing in Icelandic. MS. University of Tromsø. Paper presented at 14th Comparative Germanic Syntax Workshop, Lund, Sweden, January 8–9, 1999.

—— 1999b. *Verb Phrase Syntax in the History of Icelandic*. Doctoral dissertation. University of Tromsø. Published as *Word Order Change in Icelandic: From OV to VO*. Amsterdam and Philadelphia: John Benjamins, 2000.

—— To appear. Parameter change in Icelandic. In P. Svenonius (ed.), *The Derivation of VO and OV*. Amsterdam and Philadelphia: John Benjamins.

HUANG, YAN. 1995. On null subjects and null objects in generative grammar. *Linguistics* 33.1081–123.

HUDSON, R. 1995. Measuring Syntactic Complexity, MS. University College London.

HULK, AAFKE, and ANS VAN KEMENADE. 1993. Subjects, nominative case, agreement and functional heads. *Lingua* 89.181–215.

—— 1997. Negation as a reflex of clause structure. In D. Forget, P. Hirschbuehler, F. Martineau, and M.-L. Rivero (eds.), *Negation and Polarity: Syntax and Semantics*, 183–207. Amsterdam and Philadelphia: John Benjamins.

HULST, HARRY VAN DER, and J. VAN DE WEIJER. 1995. Vowel harmony. In J. A. Goldsmith (ed.), *The Handbook of Phonological Theory*, 495–534. Cambridge, MA and Oxford: Blackwell.

HURFORD, J. 1987. *Language and Number*. Oxford: Blackwell.

—— 1999. The evolution of language and languages. In R. Dunbar, C. Knight, and C. Power (eds.), *The Evolution of Culture*, 173–93. Edinburgh: Edinburgh University Press.

—— 2000, to appear. Expression/induction models of language evolution: Dimensions and issues. In Briscoe (ed.).

—— M. STUDDERT-KENNEDY, and C. KNIGHT (eds.). 1998. *Approaches to the Evolution of Language*. Cambridge: Cambridge University Press.

HYAMS, N. 1986. *Language acquisition and the theory of parameters*. Dordrecht: Reidel.

HYMAN, LARRY. 1975. On the change from SOV to SVO: Evidence from Niger-Congo. In Charles N. Li (ed.), *Word Order and Word Order Change*, 113–47. Austin, TX: University of Texas Press.

IATRIDOU, SABINE, and ANTHONY KROCH. 1992. The licensing of CP-recursion and its relevance to the Germanic verb-second phenomenon. *Working Papers in Scandinavian Syntax* 50.1–24.

INDRIÐASON, ÞORSTEINN. 1987. Skyrsla um orðaröð í sagnlið. MS. University of Iceland.

JACK, G. 1978a. Negative adverbs in Early Middle English. *English Studies* 59.295–309.

—— 1978b. Negation in later Middle English prose. *Archivum Linguisticum* (n.s.) 9.58–72.

—— 1978c. Negative concord in Early Middle English. *Studia Neophilologica* 50.29–39.

JESPERSEN, O. 1917. *Negation in English and Other Languages*. Det Kgl. Danske Videnskabernes Selskab. Historisk-filologiske Meddelelser 1.1–151. Copenhagen.

JOHNSON, KYLE. 1996. In search of the English middle field. MS. University of Massachusetts, Amherst, MA.

JONES, MICHAEL. 1993. *Sardinian Syntax*. London: Routledge.

JÓNSSON, JÓHANNES GÍSLI. 1991. Stylistic fronting in Icelandic. *Working Papers in Scandinavian Syntax* 48.1–43. Dept. of Scandinavian Languages, Lund.

JOSEFSSON, G., and C. PLATZACK. 1998. Short raising of V and N in Mainland Scandinavian. In *Working Papers in Scandinavian Syntax* 61. Dept. of Scandinavian Languages, Lund.

KAGER, RENÉ. 1999. *Optimality Theory*. Cambridge: Cambridge University Press.

KAPLAN, RONALD, and JOAN BRESNAN. 1982. Lexical-Functional Grammar: A formal system for grammatical representation. In Joan Bresnan (ed.), *The Mental Representation of Grammatical Relations*, 173–281. Cambridge, MA: MIT Press. Reprinted in Dalrymple *et al.* (eds.), 29–130.

KAUFFMAN, S. 1993. *The Origins of Order: Self-Organization and Selection in Evolution*. New York: Oxford University Press.

KAYNE, RICHARD S. 1984. *Connectedness and Binary Branching*. Dordrecht: Foris.

—— 1994. *The Antisymmetry of Syntax*. Linguistic Inquiry Monograph 25. Cambridge, MA and London: MIT Press.

—— 1998. Overt vs. covert movement. *Syntax* 1.128–91.

—— 1999. Prepositional complementizers as attractors. *Probus* 11.39–73.

KELLER, R. 1994. *On Language Change: The Invisible Hand in Language*. London: Routledge.

KEMENADE, ANS VAN. 1987. *Syntactic Case and Morphological Case in the History of English*. Dordrecht: Foris.

—— 1997a. V2 and embedded topicalization in Old and Middle English. In Kemenade and Vincent (eds.), 326–352.

—— 1997b. Negative-initial sentences in Old and Middle English. In *A Festschrift for Roger Lass on his Sixtieth Birthday. Studia Anglica Posnaniensia* 31.91–104.

—— 1999. Sentential negation and clause structure in Old English. In Tieken-Boon van Ostade, Tottie, and van der Wurff (eds.), 147–65.

—— To appear. *Verbal Syntax and Negation in the History of English*.

—— and A. HULK (eds.). 1993. *Null Subjects in Diachrony*. Special issue of *Lingua* 89:2/3.

KEMENADE, ANS VAN and NIGEL VINCENT (eds.). 1997. *Parameters of Morpho-syntactic Change*. Cambridge: Cambridge University Press.

KENISTON, H. 1937. *The Syntax of Castilian Prose. The Sixteenth Century*. Chicago: The University of Chicago Press.

KENSTOWICZ, M. 1994. *Phonology in Generative Grammar*. Cambridge, MA and Oxford: Blackwell.

KING, TRACY HOLLOWAY. 1996. Slavic clitics, Long Head Movement, and Prosodic Inversion. *Journal of Slavic Linguistics* 4.274–311.

KIPARSKY, PAUL. 1996. The shift to head-initial VP in Germanic. In H. Thráinsson, S. D. Epstein, and S. Peter (eds.), *Studies in Comparative Germanic Syntax*, II.140–79. (Studies in Natural Language and Linguistic Theory 38.) Dordrecht: Kluwer.

—— 1997. The rise of positional licensing. In van Kemenade and Vincent (eds.), 460–94.

KIRBY, S. 1997. Competing motivations and emergence: explaining implicational hierarchies. *Language Typology* 1.5–32.

—— 1998. Fitness and the selective adaptation of language. In Hurford, Studdert-Kennedy, and Knight (eds.), 359–83.

—— 1999. *Function, Selection and Innateness: The Emergence of Language Universals*. Oxford: Oxford University Press.

—— 2000, to appear. Learning, bottlenecks and the evolution of recursive syntax. In Briscoe (ed.).

—— and J. HURFORD. 1997. Learning, culture and evolution in the origin of linguistic constraints. In P. Husbands and I. Harvey (eds.), *4th European Conference on Artificial Life*, 493–502. Cambridge, MA: MIT Press.

KLOOSTER, W. 1994. Negation and the Comparative Construction: A Note on Dutch Comparative Construction. MS. University of Amsterdam.

—— 1998. Monotonicity and Scope of Negation. MS (preliminary draft). Holland Institute of Generative Linguistics/University of Amsterdam.

KOCK, E. A. 1902. Introduction. In E. A. Kock, *Three Middle English Versions of the Rule of St Benet*. London: Early English Text Society OS 120.

KOOPMAN, HILDA. 1984. *The Syntax of Verbs: From Verb Movement Rules in the Kru Languages to Universal Grammar*. Dordrecht: Foris.

—— and ANNA SZABOLCSI. 1997. The Hungarian Verbal Complex: Incorporation as XP-movement. MS. UCLA.

KOOPMAN, W. 1990. Word order in Old English with Special Reference to the Verb Phrase. Ph.D. dissertation. University of Amsterdam.

—— 1996. Evidence for clitic adverbs in Old English: An evaluation. In D. Britton (ed.), *English Historical Linguistics 1994*, 223–45. Amsterdam and Philadelphia: John Benjamins.

KOSTER, JAN. 1995. Predicate incorporation and the word order of Dutch. In G. Cinque, J. Koster, J.-Y. Pollock, L. Rizzi, and R. Zanuttini (eds.), *Paths to Universal Grammar: Studies in Honor of Richard S. Kayne*, 255–76. Washington, DC: Georgetown University Press.

KROCH, ANTHONY. 1989*a*. Function and grammar in the history of English: Periphrastic *do*. In Ralph Fasold and Deborah Schiffrin (eds.), *Language Change and Variation*, 133–72. Current Issues in Linguistic Theory 52. Amsterdam and Philadelphia: John Benjamins.

—— 1989*b*. Reflexes of grammar in patterns of language change. *Language Variation and Change* 1.199–244.

—— 1992. Syntactic change. In W. Bright (ed.), *Oxford International Encyclopaedia of Linguistics* IV.111–14. New York and Oxford: Oxford University Press.

—— 1994. Morphosyntactic variation. In K. Beals *et al.* (eds.), *Papers from the 30th Regional Meeting of the Chicago Linguistics Society* II, 180–201. Chicago: Chicago Linguistic Society.

—— and ANN TAYLOR. 1994*a*. Remarks on the XV/VX Alternation in Early Middle English. MS. University of Pennsylvania.

—— —— (eds.). 1994*b*. *Penn–Helsinki Parsed Corpus of Middle English*. Philadelphia: Department of Linguistics, University of Pennsylvania. 1st edn. Accessible via www.ling.upenn.edu.

—— —— 1997. Verb movement in Old and Middle English: Dialect variation and language contact. In van Kemenade and Vincent (eds.), 297–325.

—— —— (eds.). 2000. *Penn–Helsinki Parsed Corpus of Middle English*. Philadelphia: Department of Linguistics, University of Pennsylvania. 2nd edn. Accessible via www.ling.upenn.edu.

—— —— and D. RINGE, Jr. 2000. The Middle English verb-second constraint: A case study in language contact and language change. In S. Herring, P. van Reenen, and L. Schoesler (eds.), *Textual Parameters in Older Languages*. Amsterdam and Philadelphia: John Benjamins.

KURYŁOWICZ, JERZY. 1949. La nature des procès dits 'analogiques'. *Acta Linguistica* 5.15–37.

LABOV, W. 1994. *Principles of Linguistic Change* I: *Internal Factors*. Oxford: Blackwell.

LADUSAW, W. 1992. Expressing negation. *Semantics and Linguistic Theory (SALT)* II.237–59. Ithaca, NY: Cornell University Press.

LAING, M. 1993. *Catalogue of Sources for a Linguistic Atlas of Early Medieval English*. Cambridge: D. S. Brewer.

LAKA, I. 1990. Negation in Syntax: On the Nature of Functional Categories and Projections. Ph.D. dissertation. Massachusetts Institute of Technology.

—— 1993. Unergatives that assign ergative, unaccusatives that assign accusative. In Jonathan D. Bobaljik and Colin Phillips (eds.), *Papers on Case and Agreement* I. MIT Working Papers in Linguistics 18.

LANGACKER, RONALD. 1977. Syntactic reanalysis. In C. Li (ed.), 57–139.

—— 1987. Nouns and verbs. *Language* 65.53–94.

LAPESA, R. 1961. Del demostrativo al artículo. *Nueva Revista de Filología Hispánica* 15.23–44.

LARM, K. 1936. *Den bestämda artikeln i äldre fornsvenska. En historisk-semologisk studie*. [The definite article in Early Old Swedish]. Stockholm.

LARSON, R. 1991. Some issues in verb serialization. In C. Lefebvre (ed.), *Serial Verbs: Grammatical, Comparative and Cognitive Approaches*, 185–210. Amsterdam and Philadelphia: John Benjamins.

LASNIK, HOWARD. 1992. Case and expletives: notes towards a parametric account. *Linguistic Inquiry* 23.381–405.

—— 1999. *Minimalist Analysis*. Oxford: Blackwell.

LATTEWITZ, KAREN. 1996. Movement of Verbal Complements. MS. University of Groningen.

LEDGEWAY, ADAM. 1998. Variation in the Romance infinitive: The case of the Southern Calabrian inflected infinitive. *Transactions of the Philological Society* 96.1–61.

LEHMANN, CHRISTIAN. 1985. Grammaticalization: Synchronic variation and diachronic change. *Lingua e Stile* 20.303–18.

LEMA, JOSÉ, and MARÍA-LUISA RIVERO. 1989. Long Head Movement: ECP vs. HMC. *North Eastern Linguistics Society* 20.333–47.

LEONETTI, M. 1996. Determinantes y contenido descriptivo. *Español Actual* 66.5–23.

LI, C., and S. THOMPSON. 1973. Serial verb constructions in Mandarin Chinese: Subordination or coordination? In C. Corum, T. C. Smith-Stark, and A. Weiser (eds.), *You Take the High Node and I'll take the Low Node: Papers from the Comparative Syntax Festival*. 96–103. Chicago: Chicago Linguistic Society.

—— —— 1974. An explanation of word order change SVO > SOV. *Foundations of Language* 12.201–14.

—— —— 1977. A mechanism for the development of copula morphemes. In Li (ed.), 419–44.

—— (ed.). 1977. *Mechanisms of Syntactic Change*. Austin, TX: University of Texas Press.

LI, Y. 1993. Structural head and aspectuality. *Language* 69.480–504.

LI, Y. H. A. 1990. *Order and Constituency in Mandarin Chinese*. Dordrecht: Kluwer.

LIEBERMAN, P. 1991. Preadaptation, natural selection and function. *Language and Communication* 11.67–9.

LIGHTFOOT, DAVID. 1976. The base component as a locus of linguistic change. In W. Christie (ed.), *Current Progress in Historical Linguistics*, 22–5. Amsterdam: North Holland.

—— 1979. *Principles of Diachronic Syntax*. Cambridge: Cambridge University Press.

—— 1991. *How to Set Parameters: Arguments from Language Change*. Cambridge, MA: MIT Press.

—— 1997. Shifting triggers and diachronic reanalyses. In van Kemenade and Vincent (eds.), 253–72.

—— 1999. *The Development of Language: Acquisition, Change, and Evolution*. Malden, MA and Oxford: Blackwell.

—— and NORBERT HORNSTEIN (eds.). 1994. *Verb Movement*. Cambridge: Cambridge University Press.

LINDBLOM, B. 1998. Systemic constraints and adaptive change in the formation of sound structure. In Hurford, Studdert-Kennedy, and Knight (eds.), 242–64.

LIPSKI, JOHN. 1991. In search of the Spanish personal infinitive. In D. Wanner and D. Kibbee (eds.), *New Analyses in Romance Linguistics*, 210–20. Amsterdam and Philadelphia: John Benjamins.

LLORENS, E. 1929. *La negación en el español antiguo con referencia a otros idiomas*. Madrid: Anejo 11 de la Revista de Filologia Española.

LONGOBARDI, GIUSEPPE. 1994. Reference and proper names. *Linguistic Inquiry* 25.609–65.

—— 1996. Formal syntax and etymology: The history of French *chez*. Paper delivered at the Fourth Diachronic Generative Syntax Conference, Montreal, October 1995.

LOPORCARO, MICHELE. 1986. L'infinito coniugato nell'Italia centro-meridionale: ipotesi genetica e ricostruzione storica. *L'Italia dialettale* 49.173–240.

LORD, C. 1973. Serial verbs in transition. *Studies in African Linguistics* 4.269–96.

—— 1976. Evidence for syntactic reanalysis: From verb to complementizer in Kwa. In S. Steever, C. Walker, and S. Mufwene (eds.), *Papers from the Parasession on Diachronic Syntax.* 179–91. Chicago: Chicago Linguistic Society.

—— 1982. The development of object markers in serial verb languages. In P. Hopper and S. Thompson (eds.), *Studies in Transitivity.* Syntax and Semantics 15.277–99. New York and San Diego: Academic Press.

LURAGHI, SILVIA. 1997. Omission of the direct object in Latin. *Indogermanische Forschungen* 102.239–57.

McCOLL, J. H. 1995. *Probability.* London: Edward Arnold.

McMAHON, A. 1994. *Understanding Language Change.* Cambridge: Cambridge University Press.

MACROBERT, C. M. 1980. The Decline of the Infinitive in Bulgarian. D. Phil. thesis. University of Oxford.

McWHORTER, J. 1997. *Towards a New Model of Creole Genesis.* New York: Peter Lang.

MALING, JOAN. 1990. Inversion in embedded clauses in Modern Icelandic. In Maling and Zaenen (eds.), 71–90.

—— and ANNIE ZAENEN (eds.). 1990. *Syntax and Semantics 24: Modern Icelandic Syntax.* New York and San Diego: Academic Press.

MANZOTTI, E., and A. RIGAMONTI. 1991. La negazione. In L. Renzi and G. Salvi (eds.), *Grande grammatica italiana di consultazione* II: *I sintagmi verbale, aggetivale, avverbiale; La Subordinazione,* 245–317. Bologna: Il Mulino.

MARTINS, ANA MARIA. 1996. Aspectos da negação na história das línguas românicas: Da natureza de palavras como nenhum, nada, ninguém. *Actas do XII encontro nacional da Associação Portuguesa de Linguística,* 179–210. Lisbon: Associação Portuguesa de Linguística.

—— 1999. On the origin of the Portuguese inflected infinitive. Paper delivered at ICHL14, UBC, Vancouver, 9–13 August 1999.

MATTHEWS, P. H. 1981. *Syntax.* Cambridge: Cambridge University Press.

—— 1991. *Morphology.* Cambridge: Cambridge University Press. 2nd edn.

MAUGER, G. 1968. *Grammaire pratique du français d'aujourd'hui. Langue parlée, langue écrite.* Paris: Hachette. 6th edn.

MAURER, THEODOR. 1968. *O infinito flexionado português. Estudo histórico-descritivo.* São Paulo: Editora Nacional.

MAYLEY, G. 1996. Landscapes, learning costs and genetic assimilation. In P. Turney, D. Whitley, and R. Anderson (eds.), *Evolution, Learning and Instinct: 100 Years of the Baldwin Effect.* Cambridge, MA: MIT Press.

MAYNARD-SMITH, J. 1998. *Evolutionary Genetics.* Oxford: Oxford University Press. 2nd edn.

MEI, T. 1990. Tang-Song chuzhishi de laiyuan [The origin of the disposal construction during the Tang and Song dynasties]. *Zhongguo yuwen* 3.191–216.

MEILLET, A. 1912. L'évolution des formes grammaticales. Repr. in A. Meillet, *Linguistique Historique et Linguistique Générale,* 130–48. Paris: Champion, 1958.

MENÉNDEZ-PIDAL, R. (ed.). 1946. *Cantar de Mio Cid: texto, gramática y vocabulario* III. Madrid: Espasa-Calpe. 5th edn. 1980.

MEYER-LÜBKE, W. 1900. *Grammaire des langues romanes* III: *Syntaxe.* Paris: H. Welter. Translated from *Grammatik der romanischen Sprachen: Syntax.* Leipzig, 1899.

MILLER, G. A., and N. CHOMSKY. 1963. Finitary models of language users. In R. D. Luce, R. R. Bush, and E. Galanter (eds.), *Handbook of Mathematical Psychology* II. 419–91. New York: Wiley.

MILNER, J. C. 1979. Le système de la négation en français et l'opacité du sujet. *Langue française* 44.80–106.

MILSARK, GARY. 1974. Existential Sentences in English. Ph.D. dissertation. MIT.

MITCHELL, B. 1985. *Old English Syntax*. Oxford: Clarendon Press.

MOLINELLI, P. 1988. *Fenomeni della negazione dal latino all'italiano*. Firenze: La Nuova Italia.

MORRIS, R. 1969. *Old English Homilies: First Series*. New York: Oxford University Press.

MOSSÉ, FERNAND. 1952. *A Handbook of Middle English*. Baltimore: The John Hopkins Press.

MOUREK, V. E. 1903. *Zur Negation im Altgermanischen*. Prague: Verlag der kgl. Böhmischen Gesellschaft der Wissenschaften.

MUGGLETON, S. 1996. Learning from positive data. *Proceedings of the 6th Inductive Logic Programming Workshop*, Stockholm.

NASH, L., and A. ROUVERET. 1997. Proxy categories in phrase structure theory. *NELS* 27.287–304.

NEWMEYER, FREDERICK. 1998a. *Language Form and Language Function*. Cambridge, MA: MIT Press.

—— 1998b. On the supposed 'counterfunctionality' of Universal Grammar: Some evolutionary implications. In Hurford, Studdert-Kennedy, and Knight (eds.), 305–19.

NEWPORT, E. 1977. Motherese: The speech of mothers to young children. In N. Castellan, D. Pisoni, and G. Potts (eds.), *Cognitive Theory* II.177–217. Hillsdale, NJ: Lawrence Erlbaum.

NICHOLS, JOHANNA. 1986. Head-marking and dependent-marking grammar. *Language* 62.56–119.

NIKIFORON, S. D. 1952. *Glagol: ego kategorii i formy v russkoj pis'mennosti vtoroj poloviny XVI v.* [The verb: Its categories and forms in Russian written texts of the second half of the sixteenth century]. Moscow: Izdatel'stvo Akademii Nauk SSSR.

NIYOGI, PARTHA. 1996. The informational complexity of learning from examples. MIT AI Lab TR-1587.

—— 2000, to appear. Theories of Cultural Change and their Application to Language Evolution. In Briscoe (ed.).

—— and ROBERT C. BERWICK. 1996. A language learning model for finite parameter spaces. *Cognition* 61.161–93.

—— —— 1997. A dynamical systems model for language change. *Complex Systems* 11.161–204.

NORDLINGER, RACHEL. 1998. *Constructive Case. Evidence from Australian languages*. Stanford, CA: CSLI.

NUNES, J. 1998. Bare X-bar theory and structures formed by movement. *Linguistic Inquiry* 29.160–8.

OHALA, JOHN. 1993. The phonetics of sound change. In Charles Jones (ed.), *Historical Linguistics: Problems and Perspectives*, 237–78. London and New York: Longman.

OLSVANGER, I. 1947. *Royte Pomerantsen* [Red Oranges]. New York: Schocken.

PANZER, BALDUR. 1967. *Der slavische Konditional: Form–Gebrauch–Funktion.* Forum Slavicum 14. Munich: Wilhelm Fink Verlag.

PAUL, W. 1999. Proxy categories in phrase structure theory and the Chinese VP. MS. Paris: EHESS-CNRS.

PAULINY, EUGEN. 1981. *Slovenská gramatika (Opis jazykového systému)* [A Slovak grammar (A description of the linguistic system)]. Bratislava: Slovenské Pedagogické Nakladatel'stvo.

PEAK, D., and M. FRAME. 1994. *Chaos under Control: The Art and Science of Complexity.* New York: Freeman.

PERES, J. 1997. Extending the notion of negative concord. In D. Forget, P. Hirschbühler, F. Martineau, and M.-L. Rivero (eds.), *Negation and Polarity. Syntax and Semantics,* 289–310. Amsterdam and Philadelphia: John Benjamins.

PESETSKY, DAVID. 1997. Optimality theory and syntax: Movement and pronunciation. In Archangeli and Langendoen (eds.), 134–70.

PETTER, MARGA. 1998. *Getting PRO under Control.* The Hague: Holland Academic Graphics.

PEYRAUBE, A. 1985. Les structures en 'ba' en chinois mediéval et moderne. *Cahiers de linguistique Asie Oriental* 14.193–213.

—— 1986. Shuangbin jiegou cong handai zhi tangdaide lishi fazhan [The historical developments of double object constructions from the Han to the Tang dynasty]. *Zhongguo Yuwen* 3.204–16.

—— 1996. Recent issues in Chinese historical syntax. In C.-T. J. Huang and Y.-H. Li (eds.), *New Horizons in Chinese linguistics,* 161–213. Dordrecht: Kluwer.

—— and T. WIEBUSCH. 1995. Problems relating to the history of different copulas in Ancient Chinese. In *Linguistics Essays in Honor of William S.-Y. Wang,* 383–404.

PHILIPPI, J. 1997. The rise of the article in the Germanic languages. In van Kemenade and Vincent (eds.), 62–93.

PIERONI, SILVIA. 1999. Subject properties and semantic roles in Latin. Paper delivered at Xth International Colloquium on Latin Linguistics, Paris, 19–23 April 1999.

PINKER, S. 1989. *Learnability and Cognition: The Acquisition of Argument Structure,* Cambridge, MA: MIT Press.

—— and P. BLOOM. 1990. Natural language and natural selection. *Behavioral and Brain Sciences* 13.707–84.

PINTZUK, SUSAN. 1991. Phrase Structures in Competition: Variation and change in Old English word order. Ph.D. dissertation. University of Pennsylvania.

—— 1993. Verb seconding in Old English: Verb movement to Infl. *The Linguistic Review* 10.5–35.

—— 1996a. Variation and change in Old English clause structure. *Language Variation and Change* 7.229–60.

—— 1996b. Cliticization in Old English. In Halpern and Zwicky (eds.), 375–409.

—— 1997. From OV to VO in the History of English. MS. University of York.

—— 1998. Syntactic change via grammatical competition: Evidence from Old English. In Paolo Ramat and Elisa Roma (eds.), *Sintassi storica,* 111–25. Rome: Bulzoni.

—— 1999. *Phrase Structures in Competition: Variation and Change in Old English Clause Structure.* Revision of Pintzuk 1991. New York: Garland.

—— and ANTHONY KROCH. 1989. The rightward movement of complements and adjuncts in the Old English of *Beowulf. Language Variation and Change* 1.115–143.

PINTZUK, SUSAN, ERIC HAEBERLI, ANS VAN KEMENADE, WILLEM KOOPMAN, and FRANK BETHS (eds.). 2000. *The Brooklyn–Geneva–Amsterdam–Helsinki Parsed Corpus of Old English.* York: Department of Language and Linguistic Science, University of York.

PLANK, F. 1984. The modals story retold. *Studies in Language* 8.305–64.

PLATZACK, CHRISTER. 1983. Three syntactic changes in the grammar of written Swedish around 1700. In Erik Andersson, Mirja Saari, and Peter Slotte (eds.), *Struktur och variation, Festskrift till Bengt Loman, 7.8.1983*, 43–63. Åbo: Åbo Akademi.

—— 1987. The Scandanavian languages and the null-subject parameter. *Natural Language and Linguistic Theory* 5.377–401.

—— 1988. The emergence of a word order difference in Scandinavian subordinate clauses. *McGill Working Papers in Linguistics: Special issue on comparative Germanic syntax*, 215–38.

—— and ANDERS HOLMBERG. 1989. The role of Agr and Finiteness in Germanic VO languages. *Working Papers in Scandinavian Syntax* 43.51–76. Dept. of Scandinavian Languages, Lund.

POLLARD, CARL, and IVAN SAG. 1994. *Head-driven Phrase Structure Grammar.* Chicago and London: The University of Chicago Press.

POLLOCK, J.-Y. 1989. Verb movement, Universal Grammar, and the structure of IP. *Linguistic Inquiry* 20.365–424.

PORTNER, PAUL. 1992. Situation Theory and the Semantics of Propositional Expressions. Dissertation. University of Massachusetts at Amherst.

POSNER, R. 1984. Double negatives, negative polarity and negative incorporation in Romance: A historical and comparative view. *Transactions of the Philological Society*, 82.1–26.

POSTMA, G. 1995. *Zero Semantics: A Study of the Syntactic Conception of Quantificational Meaning.* HIL Dissertations 13. The Hague: Holland Academic Graphics.

POUNTAIN, CHRISTOPHER. 1998. Learned syntax and the Romance languages: The 'Accusative and Infinitive' construction with declarative verbs in Castilian. *Transactions of the Philological Society* 96.159–201.

PRIESTLEY, L. 1955. Reprise constructions in French. *Archivum Linguisticum* 7.1–28.

PROGOVAC, LJILJANA. 1996. Clitics in Serbian/Croatian: Comp as the second position. In Halpern and Zwicky (eds.), 411–28.

QUER, J. 1993. The Syntactic Licensing of Negative Items. MA dissertation. Universitat Autònoma de Barcelona.

QUIRK, R. 1985. *A Comprehensive Grammar of English.* London: Longman.

RAMAT, P. 1998. Perché veruno significa 'nessuno'? Sintassi Storica. *Atti del XXX Congresso. Società Linguistica Italiana*, SLI 39. Roma: Bulzoni.

RAMBOW, O., and A. JOSHI. 1994. A processing model of free word order languages. In C. Clifton, L. Frazier, and K. Rayner (eds.), *Perspectives on Sentence Processing*, 267–301. Hillsdale, NJ: Lawrence Erlbaum.

RAPOSO, EDUARDO. 1987. Case theory and Infl-to-Comp: The inflected infinitive in European Portuguese. *Linguistic Inquiry* 18.85–109.

RIDLEY, M. 1990. Reply to Pinker and Bloom. *Behavioral and Brain Sciences* 13. 756.

RIEMSDIJK, H. VAN. 1982. Locality principles in syntax and phonology. *Linguistics in the Morning Calm. Selected Papers from SICOL-1981*, 693–708 (edited by the Linguistic Society of Korea). Seoul: Hanshin Publishing Company.

RISSANEN, M. 1994. The position of *not* in Early Modern English questions. In D. Kastovsky (ed.), *Studies in Early Modern English*, 339–48. Berlin: Mouton de Gruyter.

—— 1999. *Isn't it?* or *Is it not?* On the order of postverbal subject and negative particle in the history of English. In Tieken-Boon van Ostade, Tottie, and van der Wurff (eds.), 189–205.

RITTER, E. 1988. A head movement approach to construct state noun phrases. *Linguistics* 26.909–29.

RIVERO, MARÍA-LUISA. 1991. Long Head Movement and negation: Serbo-Croatian vs. Slovak and Czech. *Linguistic Review* 8.319–51.

—— 1993. Long Head Movement vs. V2, and null subjects in Old Romance. *Lingua* 89.217–45.

—— 1994. Clause structure and V-movement in the languages of the Balkans. *Natural Language and Linguistic Theory* 12.63–120.

RIZZI, LUIGI. 1982. *Issues in Italian Syntax*. Dordrecht: Foris.

—— 1986. Null objects in Italian and the theory of pro. *Linguistic Inquiry* 17.501–57.

—— 1990. Some speculations on residual V2 phenomena. In J. Mascaro and M. Nespor (eds.), *Grammar in Progress: GLOW Essays for Henk van Riemsdijk*, 375–86. Dordrecht: Foris.

—— 1997. The fine structure of the left periphery. In L. Haegeman (ed.), *Elements of Grammar*, 281–337. Dordrecht: Kluwer.

ROBERTS, IAN. 1985. Agreement parameters and the development of English modal auxiliaries. *Natural Language and Linguistic Theory* 3.21–58.

—— 1993*a*. *Verbs and Diachronic Syntax: A Comparative History of English and French*. Dordrecht, Boston, London: Kluwer.

—— 1993*b*. A formal account of grammaticalization in the history of Romance futures. *Folia Linguistica Historica* 13.219–58.

—— 1995. Object Movement and Verb Movement in Early Modern English. In H. Haider, S. Olsen, and S. Vikner (eds.), *Studies in Comparative Germanic Syntax*, 269–84. Dordrecht: Kluwer.

—— 1997. Directionality and word order change in the history of English. In van Kemenade and Vincent (eds.), 397–426.

—— 1999. Verb movement and markedness. In M. DeGraff (ed.), 287–327.

—— and ANNA ROUSSOU. 1999. A formal approach to 'grammaticalization'. *Linguistics* 37.1011–41.

ROBERTS, S. 1998. The role of diffusion in the genesis of Hawaiian creole. *Language* 74.1–39.

ROCA, F. 1997. La determinación y la modificación nominal en español. Doctoral dissertation. Universitat Autònoma de Barcelona.

—— 1999. La estructura del sintagma nominal. MS. Universitat de Girona.

ROCA, IGGY (ed.). 1997. *Derivations and Constraints in Phonology*. Oxford: Oxford University Press.

RÖGNVALDSSON, EIRÍKUR. 1987. OV word order in Icelandic. In R. D. S. Allen and M. P. Barnes (eds.), *Proceedings of the Seventh Biennial Conference of Teachers of Scandinavian Studies in Great Britain and Northern Ireland*, 33–49. University College, London.

RÖGNVALDSSON, EIRÍKUR. 1991. Quirky subjects in Old Icelandic. In H. Á. Sigurðsson (ed.), *Papers from the Twelfth Scandinavian Conference of Linguistics*, Háskoli Íslands, Reykjavík.

—— 1994/1995. Breytileg orðaröð í sagnlið. *Íslenskt mál og almenn málfræði* 16/17.27–66.

—— 1996. Word order variation in the VP in Old Icelandic. *Working Papers in Scandinavian Syntax* 58.55–86. Dept. of Scandinavian Languages, Lund.

—— and HÖSKULDUR THRÁINSSON. 1990. On Icelandic word order once more. In Maling and Zaenen (eds.), 3–38.

ROORYCK, J. 1994. On two types of underspecification: Towards a theory shared by syntax and phonology. *Probus* 6.207–33.

ROSS, C. 1991. Coverbs and category distinctions in Mandarin Chinese. *Journal of Chinese Linguistics* 19.79–115.

ROSS, J. R. 1967. *Constraints on Variables in Syntax*. Ph.D. dissertation. MIT. Published as *Infinite Syntax!* Hillsdale, NJ: Erlbaum, 1986.

SAFIR, KEN. 1985. Missing subjects in German. In Jindrich Toman (ed.), *Studies in German Grammar*, 193–229. Dordrecht: Foris.

SAMEK-LODOVICI, VIERI. 1996. *Constraints on Subjects. An Optimality Theoretic Analysis*. Ph.D. dissertation. Rutgers University.

SÁNCHEZ VALENCIA, V., T. VAN DER WOUDEN, and F. ZWARTS. 1993. Polarity and the flow of time. In A. de Boer, J. de Jong, and R. Landeweerd (eds.), *Language and Cognition* 3, 209–18. Yearbook 1993 of the research group for Theoretical and Experimental Linguistics of the University of Groningen.

SANTORINI, BEATRICE. 1992. Variation and change in Yiddish subordinate clause word order. *Natural Language and Linguistic Theory* 10.596–640.

—— 1993. The rate of phrase structure change in the history of Yiddish. *Language Variation and Change* 5.57–283.

—— 1994. Some similarities and differences between Icelandic and Yiddish. In Lightfoot and Hornstein (eds.), 87–106.

SAPIR, E. 1921. *Language: An Introduction to the Study of Speech*. New York: Harcourt, Brace, Jovanovich.

SCHÜTZE, H. 1997. *Ambiguity in Language Learning: Computational and Cognitive Models*. CLSI Series. Stanford, CA: Cambridge University Press.

SIEWIERSKA, ANNA. 1999. Reduced pronominals and argument prominence. In Butt and King (eds.).

SIGMUND, K. 1993. *Games of Life: Explorations in Ecology, Evolution and Behaviour*. London: Penguin.

SIGURÐSSON, HALLDÓR. 1988. From OV to VO: Evidence from Old Icelandic. *Working Papers in Scandinavian Syntax* 34. Dept. of Scandinavian Languages, Lund.

—— 1989. *Verbal Syntax and Case in Icelandic*. Dept. of Scandinavian Languages, Lund.

—— 1990. V1 declaratives and verb raising in Icelandic. In Maling and Zaenen (eds.), 41–70.

—— 1993. Argument-drop in Old Icelandic. *Lingua* 89.247–80.

SISAM, C. 1951. The scribal tradition of the Lambeth Homilies. *The Review of English Studies* 2(6).105–13.

SIVIA, D. S. 1996. *Data Analysis: A Bayesian Tutorial*. Oxford: Clarendon Press.

SKYTTE, GUNVER. 1978. Il cosiddetto costrutto dotto di accusativo con l'infinito in italiano moderno. *Studi di Grammatica Italiana* 7.281–315.

SŁAWSKI, FRANCISZEK. 1946. *Miejsce enklityki odmiennej w dziejach języka bułgarskiego* [The position of the inflected enclitic in the history of the Bulgarian language]. Prace Komisji Językowej 30. Cracow: Polska Akademia Umiejętności.

SOBOLEVSKIJ, A. I. 1962 [1907]. *Lekcii po istorii russkogo jazyka.* [Lectures on the history of the Russian language]. The Hague: Mouton. 4th edn.

SPASOV, D. 1966. *English Phrasal Verbs.* Sofia, Bulgaria: Naouka i Izkoustvo.

SPEAS, MARGARET. 1997. Optimality theory and syntax: Null pronouns and control. In Archangeli and Langendoen (eds.), 171–99.

SPROUSE, REX A., and BARBARA VANCE. 1999. An explanation for the decline of null pronouns in certain Germanic and Romance languages. In M. DeGraff (ed.), 257–83.

STADDON, J. E. R. 1988. Learning as inference. In R. Bolles and M. Beecher (eds.), *Evolution and Learning.* Hillside NJ: Lawrence Erlbaum.

STÅHLE, C. I. 1988. Studier över östgötalagen [Studies into the provincial law of Östergötland]. Samlingar utgivna av Svenska fornskrift-sällskapet 77. Lund: Bloms Boktryckeri.

STANISLAV, JÁN. 1967–73. *Dejiny slovenského jazyka* [History of the Slovak language]. 5 vols. Bratislava: Vydavateľstvo Slovenskej Akadémie Vied.

STEELS, L. 1998. Synthesizing the origins of language and meaning using coevolution, self-organization and level formation. In Hurford, Studdert-Kennedy, and Knight (eds.), 384–404.

STOCKWELL, R. P. 1976. Reply to Lightfoot. In W. Christie (ed.), *Current Progress in Historical Linguistics*, 32–4. Amsterdam: North Holland.

STONE, GERALD. 1993. Sorbian (Upper and Lower). In B. Comrie and G. Corbett (eds.), *The Slavonic Languages*, 593–685. London: Routledge.

STOWELL, TIM. 1981. The Origins of Phrase Structure. Ph.D. dissertation. MIT.

—— 1982. On tense in infinitives. *Linguistic Inquiry* 13.561–670.

SUN, C. 1996. *Word-Order Change and Grammaticalization in the History of Chinese.* Stanford, CA: Stanford University Press.

SUÑER, MARGARITA. 1988. Null definite objects in Quiteño Spanish. *Linguistic Inquiry* 19.511–19.

—— 1995. Negative elements, island effects and resumptive *no. The Linguistic Review* 12. 233–73.

SYBESMA, R. 1992. *Causatives and Accomplishments: The Case of Chinese* ba. Dordrecht: Holland Institute of Generative Linguistics.

TAKAHASHI, CHIOKO. 1997. Object Shift in Chinese: The *Ba*-construction Meets the Minimalist Program. MS. Yale University.

TARALDSEN, KNUT TARALD. 1990. D-projections in Norwegian. In J. Mascaró and M. Nespor (eds.), *Grammar in Progress*: GLOW Essays for Henk van Riemsdijk, 419–31. Dordrecht: Foris.

—— To appear. V-movement versus VP-movement in derivations leading to VO order. In P. Svenonius (ed.), *The Derivation of VO and OV.* Amsterdam and Philadelphia: John Benjamins.

TAYLOR, ANN. 1994. The change from SOV to SVO in Ancient Greek. *Language Variation and Change* 6.1–37.

THRÁINSSON, HÖSKULDUR. 1993. On the structure of infinitival complements. *Harvard Working Papers in Linguistics* 3.181–213.

THRÁINSSON, HÖSKULDUR. 1996. On the (non-)universality of functional categories. In W. Abraham *et al.* (eds.), *Minimal Ideas*, 253–81. Amsterdam and Philadelphia: John Benjamins.

TIEKEN-BOON VAN OSTADE, INGRID, GUNNEL TOTTIE, and WIM VAN DER WURFF (eds.). 1999. *Negation in the History of English*. Berlin: Mouton de Gruyter.

TIMBERLAKE, ALAN. 1977. Reanalysis and actualization in syntactic change. In Li (ed.), 141–77.

TOLKIEN, J. R. R. 1929. *Ancrene Wisse* and *Hali Meithhad*. *Essays and Studies* 14. 104–26.

TOMIĆ, OLGA MIŠESKA. 1996. The Balkan Slavic clausal clitics. *Natural Language and Linguistic Theory* 14.811–72.

TRAUGOTT, E. C. 1992. Syntax. In Hogg (ed.), 168–289.

—— and B. HEINE. 1991. *Approaches to Grammaticalization*. Amsterdam and Philadelphia: John Benjamins.

TRIPS, C. 1999. Scandinavian characteristics in the *Ormulum*: Evidence for Scandinavian influence on word order change in Early Middle English. MS. University of Stuttgart. Paper presented at ConSOLE 8, Vienna.

UTLEY, F. L. 1972. Debates, dialogues, and catechisms. In J. B. Severs and A. E. Hartung (eds.), *A Manual of the Writings in Middle English, 1050–1500*, 669–745. New Haven: Connecticut Academy of Arts and Sciences.

VÄÄNÄNEN, V. 1968. *Introducción al latín vulgar*. Madrid: Gredos.

VAILLANT, ANDRÉ. 1948. *Manuel du vieux slave*. Paris: Institut d'Études Slaves.

—— 1977. *Grammaire comparée des langues slaves*, V. Paris: Éditions Klincksieck.

VALIN, ROBERT VAN. 1985. Case marking and the structure of the Lakhota clause. In Johanna Nichols and Anthony Woodbury (eds.), *Grammar inside and outside the Clause*, 363–413. Cambridge: Cambridge University Press.

VALLDUVÍ, E. 1994. Polarity items, n-words, and minimizers in Catalan and Spanish. *Probus* 6.263–94.

VANCE, BARBARA. 1993. Verb-first declaratives introduced by *et* and the position of *pro* in Old and Middle French. *Lingua* 89.281–314.

—— 1997. *Syntactic Change in Medieval French: Verb Second and Null Subjects*. Dordrecht: Kluwer.

VANGSNES, Ø. A. 1996. A configurational approach to noun phrase interpretation. In João Costa *et al.* (eds.), *Proceedings of ConSOLE* 4.313–35.

VEČERKA, RADOSLAV. 1989. *Altkirchenslavische (altbulgarische) Syntax* I: *Die lineare Satzorganisation*. Monumenta Linguae Slavicae Dialecti Veteris 27. Freiburg: U. W. Weiher.

—— 1995. Eine Skizze zur altkirchenslavischen Syntax: Die Negation. *Byzantinoslavica* 56.511–22.

VERGNAUD, J. R., and M. L. ZUBIZARRETA. 1992. The definite determiner and the inalienable constructions in French and in English. *Linguistic Inquiry* 23.595–652.

VIKNER, STEN. 1994. Finite verb movement in Scandinavian embedded clauses. In Lightfoot and Hornstein (eds.), 117–148.

—— 1995. *Verb Movement and Expletive Subjects in the Germanic Languages*. New York: Oxford University Press.

VINCENT, NIGEL. 1993. Head- versus dependent-marking: The case of the clause. In Greville Corbett *et al.* (eds.), *Heads in Grammatical Theory*, 140–63. Cambridge: Cambridge University Press.

—— 1996. Appunti sulla sintassi dell'infinito coniugato in un testo napoletano del '300. In P. Beninca *et al.* (eds.), *Italiano e dialetto nel tempo*, 387–406. Rome: Bulzoni.

—— 1997. The emergence of the D-system in Romance. In van Kemenade and Vincent (eds.), 149–69.

—— 1998. On the grammar of inflected non-finite forms (with special reference to Old Neapolitan). In Iørn Korzen and Michael Herslund (eds.), *Clause Combining and Text Structure*, 135–58. Copenhagen Studies in Language 22. Frederiksberg: Samfundslitteratur.

—— To appear. Il gerundio in toscano antico e napoletano antico. To appear in a special issue of *Lingua e Stile*.

—— and KERSTI BÖRJARS. 1996. Suppletion and syntactic theory. In M. Butt and T. Holloway King (eds.), *Proceedings of the 1st LFG Colloquium*, 448–62. Grenoble: RXRC.

VISSER, F. Th. 1966. *An Historical Syntax of the English Language* II. Leiden: E. J. Brill.

WADDINGTON, C. 1942. Canalization of development and the inheritance of acquired characters. *Nature* 150.563–5.

—— 1975. *The Evolution of an Evolutionist*. Edinburgh: Edinburgh University Press.

WAL, S. VAN DER. 1996. *Negative Polarity Items and Negation: Tandem Acquisition*. Groningen Dissertations in Linguistics 17.

WANG, L. 1958. *Hanyu shi gao* (zhong) [A draft history of Chinese (Part II)]. Beijing: Kexue chubanshe.

WANNER, E., and L. GLEITMAN. 1982. Introduction. In E. Wanner and L. Gleitman (eds.), *Language Acquisition: The State of the Art*, 3–48. Cambridge, MA: MIT Press.

WARNER, A. 1982. *Complementation in Middle English and the Methodology of Historical Syntax*. University Park, PA: The Pennsylvania State University Press.

—— 1993. *English Auxiliaries: Structure and History*. Cambridge: Cambridge University Press.

—— 1997. The Structure of Parametric Change, and V-movement in the History of English. In van Kemenade and Vincent (eds.), 380–93.

WEERMAN, F. 1997. On the relation between morphological and syntactic case. In van Kemenade and Vincent (eds.), 427–59.

WEINREICH, U., W. LABOV, and M. I. HERZOG. 1968. A theory of language change. In W. P. Lehmann and Y. Malkiel (eds.), *Directions for Historical Linguistics*, 97–195. Austin, TX: University of Texas Press.

WENNING, A. 1930. *Studier över ordföljden i fornsvenska* [Studies in the word order of Old Swedish]. Lund: Lindstedts universitetsbokhandel.

WEXLER, K., and P. CULICOVER. 1980. *Formal Principles of Language Acquisition*. Cambridge, MA: MIT Press.

—— and R. MANZINI. 1987. Parameters and learnability in binding theory. In T. Roeper and E. Williams (eds.), *Parameter Setting*, 41–76. Dordrecht: Reidel.

WILLIS, DAVID W. E. 1998. *Syntactic Change in Welsh: A Study of the Loss of Verb-Second*. Oxford: Oxford University Press.

WOOD, M. M. 1993. *Categorial Grammars*. London: Routledge.

WOUDEN, T. VAN DER. 1994. Polarity and 'illogical negation'. In M. Kanazawa and C. J. Piñon (eds.), *Dynamics, Polarity, and Quantification*. Stanford, CA: CSLI.

WOUDEN, T. VAN DER. and F. ZWARTS. 1993. A semantic analysis of negative concord. *Semantics and Linguistic Theory (SALT)* III.202–19. Ithaca, NY: Cornell University Press.

WRIGHT, SEWALL. 1931. Evolution in Mendelian populations. *Genetics* 16.97–126.

WURFF, WIM VAN DER. 1993. Null objects and learnability: The case of Latin. Paper presented at ICHL10, UCLA, August 1993.

—— 1997. Deriving object–verb order in late Middle English. *Journal of Linguistics* 33.485–509.

—— 1999. Objects and verbs in Modern Icelandic and fifteenth century English: A word order parallel and its causes. *Lingua* 109.237–65.

WYNGAERD, GUIDO VAN DEN. 1994. *PRO-legomena. Distribution and Reference of Infinitival Subjects*. Berlin: Mouton de Gruyter.

ZAMPARELLI, R. 1996. Layers in the Determiner Phrase. Ph.D. dissertation. University of Rochester, NY.

ZANUTTINI, R. 1991. Syntactic Properties of Sentential Negation: A comparative study of Romance languages. Ph.D. dissertation. University of Pennsylvania.

—— 1994. Re-examining negative clauses. In G. Cinque, J. Koster. J.-Y. Pollock, L. Rizzi, and R. Zanuttini (eds.), *Paths Towards Universal Grammar. Studies in Honor of Richard S. Kayne*, 427–51. Washington DC: Georgetown University Press.

—— 1997. *Negation and Clausal Structure: A Comparative Study of Romance Languages*. New York and Oxford: Oxford University Press.

ZOU, K. 1993. The syntax of the Chinese BA construction. *Linguistics* 31.715–36.

ZWART, C. JAN-WOUTER. 1993. Dutch Syntax: A Minimalist Approach. Doctoral dissertation. University of Groningen.

—— 1996. Verb clusters in continental West Germanic dialects. In J. R. Black and V. Motapanyane (eds.), *Microparametric Syntax and Dialect Variation*, 229–58. Amsterdam and Philadelphia: John Benjamins.

—— 1997. *Morphosyntax of Verb Movement: A Minimalist Approach to the Syntax of Dutch*. Dordrecht: Kluwer.

ZWARTS, F. 1993. Three Types of Polarity. MS. University of Groningen.

—— 1995. Nonveridical contexts. *Linguistic Analysis* 25.286–312.

ZWICKY, ARNOLD M. 1977. *On clitics*. Bloomington: Indiana University Linguistics Club.

Index

Printed in Great Britain
by Amazon